Blood, Body and Soul

Also edited by Tamy Burnett and AmiJo Comeford

The Literary Angel: Essays on Influences and Traditions Reflected in the Joss Whedon Series. 2010

Worlds of Whedon Series

Joss Whedon Versus the Corporation: Big Business Critiqued in the Films and Television Programs. Erin Giannini. 2017

Joss Whedon's Big Damn Movie: Essays on Serenity. Edited by Frederick Blichert. 2018

The Whedonverse Catalog: A Complete Guide to Works in All Media. Don Macnaughtan. 2018

Joss Whedon, Anarchist? A Unified Theory of the Films and Television Series. James Rocha and Mona Rocha. 2019

Sexualties in the Works of Joss Whedon. Lewis Call. 2020

Blood, Body and Soul: Essays on Health, Wellness and Disability in Buffy, Angel, Firefly *and* Dollhouse. Edited by Tamy Burnett and AmiJo Comeford. 2022

Re-Entering the Dollhouse: Essays on the Joss Whedon Series. Edited by Heather M. Porter and Michael Starr. 2022

Welcome to the Hellmouth: Essays on Trauma and Memory in the Whedonverse. Edited by Alyson R. Buckman, Juliette C. Kitchens and Katherine A. Troyer. 2022

Blood, Body and Soul

Essays on Health, Wellness and Disability in Buffy, Angel, Firefly *and* Dollhouse

Edited by Tamy Burnett *and* AmiJo Comeford

Worlds of Whedon
Series Editor Sherry Ginn

McFarland & Company, Inc., Publishers
Jefferson, North Carolina

This book has undergone peer review.

Library of Congress Cataloguing-in-Publication Data

Names: Burnett, Tamy, 1979– editor. | Comeford, AmiJo, 1977– editor.
Title: Blood, body and soul : essays on health, wellness
and disability in Buffy, Angel, Firefly and Dollhouse /
edited by Tamy Burnett and AmiJo Comeford.
Description: Jefferson, North Carolina : McFarland & Company, Inc., Publishers, 2022 |
Series: Worlds of Whedon | Includes bibliographical references and index.
Identifiers: LCCN 2022001984 | ISBN 9781476667638 (paperback : acid free paper) ♾
ISBN 9781476646275 (ebook)
Subjects: LCSH: Whedon, Joss, 1964—-Criticism and
interpretation. | People with disabilities on television. | Fantasy
television programs—United States—History and criticism. |
Science fiction television programs—United States—History
and criticism. | BISAC: PERFORMING ARTS / Television /
Genres / Science Fiction, Fantasy & Horror | SOCIAL
SCIENCE / People with Disabilities
Classification: LCC PN1992.4.W49 B58 2022 | DDC 791.4302/33092—dc23/eng/20220210
LC record available at https://lccn.loc.gov/2022001984

Brit2sh Library cataloguing data are available

ISBN (print) 978-1-4766-6763-8
ISBN (ebook) 978-1-4766-4627-5

Printed in the United States of America

McFarland & Company, Inc., Publishers
Box 611, Jefferson, North Carolina 28640
www.mcfarlandpub.com

Acknowledgments

Seeing this collection in print has been a long journey, and we are first and foremost grateful for our contributors for their continued energy, enthusiasm, and patience during the process. We are similarly grateful to the community of scholars who study these television series for their ongoing interest and support for this volume. Our gratitude extends also to our colleagues, friends, and families, who have cheered and supported our work on this volume. Deepest thanks to Rose Wehrman, for her help with all things citation; to Rhonda V. Wilcox for her thoughtful, detailed, and gracious review of this volume; Sherry Ginn for her careful editing; and to Layla Milholen at McFarland for her unwavering enthusiasm and support.

Table of Contents

Introduction

TAMY BURNETT *and* AMIJO COMEFORD

Among the most poignant and powerful episodes of *Buffy the Vampire Slayer* is "The Body" (5.16), where Buffy comes home to discover her mother's dead body. The horror of this episode is found in the fact that Joyce Summers died from natural causes, a brain aneurysm, rather than a supernatural monster or ailment that her daughter can fight or reverse with magic, as is explored so eloquently in Lawson Fletcher's essay "'Is She Cold?': Telaesthetic Horror and Embodied Textuality in 'The Body.'" Indeed, the episode nearly concludes without Buffy facing any supernatural foes; it is only in the last few minutes that she fights a vampire in the hospital morgue, where her younger sister Dawn has snuck off to in an attempt to understand the loss of their mother by seeking out Joyce's body. Whereas this episode might be the most emotionally powerful engagement with the physical body and its inherent vulnerabilities, this is not the only time in *Buffy* that the physical is paramount to a story.

In the Whedonverse, all transformative monsters—vampires, werewolves, and zombies—are the healthy, abled body perverted into something other, something dangerous. And indeed, for the show's titular monster, the vampire, the healthy body in the form of blood is needed to sustain undead life. As Spike says in "The Gift" (5.22) when the gang discovers Dawn's blood will open a dangerous mystical portal which will only close when her blood stops flowing and she dies, "it's always got to be blood. [...] Blood is life [...] makes you warm. Makes you hard. Makes you other than dead. Course it's her blood." Blood is the ultimate metaphor here and elsewhere in the series for the role and value of the body.

Just as Dawn sought out her mother's physical body in an attempt to process her grief, so too does this collection seek greater understanding of the physical body in four television series spanning just over a decade in the late 1990s and early 2000s that are linked by the collaborative output of individuals behind and in front of the camera, whose creative lineage grew out of the first of these, *Buffy the Vampire Slayer.* The additional series are the *Buffy* spinoff *Angel*, the space-western *Firefly* (including its feature film sequel/conclusion *Serenity*), and the sci-fi dystopian thriller *Dollhouse* (2009–2010). Together, we call these "the Whedonverses" throughout this volume, borrowing a term familiar to the academic circles wherein the largest audience for this volume resides and used colloquially to refer to work attributed largely to Joss Whedon, who created or co-created and executive produced all of these series.

However, this volume goes to press during a time in which a shift is occurring within the aforementioned scholarly circles, away from an auteurist approach and toward emphasizing the undeniable collaborative nature of television production. This shift is reflected in a 2021 rebranding of the *Slayage* journal and discussions about the future of the academic association known as the Whedon Studies Association (as of April 2021) to reflect movement away from a focus on one individual and onto a broader analysis of creative collaborations around these productions, in part to address issues of diversity and inclusive excellence. As a result of these changing scholarly understandings of how we approach inquiry and analysis of works in the Joss Whedon oeuvre—and with recognition that the essays contained herein were all completed well before the scholarly conversations about best practices for this area of study began in earnest—we have attempted to de-center Whedon as auteur and focus instead on the texts and the collective contributions of writers, cast, and crew, whose talents helped bring these episodes and series to the small screen. Our intent is not to deny the impact or influence Joss Whedon has had on these works, but to acknowledge his contributions alongside those of other writers and directors, of the actors, and of the various crew members who are essential in bringing these narratives to life.

We specifically chose these four series as our scope of inquiry because they represent a specific period in Joss Whedon's creative life on network television. *Buffy* (1997–2003) and *Angel* (1999–2004) share a narrative universe, and with *Firefly* (2002), they represent the height (to date) of Whedon and his collaborators' simultaneous work on television.[1] *Dollhouse* (2009–2010) may seem an outlier, but even leaving aside the intertextual casting of *Buffy*'s/*Angel*'s Faith (Eliza Dushku) as the *Dollhouse* lead Echo; *Angel*'s Fred (Amy Acker) as Dr. Claire Saunders/Whiskey; *Buffy*'s/*Angel*'s Wesley (Alexis Denisof) as Senator Daniel Perrin; and *Firefly*'s Wash (Alan Tudyk) as Alpha and River (Summer Glau) as Bennett Halverson,[2] this latter series clearly engages similar themes to the earlier series related to empowerment, identity, existentialism, and agency. Additionally, these four shows are original content; they are not beholden to outside source material, the way Whedon-affiliated properties in the Marvel Cinematic

Universe are, including the first two *Avengers* films (2012 and 2015) and *Agents of S.H.I.E.L.D.* (2013–2020).[3]

The televisual worlds of *Buffy, Angel, Firefly,* and *Dollhouse* inhabit many genres ranging from drama to comedy, from horror to western, from science fiction to fantasy. Yet all are also series grounded in action shared via a medium that privileges the visual as much as the auditory and linguistic. For shows whose storylines feature physical fights, injury, and death (and even resurrection) on a fairly regular basis, the vast majority of the scholarship on Whedon, his collaborators, and the television shows they created in the late '90s and early 2000s focuses on the psychological, the philosophical, and the metaphysical, on symbolism and thematic readings. Indeed, many Whedonverse scholars' home disciplines are literature or film, and the scholarship often reflects the practices of those fields. These are certainly worthy areas of study; indeed both of this volume's editors hold degrees in literary studies and have previously published on the Whedonverses using these methodologies. While Whedonverse scholarship has branched out to embrace approaches from a variety of disciplines (although still most commonly the humanities and social sciences), it has been slower to integrate considerations of more corporeal elements of these series into the scholarly conversation. In fact, overall, analysis on how Whedon and his collaborators carry out thematic concerns via the bodies of their characters is, at present, a fairly sparse area of scholarship, which is something this collection of essays seeks to address.

We do not mean to suggest that no scholarly work has been done in this area. Indeed, much of the Whedonverse scholarship available in this vein was published after this project was undertaken, suggesting both an area ripe for new scholarship and a desire for critical investigations in this direction. For example, in terms of consideration of the physical body, Ian Klein offers insightful analysis of *Dollhouse*'s Whiskey's scars and how her physical "disfigurement" is central to the character's new identity as Dr. Saunders in "'I Like My Scars': Claire Saunders and the Narrative of Flesh." Similarly, Katherine E. Whaley provides an astute reading of *Buffy*'s Xander as disabled by virtue of his purely humanness in a world of supernatural and superpowered beings in "'There's Nothing Wrong with My Body': Xander as a Study in Defining Capability of the Disabled Body in *Buffy the Vampire Slayer*." Editors Alyson R. Buckman, Juliette C. Kitchens, and Katherine A. Troyer are additionally working on a separate volume about trauma, memory, and disability in the Wheondverse.[4]

A fair number of critics have utilized a gendered/sexuality studies lens to consider bodies, including critics like Lorna Jowett and Marcus Recht, who have explored the gendered body in Whedon's works, especially in *Sex and the Slayer* and *Der Sympathische Vampir* (written in German), respectively. Likewise, Josefine Wälivaara connects the physical space/place of Sunnydale to physical bodies in *Buffy*, as well as their expressions of gender and sexuality in "Welcome to Buffydale." Kelsie Hahn has critiqued Whedon's depictions of the physically traumatic deaths of *Firefly*'s Wash, *Buffy*'s Tara, and *Doctor Horrible*'s Penny in "Lady Killer: Death of the Feminized Body in the Whedonverse," just as Alyson Buckman has eloquently articulated the implications of the physicality of Penny's death in "'Go Ahead, Run Away! Say it was Horrible!': *Dr. Horrible's Sing-Along-Blog* as Resistant Text." Additionally, both Bronwen Calvert ("Inside Out") and Jacqueline Potvin ("Pernicious Pregnancy"), among others, have written on the depictions and characterization of the pregnant body in *Angel*.

Exploration of depictions of mental health are also available, including Alex Fixler's "'The Hardest Thing in This World Is to Live in It': Identity and Mental Health in *Buffy the Vampire Slayer*" and Margaret A. Shane's "River Tam as Schizoanalysand." Perhaps the earliest scholarly engagement with this topic comes from Caitlin Peeling and Meaghan Scanlon, who offered a feminist reading of Buffy's "madness" in "Normal Again" in their conference presentation at the first Slayage Conference in 2004.

Some Whedonverse scholars have expanded beyond the shows around which this collection is focused. Examples include Lewis Call's keen analysis of kink and the disabled sexual body in Whedon's run authoring *The X-Men* comics in "'That Weird, Unbearable Delight': Representations of Alternative Sexualities in Joss Whedon's *Astonishing X-Men* Comics"; Derrick King's consideration of the value of bodies in the 2012 horror film *A Cabin in the Woods* (directed by Whedon collaborator Drew Goddard and co-written by Whedon and Goddard) in "The (Bio)political Economy of Bodies, Culture as Commodification, and the Badiouian Event: Reading Political Allegories in *The Cabin in the Woods*"; and Masani McGee's reading of male Avenger bodies in "Big Men in Spangly Outfits: Spectacle and Masculinity in Joss Whedon's *The Avengers*."

For this collection, then, we specify that we are interested in issues related to the body, particularly in two areas: first, how we might think about and understand the representation of characters who are injured, ill, or differently abled, and second, what we can learn from explorations related to specific physical experiences or states of the body. We do include considerations of mental health or wellbeing when they are connected to physical causes (e.g., trauma) or medically diagnosed conditions. We do so with full recognition that medical and cultural understanding of mental and emotional health is an ever changing and rapidly evolving field, and our choice to make this distinction today may not make as much sense in the future. Within these frameworks, we are specifically interested in how both of these particular areas of inquiry intersect with or enhance the more common directions for scholarship on the four television series previously identified: *Buffy*, *Angel*, *Firefly*, and *Dollhouse*.

As such, this collection of essays is divided into two halves, with the first focused on theorizing (dis)ability, health care, and what it means to be well. Mary Ellen Iatropolous begins this section and the volume with an insightful essay about the Whedonverses' approach to a disability narrative ethic by comparing the treatment of *Angel*'s Lindsey McDonald, *Dollhouse*'s Bennett Halverson, and *Buffy*'s Xander Harris. She contends that the narrative impairment arcs for these three characters offer us greater insight into the use of the individual choice to accept or reject socially-constructed paradigms for differently-abled or impaired individuals, and that the choices these characters make aligns with their ethical positioning as "good" or "evil." Notably, Iatropolous was recognized for an earlier version of this essay with a "best conference paper" Mr. Pointy at the 2012 Slayage Conference on the Whedonverses in Vancouver, BC.

Next, Cynthia Headley builds on these theoretical frameworks in a thoughtful comparison of *Buffy*'s Buffy and *Firefly*'s River, with an emphasis on positing them as differently-abled rather than disabled. Specifically, Headley suggests that both characters' storylines offer a bridge of sorts, one that overcomes the gaps between the social and medical models of disability.

Lorna Jowett subsequently offers a perceptive analysis of *Angel*'s "female freaks," women in the series who are differently abled. Jowett primarily examines reoccurring characters Gwen Raiden (Season Four), also known as "electro girl," and Angel's romantic interest in Season Five, Nina the werewolf, against a backdrop of others including, of course, Cordelia Chase, whose character arc was dramatically impacted and cut short in response by actress Charisma Carpenter's real life pregnancy in Season Four.

Elizabeth K. Switaj then examines slayerhood through the social model of disability, comparing the representation of different slayers in the series. She starts by considering Buffy, Kendra, and Faith in contrast to one another and to non-slayer Scoobies Willow and Xander. She then expands her analysis to the army of slayers activated in the television series finale and mobilized in the Season Eight comics. Switaj offers an astute argument about the ways in which *Buffy* interacts with the social model of disability precisely because of the series' evolving mythos moving from one slayer at a time to all potential slayers being activated simultaneously.

Barbara Stock next asks us to shift perspective and consider not physical but intellectual disability in her essay exploring the Dolls from *Dollhouse* as intellectually-disabled individuals. As Stock notes, "intellectually disabled" is not a monolithic category, and thus her keen analysis explores the Dolls within the broader category of intellectual disability. Ultimately Stock asks us to perhaps reconsider our understanding of intellectual disability and what it means for an individual.

Roslyn Weaver returns us to the earliest series in the Whedonverses in her shrewd exploration of mental health in *Buffy*. Weaver's analysis focuses primarily on the episode "Normal Again" (6.17), where Buffy's perspective switches back and forth between the world of Sunnydale and an alternative reality in which she is an institutionalized, mentally-ill girl who created Sunnydale entirely in her mind. The allure of the alternate world is strong, as Buffy's mother is alive and Buffy is free from the many responsibilities she faces in Sunnydale, ranging from caring for her younger sister Dawn to saving the world on a regular basis as the Slayer. Buffy's struggle in this episode, Weaver suggests, offers a model for understanding the ways that mental health and social ideas of "normality" intersect.

Next, Brett S. Stifflemire offers thoughtful insight into competing medical models of health care, using the doctors of *Firefly* and *Serenity* as examples. Stifflemire's analysis focuses on Dr. Simon Tam, positioning him within a long history of television and film doctors and representations of medical approaches on screen, especially within the Western genre context. Over the course of the series, Simon evolves and so too does his approach to health care and disability—especially as exhibited in the person of his sister, River.

Madeline Muntersbjorn concludes the first half of the volume with a philosophy-based inquiry into how suffering impacts individuals. Muntersbjorn expertly explores the connections between suffering and strength, and between identity and the soul. As readers of this collection likely already know, the soul and the internal self is a favorite common theme in these series. Muntersbjorn's astute analysis suggests that considerations of suffering—physical and mental—must account for the impact of that suffering on the soul.

Building upon the theoretical frameworks of the first half, the second half of this volume contains essays exploring questions about bodies or specific body parts, traumatic experiences, and recovery. This section begins with Cynthea Masson's examination of beheading, specially looking at beheading in Pylea, the alternate universe from which *Angel*'s Lorne hails and which Team Angel visit at the end of *Angel*'s Season Two. Masson astutely argues that beheading in Pylea is ultimately about power. Understanding how Team Angel seeks to confront the beheading topos in Pylea offers insight for resistance of evil (ab)uses of power in the real world.

Next, Erin Hollis explores the act of torture and the impact on the body in an insightful consideration of torture in these television worlds, primarily through the lens of *Buffy*'s "Hush" (4.10). Hollis also asks readers to consider how fictionalized representations of and responses to torture impact their response to torture in the real world, drawing connections to Whedon's public condemnation of "torture porn" in 2007.

Brian Cogan next offers an analysis of Xander's loss of an eye and need for an eye patch in Season Seven of *Buffy* within the long history of visibly representing disability in theater, film, and television. Cogan reinforces Iatropolous' earlier reading of how Xander navigates his response to his impairment, suggesting that Whedon and his collaborators "flip the script" on traditional, historic positioning of a visibly disabled character as "evil" through Xander's reintegration into the core Scooby team for the final battle at the Hellmouth in "Chosen" (*Buffy* 7.22) and into the *Buffy* Season Eight comics.

J. Bowers next asks us to consider Spike within the context of his human self from the 1880s and a nineteenth-century disease: neurasthenia. This masculine counterpart to the more commonly known feminine "hysteria" was something of a catch-all diagnosis for a range of mental and emotional states, characterized by its positioning as opposite to Victorian social definitions of "successful" masculinity. Bowers methodically explores how the character's transition from human William to vampire William the Bloody, and then Spike, fits within the social discourse of the late 19th and early 20th centuries about neurasthenia and its treatments.

Emily James Hansen and Katheryn Wright bring us back to the present and future with their analysis of the affective body in *Firefly* and *Dollhouse*, specifically within the context of trauma and technology. Hansen and Wright suggest that technology—whether that of the Dollhouse, *Firefly*'s futuristic technology, or social networking technologies readers engage with on a daily basis in their everyday lives now in the early twenty-first century—has the power to offer one the experience of being an affective body, as defined by seventeenth-century philosopher Baruch Spinoza. They argue that the connections of chosen family offers a mechanism for addressing the challenges that embodied affective experience presents.

Next, Sherry Ginn tackles what is so often the "elephant in the room" when thinking about bodies in film and television: the unrealistic physical representations that Hollywood bodies—especially female bodies—offers, including the ways that "larger" bodies are portrayed. Ginn offers a discerning analysis of what she tongue-in-cheek calls the "token fatty" characters of *Buffy* (Tara), *Firefly/Serenity* (Kaylee), and *Dollhouse* (Mellie). Using these actresses' Body Mass Index (BMI) scores and comparing them to the other female regulars on these series, Ginn highlights the often troubling ways these "bigger" female characters are depicted.

Kelly L. Richardson also explores the physicality of bodies in an insightful examination of how bodily transformations in Seasons Six and

Seven of *Buffy* reinforce the season's themes about transitioning into adulthood. In comparing Buffy's resurrection and Willow's descent into and return from "Dark Willow," Richardson offers not just insight into the process of transformation and its immediate aftermath but also long term insight into healing processes and the integration of the new/changed body into the post-recovery understanding of self.

Frances Sprout continues the consideration of Willow during this point in *Buffy*'s run with a perceptive analysis of the role of skin in the series. Specifically, Sprout contrasts three moments from *Buffy* Season Six and Seven: when Willow's skin is overwritten by the dark magic she literally pulls out of books and into herself following Tara's death; when Willow removes the skin of Warren, Tara's murderer, by magically flaying him alive; and when, upon her return to Sunnydale after her recovery, Willow is captured by the Gnarl demon who methodically peels off her skin to eat. Mediating between Bakhtinian and Foucauldian understandings of the body, Sprout follows Willow's descent into monstrosity and her eventual healing.

This section and the collection conclude by bringing us full circle with Tamy Burnett's analysis of Lindsey's and Spike's hand amputation narratives in *Angel*. Through a thoughtful comparison of these two characters' story arcs and their response to amputation and transplantation (Lindsey) or reattachment (Spike) of their missing limbs, Burnett contends, much like Iatropolous, that it is one's response to impairment that defines one's positioning in the great balance of good vs. evil.

From these fictional worlds we can take real-life lessons about our own responses to disability, impairment, trauma, illness, or other shifts in our understanding of our body as part of our identities. Likewise, how we respond to others' (dis)ability will also hopefully be shared for the better through a deeper understanding of how we culturally, socially, and medically understand physical, intellectual, and mental disabilities.

Notes

1. Readers may also wonder why *Dr. Horrible's* Sing-Along Blog is not addressed in this collection. While *Dr. Horrible* certainly fits within this window of Joss Whedon's creative life, the element of the show most closely aligned with this collection's theme is the visceral depiction of Penny's injured and subsequently dead body, which has already been examined in depth by Alyson Buckman in "Go Ahead! Run Away! Say It Was Horrible!"

2. For more on intertextual casting, see Jeffrey Bussolini's "Television Intertextuality After *Buffy*," Alyson Buckman's forthcoming "We Are Not Who We Are," and K. Brenna Wardell's "Actors Assemble!"

3. *The Nevers*, although airing on HBO rather than a broadcast network, promises to offer additional original content television that very well may align with the arguments and ideas included herein, but while the first season will finish airing before this volume is published, it is not available at the time of manuscript submission to the publisher.

4. Forthcoming from McFarland.

Part I

Theorizing (Dis)Ability, Medicine, and Wellness

Defining the Whedonverse Disability Narrative Ethic

Examining Impairment Arcs in Dollhouse, Angel, *and* Buffy the Vampire Slayer

MARY ELLEN IATROPOULOS

Towards the beginning of "Willow: Goddesses and Monsters," the Willow one-shot story from the comic serial *Buffy Season 8*, Willow embarks upon the magical inter-dimensional mind-quest that is "part of a witch's path" (Whedon, "Willow"). Her guide, a steampunk girl named Muffitt who uses a wheelchair, mocks the billowing clouds and O'Keefean flowers filling the landscape crafted by Willow's subconscious: "Wow, are you ever a dyke," Muffitt sardonically muses. Willow promptly responds, "That term is offensive. Or maybe it's empowering—I can't always keep up." Later in her journey, Willow is transferred to the guardianship of Eluwyn, whose ambiguous myth-speak confounds Willow to the point of wondering aloud, "Can I have wheely-girl back?" Willow, earlier taken aback by Muffitt's offensive/empowering language, chooses later to respond in kind, similarly referring to Muffitt with the vaguely derogatory "wheely-girl." While this exchange of borderline insults may strike readers as unfriendly or even adversarial, it can also be interpreted ironically. Willow and Muffitt, mutually recognizing each other's status as marginalized outsiders due to aspects of their identity (in Willow's case, her sexuality; in Muffitt's case, her disability), regard each other in ironic articulations of mainstream pejoratives that are robbed of their malice through re-appropriation by the very groups they aim to disparage.

Such anxiety of terminology is endemic to the realm of disabilities studies, which proudly reclaims the term "disabled" as a source of door-opening political equality even as the term itself remains vexed in its use in society. The Whedonverses reflect this vexation, depicting complex, confusing, and often-contradictory images of and messages to marginalized groups seeking mainstream inclusion and representation. As I argue in this essay, investigating disability narratives in the Whedonverses reveals that behind even the most offhand snarky dialogue operates a profound anxiety about negotiating the marginalized self within oppressive society. Though manifest through troubling terms, this negotiation often creates narratological opportunity in which characters define themselves through the stories they choose to tell about themselves and who they choose to be. In this essay, I explore the Whedonverses' treatment of disability vis-à-vis the impairment arcs of three specific characters—Lindsey McDonald, Bennett Halverson, and Xander Harris—noting the complex web of competing narratives that reflect, illustrate, occasionally adhere to, and occasionally subvert competing theories of the disabled self. This contrast is especially illuminating given that these three characters inhabit three different narrative worlds—*Angel*, *Dollhouse*, and *Buffy the Vampire Slayer*, respectively—demonstrating an ongoing concern across the various projects.[1] These creative works time and again construct a framework of narrative ethics built upon choices; specifically, the choice to accept the disabling socio-cultural environment's attitude becomes something that bad or evil characters do (Lindsey, Bennett), and the choice to reject disabling society and to develop into an impairment-encompassing entity is something that good characters do (Xander). While these characters' impairment arcs may depict disabling societies and ableist paradigms, I argue that the extant ableist narratives of a disabled self are repeatedly characterized as evil, while counter-narratives of disabled subjectivity that transcend models of disabled selfhood are characterized as good, resulting in a narrative ethics of disability that overall offers viewers a path towards self-acceptance and less problematic paradigms of disabled selfhood.

Towards Defining "Disability" and Whedon's Narrative Ethics

What does it mean to become, and be, disabled? The word itself seems to disempower the very constituency it aims to describe, calling into question (if not outright negation) the *dis*-abled person's abilities, potential, and options. Yet, ever since Paul Hunt differentiated between the "the social lives and interests of 'able-bodied' and disabled people'" in his 1966 work *Stigma: The Experience of Disability*, the words "disability" and "disabled" have been reclaimed by the people to which they refer even as they hotly contest the degree to which such words are self-selected identities, narrow categorizations, and/or outright slurs (qtd. in Barnes and Mercer, *Disability*

8–10; 2003 edition). To avoid confusion, a survey of my usage of these terms is helpful. Most importantly, throughout my argument I distinguish between "impaired" and "disabled." By "impairment," I refer to the "loss of physiological or anatomical capacity," in other words the specific physical injury or trauma incurred (Howson 26). For example, in the case of Lindsey McDonald on *Angel*, impairment occurs when Angel cuts off Lindsey's hand. Bennett Halverson's impairment happens on *Dollhouse* when her arm's nerves become severed after being trapped under debris following an explosion, and for Xander Harris on *Buffy*, impairment occurs when the evil preacher Caleb gouges out his eye. In each case, the impairment refers to the literal physical injury sustained.

I will use "disability," by contrast, to refer to the "repercussions of impairment and the difficulties a person may have engaging" in their lives and environments after the occurrence of impairment (Howson 26). As Howson relates, "disability" reflects "the ways in which people with impairments are typically isolated and excluded from full social participation" (26). In other words, *dis*abling society's "system of compulsory able-bodiedness [...] in a sense produces disability" by creating social norms that obstruct or contest the impaired individual's right to citizenship and selfhood (McRuer 2). Put short, "impairment" refers to the physical and "disability" refers to the socially constructed.[2] Disability studies exposes that construction as a type of discrimination called ableism. Ableism, sometimes referred to as disablism, disability discrimination, or able-bodied bias, refers to the general attitude that mirrors or internalizes discriminatory and *dis*abling forces of social normativity (Barnes and Mercer, *Disability* 10; 2003 edition). Ableism takes many shapes in society, some aggressively discriminatory and some disguised as harmless, as disabledfeminists.com bloggers Annaham and s.e. smith relate in posts on "Liberal Ableism" and "Hipster Ableism."[3] No matter the type, exposing ableism allows the impaired, disempowered individual to construct a counter-narrative of the disabled self, one that empowers the self to own its bodily impairments and to reclaim subjectivity that encompasses but is not limited to disability.

Yet as illustrated with the scene between Willow and Moffitt, the systematic marginalization and oppression articulated and attacked through discourse goes much deeper than mere terminology. To put it another way, to spend too much time focusing on terminology is to ignore, in the words of s.e. smith, that "the problem isn't the *word*, it's what lies behind it. It's what the word reinforces and reveals. It's not that people call me a crip. It's what they think that means" (smith, "Language," emphasis in original). To wit: elements of this very vexed language run rampant in the Whedonverses, spouted from both good and evil characters alike.

The recently-turned-evil Angelus of *Buffy*'s Season Two, for example, makes repeated jabs at Spike's broken back, which necessitates his use of a wheelchair (e.g., he says "things change, Spikey. You've got to roll with the punches. Well, you pretty much got that part down, haven't you?" in "I Only Have Eyes for You," 2.19), even as our beloved Buffy and her Scoobies casually and consistently use the word "lame" as a synonym for underwhelming, disappointing, or pathetic (as in "Gingerbread" [3.13], when Buffy gripes "M.O.O? … Who came up with that lame name?"). The word "retard" also appears, as when at the end of *Buffy* Season Six a harried Xander laments having to baby-sit Jonathan and Andrew, calling them "a pair of social retards" ("Grave" 6.22). I mention this troubling language because, as s.e. smith writes, the language matters, but what these semantic choices reveal or reinforce about the Whedonverses matters more. What such language—and the images of impairment and disability that accompany and contextualize that language—reveals is that problematic depictions of ableist behavior and language do not necessarily translate to the earnest endorsement or valorization of ableism itself.

Indeed, Whedon has a history of presenting issues in order to problematize them. Calling *Buffy* "a sustained moral argument" in which "difficult hypothetical cases are imagined and various ways of dealing with them considered," J. Michael Richardson and J. Douglas Rabb suggest that Whedon's shows often portray complex, conflicting, and contradictory messages in order to pose difficult questions, each portrayed without necessarily being promoted by the show (*The Existential* 52). Considering the depictions of disability via impairment arcs in *Buffy*, *Angel*, and *Dollhouse* as examples of Richardson and Rabb's "difficult hypothetical cases," we see that when Lindsey, Bennett, and Xander become impaired, they must navigate the often-disabling forces of their social environments by choosing from among many "various ways of dealing with" impairment. As these hypothetical cases will illustrate, impairment arcs enact the existentialist choice Richardson and Rabb identify in the Whedonverses, "one which must be made continuously, as it is that which makes us who we are, and we are always in progress" (133). Howson theorizes disability studies with similar language, saying that disability can be seen "as an ongoing process of negotiation and interaction with others" (28). Since characters who become impaired must navigate between their former roles, their new physical adjustments, and the disabling pressure of able-bodied society, impairment arcs comprise exactly such sites of ongoing negotiation of identity. The continuous process of negotiating disabled identity presents itself in characters selecting from competing theories of the disabled self (choosing a mentality to guide their navigation of impaired life) as well as competing narratives (choosing what stories to tell and believe about themselves). Rabb and

Richardson describe this process of perpetual choice as shedding light onto both that person's ethics and the values they represent within the ethical framework of the overall show ("Memory"). This intersection of disabled self-theory and narrative ethics becomes readily apparent when reading the arcs of characters that become impaired over the course of their respective television series. By considering Lindsey McDonald from *Angel*, Bennett Halverson from *Dollhouse*, and Xander Harris from *Buffy the Vampire Slayer*, reading disability through narrative ethics in the Whedonverses reveals the many ways in which characters' selections of their own disability narratives serve to characterize their goodness or evilness, in turn demonstrating that Joss Whedon presents ableism as an existential choice to be avoided by rejecting (rather than internalizing) disabling social institutions and working to create communities that support the impaired individual and encourage (rather than suppress) frank conversations about disability. In other words, the Whedonverses depict impaired individuals navigating disabling institutions and constructing supportive social environments as good and disabling/suppressive institutional environments as evil.

Disability as Choice of Models: The Impairment Arc of Lindsey McDonald

Angel presents a number of episodes involving impairment, so many that in her book *Angel*, Stacey Abbott surmises that bodies on *Angel* are "presented and described as vessels to be cut open, emptied, or hollowed out" (57). Indeed, Lindsey McDonald, whose manual impairment arc features his body as just such a malleable vessel, becomes impaired on the job and is then disabled by his social environment (the hierarchical corporate law firm Wolfram & Hart). Lindsey's impairment arc illustrates what the realm of disability studies refers to as the "biomedical" and "personal tragedy" models of disability. According to the biomedical model of disability, when people sustain physical harm or injury, society thereafter considers them a problem that must be fixed (Howson 26–7). Under the biomedical model, "people with impairments are typically isolated and excluded from full social participation" by the discriminatory and/or disempowering "social and cultural contexts in which it [the impairment] occurs or is acquired" (26). The relative inclusivity or exclusivity of the socio-cultural environment in which impairment occurs marks the difference between impairment and disability. As Howson relates, a famous study of Martha's Vineyard in the 1940s found that the town's large Deaf population had hearing impairments, but due to the widespread knowledge and use of sign language, was "not viewed as separate from the community because they formed a significant part of it" (26). By contrast, when people with impairments are labeled as "disabled," that act of categorization based on difference "leads to social distinctions that may be stigmatizing in their consequences" (26). Seen as a problem to be "fixed," the stigma of the biomedical model leads to the impaired person developing or internalizing the "personal tragedy" narrative of disability, which collaborates with the biomedical model to render people with impairments "less than whole" and therefore "unable to fulfill social roles" (Barnes and Mercer, *Disability* 2; 2003 edition). This prescription of dependency and "broken" status often confers "denial or despair that any recovery is possible, leading to anger at others" (5). The personal tragedy mindset is also a disabling force: just as the biomedical model tries to "fix" what it disables, the personal tragedy narrative "fixes" the identities of those whom they involve to stories of despair and resentment.[4] Along these lines, to what degree depictions of disability reinforce or repudiate ableism lies largely in the interplay between the impaired individual's mentality and his/her environment's influence.

Lindsey McDonald's impairment occurs during the *Angel* Season One finale "To Shanshu in L.A." (1.22) during a standoff with Angel following a battle. The two threaten each other while Lindsey holds a scroll with the important Shanshu prophecy out of Angel's grasp, threatening to destroy it; just then, Angel hurls a scythe at Lindsey and saves the prophecy from destruction by slicing off Lindsey's right hand. From this moment on, Lindsey nurtures a not-so-secret rage and desire for revenge against Angel, harboring the anger indicative of a personal tragedy mindset. This disabling mentality is further encouraged by Wolfram & Hart in "Judgment" (2.01), when colleague Lilah Morgan maliciously quips "you're not handicapped, you're handi-capable," to devalue Lindsey with a taunting turn of phrase. Lindsey's "personal tragedy" mindset, informed by an unsupportive environment, causes him to initially internalize ableism, as seen in "Dead End" (2.18). The episode's opening shots are cinematographically poised to invoke pity for Lindsey's impairment, as the camera follows Lindsey through his morning routine, while emphasizing his physical struggles (for example, the camera shows him shaving with one hand while occasionally sighing). Discomfort with adjusting to impairment fits with actual lived experiences of newly impaired people (clearly, when one's body changes, one must adapt). Lest we interpret Lindsey's attitude as neutral, though, he opens the door to his closet and his eyes are drawn to a guitar resting unused in the corner. The camera zooms in to Lindsey's somber face as mournfully contemplative music swells, implying hints of regret, frustration, and anger as he looks at the guitar he can no longer play. Lindsey sighs audibly and shuts the door. This scene imbues Lindsey with the personal tragedy narrative of disability, for the longing gaze at the guitar indicates Lindsey's use of his former "able-bodied normality" as a standard against which he judges his currently impaired situation, a standard bound to make Lindsey feel broken or "less than human" (Barnes and Mercer, *Disability* 26; 2003 edition).

The corporate structure of Lindsey's immediate socio-cultural environment suppresses his feelings about impairment. Nathan Reed, his boss, begins to say: "I realize what he did to you was"—and on the next word, the camera cuts to Lindsey's prosthetic hand—"heartless," but this is superficial sympathy, as Reed goes on to say it is unprofessional to "air those feelings" of resentment ("Dead End"). Reed's true concern is not for Lindsey's well being, but for how Lindsey's attitude might adversely affect the workplace. Here, Reed acts as the oppressive institution, disabling Lindsey's ability to negotiate the frustrations and anxieties placed on him via impairment. This difference between living in an impaired body and being forbidden to discuss the experiences of living in an impaired body marks the departure from impairment to disability. Moreover, Reed treats Lindsey's impairment as him being "broken," and he offers a biomedical fix in the form of a doctor who can attach a new hand. Even though Lindsey troublingly accepts, as said before, depiction is not necessarily endorsement, and even as Lindsey appears to be investing in the personal tragedy and biomedical models of disability, his choices are undermined by the narrative and camera work.

After the surgery, Lindsey continues feeling incomplete and unhappy, underscoring the inefficacy of the "fix" of surgery. We once again see him performing his daily morning routine. Despite using both hands now, however, Lindsey does not smile, seem glad, or give any sign of being at all "fixed," further unsettling the efficacy of the "fix" given him by Wolfram & Hart's biomedical ethic. Again, his eyes fall on the dusty guitar, and he this time picks it up and begins to strum the guitar with his new hand; it is only as he does so that viewers are given the first glimpse of any happiness the surgery gave him. Yet even this small happiness is undermined, as Lindsey discovers his new hand has been writing the words "Kill! Kill! Kill!" independent of his control ("Dead End"). Lindsey stares at the new hand, jabbing at it with a letter opener as though to confirm it is part of him. The letter opener draws blood, and Lindsey shrinks back in pain. He wonders aloud "who are you?," further illustrating that the real "problem" here is that he let Wolfram & Hart "fix" him. The final rug is pulled from under Lindsey's new-hand "fix" when he and Angel discover the new hand comes from a veritable orchard of bodies for the rich and privileged, where naked, half-dissected people stand suspended within large metal chambers in a dank basement, presumably waiting for another Wolfram & Hart employee, such as Lindsey, to be in need of a spare part. This is the nefarious source of Wolfram & Hart's disabling power. They own the bodies of their workers and literally succeed off the flesh of the less privileged. No wonder, then, that Lindsey's new hand has not "fixed" anything; it is indicative of a matrix of power, privilege, and ableism that continues to prey on the underclasses.

Whereas Lindsey's impairment arc poses troubling and difficult questions about power, privilege, and disability, as said before, depiction and endorsement are not necessarily the same things. Given the show's use of the biomedical model and personal tragedy narrative to expose such thinking as disabling and false, we can interpret Lindsey's initial investment in ableist attitudes as, ultimately, something the show itself critiques, seeing as how the environments which encourage and enforce the internalization of ableism and the "personal tragedy" mindset are characterized as evil. Through the vehicle of Wolfram & Hart, the show portrays evil as that which turns impairment into disability. Seeing as how Lindsey ends the episode quitting Wolfram & Hart and sardonically citing "evil hand issues" as his reason, the show portrays the impaired individual rejecting the evil disabling institution and choosing instead to forge a narrative path that encompasses but is not limited to impairment. Along these lines, the impairment arc of Lindsey McDonald illuminates the impaired individual's ability to recognize ableist oppression and agency to change his/her situation.[5]

Disability in Dollhouse: *The Impairment Arc of Bennett Halverson*

Dollhouse's second season offers an opportunity to observe impairment arcs as intersections between disability studies and narrative ethics in the character of Bennett Halverson, a Rossum employee and programmer at the D.C. Dollhouse who is also impaired. Bennett's impairment arc closely resembles that of Lindsey McDonald in that, following the biomedical and personal tragedy models of disability, she internalizes ableism and chooses a narrative that disables her. Although we only see Bennett in four episodes of *Dollhouse* ("The Public Hand" 2.05, "The Left Hand" 2.06, "Getting Closer" 2.11, and in a video in "Epitaph Two" 2.13), through flashbacks we see the entirety of her impairment arc, obtaining access to Bennett before, during, and after her impairment occurs. Julie Hawk asserts that "*Dollhouse* highlights how identity is constructed and reconstructed through lived and remembered experiences," and indeed, the use of flashbacks in Bennett's narrative serve to illustrate how Bennett's negotiation of impairment occurs within a disabling institution and prompts her to internalize ableism (par. 17). We can perhaps see ableism simply reflected in the fact that so much of Bennett's screen time concerns her disability. While certainly, impairments often require priority, stereotypical media portrayals of characters with impairments often foreground that impairment and emphasize disability as their primary defining characteristic.[6] *Bitch Magazine* blogger Anna_Palindrome describes this as the "Poster Child" effect: for example, when a character in a wheelchair exists to invoke pity, and that is the entirety of their characterization. Of course, in reality, people with disabilities are first and foremost people, and although they negotiate impairment, it does not necessarily define them.

Bennett complicates this stereotype, as she both is and is not introduced to us through her impairment. Her first appearance in *Dollhouse* features her impairment as visually emphasized but unarticulated: she is hard at work in the D.C. Dollhouse, typing with one hand on a specially designed vertical curved keyboard ("The Public Eye"). Her impairment is present and obvious—her arm rests in a sling by her side as she reaches for a cup of tea—but does not enter the dialogue. Her work environment has invested in accommodations, and yet, this is not an emotionally supportive environment. Bennett's speech is stilted and awkward as she discourages a co-worker from chatting with her by saying, "We can't.... We have the privilege of living in the human heart, and for that we give up everything." She pauses and looks off into the distance, as though her thoughts linger on what she gave up. She repeats, muttering, "We give up everything," an embittered behavior that implies that Bennett regards her impairment through a "personal tragedy" worldview.

Bennett's introduction to her L.A. counterpart Topher (both are the technological geniuses of their respective Dollhouses) encapsulates anxieties of terminology and illustrates how Bennett has internalized her socio-cultural environment's attitude that disabilities are disfiguring and damaging. In the midst of expressing admiration towards her when they meet, Topher exclaims: "What's up with your arm?" Visibly taken aback by Topher's bluntness, Bennett responds that the nerves are severed and then changes the subject ("The Left Hand"). He asks if it was weird to ask about her arm, and she says, "Honestly, it's refreshing," echoing the Willow/Muffitt scene's ambiguous attitude about the anxieties of offensive language. Despite his crush on Bennett, Topher still exhibits a disabling assumption that since she is beautiful and impaired, she must be a damaged Doll like Whiskey who has been repurposed, reinforcing the idea that disabled people are damaged or less than human (or, as Topher puts it, "rendered unengagable"). Bennett replies that she could not be a Doll because Dolls are beautiful, suggesting that she sees her disability as both physically and emotionally disfiguring, an attitude of internalized ableism. In this exchange, we see the mainstream paradigm operating as well as the pain Bennett feels negotiating between living with and hating her disabled body. That Bennett's investment in this disabling model of selfhood is portrayed as spiteful and sadistic opens up the interpretation that *Dollhouse* portrays this ableism in order to expose the violent (self)hatred such thinking promotes.

In addition to exhibiting (and apparently investing in) this sort of biomedical thinking, we learn that Bennett endorses the personal tragedy model of disability as well, blaming her impairment on Caroline and regarding her arm as physical proof of Caroline's betrayal. After all, Bennett and Caroline once were partners in crime, as we learn in a flashback scene in "The Left Hand" featuring a bleeding Bennett struggling under fallen debris following an explosion. While Bennett begs her partner for help, Caroline flees, saying "Sorry, sister. If I stay, we both get nabbed." Bennett bitterly blames Caroline for the impairment she sustained during the explosion, as for example when she angrily gestures to her arm and tells Topher, "I was her [Caroline's] best friend. This is what I got for it. This is my gift from Caroline." Following the grief and despair assigned to her "gift" by the personal tragedy narrative, Bennett takes revenge on Caroline (via Echo, the Doll who Caroline's body becomes) by imprinting Echo with her memories of the impairing event ("The Left Hand"). Bennett makes the imprint as tortuously painful as possible as she "deliberately and (it seems) unemotionally inflicts pain on Echo" (Calvert, "Mind" par. 8). Bennett gives Echo memories of "what you did to me. Not just to my arm, to me. I want you to feel this. There is something worse than pain." As Rabb and Richardson relate, "The kind of narrative we accept will influence the kind of person we become and the sorts of goals we are likely to choose" ("Memory"). Here, we see Bennett accepting the narrative of betrayal and formulating the goal of torturing Caroline accordingly. The fact that Bennett's goal is to inflict pain and impairment upon Caroline in retribution emphasizes the degree to which Bennett disables herself, limiting her identity to the goal of inflicting pain (thus characterizing her as evil).[7] Moreover, meeting the goal of revenge does not "fix" or placate Bennett, underscoring the fallacy of investing in the biomedical/personal tragedy model. Even after torturing Echo with her memories of impairment, Bennett is still preoccupied with "what it's like ... to be betrayed. To be abandoned" ("The Left Hand"). Unable to imagine a role other than disabler or disabled, Bennett chooses an identity that hinges on hating her impairment (or at least what it means to her).

Yet, as Rabb and Richardson note in "Memory and Identity in Whedon's Narrative Ethics," in the Whedonverses "our memories themselves are actually interpretations of what we have experienced." We are introduced to Bennett's memory of Caroline through the interpretive lens of Bennett's own vengeful preoccupation, but the subsequent episode "Getting Closer" (2.11) encourages viewers to revisit and re-think Bennett's interpretation of her impairment. This encouragement arrives in the form of flashbacks, which prove that, in the words of Hawk, "what one comes to know as oneself [...] is not the whole story" (par. 4). "Getting Closer" delivers narrative expansion on the flashbacks we glimpse from Bennett's memory of Caroline in "The Left Hand" where Caroline flees the destroyed Rossum lab, leaving Bennett pinned under fallen debris. The flashbacks in "Getting Closer" expand this memory, however, as we get additional data to inform our available interpretations of the earlier flashback. For example, the flashbacks show Bennett and Caroline developing rapport as students, offering glimpses of Bennett's pre-impairment personality. While always genius-smart, she was not previously violent, as shown when she tries to reason with, not attack, snobby girls at a lunch table. Given her sadism in the present moment of the *Dollhouse* narrative, these additional flashbacks clarify Bennett's arc, revealing the severity of her transformation from innocence into duplicity.

We also find out why Caroline and Bennett were in the explosion, learning that they had been conspiring to infiltrate a Rossum building to strategically plant bombs. But while doing this, Caroline discovers a human orchard visually similar to *Angel*'s "Dead End." Partially dismembered bodies lay on tables and are suspended inside large metal chambers with glass doors ("Getting Closer"). This unequivocally characterizes Rossum's capacity as a disabling institution; like Wolfram & Hart, Rossum views people's bodies as materials to use as replacements for the wealthy and elite. Whereas the viewer shares Caroline's perspective in discovering and being horrified by this clinical body orchard, however, Bennett does not since she is only connected to Caroline via an audio feed. She urges Caroline to leave, knowing nothing of Caroline's startling discovery, only watching the seconds tick down. When Caroline's delay causes the two women to still be inside the building as it explodes, we move back into the familiar scene of the memory we have already seen. But now, Caroline stands above the trapped Bennett, struggling to move the debris and free her. When Caroline realizes she cannot lift it, she comes up with a plan to save Bennett from being captured by the Dollhouse: "You were working late. The building was attacked. They'll find you. You'll be fine." Bennett begs Caroline not to leave her, and we hear the familiar lines, this time imbued with more than one meaning: "Sorry, sister. I stay, we both get nabbed"; however, the scene continues, offering clarification from Caroline: "and I'm gonna make sure it's just me." These additional flashback scenes reveal Bennett's interpretation of her impairment to be but one among many possible interpretations. With these flashbacks we know that Bennett *could* choose to believe that Caroline honestly tried to do right by Bennett, or she *could* choose to believe that Caroline didn't betray Bennett but rather saved her from jail by taking the blame. Given that, from among these choices, Bennett chooses an attitude of resentment, revenge, and internalized ableism, we can read this narrative choice as Bennett accepting society's disabling influence and biomedical mindset. With some relief, we can also note that this choice is made by a character willingly aligned with an evil institution. Even until the end, Bennett's resentment towards Caroline dictates her goal and character, as Bennett only agrees to help the L.A. Dollhouse (where she is killed) as part of a deal made with Echo to continue torturing Caroline's body. Thus Bennett's choice to pursue the vengeful goal, limited by her interpretation of the past, determines her present and disables her future.

Interestingly, Echo says in "Meet Jane Doe" (2.07) that her multiple-imprint wielding self really came alive as a result of Bennett's attempt to disable her. Bennett had imprinted Echo with her memories of being betrayed by Caroline. In "Meet Jane Doe," Echo reveals that the only reason she was able to evolve into the Echo super-being is "because of Bennett.... She showed me something Alpha didn't. Caroline.... I didn't like it." Bennett's memory reveals aspects of Caroline that Echo does not have, that Echo does not want to have, causing a shift in Echo's self-identity: "I've been saving this body for her, but I'm not her." In other words, while Bennett's biased memory of Caroline prompts her to want to disable Caroline/Echo retributively, this misguided retribution actually enables Echo to evolve beyond the one-brain/one-imprint limitation. In terms of narrative ethics, Bennett's insistence on blaming Caroline and the narrative goal she chooses in fostering that blame enacts an evil ethic that permits pain into the world. Yet ironically, the evil Bennett enacts works to pave the way for Echo to distinguish between herself as Echo and the Caroline of Bennett's memory. Echo, having felt the pain Caroline caused Bennett, realizes she does not want to be the person that caused such pain, and rejects Caroline, an act which allows Echo to fully self-differentiate from her body's original personality for the first time. This, in turn, allows Echo to choose an identity that admits the least evil into the world (enacting Richardson and Rabb's "virtue ethics"). This sort of virtuous narrative ethic is endorsed by *Dollhouse* in ways that Bennett's narrative ethic is not (namely, Echo lives). We will see this virtuous narrative ethic developed in more detail in the impairment arc of Xander Harris.

Transcending Personal Tragedy: The Impairment Arc of Xander Harris

On the other end of the existential spectrum, we have Xander Harris, a good character, loyal friend, and beloved Scooby (the self-chosen name for Buffy's group of friends) who makes a particularly poignant example of the impaired body functioning as a site in which both theoretical models of disability and narratives of disabled selfhood compete, conflict, and struggle. As Richardson and Rabb suggest in their book *The Existential Joss Whedon*, throughout the seven TV seasons of *Buffy*, Xander's role in the Scooby group make him the show's Everyman (76). Ironically (and, as fans may be temped to say, tragically), the ordinary embodiment that defines Xander becomes impaired where it hurts him most, when villain Caleb gouges out his left eye ("Dirty Girls" 7.18). In keeping with the personal tragedy mentality, this impairment is treated at first as earth-shatteringly devastating. For example, when Willow visits Xander in the hospital, they attempt to resume their typically optimistic and jocular banter but falter and mourn what has just happened ("Empty Places" 7.19). Whereas they usually laugh in the face of evil on a weekly basis, their difficulty in laughing now that Xander has been hurt marks the severity of the impairment's impact—not just to Xander but to Buffy's whole group. In fact, on the DVD commentary for "Dirty Girls," actor Nicholas Brendan and story editor Drew Greenberg discuss how the writing team felt injuring Xander (of all the characters) would best metaphorically signify that the team was falling apart ("Dirty Girls Commentary").

The Scooby Gang does not disable Xander in the same way Wolfram & Hart disables Lindsey or Rossum disables Bennett. We can see this by comparing several instances. For one thing, neither characters in the show nor production staff on the show regard Xander's eye as a problem to be fixed. Quite the opposite, as the commentary continues with Brendan specifying that he would not want there to be a supernatural healing spell, that he would want Xander to remain in his impaired body. Clearly the writers similarly felt Xander's impairment became an important part of his character, rather than a problem to be solved, given Xander's eye patch in the *Buffy Season 8* comics. Indeed, Xander's post-impairment identity eventually becomes an integrated part of his personality, as both he and the Scooby Gang work towards accepting his impaired status. Contrast this with Lindsey's situation, wherein Wolfram & Hart's disabling attitude treats impairment as a problem to be supernaturally fixed. The attitude engendered by the Scooby Gang is much more empowering. In a manner reminiscent of Dr. Claire Saunders in *Dollhouse*, who explains in "Vows" (*Dollhouse* 2.01) that she likes her scars and will not undergo plastic surgery to erase them, Xander reclaims his impairment and comfortably resides in a one-eyed body, choosing to be a person whose identity encompasses physical impairment and the negotiation of social disabling without being limited by it. As Ian Klein writes of Dr. Saunders, "In the same way that the body creates literal scar tissue over time, the mind creates metaphysical scar tissue by reframing and reinterpreting the scar" (124). While at first, Xander is clearly saddened and depressed by his impairment, he presses on past viewing himself as broken and reframes his viewpoint to negotiate life with impairment in a way that transcends the typical model. Keeping and continually reinterpreting his impairment in a difficult, on-going process of crafting the personal narrative he believes and tells other people, Xander transcends the biomedical and personal tragedy models of disabled selfhood.

Xander also differs from Lindsey and Bennett in terms of the socio-cultural environment in which he negotiates disabled identity. Recall that both Lindsey and Bennett's environments suppress the discourse of disability and encourage the impaired to view themselves as broken. Wolfram & Hart exploits workers' bodies to "fix" impairments and denies expression to the people it disables, while Rossum's Dollhouses wipe people of their personalities entirely to "fix" disabilities such as PTSD and schizophrenia. By contrast, the Scooby Gang community supports Xander's negotiation of impaired life, even when it causes the group discomfort. Immediately following the failed battle plan resulting in Xander's impairment, the Scooby/Slayer Gang mutinies against Buffy's leadership, thereby registering the severity of the trauma on the whole community. They support Xander's right to express his feelings about his impairment, even when it is uncomfortable for them, as for example in "Empty Places" when Xander tells Buffy "I'm trying to see your point here, Buff [pause] but I guess it must be a little bit to my left" (7.19). Even when the mutiny subsides and the group comes back together, Xander is not labeled as broken but rather retains his integral role. Moreover, Xander grows into this identity through an on-going process of reaffirming that selfhood amidst the occasional unintentional disabling influence of his friends. Buffy and Xander illustrate this dynamic in "End of Days" (7.21), as the anxieties of negotiating impairment-encompassing identity come to a head when Buffy asks Xander to leave town with Dawn to get out of harm's way. Xander expresses that he feels she is "putting him out to pasture," which he later jokingly defines as "you know, when a cow gets old, and loses an eye, … the farmer takes it and puts it in a different pasture so it won't have to fight." Buffy denies that she is being overprotective, but even though she says it lightheartedly, she here treats Xander according to the biomedical model's assumptions about impairment damaging people past the point of functionality: "Also, you can't shoot a bow and arrow anymore, and every time you pick up a sword I worry you're going to break one of our good lamps." While Buffy tries to support Xander's identity-in-flux, what she says and does here can be construed as offensive and ableist. Buffy means well, but even friends with good intentions contribute to society's disabling of people with impairment, especially when they are overprotective. Messages of weakness can be unconsciously sent and internalized (possibly as shown by Xander's eventual compliance with Buffy's request).

Yet, as said before, Whedon often depicts things in order to critique them, and this scene is a perfect example of the show displaying attitudes without promoting them. The show no more endorses Buffy's ableist decision-making here than it endorses Buffy's startled and flustered reaction to Willow's coming out of the closet in "New Moon Rising" (4.19). Whereas Buffy is shocked and uncomfortable at first, the show does not overall endorse homophobia. Rather, Buffy's reaction illustrates the on-going process of working through discomfort and eventually becoming more open-minded. Keeping in mind Richardson and Rabb's theory of narrative ethics, we might say that while Buffy's reaction to Willow's coming out may be homophobic, the show features this homophobia to later critique and undo it. Similarly, although the Scoobies' reaction to Xander's impairment at first upholds the biomedical/personal tragedy model, they do eventually come to see that alternative choices are available. When Xander complies with Buffy's request and coerces Dawn into leaving town, Dawn eventually makes them turn the car back. When Dawn and Xander rejoin the Scooby Gang, Dawn gives Buffy a swift, playful kick to the shin, uttering a one-word evaluation of both Buffy's plan and the biomedical assumptions of inferiority of impaired people it exemplifies: "Dumbass!" ("Chosen" 7.22). Compare this candor to *Dollhouse*, where characters refer to Bennett's impairment—in "Getting Closer" for instance, Adelle DeWitt refers to Bennett as "that troublesome one-armed creature"—but do so mostly behind Bennett's back, suggesting the hostility of the social environment of the Dollhouse. In "Chosen," Buffy's and Xander's impairment-centric comments occur in a face-to-face conversation, exchanging equal, if uncomfortable and potentially offensive, expression.

While far from perfect, the Scoobies perpetually try to support rather than disable Xander. When he bravely says, "I got hurt, but I'm not done. I can still fight" ("End of Days"), his community listens to him and respects his self-chosen narrative of ability, enacting what Richardson and Rabb call "virtue ethics grounded in care" (*The Existential* 75). The Scoobies do not treat Xander as disabled, and so while he may be impaired, he still remains a beloved central figure and holds a position of power and authority among Scoobies and Slayers alike throughout all of the *Buffy* Season 8 comics. Although his ocular impairment is present in the narrative, it is not a barrier to his ability to function in the group. It does not compromise his ability to make his own choices and decisions, nor his ability to be a sexual being, as he dates one of the Slayers and eventually Dawn. His sexual identity further marks his transcendence of the typical biomedical/personal tragedy model, which commonly presents depictions where "the 'good parts' of ordinary life—love, romance, and sex—are largely absent or not stressed in disabled characters' lives" (Barnes and Mercer, *Disability*

94; 2003 edition). Undoubtedly, Richardson and Rabb's identified "virtue ethics grounded in care" are what enable Xander to form an identity that encompasses but is not limited to impairment, as well as help to form social structures that support rather than disable people with impairments. Notably, such an environment is only provided by characters aligned with the forces of good in the Whedonverses, standing in stark contrast to the environments offered by evil-affiliated institutions.

Conclusion: Engage to Complicate

Clearly, the portrayals of disability the Whedonverses offer us are complicated, often contradictory, and very often exhibit ableism. Yet these depictions also serve to critique or undermine dominant narratives of disability by using them as a characterization device for evil, and just as often reflect the complicated realities of navigating disability in society. When we compare Lindsey's and Bennett's narrative arcs to Xander's, we see a disability narrative ethics as a characterization device, distinguishing between "good" and "evil" environments and attributes in terms of how they respond to impairment. In other words, evil disables impaired characters (as Wolfram & Hart disables Lindsey and as Rossum disables Bennett), whereas the Scoobies do not disable Xander. Moreover, while some of the language his group uses in response to Xander's eye is troubling, it still occurs within relatively free and open dialogue, standing in stark contrast to the way in which both Rossum and Wolfram & Hart discourage impaired people from expressing their frustrations publicly. Whedon models for us worlds in which good people support each other in articulating and choosing their own stories, thereby inviting viewers to do the same. As Rabb and Richardson say, we must "learn to set our own goals and write our own stories" ("Memory"). The disability narrative ethic in the Whedonverses' impairment arcs allows viewers to do just that, offering a path towards recognizing our ability to choose our own stories and define our own selves, a path that helps us reject disabling self-narratives and negotiate less problematic paradigms of disabled selfhood.

Notes

1. While the narrative universes of *Buffy the Vampire Slayer* and *Angel* co-exist and sometimes overlap, each show's respective visual style and storytelling technique render them vastly different worlds, making their treatment of common themes through wildly varied formats all the more significant when drawing conclusions across the Whedonverse shows. For further information on the differentiation of *Angel* from *Buffy*, please see Abbott, "Kicking Ass," pages 3–11.

2. As Barnes and Mercer relate, "the separation of impairment and disability characterizes schemes advanced by both UPIAS (Union of the Physically Impaired Against Segregation) and Disabled People's International": namely, the distinction between the physical and social components of constructions of disability in society (*Disability* 66; 2003 edition).

3. s.e. smith suggests that Hipster Ableism is the mistaken use of ableism as though it were edgy or transgressive ("Hipster Abelism"), and Annaham contends that Liberal Ableism appears to support disability rights activism but ceases to do so when it becomes politically inconvenient. For further variations on types of ableism, please see www.disabledfeminists.com.

4. While many more models of disability exist, I limit my discussion here to the two most prevalent in Whedon's work. For thorough analysis of the social model of disability as well as the Post-Structuralist "Foucaltian" model of disability, please see Howson at 27–30, as well as Barnes and Mercer's *Disability: Key Concepts* 6–18 (2003 edition).

5. Lindsey McDonald, for most of *Angel*, occupies a liminal space between good and evil. During Season One, for instance, he becomes morally disgusted by Wolfram & Hart's evil deeds and appeals to Angel for help leaving the firm's clutches. Yet he is almost instantly wooed back to the corporate fold when he's offered a promotion and larger office. Again, during the impairment arc discussed above, Lindsey once again seems to reject the evil institution and align himself with good, yet during Season Five he re-appears to us theoretically aligned with good (in that he is trying to take down Wolfram & Hart's senior partners) but circumstantially evil (in that he pursues this goal by trying to kill Angel, our hero). The fact that Lindsey's morality is not inherent or inborn but rather an on-going negotiation between individual and environment renders his impairment arc in Season Two all the more powerful an indication that *Angel* poses problematic scenarios not necessarily to endorse them but to feature characters navigating them.

6. This one-dimensional approach to characters with impairment/disability concerns such disability activist blogging sites as disabledfeminists.com, Bitchmagazine.com, disabilitylaw.blogspot.com, cripwheels.blogspot.com, accessibility-fail.dreamwidth.org, and disabilityvoices.wordpress.com/blog.

7. Bennett's characterization is compounded by the fact that she, as a top technician in the D.C. Dollhouse, should know better than anyone that Echo is not Caroline, and that revenge on Caroline's body is not equal to revenge on Caroline herself. That Bennett's angry obsession with revenge causes her to forget or ignore this fact demonstrates the depths of her internalization of the biomedical model. Reduced to a broken body by the disabling environment Rossum provides, Bennett seeks to reduce Caroline/Echo to a body in order to similarly "break" or disable her.

Slaying the Deficit in Disability

Exploring Buffy *and* Firefly/Serenity

CYNTHIA HEADLEY

Disability theorists such as David Mitchell criticize representations of "disability as a problem in need of a solution" or a deficit in need of a cure (15). Instead of viewing disability as something that needs a cure—whether it is society or the individual who needs curing—Susan Wendell suggests that representations of disability can show "different ways of being that give valuable perspective on life and the world" ("Unhealthy" 30). In the Whedonverses, both the television series *Buffy the Vampire Slayer* and the series/film *Firefly/Serenity* provide ways of seeing disability as an asset rather than a deficit, using characters who could be read as disabled. This essay focuses on two such characters, Buffy and River, to show how both series provide models for including the disabled within communities, with the result being that inclusion benefits the community. In the Whedonverses, the immediate communities of both Buffy and River—the Scooby gang and Mal's crew, respectively—see Buffy and River as differently-abled rather than as disabled. The two shows present narratives that challenge dominant discourses that situate disability as a disadvantage in need of fixing/curing, allowing viewers to re-conceptualize disability as different ability.

Disability studies began toward the end of the twentieth century with scholars questioning the medical model of disability, replacing the medical model with a social model. A medical model of disability locates disabilities within the individual body as impairments that need repairing, devaluing the impaired body, while a social model locates disabilities outside the body, rooted in cultural constructs. A medical model seeks to repair parts of the body within the individual and a social model seeks to "repair" social viewpoints that define particular differences as disability. In a move designed to call attention to the social construction of disability, disability theorists in the 1980s emphasized the social model, which virtually ignored the body and lived bodily experiences of people with disabilities. More recently, scholars and activists have worked to close this gap by theorizing how social constructions of disability affect individual experiences of people living with disabilities in an effort to demonstrate that disabled bodies have value. Helen Deutsch and Felicity Nussbaum call for scholars and activists to "reject definitions of disability as abnormality, lack, or absence [...] that are limited to what an individual can or cannot achieve" (3). Sharon Snyder and David Mitchell's *Cultural Locations of Disability* argues that "the devaluation of disabled bodies places in jeopardy all bodies that exist within proximity to 'deviance'" (5). Sharon Snyder, Brenda Jo Bruggemann, and Rosemarie Garland-Thomson's scholarly collection *Disability Studies: Enabling the Humanities* seeks to undermine the idea that "the disabled body is imagined as [...] an alien condition," and instead, promote it as "the universal consequence of living an embodied life" (2). I argue that both *Buffy* and *Firefly/Serenity* provide narratives that act as bridges between the social and medical models and actively promote two goals of disability studies: to undermine representations that see the disabled body as deviant or alien and to find value in the disabled body. Rather than present particular bodies as disabled, both series present those same bodies as differently-abled.

Both *Buffy* and *Firefly* give viewers models that show how community interaction with disability can ultimately benefit all within the community. As K. Dale Koontz has noted, Whedon provides viewers with narratives demonstrating that "the surest way to fight these vampires and demons is to band with others," regardless of whether the vampires and demons are literal or metaphoric (4). Similarly, Shannon Sullivan's model of transactional bodies offers insight into how individuals and groups can effectively change their environments by recognizing certain habits that constitute behaviors. Transaction "indicates dynamic entities that are continually undergoing reconstitution through their inter-constitutive relations with others" (13). In other words, bodies or entities are not whole and atomistic but, much like cellular membranes, porous and transforming. This porous nature allows for different bodies to interact, potentially transforming one another. To change mainstream views, neither of the series' immediate communities—Buffy's friends and Mal's crew—subscribe to the medical model that would institutionalize and "demonize" Buffy and River. They resist the social norm by including Buffy and River in their daily lives. Sullivan goes on to say that bodies transact with other bodies by use of "habit [...] a style or manner that is reflected throughout ones' being," and that habit can either be static or dynamic (31). If an individual changes a habit that undermines a social norm, then when that individual transacts with another, that change in habit reflects back between the two and brings with it the possibility of changing another's habit (88). Integrating Buffy and River into a smaller community begins to change a larger community's "habit" to institutionalize abnormal behavior. These changes start on a very small scale, such as viewers watching Kaylee eventually accept River, viewers who then in their own lives transact with others differently, potentially leading to more grand changes that could transform a dominant paradigm of disability.

In many ways, Buffy's super-ability functions much like a chronic illness, with unforeseen flare-ups that interrupt normal activity. According to the Americans with Disabilities Act (ADA), impairment becomes disability when it "substantially limits one or more major life activities" ("What Is the Definition"). Under this definition, Buffy's super-ability qualifies as disability: she can never move from Sunnydale, the location of the Hellmouth she must guard; she cannot make choices with potentially long commitments, as her life expectancy as a Slayer is very short (early twenties); nor can she go about normal activities, such as employment and school, without being interrupted by the necessity of saving the world. For example, while working at the Doublemeat Palace, Buffy's grisly discovery of a finger in the meat grinder causes her to rampage through the restaurant to stop people from eating, well, other people. In this case, her conclusions are wrong about the particulars that constitute the threat at the Doublemeat Palace, but her instincts that something *is* wrong are absolutely correct ("Doublemeat Palace" 6.12). Her Slayer super-ability causes her to act in a way that most would consider deviant, crazy, and abnormal. Additionally, at school, vampires attack on parent-teacher night, and Buffy's subsequent protection results in vandalism and destruction. The principal determines it is Buffy's fault and labels her a troublemaker ("School Hard" 2.03). While the label of troublemaker does not necessarily equal disability, the principal's reaction to Buffy's flare-up of Slayer-ness shows that he "regard[s]" her as "having such an impairment" ("What Is the Definition"), a view that most authority figures in the series share. Disability scholar Lennard Davis suggests that ideas of normalcy create an "imperative [...] on people to conform," a process he terms "enforcing normalcy" (101). Buffy's super-ability incurs the label of not normal, a label authority figures use as they attempt to enforce normalcy by at first demonizing the bodily difference/disability, and later, "fixing" the difference/disability.[1]

In "Normal Again" (6.17), the series provides a concrete example of society's attempts to fix/cure Buffy of her disability. Throughout most of the series, Buffy longs to be what she considers normal, a high school girl who joins the cheerleading squad, earns decent grades, and gets crushes on boys. In the episode, Buffy vacillates between two realities, one of which is a fantastical Slayer reality in which she saves the world from demons on a daily basis, and the other is a (more?) reasonable reality in which she resides in a mental hospital where her Slayer activities become hallucinations. These two alternatives stem from the larger context of the series that frames Buffy's super-ability as disability. The episode "Normal Again" gives viewers two paradigms of community interaction with disability: one demonstrating a medical model of disability that institutionalizes and isolates disability in an attempt to fix the disability, and the other demonstrating a more interactive model that invites more of the community to share in working with the disability. The institutional hospital setting also adds another layer to Buffy's disability, that of labeling abnormal behavior as mentally ill. Buffy tells Willow that after her first experience of slaying in Los Angeles (that would be the film *Buffy the Vampire Slayer*), her parents send her to a clinic. She says, "I stopped talking about it [killing vampires], and they let me go.... What if I am still there?" ("Normal Again"). Buffy's outbreak of Slayer-ness in the pre-series film, where she very visibly attacks and kills vampires, results in the authorities (police, school principal, parents) defining her actions as mentally unstable, so they institutionalize her. In order to escape her confinement, Buffy stops speaking of her success in slaying the vampires who would have destroyed most of her fellow students at the high school prom. Buffy decides that she needs to at least appear to be normal to those in positions of authority. For Tobin Siebers, "The inability to disclose is [...] one of the constitutive markers of oppression" ("Disability" 2). Buffy hides her disability with silence so that those in authority remove the classifications of mentally ill and abnormal.

Like Buffy, those outside River's immediate community label her different ability as deviant and abnormal, but they go a step further and deem her dangerous to the community. This response occurs most notably in "Safe" (1.07) when a group of hill-abiding townsfolk kidnaps both her and Simon because they need a doctor. When River reveals that she has telepathic abilities, the group's reaction is to ostracize her as a "witch" and attempt to burn her to death. In other words, the townsfolk view her "as a contagion within the community" whose "presence cannot be tolerated" (Koontz 152). Even though her ability to communicate to the mute Ruby initially produces amazement and wonder, its extraordinary nature is so beyond the bounds of normal that the community feels sufficiently threatened. They decide to enforce normalcy through silencing River in the most permanent of ways, death. River cannot use her ability because the community views it as disability, as something different and out of the range of what normal bodies should do. Indeed, the town patron, who has the most to gain by silencing River before she can reveal that he attained his position by murdering his predecessor, reinforces and encourages the town's mob-mentality reaction. In *Extraordinary Bodies: Figuring Disability in American Culture and Literature*, Rosemarie Garland-Thomson argues that dominant discourse describes the disabled body as both "wondrous and repellent," pointing out that these descriptions invoke fear and the desire to ostracize as responses (136). Clearly the episode does not sanction such a view, as it represents the townsfolk as both superstitious and ignorant, suggesting that an enlightened view would never promote such measures. This hyperbolic representation of reactions to disability makes clear that such reactions should be condemned, always. Combine that with Mal's assessment that River is "our witch," and viewers see a model of disability that has a foundation based on inclusion. Mal does not replace the "witch" label with something that erases River's disability, but instead uses the label, thus keeping and accepting its problematic and powerful associations.

Traditionally, silence and passivity define socially acceptable women, and detouring from these feminine characteristics labels the woman as undesirable and even monstrous. According to Rachel Simmons' *Odd Girl Out*, girls are socialized that normal means to be "nice" at all costs and to avoid direct confrontation (18). Certainly aggressively staking vampires through the heart or lopping off demons' heads with a bloody sword does not fit into a definition of "nice," nor is it "avoiding direct confrontation." When Buffy and River use their power, they "threaten the symbolic order" that views men as powerful and women as powerless (Creed 83). For Buffy, her gender allows those in positions of authority to define her displays of power as crazy, furthering the process that makes her flare-ups of Slayer-ness a disability.[2] For River, displaying her different ability, telepathy, generates fear from those in authority to the point where they want to permanently silence her through execution (the patron's reaction to River's knowledge foreshadows the revelation in *Serenity* about why the government so desperately wants to recapture River). In these ways, both women are "regarded as having such an impairment," for they cannot display the results of their different abilities without exposing themselves to silencing through confinement or death. Their "extraordinary" bodies are at once "wondrous and repellent" as Buffy's Slayer powers and River's telepathy mark them with extraordinary abilities, and these freak-like abilities ostracize them from the mainstream (Garland-Thomson 136). As an example of the social model of disability, society disables them in that they cannot exhibit their abilities without the consequence of silencing, either through institutionalization or permanently, through death.

To challenge this dominant response that disability is deviant, both *Buffy* and *Firefly/Serenity* present Buffy and River as having an immediate community that accepts their disabilities as different ability. For Buffy, this immediate community comes from her friends, which earlier in the series comprises of Willow, Xander, and Giles. According to Tobin Siebers, one problem with disability occurs when it symbolizes "one person in his or her entirety" ("Tender" 48). Both Xander and Willow never define Buffy wholly by her Slayer super-ability. In the first episode of the series, Xander overhears Giles trying to convince Buffy to resume her Slayer duties, and when Buffy and Giles leave the library, Xander reacts, alone, saying, "What?" ("Welcome to the Hellmouth" 1.01). His reaction reflects questioning rather than fear, suggesting that he wants more knowledge about Buffy's disability. The next episode, "The Harvest" (1.02), opens in the school library with Giles, Willow, Xander, and Buffy discussing vampires. This image suggests an acceptance of Buffy's super-ability. Certainly both Willow and Xander react with shock, but their shock stems from the new knowledge they are learning and not from a fear of difference and deviance. They immediately begin discussing the ways they can find the vampires who took Jessie, and neither Willow nor Xander think that Buffy is a freak. With the exception of Giles, and later in the series, Buffy's mother, both Willow's and Xander's reactions to Buffy contrast with that of most of the adults in authority positions. The opening image foreshadows the group's support and acceptance throughout the series, paving the way for the group to take more active parts in working with Buffy's different ability. Willow and Xander immediately accept that Buffy has these different abilities, and they do it in a way that does not allow the super-ability to define Buffy in her "entirety"; in other words, being a Slayer does not wholly define Buffy's identity in Willow's or Xander's view.

On the other hand, Giles the adult and Watcher, takes more time to recognize that the Slayer identity does not define Buffy's identity in its "entirety." In the first season, Giles puts the Slayer duties ahead of Buffy's well-being when he knows that in order to fight the Master, Buffy must die. He does not tell Buffy this piece of news; she overhears it accidentally, and it is then that Giles discusses the prophecy in more detail ("Prophecy Girl" 1.12). Giles shifts his perspective gradually as the series unfolds, and he eventually recognizes that Buffy's identity goes beyond the Slayer identity. The Season Three episode "Helpless" (3.12) underscores this change. In this episode, the Council of Watchers comes to Sunnydale to test Buffy by forcing her to face a deadly vampire without her Slayer abilities. At first, Giles participates by administering the drug that temporarily removes her abilities, and thus, aligns himself with the Council of Watchers who see the Slayer as the "entirety" of Buffy's identity, an identity that Council head Quentin Travers summarizes: "It's been done this way for a dozen centuries [...] A Slayer is not just physical prowess. She must have cunning, imagination, a confidence derived from self-reliance." When a distraught Buffy comes to Giles about her loss of strength, he replies, "I'm sure it will sort itself out." However, Giles' initial reluctance to administer the drug, combined with his later disclosure to Buffy of the test, demonstrates that he no longer defines Buffy solely by her Slayer ability. Understandably, Buffy feels as if Giles has betrayed her, and she storms out to find out that the vampire Kraylick has kidnapped her mother, so Buffy must go through with the test even though Giles' disclosure has "invalidated" it. Giles even attempts to help, but before he arrives, Buffy figures out that the vampire needs pills and puts holy water in his glass. Still, Giles helps by killing another vampire, and his actions prompt the Council to fire him. Travers says to Giles, "Your affection for your charge has rendered you incapable of clear and impartial judgment." In other words, Giles no longer sees Buffy as solely a Slayer but as Buffy, and this perspective is at odds with the status quo of the Watchers Council, or the dominant social order for Slayers and Watchers. This change in perspective took time and emotional pain for both Giles and Buffy, and it came at great personal cost for Giles. Accepting disability as part of an identity does not always come easily.

In a more complex treatment of possible perceptions of otherly-abled individuals, the series *Firefly* provides viewers with a range of responses to River's disability: some define her solely through her disability; some want to cure her of it; some react with a qualified acceptance of it. Mal's qualified acceptance summarizes two dominant responses to disability, categorically dismissing both of them. In "Safe" he discusses River with Simon: "I'm not a doctor. And I'm not your gorram babysitter." In the medical model of disability, disability needs fixing, and Mal's response that he is not a doctor for River indicates a rejection to that medical model—he will not fix River. Additionally, another common response to disability occurs when people infantilize those who are disabled, treating the disabled as children, even if they are not. Once again, Mal rejects that response, and so, his short statement rejects the two most common responses to disability, responses that fundamentally see disability as an "alien condition" that needs fixing. His rejection sets up the possibility for another way to view disability, one that ultimately sees disability in Wendell's terms as providing valuable perspective on life and the world. While in some ways one could read Mal as being wholly concerned with his own interests here—the crew is doing a job that may require Simon to "gag" River to prevent her from interrupting—Mal also allows River to be River as long as it does not interfere—which is also often a question of safety for both River and the rest of the crew. In this way, he accepts her disability. Furthermore, as Alyson Buckman notes, the series frequently gives the audience more information about River than the other characters know, allowing the audience to "identify with River and more quickly understand her gifts" ("Much Madness" 44). For example, River's seemingly incoherent "hands of blue" turns out to be a real threat, and viewers understand this threat when they see the men with "hands of blue" looking for River ("The Train Job" 1.02). Both Mal's response and the narrative technique of giving the audience more information than other characters allow audiences to see River as differently-abled rather than disabled.

As in *Buffy*, the acceptance of disability by the immediate community takes time and is fraught with missteps. In "War Stories" (1.09) River saves Kaylee's life in a shootout by killing three men with three expertly-shot bullets. Kaylee reacts with horror and is unable to meet River's eyes at the end of the episode. For River, Kaylee's reaction proves to be more of a setback in her attempts to integrate with a community than the townsfolk who deemed her a witch and tried to kill her. In this moment, Kaylee represents the ways in which even a supportive community can falter. The sheer and utter delight both girls demonstrated in the beginning of the episode gives way to fear and distrust, emotions that stem from the inability to accept differences. Both Kaylee and River lose here since fear not only ostracizes the disabled person—River—but it prevents the able-bodied person—Kaylee—from enjoying her life. No longer will either run with the "pitter patter of tiny feet in huge combat boots" throughout the ship and have the time of their lives (as Mal says in "War Stories"). Instead, both, for different reasons, will fear the other, at least for a time. The series format does not provide easy solutions, but instead allows characters the time to work through the complexities of accepting disabilities as "the universal consequence of living an embodied life" (Synder, Brueggemann, and Garland-Thomas 2). Eventually Kaylee and River become friends again, but they go through periods of distrust and fear first.

River participates in a narrative similar to Buffy: some characters try to "cure" her, whether it is her brother Simon's use of medical means, the Alliance's manipulation of her brain, or Jayne's attempts to get rid of her (thereby fixing the problem River represents to the status quo of the Serenity community). These "cures" represent a reaction to her differences, with each reaction demonstrating a lack of acceptance for her differences. Certainly Simon's reaction is more complex; as her brother, he definitely cares about her and listens to her input as he tries to help her function within the small community of Mal's crew. Still, he is a doctor, and thus his knowledge of how to help River stems from his medical background. But because many characters inhabit the world of *Firefly*, viewers see a wide range of responses to River's disability, from Mal's brand of acceptance, to Simon's somewhat collaborative attempts at a cure, to Jayne's easy "solution" of dropping her off on a planet, to the Alliance's medical experiments that completely dehumanize her. This range of character responses allows viewers to consider the complex ways in which culture constructs disability while at the same time provides a very individualized account of a disabled person.

In River, viewers once again see the cultural power of constructions of normality during the episode "War Stories." River comments that when she was playing with Kaylee, she felt like a "real girl," and the wistfulness in her voice points to the powerful longing she has to be a "real girl," suggesting that River associates the very normal activities of running and playing with "real." Like Buffy, River desires to be normal, even if the definition of normality ultimately proves elusive. In both shows, the writing teams create worlds that challenge dominant views of normal. In Buffy's world, fighting demons and vampires becomes normal, while in River's world fighting the Alliance and Reavers becomes normal. Ultimately, the characters determine definitions of normal that work for their communities, inviting viewers to do the same. Normal, then, changes for different groups of people in different settings and situations, and this context-oriented definition undermines the dominant paradigm that normal has a single definition.

In Buffy's case, transforming the dominant paradigm includes transforming both a society that would label her super-ability as disability, as well as the hierarchical Council of Watchers that guides and trains the Slayers. Buffy initiates this transformative process by redefining what it means to be a Slayer: instead of working alone in isolation, she shares the burden of Slayer-ness with Giles, her Watcher, as well as her immediate friends, Willow and Xander. Initially, she invites her immediate community to share in her Slayer disability, and all work together to banish the demon *du jour*. Since the First Slayer, Slayers have fought alone. Since Buffy's immediate community accepts her disability, she transacts in ways that begin to change the definition of Slayer, ultimately resulting in Buffy sharing her Slayer powers, making this status of differently-abled desirable rather than ostracized.[3] To "heal" her Slayer disability, others in various social positions—authority figures, friends, parents, etc.—must participate, creating a micro-community that act as a family.[4] In Season Four's big battle scene against the enemy Adam in the episode "Primeval" (4.21), the gang literally bands together to defeat the enemy. Willow casts a spell to infuse Buffy with all of their collective power, incorporating a strength of each person present: Giles' knowledge of Sumerian, Xander's soldier training, Willow's magical ability, and Buffy's Slayer reflexes. In the heat of the battle between Buffy and Adam, the spell works and Buffy says, "We are forever.... You could never hope to grasp the source of our power. But yours is right here" and then calmly rips Adam's power source from his chest. When Buffy uses the word "forever" to describe their power, she does not mean it in the sense that they will live forever; she means that it is impossible to tell where Willow's power ends and begins, or where Xander's, Giles', and Buffy's power ends and begins because their power lives "across and through" the "skins" of each, having no beginning and no ending, in line with Shannon Sullivan's work in *Living Across and Through Skins: Transactional Bodies, Pragmatism, and Feminism*. Through communication and discussion with each other, the group shares "power whenever they can, rather than relying on a patriarchal model that organizes power and leadership linearly and hierarchically" (Sharon Ross 241). The friends, the micro-community, claim victory again, but only because they share in the Slayer disability. Rather than work the traditional Slayer way, alone and under the direction of a (male) Watcher and mostly male Council of Watchers, Buffy decides to cultivate relationships and build a community, demonstrating what Richardson and Rabb call "communitarian existential love ethics" (*The Existential* 174).[5]

These communitarian ethics form the basis of a value system that can potentially move disability beyond either a medical model or a social model. In a medical model, the hierarchy of doctor and patient reduces the community to a single pairing of non-peers. In a social model, the community needs to cure itself of social "dis-ease" and remake the community in a way that accommodates the disability into extinction (Wilentz 127–129). Either way, the "culture views disability as a problem in need of a solution" (David Mitchell 15). Somewhere in the middle of this either/or construct, *Buffy* finds a way of constructing disability not as a problem, but as an asset. The disability does not go away; rather the community steps in to participate in the disability. But, the community does not step in without Buffy nudging them in that direction. Soon after learning of her Slayer illness, Buffy shares that knowledge with her friends. Rarely does Buffy confront the legions of darkness alone; in fact when she does, destructive results always follow. Rather, she asks for help from people who are not traditionally considered experts in curing illnesses and even defends these choices to the Council of Watchers in Season Five. The Council questions the roles her "civilian" (e.g., non-expert) friends play, and Buffy exclaims, "We're talking about two very powerful witches and a thousand year-old ex-demon." When a Council member points to Xander and sneers, "The boy? No power there," Buffy quickly corrects his characterization of Xander: "The *boy* has clocked more field time than all of you combined" ("Checkpoint" 5.12, emphasis mine). These non-experts have valuable roles to play, and their interactions with Buffy have allowed them to grow powerful—for example, Willow as a witch and Xander's ability to save the world in Season Six. Because they aid and accept Buffy, Buffy helps them in ways that enhance their own abilities.

In *Firefly/Serenity* River undergoes a process similar to Buffy in which her immediate community works with her disability, but her process has some clear differences worth noting. Where Buffy initiates some of the processes that invite her community to share her disability, River does not have many opportunities to do so. Where *Buffy* only contains one episode in seven seasons that deals directly with institutionalizing disability, *Firefly/Serenity* has several in its short run, and thus deals more directly with the problems of institutionalization. Unlike Buffy who knows she is a Slayer from an early age, River is not aware of her "freakish" abilities and cannot access them in the way Buffy can. Additionally, River is not in situations that would allow her the same kind of access; in fact, she is confined and institutionalized as the abilities develop (or are forced upon her?). This confinement does not give River the opportunity to see that she can be different and function with others, and so, she tends to view her own differences as more than abnormal, as somehow wrong, as not a "real girl" (as she says in "War Stories"). Where Buffy sees her own differences as abnormal, with the exception of "Normal Again," she does not really see them as wrong. For River, this sense of wrongness permeates her self-perception in *Firefly/Serenity*, a perception underscored by representatives of the Alliance, a totalitarian government institution that want to make "wrong" people "right." They do this by releasing G-32 Paxilon hydrochlorate (the "pax") into Miranda's atmosphere, which was supposed to cure aggressive behavior. "We were trying to make people better," the scientist says, a view the Operative echoes when he claims that the Alliance is making a "better world" (*Serenity*). Both representatives of the institution eventually realize the problems with trying to "better" people, but this notion certainly represents the Alliance's position.

The word "better" resonates with illness and cure connotations. When someone is sick, people usually respond with something like, "I hope you get better," which suggests a value judgment: being sick is worse than being healthy. And while there is a kind of truth to this statement—being sick can be a terrible experience—there is also the danger of both devaluing the sick body and perhaps even more problematic, defining the sick body in the way the Alliance does. The Alliance determines that aggressive behavior is an illness that needs curing, and thus develops the cure, the "pax," for that illness. In a clear case of the cure is worse than the disease, Reavers result from the "pax" working differently on their bodies than other bodies, although according to the scientist, none of the results were "expected" (*Serenity*). While I am in no way advocating for scientists to stop studying treatments and cures for illness and disease, *Serenity* demonstrates the problems of defining differences and abnormalities as illness and disease that need curing. The Alliance pathologizes all aggressive behavior, defining it as illness and disease so that they can control the population, taking the concept of "enforcing normalcy" to the extreme. The Alliance defines normal as compliant, non-aggressive behavior, and this eugenics ethos allows them to take measures that make everyone the same. Rather than regarding "abnormal" behavior along a spectrum—surely there are situations in which aggressive behavior could be advantageous and desirable (say, a football game)—and instead pathologizing it, the Alliance negates such possibilities. Indeed, there is an insidious implication that the Alliance is interested in controlling/eliminating not just aggressive behavior but also dissenting behavior, such as that which led to the Independents opposing them and leading to a civil war—a far more chilling idea than the supposed peace/pax they claim to seek with their medical intervention. As with *Buffy, Serenity* in no way endorses this viewpoint, for the series and film consistently represent the Alliance as a totalitarian regime that needs toppling. Further, by allowing the audience to identify with River, the film and series undermines the Alliance's use of a single trait to define River in her entirety, that of a weapon.[6] Instead, because Mal and his crew eventually see "all" of River—the girl, the psychic, the friend, the weapon, etc.—she is able to assist them when they need her.

Both Buffy and River provide benefits to the larger community because their immediate communities—Buffy's created family and Mal's crew—accepted their disabilities. River becomes "River the Reaver Slayer," the weapon that protects her smaller community for the time necessary for Mal to broadcast the truth about the pax and the Reavers (Buckman, "Much Madness" 48). Buffy's larger Sunnydale community gains in the obvious way by being protected from that week's apocalypse, but the community also gains by having another way of seeing the world, the world through a Slayer's eyes. Disability activists contend (and I agree) that the experiences of the disabled create "different *ways of being* that give valuable perspective on life and the world" (Wendell, "Unhealthy" 30, emphasis Wendell's). What may happen if both Buffy and River's disability becomes viewed as an asset?[7] What may happen if people, instead of deciding that Buffy's bouts of Slayer-ness are social transgressions of irresponsibility, decide to support her sudden need to leave the office? Perhaps incorporating this flexibility may extend that flexibility to include and benefit the rest of her co-workers (27). What may happen if people listen to River rather than pathologize her? When others viewed their differences as difference rather than pathology, both Buffy and River were able to make valuable contributions.

In the series finale of *Buffy*, "Chosen" (7.22), each "differently-abled" person has a valuable contribution to make. They are up against the First Evil this time, the entity that "started" all evil, and since the series is about to end, this enemy is the final enemy, so the group must use every method at their disposal if they are to have any chance of defeating it. In this episode, Willow casts a spell to grant all potential Slayers the power to choose to be Slayers; Buffy discovers and wields an ancient, powerful weapon; Spike wears an amulet to channel more power; Xander, Giles, Robin, Dawn,

Anya and Andrew fight above ground; and the forty or so potentials/Slayers fight underground. In the final battle scene, *Serenity* too offers a similar narrative that values each individual contribution. All members of the community are necessary to heal the world: in *Buffy*, they stop the First from overrunning the world with evil; in *Serenity*, they provide the planets with the truth about Reavers and Miranda.

Buffy takes these benefits even further: all work together to replace the existing hierarchal power structure, that of a Watchers Council choosing one Slayer, with a new power structure, one where many girls choose for themselves to be Slayers. Now, being a Slayer no longer means being chosen and singled out as deviant or crazy; instead being a Slayer means choosing to be super-abled. Where before there was only one living the experience, now many share the experience, and because many share the experience, being a Slayer no longer means being ostracized and disabled by society. Being a Slayer no longer is a stigma.[8] For the purpose of this paper, healing does not mean that the disability gets cured; on the contrary, the disability remains, but the community gets cured of its inability to work with the disability. Slayer-ness still exists, but since many can participate (at various levels), Slayer-ness no longer is a "freak" show, but a show of community strength.

Disability activists maintain that the disabled have valuable contributions to make to society, and to silence those voices silences possibility. As Rhonda Wilcox and David Lavery note, Whedon's television oeuvre "encourages active viewing," in which "the mediation is the message" (Wilcox and Lavery xix). While shows like *Buffy* and *Firefly/Serenity* are set in the realm of fantasy, they allow us to explore complex emotional and social issues—in other words, to mediate a message—without much personal risk. I have attempted one such mediation, showing how the series model ways of incorporating disability into our lives. We cannot really imagine the results that may come with changing many current views of disability from a liability to a possible asset. Strangely, or maybe not so strangely, a fantasy show can help to dispel a fantasy definition. There is no single definition of being a "real girl," nor is there a "normal again," because really, there is no single version of "real" and "normal" that we all can share. Building communities that include, rather than exclude, the differences of the disabled can bring us into a reality where there is no normal. After all, who wants to be normal anyway?

Notes

1. In "Helpless" (3.12), Giles refers to Buffy's temporary lack of Slayer strength as being "disabled," and Buffy has conversations with both Willow and Angel about what she will do if she does not get her powers back, asserting that of course she will figure out a way to live but she would prefer not to. This is an alternative reading of the relationship between Slayer

abilities and (dis)ability, but notably, it is only Buffy's friends who perceive her Slayerhood as a super-ability rather than a disability.

2. For an account of the ways in which reason became opposed to madness, see Michel Foucault's *Madness and Civilization: A History of Insanity in the Age of Reason*. Foucault describes changes in European societies' view of insanity and reason, theorizing why the two have become opposites. By creating this diametric opposition, "madness" can be used as a way of ostracizing "undesirables." In *The Madwoman in the Attic: The Woman Writer and the Nineteenth-Century Literary Imagination*, Sandra Gilbert and Susan Gubar further interrogate diametric oppositions, such as the angel/monster images in literature that uphold feminine values that oppress women.

3. This is true in the television series; the future twists and turns of the *Buffy* comics' narrative complicate this reading.

4. As an example of this kind of family, see Donna Haraway's "A Manifesto for Cyborgs," in which she interrogates kinship based on affinity and choice rather than on biology.

5. For Richardson and Rabb, communitarian existential love ethics form the basis of the philosophy and morality in the series *Buffy the Vampire Slayer*, and though these ethics are largely absent in *Firefly*, they appear again near the end of *Serenity*. Richardson and Rabb "regard Whedon's entire corpus as a single moral argument which represents and examines ethical thinking as narrative and metaphor rather than as grounded in axioms, moral principles, or rules of behavior" (*The Existential* 4).

6. See Michael Marano's "River Tam and the Weaponized Women of the Whedonverse."

7. Pamela Cushing and Tanya Lewis' article, "Negotiating Mutuality and Agency in Care-giving Relationships with Women with Intellectual Disabilities," gives a real-world example of viewing disability as an asset. They describe relationships between caregivers and women with intellectual disabilities at L'Arche and conclude that the caregiver and the woman with the disability can have a relationship of mutuality. By recognizing the value of the disabled person as well as the value of the intellectual disability, both the disabled and non-disabled benefit from the relationship.

8. This resembles Nora Groce's *Everyone Here Spoke Sign Language*. Groce interviews the residents of Martha's Vineyard, putting together an ethnographic account of a community's adjustment to its deaf members. Since "everybody" spoke sign language, hearing and deaf alike, being deaf did not have a stigma attached to it. As previously mentioned, the model of all embracing the power of Slayerhood that the television show ends on is complicated in the comics.

Angel's Female Freaks

(Dis)Abilties, Professional, and Personal Life Limitations

Lorna Jowett

Are superpowers (or supernatural powers) a curse or a gift, abilities or disabilities? Do they make their bearer a superhero or just a freak? These are common questions posed by superhero fictions and addressed in successful fantasy TV shows, including those being examined in this volume. The tension between normality and freakishness is a driving force behind the character of Buffy Summers in *Buffy the Vampire Slayer*, who often expresses a desire to be a normal girl, to have a normal life. However, her role as the Slayer means she is destined to sacrifice these desires, and any personal ambitions, for the greater good. Whereas Buffy often resents her special powers and what they mean for her personally, Angel, title character of *Buffy*'s spin-off show, generally accedes to the standard superhero line that with great power comes great responsibility. (Though as a vampire with a soul, seeking redemption for more than a century of misdeeds, it could be argued that personal interest motivates Angel's mission to "help the helpless" at least in part.) *Angel* continually debates the pros and cons of having special abilities (or disabilities) and the cost of them to personal life. While this is often done by comparing Angel with other (male) protagonists such as Wesley and Gunn (who do not have special powers but share Angel's mission), several female characters with (dis)abilities also shed light on this central theme.

Like other supergirl protagonists,[1] most of these female "freaks" are constructed as alienated. They strive for a sense of belonging or desire to be "normal," but their superpowers inevitably set them apart from other people. Because these special powers are inherent in their genetic makeup (a recognizable version of the superhero) and because of the imperatives of commercial television, the presentation of female freak characters is strongly tied to negotiations of the body, of sexuality, and of normality in relation to both. Several of these characters, while potentially disabled by their special powers, transform their (dis)abilities into professional assets. Series regular Cordelia is perhaps the most obvious example, when she is passed the visions designed to help Angel fight the good fight by half-demon Doyle at the end of Season One. However, most view their freakish bodies as problematic for more personal interactions and as a barrier to intimacy. This essay focuses primarily on recurring characters "electro girl" Gwen Raiden from Season Four (as one character calls her in "Ground State" 4.02), and werewolf Nina Ash from Season Five. The inclusion of such characters alongside series regulars reinforces and complicates *Angel*'s (and the Whedonverses') concern with (dis)ability and with balancing social/professional and personal life.

The Americans with Disabilities Act (1990) and its Amendments (2008) defines disability through the "substantial limitation" of what it calls "major life activities." Under this definition, several characters from *Angel* have a disability. (Angel, as a vampire, does not breathe, for example. Nina's lycanthropy, an episodic or recurring condition, limits many major life activities.) However, these "major life activities" are day to day acts of (physical) living and the Act cannot ensure quality of life. As Joshua David Bellin observes, the passing of the ADA encouraged "a growing awareness that bodily disability—or ability, for that matter—*is* culturally constructed" (177). The Act is largely concerned with regulating access to the public sphere (since it notes "discrimination against individuals with disabilities persists in such critical areas as employment, housing, public accommodations, education, transportation, communication, recreation, institutionalization, health services, voting, and access to public services") and, therefore, focuses on Americans with disabilities as social citizens. The barriers to "normal" lives encountered by many who are seen as different (minorities, those with disabilities, fictional superheroes or "freaks") may be reduced through access to the public sphere and meaningful work, but what about personal lives? How does this fit with any American citizen's unalienable right not just to life and liberty, but to the pursuit of happiness?

Of course, the pursuit of happiness is often designated as a social concept, rather than a personal one, reflecting and shaping the tension between individual desire and community benefit in U.S. society. Thus Angel's belief that a superpower should be used for the greater good and that this mission trumps personal fulfillment is an iteration of what John Shelton Lawrence and Robert Jewett call the American monomyth. Lawrence and Jewett draw attention to "some paradoxes associated with these American superheroic fantasies":

> Why, for example, in an era of sexual liberation, do we still have heroes marked by sexual renunciation? ... And why do women and people of color, who have made significant strides in civil rights, continue to remain almost wholly subordinate in a mythscape where communities must almost always be rescued by physically powerful white men? [7–8]

At first glance, *Angel* seems to present its female freaks in exactly this fashion. However, on closer examination, insistence on the chaste male superhero is challenged through the development and evolution of Angel's character and through his interaction with female freaks like Cordelia, Gwen, and Nina. Long term female characters on *Angel* are often problematic given the show's focus on masculinities (see Abbott, *Angel* and other scholarship; Calvert, "The Shell I'm In"; Jowett, *Sex and the Slayer*; and Rambo, "'Queen C' Goes to Boys' Town") and a series regular like Cordelia has already been the focus of *Angel* scholarship. However, partly because her representation is sustained over time, it is more complex and nuanced than that of guest star characters like Gwen and Nina, who follow more closely the pattern of reluctant female superhero or freak. Cordelia does not choose to inherit the visions from Doyle, but she already knows that her power has a purpose—to help Angel in his fight against evil—and she does not resist it. Moreover, although Cordelia's power initially causes physical symptoms and eventually becomes part of her genetic makeup when she becomes part-demon in order to handle the visions without dangerous levels of pain ("Birthday" 3.11), she is not primarily represented as having a physical (dis)ability.[2] Once she becomes part-demon, the visions stop being physically problematic and do not appear to substantially limit her major life activities. However, the nature of Gwen and Nina's abilities is emphasized as physical from the outset, offering a more immediate embodiment of the female freak.

Employment and Professionalism: (Dis)abilities

Christine Garbett, discussing social attitudes to disability, notes that "Physical, or visible, disabilities are the least acceptable and have traditionally been hidden from society's view" (44). *Angel*'s plethora of demon characters works to normalize Other physicalities by making them visible, yet in doing so it also provides spectacle. Thus, to a certain extent, *Angel*'s freaks enact a visual exploitation of difference, "meant to be arresting in the sense of what Robert Bogdan has termed the 'pornography of disability'" as Moe Folk argues (2) of the carnies in *Carnivàle* (2003–5). This is something of a double bind. Bellin notes that freaks were removed from sideshows only to become prominent in monster films (169), but television operates rather differently. *Angel* does use its demon characters as spectacle and they provide the novelty necessary to serial fantasy drama. However, the show expands the definition of what normal is by moving beyond the human, and recurring characters like the demon Lorne become "normal" simply through the repetition and familiarity of a weekly television series. *Angel* also includes "freaks" whose embodied (dis)abilities are not visible: Angel, Gwen, Nina, Cordelia, and telekinetic Bethany Chaulk ("Untouched" 2.04) can all "pass" in the daylight world of human L.A. until they use their powers, or unless there is a full moon. Although Angel, Gwen, and Nina's freakish nature is physical, it is not (usually) visible in the way that Lorne's green skin and red horns announce he is a demon. Whereas demon characters might allegorize issues of race and ethnicity, the show's representation of difference inherent in less visible freakish powers or abilities demonstrates how disabilities can be pathologized and labeled pejoratively. Bethany, argues Anika Stafford, eventually changes her perception of telekinesis, so that "Whedon's depiction of Bethany's telekinetic power is not as a sign of illness to be overcome" but rather "a tool that will enable her to end abusive dynamics and take control over her life," which Stafford sees as a trajectory "paralleled with self-reclamation from abuse" (93).

Moreover, Bethany is valued by law firm Wolfram & Hart because of her special ability. Their representative, Lilah Morgan, tells her, "You're special, Bethany. In the old, non-retarded sense of the word" ("Untouched"), highlighting that what others might see as a negative deviation from the norm can be positive. *Angel* offers many examples of "freaks" whose skills are valued, like seer Cordelia, freelance burglar Gwen, aura-reading karaoke club owner Lorne, or vampires working for various national governments during World War II ("Why We Fight" 5.13). Employment brings financial security and offers a sense of social worth to those who may be perceived as different. As Garbett observes, "The 'normal' citizen is a contributor—not a dependent" (46). Characters like Vanessa Brewer, the blind assassin ("Blind Date" 1.21), Cordelia from Season Two onwards, and Gwen manage to create an identity that includes their special powers as part of their profession, so their (dis)abilities become a valuable asset.[3]

The episode that introduces Gwen ("Ground State") focuses on professionalism and competence by borrowing elements of the heist narrative (as already seen in "Blind Date" and "The Shroud of Rahmon" 2.08). Gwen's skills are reinforced in comparison with Angel Investigations' amateurism, which is also set against the new organization headed by Wesley (following his split with Angel Investigations at the end of Season Three). Like the Wolfram & Hart lawyer, Lilah, Gwen operates successfully in a professional sphere that is (from what we see) almost exclusively male. Lilah is often undermined by male superiors and colleagues, and when Gwen displays her body in a skin-tight outfit to meet Elliot, her employer, in a bar, he reacts aggressively: "You know Gwen, you came to me very highly recommended for your, ah, for your talents. But I have to admit, I was expecting someone a bit more—professional" ("Ground State"). On the one hand, Elliot's accusation can be read as a desire for discretion, so that Gwen's exhibitionism is at fault. However, since that lack of discretion is made apparent through her female body and its display, Elliot's continuing hostility can be read as gendered (he also calls her "young lady"), especially via Gwen's response, "I am a professional. And we professionals don't like taking the bone." One implication of Gwen's interactions with Elliot is that he tries to "screw" her (as she says later) simply because she is a woman. Moreover, the accusation of unprofessional behavior is refuted during the theft. Gwen succeeds admirably until Angel Investigations fouls it up.

Angel, Fred, and Gunn have a largely personal motivation for trying to steal the object of the heist, the Axis of Pythia (they want it to find the missing Cordelia); it is just another job to Gwen. The show contrasts the two female characters involved, Gwen and Fred, in terms of their emotional response to the heist. Fred takes charge of planning for Angel Investigations, yet afterwards she breaks down, upset by Gunn's momentary "death" during their altercation with Gwen. (Gwen accidentally electrocutes Gunn, killing him, but manages to revive him again using her electro-powers: "Just like starting a Chevy.") Fred confesses to Gunn, currently her lover, that she is "sick of taking care of everything, and paying bills, and making peace and plans, and keeping my chin up." While loner Gwen seems to remain cool, ultimately she lends the Axis to Angel, implicitly persuaded by the emotion driving his quest to find Cordelia (though she still profits hugely from the sale of the Axis, as we see in "Long Day's Journey" [4.09]). The team at Angel Investigations misses Cordelia's warmth and nurturing in "Ground State," and Gwen's flippancy is contrasted here with the more emotional Fred, and in later episodes with Cordelia herself.

Coolness and attitude are clearly presented as strategies that allow Gwen to keep her distance and thus control her power. Her parents' choice of school for her as a child is obviously based on its catering to "special" students ("Ground State"), though the death of a young boy when Gwen accidentally electrocutes him via touch suggests that the school is not really prepared for the extent of her (dis)ability or the "substantial limitation" (in the language of the ADA) it places on her interactions with others. The way Gwen subsequently reclaims the pejorative term "freak" suggests that she continues to fight for equal treatment in the face of abuse about her (dis)ability, yet, as Angel witnesses in "Ground State," it still affects her emotionally. "What I don't appreciate, Elliot," she explains, moving towards her double-crossing employer in a threatening fashion, "is being called a freak.

That's *my* word. And I get cranky when people like you use it." In "Players" (4.16) despite trying to mislead Gunn into thinking she is working for a foreign power, he deduces that her desperation to acquire the LISA technology (Localised Ionic Sensory Activity, "a device that can regulate body chemistry" as Ruditis and Gallagher describe it [235]) is for herself. "Look, there are two things that make me a good thief," she tells him, "I steal what I'm paid to steal, and I don't ask too many questions." He responds, "Liar. You're not stealing it for someone else. It's for you. You think it'll fix you." Gwen's desire to have a normal personal life motivates this, as discussed in the next section, even though it would mean losing special skills that help with her profession.

In contrast with Gwen, potential love-interest for Angel and new werewolf Nina is a student (just a nice "art school chick," she admits in "Smile Time" [5.14]), not a worker. She does not operate in the professional sphere and is shown almost entirely in the personal/domestic arena. In addition, rather than having marketable skills, Nina is positioned as a victim from her first appearance, both of the werewolf attacks that infect her, and then of a gourmet club that seeks out and eats rare species ("Unleashed" 5.03). While Dr. Royce, a "cryptozoologist" working for Wolfram and Hart (and therefore Angel in the fifth season), describes the werewolf that attacked (and infected) Nina as unusual, "*Lycanthropus exterus*. Undocumented in North America ... until now, obviously," and goes on to explain differences in the canine teeth and arm span, Angel rejects this objectification, retorting, "I don't care about that. All I care about is the girl." Royce is interested in the species as a rarity, but to Angel, Nina is vulnerable, another damsel in distress for him to save. Later, it is revealed that Royce is connected with the gourmet club and Nina is presented to them "garnished" on a platter. She is either a commodity or a case, introduced as the victim (twice over), never acting as part of the team, never desiring to be a professional, or a superhero. Nina does not actively use her werewolf abilities until the *Angel: After the Fall* sequel comics (Lynch and Whedon), when she bands together with other "freaks" to help the helpless in L.A.-gone-to-hell.

However, is the employment of freaks in *Angel* an example of equal opportunities or of exploitation? Since many of the gainfully employed "freaks" (such as the blind assassin; rogue Slayer Faith in "Five by Five" [1.18]; the fez-wearing brain man from "That Vision Thing" [3.02]; ex-Sunnydale High vampire Harmony in Season Five) are hired by corporate Big Bad Wolfram & Hart, this is a complex representation. Certainly, the free market model encourages selling to the highest bidder rather than embracing an unpaid moral mission. Gwen is initially sidelined by Angel Investigations because she is not fighting the good fight, and her mercenary motivation causes the team to suspect her (wrongly) in "Long Day's

Journey" when Manny is killed in her high-security apartment. Being a thief-for-hire allows her to use her (dis)ability constructively but places her on the margins of society. As she tells Gunn in "Players," "I'm a freak. Being a thief makes me a part of something and not a part at the same time." Sharon Sutherland and Sarah Swan argue that lawyer Lilah actively chooses evil, plays by the rules, and, therefore, "is not a victim" (58), noting the importance of choice for women (61). For female "freaks" those choices are more limited. When Angel is surprised to find Harmony working at Wolfram & Hart, she exclaims, "Well, duh! I'm a single undead gal trying to make it in the big city—I have to start somewhere. And they're evil here, they don't judge. They've got the necrotempered glass—no burning up—a great medical plan, and who needs dental more than us?" ("Conviction" 5.01). Wolfram & Hart may have facilities and policies that attract non-normative employees, but working for them necessitates a moral choice—"they're evil here."

Sutherland and Swan observe that in "Untouched," "Lilah's cruelty is particularly shocking as she exploits the girl's [Bethany's] history of childhood sexual abuse" (59), and Wolfram & Hart's "'use" of Angel's old flame Darla and of Faith are not dissimilar exploitations of personal relationships. This is nothing unique for the Whedonverses, of course. Brain Wall and Michael Zryd have noted that "Villainy in *Buffy* and *Angel* is consistently associated with hierarchical institutions that … take on more and more explicitly modern and covert institutional configurations" (55), and Wolfram & Hart are a prime example (*Buffy*'s Initiative, *Firefly*'s Alliance, and the eponymous Dollhouses are similarly exploitative and dehumanizing institutions). "Both shows suggest a radical utopian alternative," Wall and Zryd go on to argue, "a non-alienated way of working together, of bringing various sorts of experience, knowledge, talent and ability together without exploitation and for the common good" (53). Angel Investigations, then, and its occasional alliances with other "freaks" like Gwen, offers a different way for (dis)abilities to be used constructively, still in the public interest and in a professional sphere. Yet Angel and the team's acceptance of Wolfram & Hart's offer of better resources at the end of Season Four, to become part of Wolfram & Hart in Season Five, compromises their moral position. When newly-empowered Potential (Slayer) Dana's madness makes her unfit to perform the heroic role in "Damage" (5.11), the business-model professionalism of Wolfram & Hart contrasts Andrew's unexpected competence when he takes Dana back to the Slayers. His statement that nobody in Buffy's circle trusts Angel any more may sound uncharacteristic,[4] but it juxtaposes different versions of competence and professionalism in fighting the good fight, suggesting that competent, unpaid amateurs are better than corporate lackeys. However, as Harmony is well aware, female freaks need to make a living somewhere.

Non-Normative Bodies: Personal Life and Relationships

While being a "freak" might be useful professionally, whatever the inherent moral difficulties, "normal" still applies to personal life and is withheld for many female freaks because of their (dis)ability. Moreover, as the physicality of (dis)ability is emphasized by the show's representation, so body and sexuality are also highlighted. Restraint and excess are identified by Yvonne Tasker as key to the action genre, and she notes that these modes can be mediated through "both horror and comedy" (*Spectacular Bodies* 9) as is the case for many male characters in *Angel*.[5] The excesses of female characters, especially those discussed here, tend to be mediated through horror and action, linked to representations of sexuality.[6] Biology threatens to be destiny for many characters in *Angel*, and female freaks are no exception. Their difference is centered in their physical bodies.

This may suggest that female characters are more restricted by genre conventions. In the early 1990s, Tasker argued that the sexuality of the female action hero was emphasized as a kind of compensation, indicating "her availability within traditional feminine terms" (*Spectacular Bodies* 19). A decade later, Jeffrey A. Brown maintains a similar reading, "every action heroine is a combination of conventional sexual attractiveness and violent abilities, symbols of fear and desire" (68). This seems to hold true for *Angel*'s female freaks, even those not presented as action heroes, like Nina. Yet Angel's power to do good, to be a Champion, is also intimately bound up with sexuality. He assumes that because of the gypsy curse (detailed in *Buffy the Vampire Slayer* "Becoming Part 1" 2.21), if he has sex he will lose his soul and revert to the evil Angelus, and his sexual energy seems to be displaced onto his drive for redemption through helping others. In addition, Tasker observes that most film narratives "reaffirm the idea that women are a disruptive force who somehow bring sexuality into the (male) world of work" (*Working Girls* 75). This too appears to hold true for *Angel*'s female freaks, especially given Elliot's response to Gwen, discussed above. Yet male *and* female sexuality are presented as disruptive forces in *Angel*, and the uses of sexuality are more complex when situated in the context of five years of character, narrative, and thematic development rather than in the enclosed film narratives Tasker examines. Female sexuality is mobilized in different ways in *Angel* via the female freak characters in order to highlight a range of agendas or themes, often reflecting back on Angel and other male characters.

One of the first female freaks to appear on *Angel* is Jhiera, a demon from another dimension ("She" 1.13). Jhiera runs an underground railroad, helping women from her world, Oden Tal, escape abuse and oppression. She explains to Angel, "what you call personality—our passions, those impulses—sit in an area of the body we call the Ko.... When the females come of age, Ko controls our physical and sexual power." Removing the Ko means that the women of her world will "marry who they command, serve without questioning ... leave behind dreaming." Many viewers assumed that this was a kind of female genital mutilation[7] and it certainly functions as a strict regulation of sexuality but, as Nikki Stafford points out, there is confusion here between personality and physicality (*Once Bitten* 129). The overt message seems to be that the women of Oden Tal cannot control the heat of the Ko (desire), yet as the episode unfolds, Stafford observes, it is men who seem to lack control (*Once Bitten* 129) as if the women's (sexual/physical) power causes men to lose it. This is an early example of the show keeping space open for different, even opposing, interpretations of what seems to be conventional representation of gender. At the end of the episode, both Jhiera and Angel control their sexual attraction to each other in order to continue their work; personal physical desire is repressed in the interest of the mission.

Another early female freak is Bethany, a young woman with telekinetic powers ("Untouched"). Bethany is a tool to Wolfram & Hart; a case to Angel Investigations; a "damsel in distress" for Angel to save. Following a familiar story from the horror genre, her powers seem to stem from her position as a female/sexual victim. (See Anika Stafford for a detailed analysis of Bethany as an abuse survivor.) When Wesley (inspired by his own unhappy family background) suggests they send her home to her father, her power manifests violently. Wesley explains to Cordelia, "The sort of trauma that can produce this level of psychic power usually involves abuse of some kind—very early on.... Statistically speaking, the father was the best guess." When Cordelia picks up on Bethany's sexual "vibe," she privately warns her "don't bone my boss" (employing the same phallic vocabulary as Gwen) and Bethany's history is elaborated when she attempts to seduce Angel. Bethany's (dis)ability is directly connected to sexuality, and she must learn (from Angel) to control it. When she visits Angel's bedroom and asks, "What, you think I'm some frightened little mouse? I've done stuff. I can make you happy," Angel merely uses his standard line, "You wouldn't like me when I'm happy," reminding us that his own (dis)ability and identity are related to sexuality. This discrete narrative ties into a larger season arc dealing with sex and control (Wolfram & Hart are simultaneously using Darla to seduce Angel in his dreams), as well as feeding a series-long preoccupation with sexuality, power, and identity.

Unlike Bethany's mental ability, Gwen's "freakishness" is entirely located in the body and the electricity she wields makes even touching dangerous. She is initially presented as a smart-mouthed, amoral, professional thief and this nudges her into bad girl territory, helped by her clothes. Every episode in which she features makes a fairly extended comment about her body-hugging "Spandexia" outfits (as Manny describes them in "Long Day's Journey"), drawing attention to her clothes, her body, and the way others respond to these. Gwen is seen as sexualized or as sexual competition (Cordelia calls her "supertramp" in "Long Day's Journey," for instance), and it is implied that she enjoys this kind of attention—she works to present herself as sexually attractive, if not available.

Despite this, Gwen is a virgin. Logically, her condition prevents her from touching other people. In "Players" Gunn works this out: "So if you couldn't touch, I guess that means you've never—." The fact that she *can* touch Angel without dire consequences is part of his attraction during "Ground State." Rather than killing him, Gwen's electricity at one point makes him live, or rather, makes his heart beat, emphasizing the physical nature of her (dis)ability, its effect on and location in the body, as well as Angel's own "special" physicality. The stage directions describe it thus: "AN INTERNAL-ORGAN VERSION OF ANGEL'S BODY, as we see his SHRIVELLED DEAD HEART CONVULSE, as though zapped with electricity, before FILLING WITH BLOOD and beginning to BEAT. We HEAR; THA-DUMP, THA-DUMP" (in Ruditis and Gallagher 173). Following this detailed image, Angel says to Gwen, "You felt that? My heart—" and she continues, "It was beating. It doesn't, does it?" Once again a female freak is used to illuminate, here in quite a startling way, ongoing concerns about Angel's non-normative body. Both Angel and Gwen feel that their unique (dis)ability places others in danger and, therefore, that they must isolate themselves, especially from sexual intimacy. However, as Garbett notes of *Pushing Daisies* (2007–2009) protagonists Ned and Chuck, such isolation "maintains that part of their relationship which is lacking or abnormal" (51), further entrenching their sense of themselves as "freaks" who can never enjoy a normal personal life.

In "Players," Gunn's body also features, developing his anxiety that he is only "the muscle" to Angel Investigations. The episode begins with typical comments about Gwen's clothes but goes on to dress Gunn up as the "suave guy in a tight spot" Gwen needs to accomplish her task. Eventually he realizes that she chose him because Angel would never have passed the scans to get into the function they are crashing: "Security scan of a dead guy might have raised a few eyebrows." He then helps her install the LISA technology, an artificial means of control, into her body and, validating her hope that this "fix" will allow her to experience "normal" physical intimacy, introduces her to sex. While this story may have the most conclusive re/solving of a female freak's Othered body and its (dis)ability (by "fixing" her), its relation to ongoing themes and treatments of the body again keeps questions open (and Gwen's power is restored in *Angel: After the Fall*).

Gwen gains control over her body via an implant, yet Gunn's major test is still to come in Season Five, when his anxiety about his place in the team is intensified after the move to Wolfram & Hart and their ability to provide "enhancements" for employees[8] (another example of exploitation?). Gwen's episodes also cross into the period of Cordelia's pregnancy following sex with Connor, and of Wesley's liaison with Lilah, further explorations of non-normative sexualities that blur boundaries between the characters' personal and professional lives.

Nina's position, in contrast to Gwen, who takes a leading role in her three episodes, is always marginal—she is first a case and then simply the love interest. Lycanthropy locates her freakishness within the body, a body she is powerless to control at times (and lycanthropy has a history of being presented as a disease). Nina's arc seems to be about domestication of the werewolf, and then of Angel's curse (which, despite several incidents proving otherwise, is still interpreted by him as ruling out sex). As Angel's sexual partner, and a werewolf who regularly transforms, Nina is often shown naked or semi-clad, emphasizing her body and sexual function. Despite the freakishness of her werewolf body, as a human she is conventionally feminine: soft, pretty, artistic, and blonde. Furthermore, she does not see herself as "special." "You've got this whole, complicated, important life going on," she says to Angel, "and the last thing you need to deal with is a crush from monster girl, some charity case" ("Smile Time"). Arguably, he is attracted to her because while she might be a "monster girl" and, therefore, hardly likely to quibble about him being a vampire, she is far from complicated or important. Rather, she is conventional. Just as Buffy chooses Riley on the rebound from Angel because she thinks he is normal, Angel chooses Nina after his loss of Buffy and Darla. Nina may feel like a "charity case" in need of his professional help, but he needs the emotional and physical intimacy she offers.

There is little tension for Nina between freakishness and normality after "Unleashed": she manages what the other female freaks long for, to be normal, even suggesting that Angel can be too. The success of their sexual relationship may prove that she is not important enough to bring about Angelus' return, but it offers hope that he can enjoy physical and sexual intimacy, if not the perfect happiness stipulated by the curse. Nina achieves "normality" because her (dis)ability is regulated from the outset and she remains fairly conventional in terms of gender and sexuality. That is, unlike the other female freaks, her sexual power does not disrupt. On the contrary, it normalizes Angel's sexuality. In terms of the wider context Nina helps illuminate, it is worth noting that she debuts while Spike is still incorporeal (following his "death" in Sunnydale at the conclusion of *Buffy the Vampire Slayer*), guest stars in "Smile Time" when Angel is turned into a puppet while investigating a children's television show, but is never in the same scene as Illyria (a major vehicle for issues relating to identity and the body[9]). All these treatments of the non-normative body reinforce its importance as a major trope in the show. Nina demonstrates most obviously that a (dis) abled person can enjoy the same relationships as a "normal" person, though both ghost-Spike and puppet-Angel eventually approach "normal" interactions with others before reverting to their usual non-normative bodies.

The ADA's major life activities likely to be limited by a disability include operation of the reproductive system, and family life, like romance/ sex, would seem to be a "normal" expectation, both socially and personally. Like sex, family is problematic for other female freaks on *Angel* and Nina is "normal" because she has both a loving family and sexual relationship, even after being bitten. Prologue flashbacks in "Ground State" show young Gwen being (effectively) abandoned by her family to a boarding school. Bethany's abusive father is the root of her problem and possibly her talent, and she is quick to respond negatively to mention of family. Alternatively, Nina responds warmly. In conversation about Angel, Fred tells her that "it's not like he doesn't have anyone. We all, we try to be there for each other." Nina immediately replies, "Like a family." "Yeah. A demon-hunting, helpless-helping, dysfunctional family," concludes Fred ("Unleashed"). Nina's concern for her own family is integral to her story. She worries that they would be harmed if she changed out of Angel's protective custody; her initial werewolf transformation involves her "wanting to rip her [niece's] throat out," and her return to them restores her sense of normality. Nina's family is "normal" in the sense of functional, yet it is entirely composed of women. Her sister and niece apparently live without men at home, and Nina never mentions her parents, or her niece's father, a neat way of feminizing her character. Her all-female family reminds us that Nina may appear normal in relation to *Angel*'s other characters, but this normality does not necessarily align with the traditional patriarchal ideal.

Superheroes Aren't Special?

Anika Stafford argues that Angel connects with Bethany because he offers peer support not professional help. I would suggest that he offers both. Angel forges relationships with all the female freaks by telling them they have a common experience of being "different than most people" ("Untouched"). Although in general, Nina appears normal, werewolf narratives tend to contrast before and after being bitten, and one of her first conversations with Angel revolves around normality and freakishness. At first Nina berates him, "You didn't wake up and find out you're a … monster. You don't know anything," but eventually his insistence that he is "a monster too" convinces her of his good intentions ("Unleashed"). This conversation does demonstrate Angel's ability to make a personal connection with the female freaks because of his own experience of non-normative physicality, reflecting the way that "Narratives of superheroic redemption have become occasions for confessional statements of personal transformation and new trajectories of life meaning" (Lawrence and Jewett 9).

Yet it also highlights Angel's investment in the damsel in distress archetype: when Nina asks if Angel can cure her he replies, "No. But I can keep you safe." This is one aspect of *Angel* that situates it as primarily concerned with, and potentially valorizing, masculinity. Elizabeth Rambo, for instance, notes that female characters "ultimately ... appear to minister to Angel, in Angel's house, Angel's town—but then, it's Angel's show" (15; see also Abbott's *Angel* and Calvert's "The Shell I'm In"). As I have argued elsewhere,[10] however, what might initially seem like a conventional, if not stereotypical, representation, can on closer inspection be seen as the interpretation of other characters, neatly displacing the apparent contradictions and problems of representation onto the multiple perspectives of *Angel*'s ensemble cast. Often, the idealization of female characters is identified as Angel's point of view, just as Gwen's sexualization is seen through the eyes of others, presenting both as a forceful reading but simultaneously keeping open the potential for challenging traditional masculinist or patriarchal attitudes. Thus Anika Stafford observes that as early as "Untouched" Cordelia critiques Angel's desire to see women as damsels in distress (94).

Angel also offers advice to the female freaks from professional experience as well as from his personal life. As an investigator and Champion, Angel is an agent of the law and he encourages the female freaks to regulate their non-normative bodies. This done, they can, apparently, be removed from the narrative, their "problem" re/solved. Yet Angel's role as a regulator, an upholder of (moral) law is consistently deconstructed, and his own personal life intrudes on his mission and his professionalism as much as it does for the female freaks. Their stories demonstrate that female freaks are *similar to* male characters such as Angel or Gunn, as well as suggesting gender differences, simultaneously exposing a gender gap and blurring traditional gender traits. For instance, whereas the notion of tirelessly and silently sacrificing oneself for others is often associated with women, here it is strongly exemplified by male characters—Angel gives up hope of "being a real boy" repeatedly to continue the mission. Moreover, as Lawrence and Jewett note, traditionally, "[m]onomythic heroes suppress their needs in order to achieve a selfless perfection that requires no personal fulfilment ... transcending the nurturing values of sexuality" (357). In *Angel*, isolation is a consequence for all those fighting the good fight, not just female freaks whose (dis)abilities preclude intimacy, but it does not go unchallenged.

From the outset of Angel's mission in L.A. he is told by Doyle that he needs to connect with people, to avoid becoming alienated. "You see this vampire, he thinks he's helping," Doyle says, "Fighting the demons. Staying away from the humans so as not to be tempted.... But he's cut off. From everything. From the people he's trying to help" ("City of..." 1.01).[11] Even loner Gwen comes to Angel about the strange events happening in "Long Day's Journey," because she knows he will tell her, "freak to freak," what's going on. Her trust, based on their shared non-normative identity, is justified and she stays to help the team, becoming, if briefly, part of the community of freaks Angel gathers around him. Nina's sexual relationship with Angel, then, is the culmination of increasing intimacy and connection for "freaks" who previously considered themselves isolated.

Overall, therefore, *Angel*'s ongoing project seems to be more of a critique than a perpetuation of the American monomyth, including challenges to its gender bias and the superhero paradox of (dis)ability. Admittedly, one TV show is unlikely to change social perception of disability. Yet if nothing we do matters, then all that matters is what we do (as Angel says in "Epiphany" 2.16). Whedon does television, and he believes that changing perception can only happen via a popular medium like TV.[12] At times, *Angel*'s negotiation of personal and professional life might not seem any different to other TV dramas about professionals wrapped up in their work and alienated from those they should be close to. Arguably, drawing on such established conventions of character and situation helps normalize communities of "freaks" in Whedon fictions. Does anyone, "normal" or otherwise, enjoy a personal life? Aren't many American (and other) citizens expected to sacrifice their personal life to their social or professional duty? Yet Whedon's fictions, and *Angel* in particular, insist that these freaks are not only denied a personal life because they are superheroes with a moral obligation, but also because their (dis)ability (visible or not) substantially limits major life activities, including intimacy with others. The fact that Gwen, Nina, and even Angel, look for a "cure" for their (dis)abilities reflects continuing pathologization of and negative social attitudes to non-normative bodies. *Angel*'s optimism lies in the fact that by watching regularly and engaging with freak characters, we come to see them as normal and, at times, the freaks themselves enjoy the privileges of normativity.

Notes

1. Such as X-Men's Rogue, and especially contemporaneous or subsequent TV characters like Max from *Dark Angel* (2000–2) or Claire Bennet from *Heroes* (2006–10).

2. This is not to deny that, at certain points, Cordelia's representation emphasizes physicality and sexuality as part of her freakishness. The life-endangering nature of her

visions is one example; her possession and pregnancy during Season Four is another spectacular instance that I do not have time to do justice to here.

3. While Cordelia's visions are undoubtedly an asset to Angel's mission, they do not necessarily help with Angel Investigations' paying clients. Cordelia is *sent* her visions and is therefore not quite in control of her power, placing her in a slightly different position than Gwen or Vanessa, who learn to direct their abilities for professional gain.

4. See Nikki Stafford, *Once Bitten* 316.

5. See, for example, Stacey Abbot, "'Nobody Scream… Or Touch My Arms': The Comic Stylings of Wesley Wyndham-Pryce."

6. Harmony is an exception, since she is a comic character, see Lorna Jowett, "Biting Humor."

7. See, for example, Nikki Stafford, *Once Bitten* 129.

8. See also Stacey Abbott, *Angel.*

9. See Bronwen Calvert, "The Shell I'm In."

10. See Lorna Jowett, "Lab Coats and Lipstick: Smart Women Reshape Science on Television."

11. At this point Doyle notes that Cordelia will help Angel make the necessary connection to the human world, positioning her as more "normal" than "freak." Even after complex character development across several seasons, by the end of her time on the show Cordelia represents the "normal" in terms of a loving relationship that Angel still believes he is barred from enjoying.

12. "The idea of changing the culture is important to me, and it can only be done in a popular medium" (qtd. in Lavery par. 15).

"The Cliff Notes version? I want a normal life"

Slayerhood as Social-Model Disability

ELIZABETH K. SWITAJ

"I wish I could be a lot of things.... A great student, a star athlete, remotely normal. I'm not" ("Graduation Day, Part One" 3.21). These are the words of a young woman struggling with a "unique condition"[1] that interferes with her efforts to live what she sees as a normal life. This condition causes her to miss classes and social occasions. It keeps her up late, and what sleep she does get gives way, on occasion, to horrific nightmares, even night terrors. She dies once before graduating from high school ("Prophecy Girl" 1.12) and a second time before she can legally drink ("The Gift" 5.22); the first time, a friend saves her by performing CPR, but the second incident requires more dramatic intervention ("Bargaining" 6.01–6.02). If it did not come with increased strength and agility, slayerhood, as depicted in *Buffy the Vampire Slayer*, would easily be recognized as a disability, and even given these positive traits of strength and agility, slayerhood still functions as a disability according to the social model. Reading the disability of slayerhood through this particular social model accounts for the different degrees of social marginalization slayers from different societies and social positions experience, as well as for the divergent experiences of slayers and "civilians" who also battle monsters. The importance of these distinctions shifts as society changes near the end of the television series and during and throughout the subsequent *Buffy* comics.

Slayerhood, Disability, and Impairment

While the medical or personal-tragedy model of disability locates disability in the impairment and reduced functioning of an individual body alone,[2] the social model, as its name indicates, considers institutional, structural, and social factors that cause individual needs to become disabilities that interfere significantly with a person's capacity to participate in social, professional, or educational contexts.[3] As Colin Barnes, Michael Oliver, and Len Barton describe it, "This model does not deny the significance of impairment in disabled peoples' lives, but concentrates instead on the various barriers, economic, political and social, constructed on top of impairment. Thus 'disability' is not a product of individual failings, but is socially created" (5). An impairment that limits an individual's capacity to engage in certain activities only becomes a disability in a society that expects "normal" people to engage in those activities, and it becomes a more severe disability when those expectations are particularly strong and accommodations unavailable. For example, being unable to walk is always an impairment, but it only functions as a disability in societies that have developed around the assumption that normal people can walk; the disability has a more severe impact in a society that does not require buildings to have wheelchair ramps or if the disabled person cannot afford a wheelchair. Barnes, Oliver, and Barton write about "disabled people" rather than "people with disabilities" in part because according to the social model, social or institutional structures are disabl*ing* to people who therefore become disabl*ed*. As individuals and organizations whose thinking is shaped by the social model often prefer "disabled people" to "people with disabilities," I use the former term preferentially in this essay.

According to the social model, disability only occurs when social barriers overlay an impairment; it does not imply that anyone with any kind of social disadvantage should identify as disabled. Buffy Summers' need to fight demons can be understood as a disability in part because the impairment is a "destiny" or "calling" inherent to her. Kendra in "What's My Line, Part Two" (2.10) tells her, "You talk about slaying like it's a job. It's not. It's who you are," and Buffy makes this same distinction when contrasting her position with Riley's in "Doomed" (4.11). Even when Buffy resists this aspect of herself, she always ends up fighting demons. Indeed, near the end of the television series, it is confirmed that Buffy's slayerhood forms a mystical part of her body; in "Get It Done" (7.15), she learns that infection with demonic energy confers this condition. This infection points to the extent to which Buffy's impairment literalizes the phrase "battling one's demons" a cliché metaphor for struggling with mental illness that originates in the historical attribution of disorders to demonic possession. Texts that form the foundation of Western thought, such as the Bible, connect impairment and disability to demonic possession (Coleridge 72).[4] Making metaphors literal is part of the *modus operandi* of *Buffy the Vampire Slayer*, as numerous critics writing for both popular and academic sources have noted. Hillary Frey writes in *Slate* that "Joss Whedon, the series creator, transformed insensitive jocks and nightmarish roommates into actual demons for Buffy to take down." Steroids transform star swimmers who already prey or pick on the weak into actual monsters rather than merely making them more aggressive ("Go Fish" 2.20). A college roommate whose intrusiveness and musical taste make Buffy's first few weeks at university hellish turns out to be a soul-stealing demon ("Living Conditions" 4.02). Rhonda Wilcox contrasts this type of incident with those that occur in the "very special episodes" of television series set in seemingly more realistic (that is to say, demon-free) worlds: "In Buffy's world ... the problems teenagers face become literal monsters. Internet predators are demons; drink-doctoring frat boys have sold their souls for success in the business world; a girl who has sex with even the nicest-seeming male discovers that he afterwards becomes a monster" ("There Will Never" par. 1). Buffy, infected with demonic energy, literally battles her (externalized) demons. Equating disability with demonic energy may seem problematic, but in the world of *Buffy the Vampire Slayer*, demons are not always evil, though they are commonly stigmatized as such. "New Moon Rising" (4.19) makes this distinction apparent when Buffy calls Riley a "bigot" because of his single-minded refusal to view demons as anything but bad.

Though disability requires impairment, Buffy's impairment alone does not make her disabled. Rather, social expectations within the suburban, mostly white middle-class milieu of Sunnydale make her impairment a disability. Her impairment, in other words, does not become a disability because it causes missed deadlines and classes. Rather, it functions as a disability because she is expected to turn in homework on time and attend class; her impairment becomes a disability because it prevents her from doing that which is considered "normal." Moreover, the absence of accommodations for her impairment increases the severity of her disablement. During her hospitalization with influenza, her teachers send her homework via Willow because they do not expect her to be in class, but when she secretly prevents the apocalypse, no such accommodation can be provided. Her grades, rather than her identity as "normal," suffer; an individual with undiagnosed or undisclosed dyslexia might have a similar experience.

Buffy, however, while clearly aware of her slayerhood, does not consider herself disabled. When her mother, having finally accepted Buffy's slayerhood, tells her, "it's not your fault you have a special circumstance. They should make allowances for you," Buffy responds, "It's not like I need to ride a little bus to school" ("Dead Man's Party" 3.02), referring to the smaller buses often used by American school districts to transport special education students. Because she does not require highly visible adaptations, such as a wheelchair or other mobility aid, she finds it difficult to see that she requires any, even sarcastically rejecting the suggestion of accommodations. Susan Wendell describes a similar experience in which her own initial reluctance to identify as disabled originated in part in her seeing herself as privileged relative to other disabled women (*The Rejected Body* 28). Furthermore, as Tanya Titchkosky argues, "coming out" as disabled to oneself no less than to others means both calling into question one's sense of belonging and denying oneself the kind of identity that society labels both normal and desirable. Buffy desires "a normal life" ("What's My Line?, Part One" 2.09) and that desire encourages her to identify as "normal." Leaving aside the heroic tradition of secret identities that would hinder Buffy publicly identifying as other than "normal," Buffy cannot ask for accommodation so long as she does not see herself as needing it.

While the invisibility of slayerhood as a condition and Buffy's own refusal to see her condition as a disability may make accommodation impossible, these factors do not change the fact that the expectations of the society in which she lives and of the institutions with which she interacts create barriers to participation for herself and other Slayers. The contours of these socially constructed barriers, and how they shape the experience of disability, become particularly clear in the contrast between Buffy, the other slayers called during the series, and other non-slayer characters who fight evil. These barriers grow less relevant late in Season Seven and throughout most of the Season Eight comics, as Buffy forges an army of potential Slayers and then full-fledged Slayers, changing the world and creating new social roles for herself and others with the help of her friends and allies.[5]

"Your life is very different than mine": Culture, Intersectionality, and Disability[6]

The three active slayers who appear during the *Buffy* television series (prior to the transformations of the final episode) come from diverse backgrounds, and their differing abilities to participate successfully in society despite their slayerhood reflect these differences. If social barriers rather than mere impairment determine disability, then individuals with the same impairment in different societies or in different social positions within the same society must face different degrees of disablement. Additionally, if the challenges disabled people face come from society rather than from their impairments alone, then disability can be understood as similar to other forms of social oppression and can play a role in intersectional oppression. Intersectionality refers to the idea that individuals with more than one socially marginalized identity do not experience each aspect of their oppression separately or in a merely additive fashion; rather the various forms of oppression interact with each other, creating a complex system of discrimination. Indeed, the contrasts between Buffy and the other two slayers called in sequence after her first death bear out the role of society and social identity in shaping disability. That the Watchers Council only takes an interest in individual solutions—in training slayers to fight demons, not in helping slayers to find a place in society—exacerbates these differences between slayers and follows the logic of the medical model. It also, ultimately, fails.

The first slayer called after Buffy's first temporary death, Kendra, is in her home society not only disabled but, in some sense, institutionalized because the structure of her society allows the Watchers Council to take full control over her life. She experiences the sort of isolation and restriction of experience that characterizes institutionalization and that contributes to the oppression and dehumanization of institutionalized people (Gleeson, *passim*). As revealed in "What's My Line, Part Two" (2.10), she has no friends and does not even remember her parents. She even lacks a family name. Though, in her few appearances, few details emerge about Kendra's family or nation of origin, certain factors suggests that her institutionalization has intersectional elements. The Watchers Council has its headquarters in England, a historical colonizer, and Kendra comes from an unspecified nation in the Caribbean and is of African descent, a historically colonized region where the British also propagated a flourishing slave trade. This history raises questions about the dynamic that led to Kendra's parents' willingness to give her to her Watcher. Where did the respect for the calling among her people to which Kendra refers originate ("What's My Line, Part Two" 2.10)? Might economic hardships have contributed to her parents' willingness to see her institutionalized? Unfortunately, the series does not provide enough information on Kendra's background for these questions to be answered with any certainty. In any case, in the context of Sunnydale, the disability of slayerhood affects Kendra more profoundly than it affects Buffy, in part because of her history of institutionalization. She stammers and looks at the floor when she meets Xander because she has never been allowed to speak with boys; she has never developed certain social skills. Nor does her institutionalization improve her impairment: when Drusilla kills her, Kendra does not return.

Within Kendra's home society, however, her disability is not hidden in the same way Buffy's is: she maintains her secret identity through her own removal from society, not because slayerhood is unknown or because she blends into her society. Thus, while Kendra's institutionalization prevents her from participating fully in society, she also does not face the same expectations to participate. Buffy, on the other hand, seems to be a "normal" Sunnydale teenager: she (usually) attends the local high school and even tries out for the cheerleading squad ("Witch" 1.3). She must hide the impairment that is her destiny, and thus the disability that society makes of her impairment must also remain invisible. Outside the Buffyverse, non-institutionalized disabled individuals also may try to hide their impairments in order to fit into society better. Passing becomes a valuable interpersonal skill rather than a sign of poor self-esteem, as indicated in a study performed by Marjorie Olney and Karin Brockelman (*passim*). For Buffy, the invisibility of her disability also reflects the more general denial in Sunnydale of the demonic. As Wilcox notes, Giles, at the end of "The Harvest" (1.02), tells the Scooby Gang (Buffy and her friends) that "'people have a tendency to rationalize what they can and forget what they can't.' And of course his words apply to the social problems of the real world just as emphatically as they do to monsters" ("There Will Never" par. 11). One way of ignoring social problems is to ignore the way social expectations negatively affect individuals by attributing their difficulties to individual shortcomings instead. Many people would prefer not to believe in vampires, demons, or social inequality. They would rather believe that someone is simply "lazy" or "weird" than that they have a disability that requires accommodation.

Because in Kendra's home society slayerhood is not entirely invisible, her parents believed she had the potential to become a Slayer. By contrast, when Buffy does reveal her impairment, she is disbelieved. After Buffy reveals her "condition," her mother asks, "Are you sure you're a Vampire Slayer?" and "Have you tried not being a Slayer?" ("Becoming, Part Two" 2.22). Indeed, in "Normal Again" (6.17), viewers learn that the first time Buffy attempted to reveal her knowledge of an involvement in the supernatural prior to the show's start, her parents institutionalized her, albeit briefly once she recanted her comments about vampires. It may seem that a young woman having to fight demons is naturally less believable than most of the conditions we would call disabilities, but the many real-world individuals with hidden disabilities have experienced other people doubting their conditions. Sally French relates having a new neighbor refuse to believe that she could be visually impaired because he had seen her walking confidently along the street ("Disability" 18); she also provides a number of examples from her childhood in which adults had a "tendency to disbelieve me and interpret my behavior as 'playing up' when I told them I could not see" ("Can You See" 68). Wendell describes the challenges of living with an adult-onset invisible disability as more socially than medically based (*The Rejected Body* 3–5). These women's experiences are common enough that there is even an online support community called *But You Don't Look Sick* (*ButYouDontLookSick.com*). None of this makes institutionalization of the sort experienced by Kendra preferable to having a hidden disability; rather, it shows how differing thresholds of believability in different societies create differing experiences of disability.

Because Buffy has not been institutionalized long-term, she has more space to rebel against the Watchers Council—most importantly, against their insistence that slayers work alone. This equates to the common emphasis placed on the value of independence for disabled people. In "What's So Great about Independence?" Sally French questions this value but also points out that the focus on independence "individualizes disability rather than viewing it in social terms" (45). Buffy dies twice and her friends bring her back to life; she depends upon her small community. Kendra has no such support. As Laura Miller has observed while arguing that Buffy's greatest achievement lies in transgressing the notion that heroism requires acting alone, "Buffy is an exceptionally powerful and long-lived slayer, and her friendships are at the heart of that" ("Bye-Bye-Buffy"). Buffy uses the equivalent of community care to survive and thrive outside the institutionalized context that is all Kendra ever knows, except during her brief stay in Sunnydale.

By contrast, in the alternate world of "Normal Again," in which vampires and Slayers do not exist outside of Buffy's mind, Buffy too experiences institutionalization in a long-term way—and her institutionalization, like Kendra's, fails. Her "lucid moments" in that world originate not in any new treatments tried by her doctors, who of course act in accord with a medical model of disability, but rather from adverse events in the Slayer-world (her death at the end of Season Five and, in the course of the episode, toxins from the Glarghk Guhl Kashmas'nik's barb). More significantly, Buffy ultimately chooses to live in the world in which she relies on community care rather than the world in which she lives in a mental hospital, sometimes drugged and restrained, even if in the mental-hospital world, the possibility of a normal life outside the institution has been promised to her. In the world in which she is institutionalized, Buffy ends up catatonic just as Kendra, who grew up institutionalized, dies. They experience very different kinds of institutions, but in neither case does institutionalization produce positive results.

While the differences between Buffy's and Kendra's experiences of the disability of slayerhood can be attributed to the different societies in which they grew up, the differences between Buffy's and Faith's experiences originate in their different positions within the same society. Faith's greater marginalization leads to her eventual turn towards evil. She fits into the common trope of the disabled person who turns evil,[7] often, though not always, due to resentment at their exclusion from society.

Faith, having fewer social resources and less support due to her working class status, is more severely affected by the disability of slayerhood than Buffy is; the intersection of class and disability leaves her far more marginalized. Before Faith allies herself with the Mayor, she lives alone in a seedy motel. Unlike Buffy, she does not have a comfortable suburban home provided by her mother and, as a slayer, she cannot hold down the kind of job that might pay enough for her to move into an apartment—even assuming she could find one paying a living wage, given her lack of education. She also does not attend high school; she claims to have dropped out ("Faith, Hope, and Trick" 3.03) but given that she has not always reported her own history honestly, she may well have been expelled. In either event, Buffy's ability to achieve a higher level of education than Faith does, despite their shared disability, depends upon the advantages of her social class. Buffy's slayer-related activities result in her expulsion from Hemery High School as well as her eventually overturned expulsion from Sunnydale High School. Faith, even if she did leave education willingly or was expelled for reasons unrelated to slaying, would certainly have risked similar punishments for similar reasons had she returned to school. After Buffy's first expulsion, her middle-class mother has sufficient resources to move to Sunnydale in order to find a school that Buffy can attend. After Principal Snyder expels Buffy ("Becoming, Part Two" 2.22), her mother has the time, energy, and understanding of the system to appeal the punishment. Though Giles' more physical intervention seems ultimately to have been the successful one, it is clear that, had Giles not intervened, Joyce would have found a way for Buffy either to re-enroll at Sunnydale or to attend another school ("Dead Man's Party" 3.2). Faith's mother, working-class and alcoholic ("Enemies" 3.17), could not intervene on her daughter's behalf to the same degree, so even had Faith remained in Boston, she would have had to face the full consequences of slayerhood alone.

Seeing ordinary social participation as impossible, she gives up on it. Instead, she seeks to take pleasure in her marginalized position; she attempts to reject social rules and make slayerhood an advantage rather than a disability. Who needs an education or a job when you can "Want. Take. Have" ("Bad Girls" 3.14)? Certainly, taking pleasure in slayerhood by itself need not harm anyone, nor is it unheard of for disabled people to take pleasure in disability. The neurodiversity movement, for instance, celebrates minds that do not function in a "neurotypical" way—e.g., those of autistic or dyspraxic people. Indeed, the possibility of taking pleasure in being disabled underlies Robert McRuer's "crip theory" which combines queer and disability theories with an avowedly liberatory aim. Faith, however, moves beyond taking pleasure in her disabled self to insisting on slayer superiority; this trajectory leads her to serve the Mayor, who not only provides her with the kind of work she can do and the economic privileges she never had but also confirms her belief in her superiority. Though she has literally found a home—the apartment he secures for her—she is removed from community with the only other living slayer. Her success comes at the price of losing her connection to others, or at least the other like her; for disabled people outside the Buffyverse, success too often comes at the price of such removal from community. They may be the only ones with a highly visible disability or may hide an invisible disability to avoid discrimination.

The community in which the other slayer lives, however, has failed Faith. Whereas Giles helped ensure that Buffy could re-enroll in high school, neither Kendra nor Faith benefit from such intervention into their social situations. Kendra's Watcher prevents her from integrating socially. After Faith comes to Sunnydale, neither Giles nor Wesley tries to improve her living conditions. They do not encourage her to attend high school or secure her a more pleasant place to live. The Watchers Council does not concern itself with the social position of slayers. Rather, it focuses exclusively on the individual battle with demons; like most of the medical establishment, it focuses on the impairment without concern for social barriers. Giles transgresses this role because of his affection for Buffy, but he does not do the same for Faith. It comes as no surprise then that much of Faith's resentment of Buffy later on revolves around her perception of Giles' favoritism. After discovering that the slayer she has been sent to assassinate in the post-series comics intends to kill Buffy, Faith thinks, "Giles sent me on this suicide mission 'cause he said it was about saving the world … but really, it was just about saving his golden girl" (Vaughn, "No Future").

That Giles' feelings for Buffy, rather than a change in philosophy, underlies the help he gives Buffy in overcoming social barriers is evident not only because he fails to assist Faith in this way but also because he later on continues to act in a way that reflects the Council's medical-model approach. In Season Six, his insistence that Buffy should learn how to live independently leads him to leave Sunnydale at the end of "Tabula Rasa" (6.08) because he believes that she had been depending on him too much. Following this rejection of dependence and interdependence, Buffy's small community begins to fall apart. In the Buffyverse, as in real life, the good intentions of non-disabled people are not enough; of the three slayers active during the television series, however, Buffy suffers the least harm from this fact.

Slayers vs. Civilians

Despite the social differences between Buffy, Kendra, and Faith, they do share one key aspect of their experience: for all three of them, slayerhood functions as a long-term, incurable disability that prevents them from living a "normal" life. By contrast with the slayers, most individuals who demons attack fight only briefly: they survive and flee, or they die. They experience the equivalent of an acute illness.[8] Survivors generally return to their normal lives, though perhaps with a changed perspective. In some cases, individuals choose to help the Slayer battle her demons. Those who choose to ally themselves with the Slayer have more flexibility about when and how to fight demons; they can work around the requirements of society more easily than slayers can. Looked at another way, society and its various institutions are designed in such a way as to enable these allies, even when they have their own impairments, to succeed more than slayers. Because among Buffy's allies, Xander and Willow have the most in common with Buffy (attending the same high school for three out of four years) and appear the most frequently in the series, the contrasts between them and Buffy have particular significance.

Xander, despite at first being on a similar level with Buffy in terms of success, is left behind when she enrolls in university. In the working world, however, he eventually attains a higher-status and higher-paying position. Throughout high school, Buffy and Xander follow a similar academic trajectory. Neither earns particularly high grades. Willow tutors both of them. Xander certainly has more time to study than Buffy does, but to what extent he uses it remains unclear. His response to Principal Snyder pressuring Willow into giving a star swimmer a passing grade is that "[i]t's a slap in the face to every one of us who studied hard and worked long hours to earn our D's" ("Go Fish" 2.20), yet in "Earshot" (3.08) Buffy overhears him wondering if he should have studied. In either case, Xander's low SAT scores reflect a similar level of ability as his regular grades would seem to show, while Buffy's significantly higher scores ("Lovers Walk" 3.08) suggest the potential for her to earn better grades. Buffy, however, lacks the same amount of opportunities to study. For instance, early in "Becoming, Part One" (2.21) Buffy, having previously expressed anxiety about her final examinations, cannot commit to a study session that evening with Willow because she must patrol; later that evening, as Buffy prepares to confront Angel, any possibility of making time to study for the following day's final evaporates.

Buffy's relative lack of time is due to the impairment of her slaying, but its impact on her grades also reflects a lack of accommodations for her in the school system. Partly because of her disability's invisibility, she is not allowed extra time on assignments or the opportunity to take a test at a later date if circumventing an apocalypse has intruded on her study time. To a degree, Buffy's difficulty in this regard resembles the experience of a teenager who has to work to support herself or her family and, certainly, a very similar ethical case could be made for granting accommodations in both situations. Moreover, both could benefit from changes to the educational system that would require no scrutiny of their particular difficulties—allowing students to work at their own pace rather than at a curricular pace, for instance—and which would redefine different paces of educational progress as "normal." What makes Buffy's case here an issue of disability is that slayerhood forms an inherent part of herself: placed in different circumstances, she would still have to slay. Placed in other circumstances, a teenager who has to work to support his/her family would no longer have to do so.

Though throughout Season Four, Xander struggles to find decent employment while his friends attend university, he does eventually find well-paid work in construction, even moving into a supervisory capacity. Because, unlike Buffy, he does not face the barriers associated with disability or gender, he can find better employment even when they have roughly the same level of education. After her resurrection, Buffy tries, in "Life Serial" (6.05), to begin a similar career, but when her impairment emerges on a worksite, and she has to slay demons, he fires her rather than trying to find a way to accommodate her. As a manager, he does not attempt to create a story to explain the incident away to the other workers, though as high school students, the Scooby gang regularly covered up Buffy's slaying in this way. Her coworkers, too, refuse to help, even though she saved their lives; had a male coworker damaged the building site in the process of killing a demon, they might well have reacted differently, considering the sexist attitudes they showed as soon as Buffy walked onto the site. In this case, Buffy's potential for a career in construction suffers from the intersection of disability (slayerhood) and gender; her disability creates the situation in which she needs accommodation, and her gender makes her coworkers unwilling to support her. That the monsters in this episode have been sent by three humans who target Buffy because of her status as the Slayer suggests a parallel with the kind of harassment that disabled people may experience due to stigmatization, to say nothing of the gendered-implications of Warren's overt misogyny.

After this, Buffy finds employment in a fast food restaurant where she has to wear a "funny"—that is to say, humiliating—hat and likely earns minimum wage. Buffy's misery over working at the "Doublemeat Palace" has two major aspects: on the one hand, she is trying to support herself and her younger sister while earning a wage that places her below the poverty line and, on the other, her working in a fast food restaurant as a career undermines her identity as a young, middle-class woman. Because of her slayerhood, as Rhonda V. Wilcox and David Lavery observe in their introduction to *Fighting the Forces*, Buffy must sacrifice not only "her life" but also "perhaps even more frightening—her social status" (xviii). By the final two televised seasons, the social status she risks goes beyond that associated with high school cliques: it is her socioeconomic class, her identity as middle class. Young, white, middle-class women, if they work in fast food, are expected to do so part-time as a sort of rite of passage or a way of earning extra pocket money, not because they need the money to survive. Society's failures to meet the needs of her demon-fighting make a middle-class existence tenuous at best for Buffy. In real life, when accommodations are not sufficient to allow disabled people to complete their education, they have little choice but to settle for lower-paying jobs; even those who do complete higher education degrees may have to work in positions that pay less than one would expect, given their qualifications, if workplaces do not provide adequate accommodations. According to the U.S. Census Bureau, twelve percent of individuals with a "nonsevere disability" and twenty-seven percent of those with a "severe disability" live in poverty; only nine percent of the non-disabled do.

Xander, a non-disabled man, can achieve greater success in employment than Buffy because he does not have to deal with the same complicating issues. By contrast, Willow never enters the workforce but, rather, throughout most of the series, achieves higher academically. Unlike Buffy, in high school, she earns the kind of grade point average one would expect given her ability to succeed on the SAT. They both attend UC Sunnydale immediately after high school, but Willow chooses to do so because she believes that it is the best place for her to continue studying magic. Buffy does so because remaining in Sunnydale allows her to best fulfill her need to slay demons. She chooses the university that best fits the needs created by her disability, even though it makes no particular accommodations for her disability (which continues to be hidden).

Eventually, Willow's interest in the dark arts develops into an impairment. After she begins to recover from her addiction, however, she is able to re-enroll ("Selfless" 7.05). Her impairment is not highly visible: overusing magic and trying to destroy the world do not fit the symptoms of any well-known condition. Because the needs that result from her impairment are not exceptional, however, she can follow established procedures. Buffy, by contrast, having been dead, has greater needs. Her death at the end of Season Five causes her to miss a registration deadline ("Life Serial" 6.05); in the aftermath of her resurrection, she also misses a deadline to apply for readmission ("As You Were" 6.15). Prior to her death, Buffy, despite the challenges of acting as a single mother had been planning to re-enroll after withdrawing for a semester ("Tough Love" 5.19). Because her disability is invisible and the relevant symptom (temporary death) is not known to allow a return to university studies, she has no avenue for appeal. After high school, Willow and Buffy both experience impairments, but only Buffy's becomes a long-term disability that disrupts her education and limits her opportunities.

"The thing about changing the world...."[9]

Xander and Willow can succeed more than Buffy in terms of career and education because they can fight demons on their own terms and so can work around the demands of society and its institutions. Buffy, who battles demons due to her destiny, must try to meet those demands in the margins of her struggles. When the world changes, however, these distinctions too begin to change, as do the differences between Faith's and Buffy's relative positions. In Season Seven, as The First Evil's army gains strength and the Hellmouth rumbles, Sunnydale's institutions crumble. Most of the population flees. The meaning of success and the demands of society change dramatically. In the series conclusion, Buffy, with the help of her friends and allies, makes a more permanent and positive change in society which leads to the creation, in the Season Eight comics, of a new kind of community in which slayerhood no longer functions as a disability. This shift, this way of ameliorating the disability, fits the demands of the social model: rather than changing the individual, Buffy and her allies change the world. Moreover, this change focuses not on creating greater independence for individual slayers but on creating a co-supportive, interdependent community.

Late in Season Seven, when most Sunnydale residents have left, slayerhood becomes irrelevant as a disability, though this change is not a positive one. Buffy's inability to work in construction can no longer be viewed as the result of disability because Xander, too, cannot work. Even if he had not lost an eye, there simply would no longer be any job opportunities in construction in an abandoned town. Similarly, her inability to complete her undergraduate education can no longer be considered evidence of a disability because Willow, too, cannot attend university. The campus, presumably, has been abandoned along with the town; whether the students have been provided with adequate support to transfer to other schools within the University of California system (or beyond) remains unknown. When the reformed Faith returns to Sunnydale, she no longer experiences slayerhood differently from Buffy because of their relative class positions; everyone in the small army lives in the same home and works toward the same goal, in a preview of what will follow, in the Season Eight comics, with the growth of the more extensive community of slayers.

Finally, in "Chosen," Buffy fully abandons the idea of individual solutions to the challenges of slayerhood. She changes the world, but not by herself. Come Season Eight, she has taken on a position of leadership at the head of an international community of slayers. Though referred to throughout Season Eight as an "army" with "squads," the term "community" better reflects the realities of a large group of young women who feel a powerful sense of connection with each other; the slayers also call themselves a "family." Their shared sense of connection also distinguishes their experience as slayers living within a slayer-run world from Kendra's isolating experience of living in a Watcher-run world. The slayers help each other to overcome their impairments by battling demons as a team, and the community expects them to be fighting demons. Because within their community, social expectations are built around this need, slayerhood no longer functions as a disability. Faith lives on the margins of this community, perhaps out of choice or perhaps due to a lack of trust in her. While the slayer community may have created a milieu in which slayerhood no longer functions as a disability, it is no utopia. Nonetheless, though this community does not survive Twilight and the destruction of the Seed of Magic, it represents an ideal of community and mutual care.

In the changed world of Buffy Season Eight, slayerhood no longer functions as a disability because a community exists in which the social expectations revolve around the assumption that everyone will have to fight demons. From the age of fifteen until the age of twenty-two, however, Buffy experiences serious social disadvantages because of a mystical aspect of herself, an infection with the demonic that literalizes an older understanding of disease and impairment. She manages for many of those years, because of her other social advantages, to build a life for herself that, however tenuous and however unsuccessful compared to the lives built by her non-slayer friends, exceeds Kendra's and Faith's possibilities for social inclusion and participation. Unsatisfied with efforts to overcome her disability as an individual, Buffy attempts to build a better world by changing the social rules and by working in a community with individuals who both do and do not share her particular challenges. Battling one's demons will never be a pleasant task and having to battle them persistently will always be an impairment. What Buffy's story shows, even if only for a brief time, is that by working in community with others, one can make a world in which impairment does not function as a disability.

Notes

1. Giles uses this phrase to describe Buffy's status as a slayer in "Never Kill a Boy on the First Date" (1.5), and the slayer infomercial in "The Chain" (Season 8, issue 5) echoes this language (Whedon, "Long Way").

2. On the medical model, see, Oliver, *The Politics* 4–5; Barnes, Oliver, and Barton 4; Finkelstein 14–15; Finkelstein and French 27–28; Coleridge 72–73; and Clogston 47.

3. For more on the social model, see Coleridge 73, Oliver "Defining Impairment," Crow, and Shakespeare. Oliver, in "Re-Defining Disability," also argues that this model could be referred to as "Social Oppression Theory" (62).

4. For a more general exploration of the attribution of disabilities and "defects" to supernatural powers, see Eberly. DeRogatis discusses a more contemporary iteration of such beliefs.

5. Society's responses to Slayers and vampires in subsequent seasons of the comics within the framework of a disability continues to evolve, exceeding the space available in this essay.

6. Kendra says this to Buffy after meeting her in "What's My Line Part Two" (2.10), drawing attention to the differences in their training, respective relationships to their Watchers, understanding of what it means to be a slayer, and their general lived experience.

7. See Dahl. Note also that the highly informal tvtropes.org wiki has an "Evil Cripple" page.

8. The precise relationship between illness and disability remains a matter of much debate (Wendell, *The Rejected Body* 19–21).

9. "Once you do it, the world's all different" (Whedon, "Long Way").

Dollhouse and Intellectual Disability

BARBARA STOCK

"Is that why you keep us so simple?" ("Needs" 1.08)

The Whedonverses include multiple images of mental illness, usually of the eloquently, poetically mad variety exemplified by vampire Drusilla and victim of government conditioning River (in *Buffy* and *Firefly*, respectively). In contrast, intellectual disability is rarely addressed. One great exception to this pattern is seen in the residents of the Dollhouse, the Dolls, or "Actives in the resting state" as they are sometimes called. In this essay, I examine parallels between the Dolls and individuals with intellectual disabilities, using these parallels to frame ethical issues affecting the intellectually disabled.

Before I outline my plan for this essay in more detail, a note about terminology: "intellectually disabled" is currently replacing the term "mentally retarded," which has fallen out of favor among people so labeled and their advocates. For example, Jill Egle, an intellectually disabled woman who served as co-executive director of the ARC of North Virginia, successfully campaigned to "get rid of the R word" in her organization's publications and also in Virginia state law (Schumitz 3). Advocates in other states have mounted similar protests, a trend that culminated in the 2010 passage of Rosa's Law, which changed references to "mental retardation" in federal laws to "intellectual disability" (Rosa's Law). Naturally, I will respect this preference in my writing, though I will preserve "mental retardation" and even older, more offensive, terms in my quoted source materials.

What exactly is intellectual disability? According to the American Association of Intellectual and Developmental Disabilities: "Intellectual disability is a disability characterized by significant limitations both in intellectual functioning and in adaptive behavior, which covers many everyday social and practical skills. This disability originates before the age of 18" ("Definition of Intellectual Disability"). Intellectual functioning, or intelligence, includes reasoning and problem solving, and it may be documented through an IQ test. Adaptive behavior includes language and conceptual skills, interpersonal skills, and practical activities of daily living, such as personal care and job skills ("Definition of Intellectual Disability"). Although intellectual disability may co-occur with mental illness, the former does not imply the latter. An intellectually-disabled person may be perfectly in touch with reality and exhibit no neuroses or emotional problems. Thus, while Topher, late in the series' timeline, showed marked deterioration in his adaptive behavior, to the point that DeWitt had to take care of him, his residual intellectual functioning disqualifies him as intellectually disabled; rather, he becomes mentally ill.

In this essay, I examine the extent to which the Dolls fit the criteria for intellectual disability, focusing on their expressive and receptive language, conceptual repertoire, engagement in activities of daily living, and problem solving skills. My goal here is not to diagnose the Dolls, but to place them in the context of the wide array of abilities shown by individuals with intellectual disabilities. More significant, I think, than the characteristics shared by the Dolls and people with intellectual disabilities are the social perceptions attached to them. Thus, I discuss how other characters' perceptions of the Dolls mirror rhetoric pertaining to the intellectually disabled, focusing on the period of American history since the mid–1800s. The many similarities include: members of both groups are compared to children and animals; both are assumed to lack normal sex drives; both are subject to paradoxical views on moral culpability; both have been placed in institutional settings for complex and often inconsistent reasons; and, while both groups inspire protectiveness in others, they are nonetheless exposed to risks to which non-members of these groups would not be exposed.

The fact that I employ a definition of intellectual disability does not imply that I am reifying intellectual disability as a category. In *Inventing the Feeble Mind*, James W. Trent, Jr., shows how medical and other professionals shaped the meaning of "mental retardation," instituting various power relations (5). This approach reflects a dominant view in disability studies: disabilities are socially constructed. That is, whether variations in human abilities are disabling depends on the demands, barriers, and supports present in the social environment. At least with regard to intellectual disability, this is not a new proposal. As far back as 1923, Stanley Davies held that "feeblemindedness ... is a relative term" (25), noting that complex, industrial societies produce more people who are unable to keep up than do simpler rural environments. Supporting or debating this approach is outside the scope of my project, though my points about rhetoric and social perceptions are certainly friendly toward it.

Because of the parallels between the Dolls and people with intellectual disabilities, the situation of the Dolls can be used to frame ethical issues relating to intellectually-disabled individuals. I consider two such issues: (1) The Doll/handler relationship illustrates, via an extreme example, the kind of caretaking relationship in which many adults with intellectual disabilities find themselves. Because of familiarity and attachment, the handler or caretaker becomes an ideal choice to speak on behalf of her/his charge. What moral pitfalls are there in this approach? (2) Is it bad for one to become a Doll? What implications does this have for evaluating the quality of life of people with intellectual disabilities?

The Dolls' Intellectual (Dis)Abilities

One part of the definition of intellectual disability that the Dolls do *not* match is the final clause: "This disability originates before the age of 18" ("Definition of Intellectual Disability"). This clause was imported directly from the definition of mental retardation; to change the wording of laws without changing the scope and impact of said laws, it was necessary to keep the official definitions of "mental retardation" and "intellectual disability" precisely the same. I am curious, however, whether the real world application of "intellectual disability" remains so strictly aligned. Suppose a twenty-five year old with average intelligence suffers brain trauma, leaving him with severe deficits in intellect and adaptive skills. It might be odd to refer to such a person as mentally retarded, as this term connotes slowness in development. At least to my ear, it does not sound wrong to say he has acquired an intellectual disability, though others may disagree.[1] In any case, the Actives are all adults; their condition did not emerge within the developmental period. As science fiction settings often require stretching concepts beyond their everyday applications, a slight mismatch with the official definition is not surprising.

Language and Concepts

Like the vast majority of people diagnosed with intellectual disabilities, the Dolls can talk. In fact, the Dolls speak quite well, showing no particular deficits in sentence structure, verb agreement, etc., and using contractions fluently. They do not display over-regularization of irregular verbs ("taked" instead of "took") as developing language users often do. The one thing that marks the Dolls' expressive language as immature is sentence length. It is typically short. For example, when Echo meets Boyd for the first time she says, "Hello. You're tall" ("The Target" 1.02). And who could forget Tango's statement that struck fear in the heart of the newly self-aware Victor? "I like pancakes" ("Needs").

Speech therapists use mean length of utterance (MLU) as a measure of expressive language development. One counts the number of morphemes (the smallest meaningful language units—for instance, walked = 2 morphemes, one for the root and one for the past tense ending) in a language sample and divides by the number of separate utterances. MLU age equivalences have been determined for young children, with two year olds typically having an MLU of 1.92, three year olds around 3.16, four year olds around 4.40, and five year olds around 5.63 (Williamson). Unfortunately, to calculate a reliable MLU, one needs a substantial language sample, preferably 100 utterances; most of the Dolls do not speak that many lines through the whole course of the series, and the most verbose, Echo, is also the least representative. So, I will just note that the bulk of the Dolls' utterances are of a length that would be typical of a four year old. However, once in a while they come out with something in the eight-plus morpheme range, such as, "I think if you always try, that's best" ("Gray Hour" 1.04).

What about receptive language? Clearly, the Dolls are sometimes confused by what others say to them, as shown in this exchange at the end of "The Target":

> ECHO: Sorry.
> DOMINIC: Are you?
> ECHO: Am I?
> DOMINIC: Sorry. Are you really sorry? Awful lot of people seem to end up dead around you. How's it make you feel? Oh, right. You don't, unless we tell you how and what and when.
> ECHO: I'm going to swim in the pool.

In this instance, Echo was probably confused by the *content* of Dominic's rant—referring to events she cannot remember—rather than the language itself. If the language used over the public announcement system is any indicator, the Dolls are expected to comprehend at a fairly sophisticated level: "We are experiencing a temporary interruption of power. We assure you there is no need to worry. Everyone please gather calmly on the main floor" ("Needs"). This sample clocks in at the seventh grade level on the Flesch-Kincaid Readability scale. If the staff had any cause for concern about the Dolls' receptive language, the content could easily have been communicated more simply: "The power went out. It will be back soon. Don't worry. Please go to the main floor."

The Dolls may not be deficient in their language *per se*, but they do seem limited in what they talk *about*. Dominic disparages them, "Four hours ago you were discussing your love for applesauce" ("Echoes" 1.07).

If it is not about a food that is naturally sweet, they are not interested! That is an exaggeration, of course; they are conversant on several topics, such as exercise, relaxing, and being one's best. They can talk about what they have just done (had a medical exam, learned that something fell on them) or plan to do (get a massage). They can express friendship and make social overtures toward each other, such as in the following exchange in "Man on the Street" (1.06). Sierra greets Victor with "Good day," and he responds by observing, "You have a book." Sierra explains, "I enjoy looking at it" and invites him to join her with "Would you like to see?"

The Dolls can even comment on rather abstract reasons that justify common actions and situations, such as how exercise helps one be one's best, how being alone can be peaceful, and how noise is upsetting. But they quickly run out of steam when a conversation steps outside their comfort zone. Tango does not know what to do with Mike's statement that the earth's core is high in potassium ("Needs"), and Victor struggles, unsuccessfully, to explain his feelings for Sierra:

> CLAIRE: Victor, can you tell me about Sierra?
> VICTOR: Sierra is beautiful.
> TOPHER: There's a lot of beautiful girls here, bro, it's pretty much the idea. Beauty.
> VICTOR: Sierra is different.
> CLAIRE: How is she different?
> VICTOR: I'm sorry. ("Man on the Street")

When asked directly how Sierra makes him feel, all he can say is "better." These limitations do not seem like language problems, but rather a sort of conceptual poverty. In their "resting state," the Actives are given the conceptual frameworks necessary for everyday encounters, but not much more. They are kept "simple."

Activities of Daily Living and Problem Solving

The Dolls can feed themselves, shower, and get dressed independently. Off-camera, they presumably brush their teeth and go to the bathroom on their own, too. Most of us take these basic activities of daily living for granted, as do many individuals with mild or moderate intellectual disabilities, though they represent real achievements for people who are more severely intellectually disabled. Beyond the basics, the Dolls also engage in fairly advanced leisure activities: they paint; they trim bonsai trees; they attend tai chi classes. Many of these activities require one to use specialized tools and follow complex instructions.

Thus, within the confines of the protective and structured environment of the Dollhouse, the Dolls are fairly self-sufficient. However, their nearly total lack of problem solving skills makes them unable to cope with any deviations from routine. When Alpha attacks, the Dolls do nothing; they do not even flee effectively. When Echo undergoes a remote wipe in "Gray Hour," she mostly curls up and babbles pathetically, though she does show some initiative near the end of the episode. This helplessness is by design. As Dominic puts it, "They shouldn't be adaptable. They should be predictable" ("True Believer" 1.05). Echo is unusual in that she is able to think outside of the parameters she is given and create her own approach to the problem, as shown in "Stage Fright" (1.03), when she endangers the woman she was supposed to protect in order to, in the long run, protect the woman from herself. Echo tends to show this problem solving ability when she is imprinted with some other personality, or when her Doll architecture starts to break down. Only once, in "A Spy in the House of Love," does she ask Topher to imprint her while she is in her Doll state.

Lacking the ability to solve the little problems and challenges that life presents, it is hard to imagine the Dolls being competitively employed. Sure, one could picture an enterprising handler exploiting Doll labor to stuff envelopes, or even to do complex manufacturing, within the shelter of the Dollhouse. But a real job, out in the world, where things do not always go as planned? No way. In this regard, the Dolls are significantly more limited than intellectually-disabled people. Take, for example, a person with a moderate intellectual disability associated with Down syndrome. She may not be able to trim the perfect bonsai and her reading skills may be rudimentary, but she can adapt to changing situations. Her problem solving skills are perhaps not up to what would be expected of her chronological age, but they are appropriate to her developmental level. Within the parameters of her cognitive abilities, she can draw upon her past experiences to figure out what to do and make decisions. Thus, unlike the Dolls, she can succeed in certain jobs outside a sheltered environment.

Parallel Perceptions

As shown above, the Dolls share many, though not all, of the characteristics of intellectual disability. The way they are viewed by others, particularly the Dollhouse staff, serves as a microcosm for how individuals with intellectual disabilities have historically been perceived and described. In this section, I explore several such parallels.

Children, Animals, or Worse. One common theme is that both the Dolls and people with intellectual disabilities are often not viewed as adult human beings. At the milder end of this attitude spectrum, they are seen as children. While orienting Boyd to the Dollhouse, Adelle DeWitt explains, "In their resting state, our Actives are as innocent and vulnerable as children" ("The Target"). In the same episode, Boyd calls the Dolls "helpless children." Echo is repeatedly referred to as Boyd's "girl"—and once, in "Stage Fright," as his "little girl." At least through the first season, there is something undeniably parental in his relationship with her. And, upon learning that Sierra had been coerced by her handler, Hearn, into having sex with him, all of the staff—even the not-so-Doll-friendly Dominic—regard Hearn with the sort of contempt accorded to pedophiles.

Individuals with intellectual disabilities are also frequently regarded as perpetual children. Pearl S. Buck's classic 1950 memoir, *The Child Who Never Grew*, introduces the author's daughter: "She is one who has never grown mentally beyond her early childhood, therefore she is forever a child, although in years she is old enough now to have been married and to have children of her own—my grandchildren who will never be" (5–6). Buck invokes the image of the forever-child clearly and intentionally, as it plays a role in explaining her own emotional journey. In documents relating to institutional care of intellectually-disabled people, this image is employed much less clearly; as shown in the following examples, it is often difficult to discern just how old the individuals being discussed truly are.

The early institutions for people with intellectual disabilities that arose in the United States in the mid-nineteenth century were primarily educational; they were training *schools*. The exact ages of pupils varied, but as one advocate for such schools explained, "There is ... far less hope of material progress in adults than in children—and it is hardly desirable that those beyond fourteen or fifteen should be placed under instruction" (Brockett 81). Yet by the latter part of the century, these early training schools had morphed into comprehensive institutions with large numbers of "custodial" cases—adults deemed unable to live in the community (Fernald, "Description" 324). Yet, the 1891 manual for the employees of Elwyn Asylum repeatedly refers to their charges simply as "the children" (Kerlin 313–316). A glowing description of the successes achieved at an institution-sponsored farm colony in 1903 refers throughout to the "boys" from the institution who toil there, while calling the male attendants "men" (Fernald, "Farm Colony"). It is only by considering remarks about the duration of time certain residents were in training that one realizes they must be well into adulthood. Reporting data on such farm colonies twenty years later, Davies clarifies, "The terms 'boy' and 'girl' are here used to denote the feeble-minded of whatever actual age" (112).

Being relegated to the ranks of children at least acknowledges that one is a member of the human race; not all of the characterizations of the Dolls and the intellectually disabled are so kind.[2] The Dolls are frequently compared to animals, with Dominic suggesting bluntly that handlers should not think of their Actives as children, but rather should "think of them as pets" ("Needs"). When Topher describes Echo, Sierra, and Victor's frequent association with each other as flocking or herding behavior, Boyd reproaches him, "They're not bison, Topher," to which Topher replies, "They're a little bit bison" ("The Gray Hour"). And, of course, there is Bennett's chilling description of how the Los Angeles Dollhouse's treatment of their Actives differs from her own House's practice: "You let them roam. They roam like free-range chickens. We keep ours more like veal" ("Getting Closer" 2.11). If you thought it could not get worse than being compared to veal, you were wrong. Echo is dubbed "a talking cucumber" in "Gray Hour" and Paul Ballard describes a client who engages Dolls for romantic encounters as "hiring zombies" ("Man on the Street"). Perhaps more disturbing are the comments that imply that the Dolls are, literally, nothing. About Echo, Dominic remarks, "There's nobody in there," and Boyd says, "She's not even a person, just an empty hat. Until you stuff a rabbit in it" ("The Target").

With regard to the intellectually disabled, Dorothea Dix, in her 1843 impassioned plea to the Massachusetts legislature to improve care of "idiots and insane persons," emphasizes that she is talking about human beings, albeit "human beings reduced to the extremest states of degradation and misery" (5–6). She chastises those who treat such people worse than they would "the lowest brutes" (11). In contrast, in 1848, Samuel Howe, when distinguishing "pure idiots" from higher functioning "imbeciles," describes them thus: "This is the maximum of idiocy; the minimum of intelligence ... in which a being in human shape is so much below even insects, and so little above a sensitive plant. [One] finds, even in our fair commonwealth, breathing masses of flesh, fashioned in the shape of men, but shorn of all other human attributes" (37). While these beings may look human, in all important respects, they are not deemed human. In the decades following, descriptions of progress attained in the training school introduced "the condition of the idiot before he has been instructed" through comparison to animals: "he often exhibits the voracity of the wolf, and the uncleanliness of the swine" (Brockett 79).

The eugenics movement in the early part of the twentieth century widely applied to humans terms typically associated with animals: breeding, stock, pedigree, etc. A piece of visual rhetoric from this era shows a "feeble-minded" mother holding her baby and looking at a family of pigs, with the caption, "After their own kind" (described in Lombardo 37). Licia Carlson charges that late-twentieth-century philosophers also trade on the comparison between intellectually-disabled individuals and animals: "the face of the beast dominates many philosophical discussions of intellectual disability, thereby placing the severely intellectually disabled in a separate domain" (130). Much of this discussion occurs in animal rights literature, where, for example, Peter Singer argues that it is only ethical to do an experiment on an animal if it would also be acceptable to do it on a "brain damaged" human with similar cognitive capacities (82–83). Singer's point is that we should be more cognizant of the suffering we cause animals, not less cognizant of the suffering we cause the intellectually disabled, and his consistent placement of *all* humans within the domain of animals weakens the case that he relegates intellectually-disabled people to a "separate domain." Still, Carlson is correct that, until recent years, if one read about intellectual disability in a philosophical argument, it is likely that animal analogies were lurking in the vicinity.

Sexuality and Culpability. "Wait, the Dolls don't have sex drives. That's part of the deal, right?" So says Sierra's handler, and sexual abuser, Hearn ("Man on the Street"). An episode earlier, in "True Believer," Topher had discovered that this is not precisely true. The Dollhouse apparently films the Actives at all times, even when showering; on the video, Topher notices Victor having a "man reaction" and freaks out: "This is a problem. This can't happen. It shouldn't happen. When they're in their Doll state, there's a limpness," he insists. While imprinted, the Actives have sex like nobody's business, but when they are Dolls they do not—moreover, they do not even want to, and they *should not* want to. The people who supervise them seem pretty invested in this fact. Part of the resistance to thinking of the Dolls as sexual beings is no doubt connected to the image of them as children and squeamishness over acknowledging sexual urges in children. Another concern targets the issue of consent: if one Doll initiates sexual intercourse with another, it is not clear that the latter has the cognitive wherewithal to agree to it.

Individuals with intellectual disabilities have, similarly, been assumed to lack normal sex drives and to be individuals who ought not have sex. As with the Dolls, the eternal child image presumably plays a role in this attitude. Yet much of the rhetoric surrounding intellectual disability and sex hinges on a different concern: eugenics. In the early twentieth century, mental and moral traits were widely believed to be hereditary, as evidenced by pedigree studies such as Henry Goddard's 1912 book on the "Kallikak" family, documenting generations of "defectiveness" within one branch of a family tree (in Zenderland 175). Harry Laughlin of the Eugenic Record Office charged that, "when a potential source of feeble-minded offspring is located, it is the duty, and should be the purpose of the state to prevent reproduction" (225). While the lowest functioning intellectually disabled were unlikely to reproduce, the highest functioning, particularly women, were considered to be at risk.[3]

Goddard's research was soundly critiqued by the 1940s; by this time the heyday of American eugenics had ended. Yet, in 1972, Wolf Wolfensberger, a pioneering writer on the rights of the intellectually disabled, described his own shocked reaction upon visiting Denmark and Sweden and learning that the culture's permissive attitude toward premarital sex extended to the "retarded." Once he got over his "hang-ups," he agreed that this stance is appropriate, though he doubted American culture would easily accept sexual relations among the more severely disabled (165–174). Even today, while sex is perhaps not explicitly prohibited, services for the intellectually disabled tend to be provided in a manner that "presumes and imposes asexuality on their recipients" (Allison Carey 3). Group homes, for example, have traditionally been single-sex. Were complete asexuality presumed, there would be no reason to separate the sexes—the Dolls, for instance, share co-ed sleeping and showering facilities. Thus, it might be more accurate to say that living arrangements for intellectually-disabled people tend to presume potential heterosexuality, yet impose asexuality in practice.

Sexuality has also played a role in perceptions of the moral culpability of individuals with intellectual disabilities, since deviant sex was seen as one of the chief causes of intellectual disability. The sexual sin might be parental adultery or sex between relatives, but Howe gets particularly worked up over "another vice, a monster so hideous in mien, so disgusting in feature, altogether so beastly and loathsome, that, in very shame and cowardice, it hides its head by day, and vampyre-like, sucks the very life-blood from its victims by night" (54). And this Big Bad is … masturbation—practiced by the parents or by the intellectually-disabled person himself. Thus, the disabled person might be judged responsible for his own condition. The Dolls share a similar paradoxical culpability. They are, at the moment, true innocents, having no awareness of any wrongdoing. Yet, as Topher notes (perhaps without complete conviction), "They volunteered for this." Boyd's response, "So we're told" ("Gray Hour"), questions the veracity of comforting assurance. Even if a Doll did agree to serve (unlike Sierra), without coercion (unlike Echo), that would hardly absolve the Dollhouse of responsibility for what it does with her once she is stripped of her ability to choose otherwise.

Institutionalization and Risk. For over 100 years, starting in the second half of the nineteenth century, a large proportion of the intellectually disabled have been housed in institutional settings—hospitals or asylums which supposedly met all their daily needs, and which they rarely left without supervision. Sound familiar? On this description, the Dollhouse qualifies as an institution, albeit a small one. To be clear, there is little resemblance between the spa-like Dollhouse, with its throw pillows and perfectly crunchy lettuce, and the deplorable conditions that existed in institutions for the intellectually disabled.[4] Yet there are striking similarities in the reasons both groups were consigned to such settings: an uneasy mixture of protecting them from the world and protecting the world from them.

The Dollhouse protects the Dolls from "a complicated world," a "world of terror and chaos" with which they would be unable to cope ("Needs"). But the Dolls are not merely helpless waifs; they are potential threats. When a small group of Dolls is allowed to escape the confines of the house, Dominic worries, "What if they make it out into the world and decide to shoot up a liquor store or jump off a roof?" This supplements his ongoing concern that one of the Dolls will develop into the next Alpha, a threat to the house, and also to the world at large.

Early rhetoric on establishing schools and institutions for intellectually-disabled individuals emphasized protecting the individuals themselves. Without facilities tailored to their needs, they ended up in jails, almshouses, inadequate private homes, or "wandering reckless and unprotected through the country" (Dix 8). But by the end of the nineteenth century, the intellectually disabled were presented as a burden to society, even a menace, responsible for crime, vagrancy, poverty, and prostitution, and increasing this threat by reproducing more of their kind. The claim was not that they were necessarily malicious, but that "they are greatly lacking in self-control; and moreover are peculiarly open to suggestion, so that they are at the mercy of bad companions" (Davies 47). Thus, we must segregate them from such bad influences, in order to protect society from them and from the vices they perpetuate.

The concept of protection leads to a final similarity between the Dolls and the intellectually disabled: despite engendering protective feelings in others, they are exposed to extraordinary risks. As an extreme example, in the 1960s, intellectually-disabled children at the Willowbrook State School were intentionally infected with hepatitis as part of a study. When challenged, researchers defended their project by pointing out that, given the unsanitary conditions at Willowbrook, the children were likely to contract hepatitis anyway. More mundanely, research shows that violence against the disabled is much higher than against members of the general population (Cushing and Lewis). The Dolls, of course, are exposed to violence and danger on a regular basis, despite having staff members who seem to care about them. For instance, in "True Believer," when DeWitt is informed of the risk to Echo of death-by-sneezure, as Topher would say, she responds, "The risks have been determined to be within acceptable margins." As Sierra might attest, being a Doll is not a safe occupation, even if one is not on a dangerous mission; besides being raped by her handler, she was also repeatedly programmed to love and have sex with someone she loathed—Nolan, the man who arranged for her to be admitted to the Dollhouse in the first place.

Ethical Issues

Because the Dolls share common characteristics with intellectually disabled individuals, and are subject to similar social perceptions, I use the Dolls to illustrate and discuss two ethical issues relating to intellectual disability: the moral pitfalls of handlers or caretakers representing the interests of those in their charge and the question of quality of life for Dolls/intellectually disabled people.

Handlers and Caretakers. In a flashback, we see Topher initiate Echo's bonding to Boyd as her handler. Boyd questions the point of the procedure: "Then what? Me and Special Needs become buddy-buddy?" Topher explains that friendship is not the goal. Rather, "It's about trust. From this point on, Echo will always trust you without question or hesitation, no matter what the circumstance. You're about to become the most important person in her life" ("The Target"). This bond allows Boyd to better protect Echo and he uses his position to advocate on her behalf—at least until, in Season Two, he is revealed to be the mastermind behind the Dollhouse, using the business to advance his own selfish ends. On the other hand, Hearn demonstrates a drawback of this sort of extreme dependence when his ongoing sexual abuse of Sierra is revealed; a Doll literally cannot refuse her handler:

HEARN: Do you trust me?
SIERRA: With my life.
HEARN: Do you want to play the game?
SIERRA: No.
HEARN: But you remember to be very quiet during the game, right?
SIERRA: Noise is upsetting.
HEARN: Lift up your dress.

The Doll/handler relationship is intense, but one-sided. All of the power belongs to the handler.

While a mildly intellectually-disabled person should attain substantial control over her own life when she reaches adulthood, someone with severe-to-profound intellectual disabilities may be stuck in a situation more like that of the Dolls. She depends on her caregiver(s), not only for daily sustenance and survival, but also to communicate with others and to exercise her basic rights. Caretakers may be parents or other family members, staff of residential facilities—typically group homes, or day program staff. I do not mean to suggest that caregivers are generally oppressive; rather, I am simply stressing the extreme level of dependence involved.

Let us focus on the relationship between a primary caregiver and an individual whose intellectual disability is such that she is nonverbal—she does not speak or reliably use a standard augmentative communication system like sign language or a communication board. That is not to say that the intellectually-disabled person (I will call her Julie) does not communicate at all—nearly everyone communicates something, somehow, even if it is just crying to express pain. But understanding what Julie communicates is a highly interpretive process. Attaching meaning to idiosyncratic nonverbal cues takes careful attention and ample experience, the sort you get from living and interacting with somebody over a long period of time (Cushing and Lewis 175). Thus, the primary caregiver is epistemologically better placed than anyone else to act on Julie's wishes and represent them to others.

All of us have certain legal rights; these rights do not go away just because of profound intellectual disability. For example, we have the right to accept or refuse medical treatment. In the 1976 *Quinlan* case, the father of a woman in a persistent vegetative state was authorized to refuse continued artificial ventilation for her. The New Jersey Supreme Court reasoned that unless a guardian can exercise Ms. Quinlan's right to refuse treatment on her behalf, this right would be lost (Cantor 33–34). The exact function of this kind of surrogate decision-making has been the subject of ethical debate. Is the surrogate supposed to be deciding as he supposes the patient would decide were she able to? What does that even mean for patients who have never been cognitively competent? Or, is the surrogate supposed to be deciding on the basis of the patient's best interest? Still, regardless of how we construe the logistics, there has been legal and philosophical consensus that certain rights may be exercised by proxy.

To apply this to our example, notice that in accessing Julie's rights, her caregiver is not simply conveying her interpretation of Julie's ambiguously-communicated wishes. Julie may really have no opinion on certain matters, such as whether to have a gastrostomy tube implanted or whether to accept service from one provider vs. another. Obviously, the caregiver ought to take Julie's interests into account (What discomfort is involved in the g-tube placement? Is Julie happy with the current service provider?), and one hopes that the same sort of privileged epistemological state with respect to communication also applies to determining interests. But when deciding on Julie's behalf, the caregiver really is deciding *for* Julie.

An obvious concern in cases of such extreme power differential is: what to do about the Hearns of the world who take advantage of their vulnerable charges? Boyd and DeWitt had a clever solution to this problem, entrapping Hearn and sending him to his death at the hands of another

Doll. However, this sort of intervention only works if more than one person is available to advocate for the disempowered party. Fortunately, moral monsters are rare. A more common ethical concern arises when a well-meaning caregiver tries to act appropriately on behalf of the person in her care but gets it wrong. Some critics, particularly from the disability rights community, have charged that this happened in the case of Ashley, a profoundly-disabled girl whose parents authorized a set of procedures that would attenuate her growth and physical maturity. Ashley's parents felt that keeping her small would facilitate her comfort and inclusion in social activities. Opponents claimed that the procedure was for the parents' convenience, violated Ashley's dignity, and perpetuated the devaluing of disabled people (Wilfond, et. al. 31–35).

I am not claiming that Ashley's parents acted improperly, but the case raises the question of how we can ensure that those who hold such power over the lives of vulnerable people *do* make good decisions for them. The short answer is: we can't. Requiring court orders or ethics committee oversight might work for life-altering decisions, as they at least ensure that the decision is not in the hands of only one or two people. But for the day-to-day stuff, a caregiver is left with her best guess, as a long-term caregiver from L'Arche explains: "Since [the intellectually disabled woman I care for] is essentially nonverbal, this means that you often aren't sure what is going on with her and I struggle to interpret her movements without imposing my own perceptions on her world" (Cushing and Lewis 184).

Quality of Life. Is it bad to become a Doll? Well, it certainly seems like it is bad for the person you used to be. As Paul Ballard explains, "The only way to imprint a human being with a new personality is to remove their own. Completely. We're talking about people walking around who may as well have been murdered. Which, to me, sounds pretty bad" ("Ghost" 1.01). A popular philosophical theory of personal identity, the psychological continuity theory, says that what makes one the same person over time is chains of mental connections, such as memories, intentions, and preferences. When someone becomes a Doll, all of these connections are severed and the original person ceases to exist. So, to reiterate Ballard's assessment, that sounds pretty bad! In some interpretations of the psychological continuity theory, there is the possibility of restoring personal identity, should the original person's memories, etc., be reinstated. The Dolls are promised this when their terms of service are complete, though, of course, it depends on their bodies and their imprints surviving long enough to be reunited.

A more interesting question is, is it bad to *be* a Doll—that is, bad for the Doll herself? Early in the first episode, Topher suggests that it is not: "Look at Echo. Not a care in the world. She's living the dream." This claim is reminiscent of something the superintendent of the facility where Buck sent her daughter said to console her: "You must remember … that these are happy children…. They will never know distress or want. They will never know struggle or defeat, nor will sorrow ever touch them…. Your child will escape all suffering" (47). This claim, like Topher's, is implausible. Barring permanent unconsciousness, nobody escapes all distress. So, neither the life of a Doll, nor the life of a person with an intellectual disability, is all hugs and puppies. But that does not mean their lives are hedonically bad either. The Dolls seem, if not happy, at least content most of the time. And the small amount of data available on the subject indicates that people with intellectual disabilities are about as happy as those without (Emerson, Hatton, and MacLean).

Yet, happiness is not everything. It has been claimed that even if people with intellectual disabilities are happy, their lives are qualitatively less rich than the lives of people with average or above average intelligence (McMahan 356, Carlson 121). Would any reasonable person choose to have his IQ reduced from, say, 120 to 50? Probably not—not even if he could be guaranteed a happy life. He might not be aware of it, the reasoning goes, but he would be missing out on so much. Like what? Actually, that is very hard to say. Michael Berube has made a practice of correcting philosophers' misperceptions of what people with intellectual disabilities can and can't do. His son, who has Down syndrome, has extensive knowledge of the Beatles' music, can speak some French, contemplates moral issues, and appreciates science fiction and fantasy (98). One can try to identify some more advanced activities that a person with a low IQ cannot do, but the more esoteric one gets, the less compelling the example will be as a determinant of life quality. My ability to do calculus does not add all that much to my quality of life.

I like being smart, and, if you are reading this book, I bet you do too. But I want to suggest that the tragedy of the Dolls is not due to their reduced intelligence so much as to the other things they are missing: deep interpersonal relationships, the ability to learn and grow, opportunities to choose for themselves. That is why we cheer when Victor and Sierra fall in love, when Echo makes cognitive progress, when any Doll makes a free choice. These are things that people with intellectual disabilities—even quite severe intellectual disabilities—can do, given appropriate opportunities and social support.

Notes

1. Indeed, there are many scenarios in which a person's intellectual ability status may change due to traumatic brain injury (TBI), which "can include impairments related to thinking or memory, movement, sensation (e.g., vision or hearing), or emotional functioning (e.g., personality changes, depression)" ("TBI: Get the Facts"). Estimates suggest anywhere from 11 to 23 percent of post–9/11 U.S. armed service personnel have suffered traumatic brain

injury (Lindquist, Love, and Elbogen), and a CDC study published in 2019 indicates that "In 2014, about 2.87 million TBI-related emergency department (ED) visits, hospitalizations, and deaths occurred in the United States, including over 837,000 of these health events among children" ("TBI: Get the Facts"). Clearly the potential for intellectual disability due to accident or injury resulting in traumatic brain injury is far from rare.

2. You might want to add mental scare quotes around the word "kind." Disability advocates have noted that seemingly benign attitudes can be subtly disempowering. Hostile regard from those in power is an obvious threat, but kindly infantilization can be equally damaging, yet harder to fight.

3. Being classified as "feebleminded" was dependent on social inadequacy, and promiscuity was a sign of social inadequacy; thus it is not surprising that feebleminded women had a reputation for hypersexuality (Lombardo 61).

4. Though, I do find the "floor coffins" the dolls sleep in to be oddly reminiscent of the rows of bed/cribs (bars on four sides) shown in Burton Blatt's 1966 exposé of state institutions, *Christmas in Purgatory*.

"I want to be healthy again"

Mental Health and Normality in Buffy the Vampire Slayer[1]

Roslyn Weaver

> "For the last six years, she's been in an undifferentiated type of schizophrenia.... Buffy's delusion is multilayered. She believes she's some type of hero.... She's surrounded herself with friends, most with their own superpowers, who are as real to her as you or me." "Normal Again" 6.17

From its first episode, *Buffy the Vampire Slayer* signals its preoccupation with "normality." In the fantastic setting of Sunnydale, Buffy Summers' attempts to live a normal life despite supernatural life-and-death battles produce an internal conflict that is difficult to resolve. This dilemma is most explicit in "Normal Again" (6.17), an episode in which Buffy must choose between her heroic life in the fantasy-world of Sunnydale and an alternative existence where she is institutionalized and suffering delusions about her identity.

One of the key ways that the series interrogates what is normal is in its representations of mental health across the seven seasons. Buffy's human and supernatural responsibilities exact a heavy toll on her mental health, and she must learn to adjust her ideas about normality with the realities of her superhero existence in Sunnydale. The following discussion draws on prior research on mental health in popular culture to explore how *Buffy* conceptualizes issues of mental health and illness.

Previous work has highlighted a range of mental health issues that intersect with *Buffy* and the other Whedonverses. These include madness (Peeling and Scanlon), gothic fear (Robert A. Davis), psychoanalysis (Kromer), mental manipulation in *Dollhouse* (Ginn), the use of *Buffy* or other vampire films as a therapeutic tool (Schlozman; Priester), and vampirism in psychiatry (Mac Suibhne and Kelly). Research suggests that some viewers can find watching *Buffy* cathartic in some ways, because of its ability to convey "important psychodynamic concepts" (Schlozman 49).

If fantasy texts such as *Buffy* and other vampire fictions can become therapeutic strategies, it is important to see how *Buffy* conceptualizes mental health for its viewers because the enduring popularity of the series has implications for how its viewers understand mental health. What we see on television and in other texts is more than a reflection of cultural attitudes to mental illness; such representations also influence our beliefs (Livingston). The concern that researchers raise with negative images of mental illness is not simply about perpetuating derogatory stereotypes but also about influencing people with mental disorders by lowering self-identity (Philo) and self-esteem and adversely affecting their likelihood of seeking treatment (Stuart). Stigma associated with mental illness can also result in lost opportunities and unfulfilled life goals, self-stigma, and "label avoidance" where people with mental disorders may not seek treatment for fear of being "labeled a 'mental patient' or suffer the prejudice and discrimination that the label entails" (Corrigan 31). Thus, the representation of mental health on programs such as *Buffy* has the potential to contribute to or subvert stigma.

This discussion of *Buffy* draws on an understanding that one's mental state is a vital aspect of health generally. According to the World Health Organization,

> Mental health is an integral and essential component of health. The WHO constitution states: "Health is a state of complete physical, mental and social well-being and not merely the absence of disease or infirmity." An important consequence of this definition is that mental health is described as more than the absence of mental disorders or disabilities. Mental health is a state of well-being in which an individual realizes his or her own abilities, can cope with the normal stresses of life, can work productively and is able to make a contribution to his or her community ["Mental Health"].

It is worth highlighting here this concept of mental health as "a state of well-being in which an individual realizes his or her own abilities, [and] can cope with the *normal* stresses of life" (emphasis added). The opening scenes of *Buffy* introduce viewers to a fantastical world of vampires and supernatural creatures, and for Buffy and her friends, this world becomes their normality, and their abilities must be realized within that context. Accordingly, mental health in the series can be understood as the characters' abilities to cope with the normal stresses of their lives in Sunnydale.

In contrast to mental health, mental illness suggests the inability to deal with normal life stresses, and I use the term mental illness broadly here, leaving the boundaries amenable to how the fictional world of *Buffy* depicts and constructs mental health and mental illness. In current usage, mental illness covers a multitude of different conditions, such as depression; schizophrenia; anxiety; autism; eating, drug and alcohol disorders; and bipolar, obsessive-compulsive, and post-traumatic stress disorders.[2] A large proportion of the general population has a mental disorder (Freeman et al.; "The Numbers Count"); among adolescents in the U.S., the most common mental conditions include disorders related to anxiety, behavior, mood, and substance abuse (Merikangas et al.).

These mental health issues are reflected in the storylines of *Buffy*. Characters find that their anxieties come to life in "Nightmares" (1.10), and again in "Fear, Itself" (4.04). When Buffy is brought back to life, twice in the series, her behavior changes ("When She Was Bad" 2.01) and she feels depression and disconnection (Season 6). The dangers of abusing alcohol are portrayed in Season Four's "Beer Bad" (4.05), and Riley experiences an addiction akin to substance abuse when he starts visiting a vampire nest—equivalent to a crack house—seeking the high of being fed upon by prostitute-like vampires ("Into the Woods" 5.10). Buffy, Joyce, and Tara suffer symptoms of mental disorders because of supernatural events (Season 5), and Dawn's storyline includes self-harm and kleptomania (Season 5 and 6). Given that most mental illnesses in adults first emerge in childhood and adolescence (Merikangas et al.; Kessler et al.), it is intriguing to analyze how a popular young adult text such as *Buffy* constructs mental health and mental illness.

By giving mental illnesses to main characters, and by regularly including storylines referencing mental health issues, the series has the potential to normalize mental health as an important aspect of adolescent life. Viewers may be more likely to treat instances of mental illness more empathetically because of the popularity of these characters. Moreover, without storylines that reveal the characters' weaknesses, the show risks becoming merely another superhero tale of superficial characters, a fantastic tale of one girl's extraordinary abilities. This area is particularly intriguing given *Buffy's* place within the action-fantasy genre that more typically valorizes enhanced abilities and superhuman skills rather than those characters with physical or psychological illness. Mental health thus becomes one way for the writers to allow viewers to empathize with the characters, and this is particularly true for Buffy. Her physical health and strength are superior to ordinary humans, and, therefore, her psychological vulnerability and fragility effectively humanize her and enable viewers to relate to her human vulnerabilities.

A Sick Girl, a Supergirl: Buffy's Dilemma

Buffy's powers might be supernatural, superhuman, but the series begins with the message that she simply wants to be normal. In the first episode of the program, "Welcome to the Hellmouth" (1.01), Buffy tells Giles, her Watcher (mentor), that she has "retired" from vampire slaying. Her reluctance to take on her supernatural responsibilities stems from very natural concerns: wanting to fit in, to make friends, to belong and "be like everybody else." Although Buffy goes on to accept her role, the normal and the supernatural exist in an uneasy juxtaposition throughout the series. When Giles demurs at the prospect of Buffy becoming a cheerleader, her answer encapsulates this dilemma: "I will still have time to fight the forces of evil, okay? I just want to have a life; I want to do something normal. Something safe" ("Witch" 1.03). Buffy's appearance is that of an ordinary girl—a blonde cheerleading student—but her identity is that of the "chosen one," the "one girl in all the world" who is able to stand against the forces of darkness ("Hellmouth").

Thus, just as the name and appearance of the town Sunnydale hides the darkness of the Hellmouth, Buffy Summers is more than her name and looks suggest. This irony informs the dialogue at many points, as when a visiting exchange student tells Buffy, "You must teach me everything about your life. I want to fit in, Buffy, just like you, a normal life," to which Buffy grimaces and replies, "One normal life, coming up" ("Inca Mummy Girl" 2.04). In this instance, both exchange student and Buffy are more than they appear—the student is an Incan mummy—reminding viewers that appearance does not tell the whole story. Each season concludes with a climactic supernatural battle, and each season begins with Buffy attempting to find her way "back to normal" ("Dead Man's Party" 3.02) and find her place in an ordinary world, whether that is high school, college, or the workforce.

Despite her wish for normality, Buffy's responsibilities and her superhuman powers weigh heavily on her psychological state. She faces stresses not of a superhero alone but also of a human girl who must deal with boyfriends, bills, employment, and (reluctantly) parenting her sister Dawn when their mother dies in Season Five. The pressure and stress she feels lead to catatonia in "The Weight of the World" (5.21) after Dawn is kidnapped, and Buffy cannot cope with the burden of responsibility: "This is—all of this—it's too much for me." Much of Season Six concerns her struggle to accept her lot after being returned to life from heaven by her friends; Buffy admits, "I've been so detached.... Every day I try to snap out of it. Figure out why I'm like that" ("Normal Again"). Her disconnection is not new; as early as Season Two Buffy was having difficulty coping with the realities of her supernatural life. When Buffy returns to Sunnydale after visiting her father in Los Angeles following her brief death in Season One's finale, her father also comments on this disconnection: "She was just, I don't know, um ... distant ... there was no connection. The more time we spent together, the more I felt like she was nowhere to be seen" ("When

She Was Bad" 2.01). Buffy's identity as the Slayer is necessarily lonely and, although her friends and eventually the Potential Slayers assist in fulfilling her duties, this theme provides much of the emotional resonance of the series.

This detachment and sense that she is simply "going through the motions" ("Once More, with Feeling" 6.07) culminates in "Normal Again" (6.17), where Buffy experiences hallucinations of an alternate reality in a psychiatric institution. It is here that she questions if her entire vampire slayer existence is, in fact, an elaborate delusion caused by schizophrenia and must make a choice as to which reality she wishes to belong. The concept of an alternate reality is not limited to this episode by any means (see Geller); viewers have already seen other episodes using the idea, and Anya even suggests that "alternate realities are neat" ("Superstar" 4.17). Yet "Normal Again" differs in that it gives Buffy a choice of existing in this alternative reality, the chance to achieve the normality she has desired since the first episode of the series.

"Normal Again" is thus one of the key episodes dealing with mental health and is worth examining more closely. In this episode, a demon's poison causes Buffy to experience life in an alternate reality where she is a patient in a mental institution. In this other reality, Buffy's parents are both alive and present, and her sister does not exist. The episode moves between the two realities and provides a rational explanation for the fantastical events of the previous seasons: Buffy has been suffering schizophrenia for six years and has imagined her entire Sunnydale existence. Her parents and doctor urge her to return to this reality by abandoning the Sunnydale delusion and rejecting her Slayer identity. Meanwhile, in the Sunnydale reality, Buffy's friends realize she has been poisoned and create an antidote to the demonic poison causing her hallucinations, and Buffy must choose whether or not to take the antidote.

In several respects there is little attraction in this alternate reality. Buffy's diagnosis is an "undifferentiated type of schizophrenia," which at times involves convulsions and hitting her head repeatedly against a wall. She is injected against her will. Her bed has restraints. Patients in the institution sit staring expressionlessly at nothing; others jerk their arms around in a straitjacket or walk slowly down corridors bent to one side. The institution scenes utilize cold, blue lighting, and costuming with monochromatic tones. In a study of mental institutions in film, Levers writes that there has been a change over time from presenting hospitals as dark and shadowed to later films portraying institutions as "bright/white/light." This is certainly the case in *Buffy*, and here the mental institution scenes are portrayed far less favorably than the Sunnydale shots, which have a *mise en scène* that comprises warm, bright, light-filled sets saturated with color, featuring a wide range of people and sounds and interaction across home, campus, and work locations. The music used in the episode is jarring to signify cuts between the Sunnydale and institution realities, and this further reinforces the disruption to Buffy's mental state as she seeks to decipher the meaning of her delusions. Her confusion is worsened by the knowledge that even in her Sunnydale existence she was institutionalized when she was younger, placed there after she first saw vampires and told her parents, and, thus, it is possible that she never left the institution.

Even the language around mental illness here is negative, offering a range of synonyms and slang that reflect our culture's attitude to mental illness: mental illness provokes words such as "cuckoo's nest" and "sick," "twisted brain" and "funny farm delusion," caused by a demon's "crazy juice." Dawn says that Buffy's "fever" is "cooking your brain" to make her believe things that are not true; Buffy's father tells her that her mind is "playing tricks on you" (6.17). Previous episodes have already established this derogatory attitude to mental illness: "Listening to Fear" (5.09) gives us "insanity," "madmen," "mental patient," "losing their marbles," "insane wacky," and "crazy." Mental illness is a "sweeping plague of madness," a "short circuit," and "something wrong." The patients are "bothering," "babbling," a "crazy guy."[3] In some ways, this language simply reflects the general irreverence of the Scoobies' chatter, a disregard for authority that manifests itself in the show's writing as black humor and nonchalance. Yet such language is hardly designed to encourage complex or sensitive portrayals of mental health issues. Because the Scoobies' world is defined and bounded by their language, because their wordplay and humorous dialogue is how they interpret, make sense and share meaning with each other, and most of all because this very language is one of the primary sources of enjoyment for many viewers, the characters' use of such negative words seems to ultimately operate as an exclusionary strategy that confirms existing social distinctions between groups. Wilson et al. point to the "vocabulary of stigmatisation" in children's television ("How Mental Illness" 440) that can be pejorative, negative, and imply a loss of control. *Buffy* deploys many of these same pejorative terms, and in this sense, the series may be said to contribute to and reinforce the negative stereotypes that can be harmful and hurtful to people with mental disorders.[4]

And yet despite these disturbing elements, this alternate reality holds much appeal for Buffy. In choosing to accept or reject the antidote, Buffy has the choice between two lives. One is characterized by normality despite the institution setting: loving parents, a secure family background, an ordinary identity as a young woman, no sister to care for. The other is bounded by difficulties: supernatural duties, human responsibility for her sister, a lonely identity as the Chosen One. Buffy reasons that her choice is between logic and fantasy: "What's more real? A sick girl in an institution … or some kind of supergirl chosen to fight demons and save the world. That's ridiculous." And even while we might decry the negative images of institution life, there is a further appeal for Buffy in its clear and defined boundaries. In the series, the unpredictability of mental illness is controlled and oppressed, almost always confined by the order and structure of mental wards and psychiatric institutions. Viewers see patients with mental disorders strapped to their beds ("Listening to Fear"); guided down corridors ("Normal Again"); and isolated to particular wards, units, and institutions rather than integrated into society. Perhaps this is a physical manifestation of the social exclusion that Byrne identifies as one of the problems around mental illness, where stigma is "a sign of disgrace or discredit, which sets a person apart from others" (65) and can lead to social isolation, shame, and secrecy. Yet this isolation and confinement is also potentially attractive to Buffy because in the institution she is no longer responsible for her own choices: she is controlled and safe compared to the risks in Sunnydale of failing her family, friends, and apocalyptic responsibilities. This institution life might be abnormal for most viewers, but it is far more ordinary than Buffy's superhero life.

Thus, the security of a more normal existence holds a powerful allure for Buffy. At one point in this episode, Sunnydale-Buffy looks at a photo of herself as a child with her parents. The photograph recalls for viewers the events of "The Weight of the World," an episode where Buffy regresses to her childhood self in her catatonic state, telling Willow "I like it here." Her parents are alive, and together, and Dawn is a newborn baby. Buffy's desire to escape the hard reality of her life for the security of her childhood in that episode is reflected here in "Normal Again," with Joyce telling Buffy "you're our little girl, Buffy, our one and only.… Mom and Dad just want to take you home and take care of you." The implication is that accepting a mental diagnosis and treating her Sunnydale life as only a delusion would be another escape, an easy way out.

A further catalyst for Buffy to reject her Sunnydale life is her relationship with Spike. In the episode, Spike threatens to publicize their relationship to her friends, a scenario Buffy is anxious to avoid because their relationship is unhealthy, founded as it is on violence and self-hatred.[5] Spike insists that Buffy stop hiding their relationship from her friends, telling her that she is "addicted to the misery" and has a martyr complex, an inflated sense of heroism that draws her away from happiness and peace. In Season Seven, Buffy explains their relationship in terms that seem to almost approach sadomasochism: "I wanted to be punished. I wanted to hurt like I thought I deserved" ("Conversations with Dead People" 7.07). Spike's threat to reveal their relationship occurs immediately before Buffy makes her choice about the antidote. If she accepts the institution reality, Buffy can avoid the consequences of her relationship with Spike. With the antidote she has the opportunity to escape her loneliness and disconnection, and the consequences of her actions; she can be normal.

Buffy rejects the cure. Viewers then see Buffy in the institution, telling her doctor and parents that she does not wish to return to her Sunnydale life: "I want to be healthy again." Buffy is told that to "get better," she must eliminate her Sunnydale friends, who are "tricks keeping you from getting healthy." This emphasis on *getting healthy* and *getting better* recurs, with the phrases used repeatedly in the next scenes in Sunnydale. Buffy's choice is not simply between two competing realities but also between two different concepts of mental health. In the institution, being healthy is refusing one's duty and accepting the security of the familial setting, which in this reality means without competition from (and responsibility for) a younger sister. In Sunnydale, being healthy is conceptualized as rejecting the desire for a normal, safe existence and instead accepting one's power and responsibilities. The message is fairly clear that a denial of power—and the attendant responsibility—may be comforting, may seem preferable, but that maturity means rejecting childhood for the hard responsibilities of adulthood, a point also discussed by Peeling and Scanlon.

When Buffy is attempting to rid herself of her Sunnydale friends and family so she can return to a more normal life, the camera position emphasizes her choice between the dependence and comfort of childhood and the power and responsibility of adulthood. In the institution, Buffy is shown huddled in a corner, and sitting on her bed, facing up as the doctors and her parents look down at her. In Sunnydale, Buffy looks down on her friends as they lie captive at her feet. These power relationships are important. In the Sunnydale reality, Buffy has always been more powerful and significant than her friends, a situation that at times causes her anguish as she feels the weight of responsibility become too heavy a burden to bear. This episode marks one of the climactic moments in Buffy's psychological journey through trauma, where she is forced to make a choice whether to accept her slayer identity and destiny and all it entails.

To embrace her institution reality, Buffy has to remove her friends in Sunnydale by allowing a demon to kill them, in essence denying her heroic abilities. And this she proves ultimately unable to do. In the closing moments, as Buffy watches the demon attacking her friends, she struggles to passively watch them die, and Joyce tells her in the institution that she must believe in herself and her own strength. This message of power and responsibility marks the return of Buffy to her Sunnydale existence: when Buffy stops doubting her identity and power, this is constructed as healthy. And so it is that she rejects the institution reality and saves her friends. In this sense she is choosing her own version of normality, adjusting her pre-conceptions to construct a more coherent view of the world that embraces her abilities and destiny despite the burden of duty. These concepts were perhaps signaled earlier in the season when Buffy sat in a college class listening to a discussion of the "social construction of reality" ("Life Serial" 6.05) that she could not follow nor understand. Here Buffy lives this construction of reality, able to choose her own version, able to comprehend in a personal way the notion of a social construction of reality.[6]

Buffy's final choice to accept her heroic identity and the attendant responsibility aligns almost precisely with WHO's definition of mental health outlined earlier, particularly in that "an individual realizes his or her own abilities, can cope with the normal stresses of life, can work productively and is able to make a contribution to his or her community" ("Mental Health"). Although Buffy's "normal stresses" are obviously fantastical, and beyond what viewers will experience, there is nonetheless the potential that Buffy's decision to accept her responsibilities can encourage and empower the audience to do the same. Given that some mental disorders such as schizophrenia may be more stigmatized than others (Mann and Himelein), associating Buffy with schizophrenia, even temporarily, may have some positive effects. Peeling and Scanlon similarly highlight this, suggesting that Buffy becomes a positive role model for viewers.

Yet there are negative implications for how the series approaches mental health because of its supernatural setting. Episodes such as "Normal Again" and "Listening to Fear" that use demons or other monsters in connection with mental illness are problematic because even as they may approach the topic of mental illness sensitively, they nonetheless inevitably draw on more traditional, negative images of the mentally ill as demonic and possessed (Butler and Hyler; Funk et al.). In *Buffy*, mental illness is indeed often caused by supernatural forces. And this perhaps recalls Sontag's protest against metaphors when she urged readers to abandon metaphors of cancer and AIDS because of the difficult implications that metaphors may have as curses or punishments for patients (*Illness as Metaphor* 99–100). If monstrosity and demonic possession—akin to curses—are metaphors for mental illness, or even literal associations as in *Buffy*, there are negative implications for real-life depictions of mental illness. As I have discussed elsewhere, the fantasy genre can be problematic when particular monsters come to represent minority groups; for every sympathetic monster that may represent disability or illness in order to speak against social injustice or unfair exclusion, there is also the undeniable truth that monsters are dangerous. Moreover, as Peeling and Scanlon point out, there are problems of presenting mental illness as a state of mind that can be escaped simply by choice.

As a popular culture text, *Buffy* plays its part in not only reflecting but also contributing to our cultural attitudes to mental health. The series produces some negative connotations by framing mental illness in ways that link disorders to demonic forces. Yet *Buffy* also opens up a space where such metaphors take on added resonance for viewers and call into question popular images of mental illness and those who suffer it. This is primarily achieved through assigning mental disorders to main characters such as Buffy. Had the writers restricted mental illness only to minor or non-speaking roles, this potential would have been lost. Television, after all, can play a significant role in raising the profile of mental disorders, increasing visibility of those with conditions and thereby reducing social stigma, as well as normalizing mental health as an important aspect of everyone's lives.

Conclusions

Throughout the series, Buffy struggles to reconcile her ideas about a normal life with the realities of her supernatural existence in Sunnydale. This dilemma culminates in the episode "Normal Again" where she is forced to actively make that choice between the normal life she craves and the difficult life she has. For Buffy, mental health is encapsulated in her ability to adjust her ideas of what is normal so that she can accept her identity and abilities with all their complexity and responsibilities, even if her life does not match her previous ideas about normality.

One of the strengths of *Buffy* is that even as the series purports to empower teenagers and particularly young women with images of strong female characters asserting themselves in supernatural battles, much of the power of this depiction is contrarily in the very human traits that show Buffy is as vulnerable and ordinary as real-world viewers. The series offers a valuable space to explore psychosocial issues relating to family, friendship, popularity, and love, as well as psychological themes about trauma, loss, mental illness, and depression, among others. The fantasy genre can be powerful in presenting real-world themes to readers, and the series' use of humor and sympathetic main characters is a powerful way to dramatize such issues. Although mental illness is often misunderstood or misrepresented in popular culture, shows such as *Buffy* offer the opportunity to create engaging and sympathetic depictions that have the potential to undermine negative stereotypes.

It is important to be wary of storytelling that aligns trauma and mental illness too closely with monstrosity, and in some cases *Buffy* displays negative stereotypes and language about people with mental disorders. Yet despite the supernatural context of vampires and demons, the psychological struggles that Buffy experiences in love, family, and friendship are not so removed from the everyday reality that viewers face, and although there are negative stereotypes evident in the series, *Buffy* nonetheless also provides some positive and sensitive images of mental illness. The particularly powerful aspect of *Buffy* is its normalization of mental health as a concept that cannot be separated from Buffy's superpowers. In this way, the series promotes a concept of mental health that involves abandoning the apparent safety of "normality" and instead acknowledging vulnerability, accepting responsibility, and believing in one's own power and ability to influence the world.

Notes

1. A different version of this essay appeared in *Mental Health Disorders on Television: Representation Versus Reality* © 2020 Kimberley McMahon-Coleman *and* Roslyn Weaver by permission of McFarland & Company, Inc., Box 611, Jefferson NC 28640. www.mcfarlandbooks.com.

2. The full list of mental illnesses runs to hundreds in the *Diagnostic and Statistical Manual of Mental Disorders 5* (American Psychiatric Association) and the World Health Organization's *International Classification of Disease* section on "Mental, Behavioural or Neurodevelopmental Disorders." See also the National Institute of Mental Health ("Any Anxiety Disorder"). There are, of course, disputes over the inclusion of many conditions as mental illnesses, and whether or not the word illness is even appropriate to describe non-physical disease (Pickering), as well as more philosophical questions about mental illness (Foucault, *Mental Illness*). Debates also focus on the terminology, with *mental illness* and *mental disorders* often used interchangeably; others distinguish between *mental illness* and *mental health problems* ("What Is Mental Health"). Such arguments about terminology are beyond the scope of this paper.

3. Elsewhere, we find a similar plethora of metaphors and analogies. Glory threatens Tara with insanity in "Tough Love" (5.19), telling her: "Imagine what you'd feel with my fingers wiggling in your brain… little pinching things that go in your ears and crawl on the inside of your skull." In "The Weight of the World," Xander calls the mental ward "the vegetable section," and Buffy's catatonic state is equivalent to being "stuck in some kind of loop" when Willow tries to reach her psychically. See Wilcox, "There Will Never," and also Kromer for more on the language of *Buffy* generally.

4. The combination of witty dialogue with derogatory words about mental disorders and those who have them provokes the question whether this contributes to negative stereotypes of mental illness that others (Pirkis et al.) have shown are already entrenched in television and films in popular culture. Yet on *Buffy*, people with mental disorders are not filmed in ways that present them as more dangerous or frightening than the supernatural monsters. Mental illness patients are just as likely to be victims as anyone else, or, as in "Listening to Fear," more so. This is in contrast with research that suggests that television and other media more frequently link mental illness with violence and danger (Allen and Nairn; Camp et al.; Diefenbach; Hyler; Hyler et al.; Wilson et al.: "Constructing Mental Illness," "Mental Illness Depictions"). *Buffy* instead tends to use its more sinister televisual techniques for the monsters of the series, and in so doing avoids some of the negative stereotypes produced in other television and film.

5. In interviews, Whedon has reinforced this link between Buffy's relationships and the concept of health. When discussing another of Buffy's boyfriends, Riley Finn, Whedon noted: "That was the problem we ran into with Riley. We said, 'Let's give Buffy a healthy relationship,'

and people didn't want it. They did some great work together. But at the same time, when they were happy, it made people crazy" (qtd. in Miller, "The Man Behind the Slayer"). Healthy in this sense is clearly linked to happy, stable relationships as well as to "normality" (unlike Buffy's vampire boyfriends, Angel and Spike, Riley was human). Part of Riley's appeal for Buffy is his apparent normality, the possibility of a "nice, safe relationship" ("Something Blue" 4.09) with someone who seems to be "Joe regular by day" ("The Initiative" 4.07). When she discovers his demon-hunting military ability, she is upset: "I really thought that you were a nice, normal guy" ("Doomed" 4.11). Riley insists that "I am a nice, normal guy," but Buffy is unconvinced. Yet at the same time as Buffy seeks a normal life with a normal relationship, she questions its value, wondering if true love can exist without pain and fighting, and such comments as well as a spell-induced romance with Spike ("Something Blue") presage her later relationship with him in Season Six. Whedon might be obeying unwritten laws of television in keeping his characters outside a "healthy relationship," but the show risks glamorizing the dysfunctional and abusive relationship of Buffy and Spike in Season Six (although perhaps Buffy's realization of her problems and Spike's later redemption mitigate this to some extent). In any case, Buffy can find little normality in her romances in Sunnydale, and at the time of "Normal Again," she is experiencing her most unhealthy romantic relationship of the series.

6. A difficulty with this episode comes at the conclusion when Buffy's doctor and parents stand over her catatonic body. Because viewers see this after Buffy has chosen her Sunnydale life, this undermines a simple explanation of Buffy's institution reality as merely the outcome of poison-induced hallucinations; instead it suggests that this alternative existence might, in fact, be real. If it were simply the product of hallucinations, once Buffy stopped hallucinating and became catatonic (returned to Sunnydale), presumably she would have no awareness of this reality and neither would the viewer. In their analysis of this episode, Peeling and Scanlon, as well as Geller, offer more on the troubling aspects of this alternative reality for *Buffy* viewers.

Dr. Simon Tam, Healer and Humanist

Medical Models of Health Care in Firefly *and* Serenity

BRETT S. STIFFLEMIRE

In the Whedonverses, the team of writers continue a long tradition of the science fiction genre to create significant characters who are affiliated with the medical profession. These figures are important in their individual texts because the narratives often place characters in situations that require medical treatment. A prime example is Dr. Simon Tam, who, in *Firefly* (2002) and the subsequent film *Serenity* (2005), functions as the medic aboard the spaceship Serenity to treat the various injuries that the crew members sustain during their travels.[1] As the ship medic and a passenger aboard Serenity, Simon develops complex relationships with the other characters through his interactions with them in both capacities. With these relationships, writers for the series do more than depict health care as a means of fixing physical bodies. They demonstrate that healing is a deeper biopsychosocial process involving understanding between patients and physicians. Simon begins his journey aboard Serenity as a body-fixer, but through serving his fellow shipmates, Simon develops into a healer whose approach to medicine is rooted in humanism. The depiction of Simon and his evolution are crafted in such ways as to privilege the humanistic healer, for humanism is the guiding principle embodied by Serenity and her crew.

The beginning of the film *Serenity* introduces two important and oppositional doctor characters—Drs. Mathias and Simon Tam. Dr. Mathias, a scientist working for the Alliance Academy, is experimenting on his "gifted" patient River Tam, who he does not yet realize is Simon's sister. Simon takes the role of observer as Mathias demonstrates his technique. River, who is sleeping strapped to a chair in the middle of an examination room, has a needle shoved into her brain by Dr. Mathias' assistant. Suddenly writhing in pain, River struggles against her restraints, a body full of vigor and emotion that contrasts with the room's cool, blue hue and cold, antiseptic atmosphere. The sterile tone of the room is echoed in Dr. Mathias' behavior, as he watches River struggle with a clinical dispassion.[2] Proud of his efforts, he boasts to Simon that "most of our best work is done when they're asleep. We can monitor and direct their subconscious, implant suggestions. It's a little startling to see at first, but the results are spectacular. Especially in this case. River Tam is our star pupil." The image of the "star pupil" being tortured by her own nightmares and by Dr. Mathias' experiments is, of course, far more than "a little startling," and this disjunction between Mathias' words and his actions help establish his role in representing a dominant, dispassionate—and undesirable—approach to medicine.

As an Alliance scientist, Mathias possesses an emotionless detachment from his subject, and he also disconnects River's special abilities from her humanity. His representation of the detached scientist becomes more concrete as he continues to describe River as a weapon to Simon: "She'll be ideal for defense deployment even with the side effects." Like a doctor on rounds, Simon asks about the side effects, and Mathias responds, "Well, obviously, she's unstable. The neural stripping does tend to fragment their own reality matrix.... Given the right trigger, this girl is a living weapon." Mathias evokes the mechanical view of the biomedical approach to health care as he describes River, his patient, as if describing a machine. Mimicking the scientist's tone, Simon asks, "How is she physically?" Mathias answers, "Like nothing we've seen. All our subjects are conditioned for combat, but River, she's a creature of extraordinary grace." By describing River as a "creature" possessing grace while she is bound to a chair with a needle stuck in her forehead and monitoring equipment attached to her, Dr. Mathias further establishes that he considers her as merely an experimental subject separate from the human race. Simon, with a robotic demeanor continuing his ruse, replies, "Yes. She always did love to dance." Mathias pauses at the contradiction between Simon's tone and words before, in a burst of action, Simon uses a device to render Mathias and his assistant unconscious so that he can rescue River from her captors. Through this scene, the Tams' necessary backstory in *Serenity* is established, but also an opposition between the good doctor and the evil scientist is set up, evoking a traditional dichotomy within the science fiction genre.

The consistent presence of doctors in film and television reveals a continuing interest in depictions of physicians and the medical profession. This long-standing interest is particularly apparent in television programs, which have ranged from *Dr. Kildare* and *Trapper John, M.D.* to more recent shows like *House* and *Grey's Anatomy*. The large number of medical dramas and medically-related films and television programs reflects continuing societal concerns about health, medicine, and the human body. Doctor characters are also recurring figures in the science fiction genre where these concerns of health, medicine, and the human body intersect with concerns of technology, individuality, and the fate of the human race. The nature of the medical profession requires that doctors have a detailed knowledge of the human body and, further, that they have an intimate knowledge of their patients' bodies. By virtue of this knowledge, doctors are in a position to be among humanity's strongest allies or greatest foes.

This view of doctor as either hero or villain is, of course, a very melodramatic idea. However, this extreme dichotomy and the reductivist moral binary it implies underlie much in the science fiction genre, especially in film and television. Indeed, Susan Sontag writes, "[S]cience fiction films are strongly moralistic. The standard message is the one about the proper, or humane, use of science, versus the mad obsessional use of science" ("The Imagination" 219). Classically, these opposing views of science—humane versus obsessional—are a motivating force in the depictions of physicians and scientists in the science fiction genre and other genres upon which it builds. For example, in science fiction films of the 1950s—the golden age of the science fiction film genre—scientists and physicians were typically depicted differently. Scientists were either humble men seeking to use science to save humankind (e.g., *When Worlds Collide*, 1951) or men blinded by hubris whose obsession with science threatens humanity (e.g., *The Thing from Another World*, 1951). However, during this period, the science fiction genre generally depicted physicians as heroes. These depictions were built on a tradition of fictional doctors motivated by the best interest of their patients, like the popular Dr. Kildare, a character featured in a series of films in the 1930s and '40s, as well as other media like radio and television in subsequent decades. In his essay "The Positive Image of the Physician in American Cinema During the 1930s," Todd Wider explains that this binary characterization of doctors and scientists emerged with the 1931 film version of Sinclair Lewis' *Arrowsmith*, which changed the novel's characters such that the "archetypal medical practitioner becomes somehow synonymous with the 'country doctor' and is out to save lives in the present, whereas the scientist emerges as a colder, more rational entity, motivated by either vainglory or the pursuit of innate truth" (141). This film marked a shift and set the precedent for decades to follow: scientists who lose their focus on the humane use of science become a threat to humanity while physicians are heroic because their work privileges helping others and is thus viewed as inherently humanistic. The impersonal threatens whereas the personal reassures.

Significantly, such depictions assume that altruistic physicians alone are the source of healing and heroism. Importantly, the faith afforded physicians during the first half of the twentieth century was the result of significant changes in the practice of medicine, particularly the introduction of the biomedical model of medical practice early in the century. The biomedical approach to medicine is founded on the direct application of knowledge gained from scientific laboratory experiments. Prior to this approach, doctors treated patients with various traditional treatments and homegrown remedies that had not been tested scientifically, and doctors' levels of training were as varied as their treatments. When the biomedical model was introduced, medicine became remarkably (even miraculously) more effective because disease and treatment were based on scientific fact. Thus, doctors during this period gained the admiration and faith of their patients because of the dramatic increase in survival rate. Family physicians became miracle workers. They were trusted and revered for their knowledge, their concern for patients, and their power to cure. As described above, this trust and reverence was reflected in representations of doctors in film and television during this time, further contributing to the popular image of the doctor-hero.

The physician-hero character is seen in the iconic 1956 film *Invasion of the Body Snatchers* in which Dr. Miles Bennell's patients and friends come to him for advice and answers as the invasion begins. Because he is a doctor, there is an expectation that he will be able to help due to his greater knowledge and ability. In the scene that opens *Serenity* and this essay, Simon Tam largely echoes this tradition as he rescues River from the machinations of Dr. Mathias. Significantly, physician-centered depictions of medicine are consistent with the model of health care that achieved prominence during the twentieth century—the biomedical model, which is "based on the premise that ill health is a physical phenomenon that can be explained, identified, and treated through physical means" (du Pré 10). This model of health care focuses on the physician—the one with knowledge and training—as the essential source of medical information. The model is based on the idea that for every symptom of disease, there is an appropriate treatment. As such, "[p]hysicians are like scientists or mechanics. They collect information about a problem, try to identify the source of it, and fix it" (10). By emphasizing the role of the physician and deemphasizing the role of the patient, the biomedical model of health care has created a gap between doctor and patient. This gap is reflected in films that portray doctors as revered and venerated heroes, who have the ability to fix whatever has gone awry because they are more knowledgeable than the untrained patient.

However, there is danger of depersonalization in the practice of the biomedical model. Further emphasizing the mechanical nature of this approach, Charles Longino writes, "Repairing a body, in this view, is analogous to fixing a machine" (14). When considering the doctor-patient relationship in terms of a mechanic fixing a machine, it is clear that the biomedical model could potentially produce impersonal physical examinations. Like with the cold, rational scientist described above, impersonal interactions threaten to dehumanize patients, similar to concerns that industrialization would turn factory workers into machines.[3] However, the biomedical model remains the main approach to medical care because its historical tradition is so strong. This model has had great success in advancing medical treatment. The biomedical approach "has been the basic premise of Western medicine for the last 100 years" since the Flexner Report was published in 1910 (du Pré 10). Prior to 1900, there was no established standard for medical education, and medical schools across the United States were not systematized. In fact, most medical schools operated like businesses rather than educational institutions and "produced thousands of physicians with little knowledge of biology or physiology" (28). Therefore, Abraham Flexner was commissioned in 1908 by the American Medical Association (AMA) to evaluate U.S. medical schools. His evaluations revealed inadequate instruction in biology and other sciences and minimal hands-on experience for students. In his report to the AMA, he made recommendations for how schools should reform their teaching practices. As a result of his report, about two-thirds of schools closed, and those that remained open "became more demanding and began to focus intensely on organic aspects of disease as well as clinical and laboratory experience" (du Pré 28). With this shift of focus to scientific rigor, the medical profession produced many advances in medical treatment, and "[t]he first half of [the twentieth] century was marked by stunning discoveries and advances in the treatment of infectious diseases. These scourges of mankind yielded to the post–Flexner report emphasis on specialization and laboratory research" (Samuel A. Banks 281). With this new standard in medicine proving to be so beneficial, it is understandable why the biomedical model was perpetuated.

However, the success of the biomedical model in treating disease is not the only reason that it remains the dominant approach to health care. Although the biomedical approach may lead to less personal doctor-patient interactions, the model is such an established standard now that it is difficult for many practitioners to accept a new, more personal approach:

> There is no rule against understanding the human situations that cause so much illness, and the [bio]medical model in no way prohibits warm, personal, sensitive interactions between doctors and patients. But the medical student soon discovers that the model *actually applied in practice* by most house staff and attending physicians is far more restricted than what was taught in the introduction to clinical medicine [Barbour 2; emphasis in original].

In practice, doctors find that they are "far more restricted" in their personal interactions with patients due to the emphasis the biomedical model places on the mechanics of obtaining medically-relevant information and performing physical examinations. Other factors like time constraints also restrict doctors from being more personal at times. In addition to the biomedical model being the accepted standard, it is also less demanding than other medical models that require more effort to acquire and assimilate information in a holistic manner: "It is so much easier simply to name a disease and prescribe a treatment. The [bio]medical model is seductive, for both doctor and patient. The patient need not assume any responsibility for the illness, and the physician need not take the time or emotional risk of exploring the life situation. Both follow the line of least resistance" (26). Success, tradition, routine, and ease are not the only reasons for the continued use of the biomedical model, but they are vital factors to consider and are helpful in understanding how the doctor-hero (especially of 1950s science fiction) possessed so much power—both narratively and socially.

Although the biomedical model has been the standard for 100 years, other medical models, specifically the biopsychosocial model, that argue for a more holistic and humanistic approach to medical care have been vying for attention within the last forty years. In the 1970s, as the biomedical model (as well as other mainstream social and political practices) was being challenged, science fiction films reflected the potential danger of a completely technical, mechanic-machine approach to medicine. In George Lucas' *THX 1138* (1971), medical care (as well as religion) has become entirely computerized and standardized. When THX visits the medical clinic, he is examined by an impersonal and inhuman robotic arm. This anticipated, dystopian future of health care envisions the progression of the medical profession from a biomedical approach to a robotic profession.[4] If the biomedical model creates doctors who dehumanize the body and systematize disease, then it is a logical progression that medicine in the future will become an entirely programmable practice in which human doctors are completely removed from the experience because medicine has become as mechanical as a computer program. In response to patient input, there is a programmed doctor output. More commonly, the science fiction genre portrays the human race as being replaced by robots, which necessitates doctors to literally become mechanics. This is seen in films such as *Blade Runner* (1982) and *I, Robot* (2004). In these films, the patient, rather than the doctor, becomes the robotic part of the medical encounter. In such a scenario, instead of the robot doctor's response being mechanical, the patient's body is literally a machine. These depictions of robots in medical situations—either as doctors, such as the one in *THX 1138*, or as patients, like in *I, Robot*—are concerned with the core negative aspect of the biomedical model. If the doctor-patient relationship shifts to that of mechanic-machine, then there is a loss of humanity in an intimately human experience.

When viewers are first introduced to Simon, his only real human connection is with River, his sister. In his other interactions, Simon is disconnected and rational, and he acts as if medical treatment is an intellectual exercise that happens to elicit the side-product of helping others. It makes sense that if a body has a hole in it, he should sew it up. If a body breaks down, he should fix it. In "Bushwacked" (1.03), Simon volunteers to help with the bodies of those who were killed by Reavers because he has "dealt with bodies." Even though Simon is not really suited for the situation, he thinks it is logical to help because his approach to his occupation is focused on bodies as objects. In "Heart of Gold" (1.13), Simon takes charge of delivering Petaline's baby. However, Inara is the one who provides comfort during the labor.[5] Simon is simply the one with the medical training; he is trained to cure, not to comfort.

As Simon Tam is depicted in the early episodes of *Firefly*, he reflects the biomedical approach of medicine and its potential of equating physicians with mechanics. This characterization of Simon is brought into sharper relief by his positioning as a romantic partner for Kaylee, Serenity's mechanic. When the crew is sitting around the table in *Firefly*'s pilot episode "Serenity" (1.01), Kaylee says to Simon, "You seem so young to be a doctor." He replies, "Yeah. You're pretty young to be a ship's mechanic." In her humble way, Kaylee responds, "Machines just got workings, and they talk to me." With this exchange, a parallel is drawn between Kaylee, the ship's mechanic, and Simon who repairs the workings of human bodies. When Shepherd Book tells her that her ability is "a rare gift," Kaylee downplays the complement, "Well, not like being a doctor. Helping fix people—that's important." Although Kaylee downplays the importance of her profession in contrast to Simon's, the parallel between doctor and mechanic is clearly established, evoking the biomedical model of health care. Throughout *Firefly*, Simon's practice of medicine is very technical, and he does little to demonstrate a humanistic, biopsychosocial approach. In fact, it seems as though the only patient he really considers as more than a body to repair is River. When Agent Dobson confronts Simon in "Serenity," Kaylee is shot, and although Simon rushes to assess her wound, he withholds treatment to force Mal to side with him and River against Dobson. His willingness to let Kaylee die seriously calls into question Simon's concern for human life, at least anyone other than River. Although his compassion for River is clearly demonstrated in his interactions with her, his interactions with others on the ship remain rather distant and impersonal, characterizing his doctoring as a business practice rather than a humanistic one. Clearly, the other characters understand Simon in this way, as evidenced by Mal's description, "The doctor knows his trade. I'll give him that." Indeed, at this point, Simon is approaching medicine as simply a trade, an occupation rather than a calling. It is not personal, not human. In fact, in the DVD commentary for this episode, Joss Whedon emphasizes this perspective when he calls Simon a "robot." This reference to the doctor being a robot calls to mind the concept of the biomedical model of health care progressing into a literally robotic practice.[6] Throughout *Firefly*, Simon remains mechanical in his relationships with others and technical in his doctoring. Late in the series, in "The Message" (1.12), when Tracey wakes up, he refers to his body in mechanical terms, telling Simon that he "runs hot." In that same episode, Kaylee continues her attempts to woo Simon, but he is insensitive to her feelings, as usual. In response to this, Kaylee echoes Whedon in calling Simon a "robot." This accusation is particularly poignant coming from the ship's mechanic. In contrast to Simon's biomedical approach to treating his shipmates, Kaylee follows a much more biopsychosocial approach in her interaction with Serenity. She often personifies the ship and even talks to it. In "Out of Gas" (1.08), when she is unable to fix the ship, she breaks down and laments that Serenity did not talk to her. The narrative uses the parallel between Simon and Kaylee in significant ways to demonstrate that Kaylee treats Serenity the way that Simon should treat his patients: with understanding and concern rooted in humanism.

Even though Simon often overtly reflects the traditional biomedical doctor-hero, he is much more complex than his outward actions initially suggest. He evolves throughout *Firefly* and *Serenity* from a biomedical model of medical care toward a more humanistic approach. His mechanical, robotic, biomedical approach to his patients and fellow crew members gives way to a more humanistic, biopsychosocial method that seeks to treat the entire person. The main argument against the biomedical model is that in focusing on the physical nature of patients, it neglects other aspects of the individual that help to define a patient's health. Because of the emphasis of the biomedical model on repairing the body through scientific knowledge,

> [t]he pendulum has swung very far in the direction of a form of medical education that places heavy demands on a student's competence in the scientific disciplines but leaves very little time for reflection, either about the broader human issues of an individual's life when confronted by the stresses of illness, or about the place of medical responsibility in relation to society and history more generally [Rogers and Barnard 4–5].

By focusing only on the physical body, medical practice becomes dehumanized and distanced from the human patient. The biopsychosocial model seeks to overcome this "technicism" (Lifton 54). In other words, "[t]he biopsychosocial model takes into account patients' physical conditions (biology), their thoughts and beliefs (psychology), and their social expectations" (du Pré 11). According to this model of health care, a patient is not viewed as a machine that must go to the doctor simply to be repaired. The biopsychosocial approach to medicine views the body as only one component of a complex system of parts that work in concert to maintain health. A person's health is influenced by a number of interconnected factors including the body, the mind, life experiences, sociality, emotions, thoughts, and feelings, which means that "illness is not solely a physical phenomenon but is also influenced by people's feelings, their ideas about health, and the events of their lives" (11). According to this model, illness is not caused simply by a patient's body falling into disrepair, nor can a simple mechanical repair truly restore a patient to full health. Barbour contends, "Human situations, problems, and stresses of many kinds are certainly the major cause of the common functional 'medical' illnesses that abound in [a doctor's] daily practice" (12). This approach requires a doctor to know the patient beyond the physical examination of the body, but it also views the patient as a vital member of the health care team. Whereas the biomedical model allows a person to follow passively the doctor's lead, the biopsychosocial model demands that the patient be active in his or her own health management. "*Healing* depends on some kind of change, action, insight, or redirection on the part of this *person*. Curing and treatment are not enough. Doctor and patient must work together" (Barbour 33; emphasis in original). Collaboration is an essential aspect of the biopsychosocial model. There is no room for passive, technical doctor-patient relationships in this approach.

The goal of the biopsychosocial approach is to humanize medicine (Rogers and Barnard 8). This means "shift[ing] from the doctor fixing what has gone wrong to what the patient needs to do for himself or herself" (Barbour 33). While this shift increases the patient's responsibility, it does not lessen the doctor's responsibility. In fact, it increases the responsibility of both doctor and patient. They must work together to create and carry out a treatment plan that will not simply fix the body but will heal the patient in a mentally, emotionally, and socially healthy way. The biopsychosocial model actually demands that "the doctor, who formulates a *clinical judgment* about the whole illness, its source, ramifications, and effects, must assume the responsibility to know this person well enough to point this all out, and to encourage the patient's interaction with the underlying personal situation" (33; emphasis in original). The doctor must understand the patient holistically, completely. Treating the patient's body is not enough because healing involves the entire person. The collaborative nature of the biopsychosocial model emphasizes that the doctor-patient relationship is a human-human relationship. Thus, it is important to recognize that both the patient and the physician are human. Humanism is an underlying guiding principle of this medical model. It is patient-focused and person-centered because good health is not simply a finely-tuned body but also a well-balanced mental, emotional, and social state. There is a humanistic morality in this approach to medical care that seeks to treat patients holistically because health and healing exist within the entire person and circumstance of the patient.

As *Firefly* progresses, Simon begins to develop his own brand of biopsychosocial humanism as he evolves from being self-interested to being concerned with the crew of Serenity. Whedon is a self-identified atheist and humanist, and his work often presents characters who make choices based on humanistic principles. Whedon often deals in morality, but it is not a religiously-defined morality of right and wrong. Rather, it is a humanistic morality based on a mutual understanding and beneficial treatment of humankind. Whedon has said, "I believe the only reality is how we treat each other. The morality comes from the absence of any grander scheme, not from the presence of any grander scheme" (TNH Videos). When he received the 2009 Lifetime Achievement Award in Humanism from the Humanist Chaplaincy at Harvard, Whedon stated, "The enemy of Humanism is not faith; the enemy of Humanism is hate, is fear, is ignorance, is the darker part of man that is in every Humanist and every person in the world" (TNH Videos). The guiding motivation behind many of the choices made by Simon is not hate, fear, ignorance, or his "darker part." Rather, he is motivated by love. As Richardson and Rabb conclude, "What makes Simon so dangerous to the Alliance is love, unconditional love for his sister" (*The Existential* 149). It is love that motivates him to defy the Alliance by giving up his career as a surgeon to rescue his sister and flee from the Alliance with her. It is his love for River that motivates him to threaten withholding medical treatment from Kaylee, so Mal will allow him and his sister to stay aboard Serenity. However, while traveling aboard the ship and while serving them, he comes to love and be loved by the Serenity crew. Thus, as his humanistic love grows to include not just River but the others, his approach toward treating them medically also grows beyond a mere mechanistic, biomedical view of medicine. Further, Simon is not the only one who is motivated by love, for love is a guiding force for the Serenity crew as a community. Indeed, as Richardson and Rabb state, "Whedon is using *Firefly* and *Serenity* … to critique rationalistic systems of ethics, such as utilitarianism, and to support his alternative communitarian love ethics, built on a foundation of existential choice" (*The Existential* 149). Humanism operates aboard Serenity as choices, based on "communitarian love ethics," that are made for the benefit of the crew. Eventually, even Simon comes to understand this as he becomes a part of the Serenity family.

When describing the set for the Serenity spaceship, Whedon explained that the infirmary is used "when people get shot, which they will because it's one of my shows" ("Joss Tours the Set"). Because *Firefly* and *Serenity* are space westerns, it is to be expected that there will be gunfights and rule-by-force on the "uncivilized" frontier. Thus, as a physician, Simon functions in a capacity to treat these wounded characters. However, he also functions as a "civilized" witness of the "uncivilized" frontier. When Simon first boards the ship in the *Firefly* pilot episode "Serenity," he is impeccably dressed, wearing a long-sleeved dress shirt under a dark vest, "civilized" attire that bears some resemblance to the traditional frontier doctor. Significantly, with this character, Whedon blends the futuristic science fiction genre with the period western genre. In her book *Faith and Choice in the Works of Joss Whedon*, K. Dale Koontz compares Simon with Bones from the original *Star Trek* television series and Michaela Quinn from *Dr. Quinn, Medicine Woman* because they are "portrayed as bearing the civilizing lamp of medical knowledge and reason in often rugged situations" (74). In reality, doctors on the frontier may not have actually had as "civilizing" an influence as these depictions may lead one to believe. Although doctors were among the few educated men on the frontier, "[m]ost frontier doctors never saw the inside of a medical school. They were educated through a medical apprenticeship, which was right out of the Middle Ages" (Dunlop 4). However meager their education may have been in comparison to today's standard of medical education, these men sought to assist those in "uncivilized" regions with their knowledge. Simon represents such an influence, but more importantly his journey to the frontier teaches him the importance of humanism and love.

In *Firefly*, Simon's clothing—dress shirt and vest—is somewhat reminiscent of the image of the frontier physician. At the beginning of the series, he wears these clothes in a very formal and proper manner. However, as the series develops, Simon changes as he becomes more accepted as a part of the Serenity crew and as he begins to adopt the principles of humanism. As he changes, so does his attire, and he begins to wear his clothes less formally—such as a shirt without a vest. Ultimately, he divests himself even of the collared shirt and vest in favor of sweaters and slacks. The transition is sharply apparent in *Serenity*, in which he wears extremely formal attire within the premises of the Alliance Academy but then wears casual attire of a sweater and slacks after rescuing River and leaving the realm of the Alliance.

Of significant note when considering Simon's apparel is the single-most recognizable article of clothing associated with doctors—the long white coat. The only time that Simon wears the white coat is in the episode "Ariel" (1.09). In this episode, Simon devises a plan to infiltrate the Alliance hospital on Ariel with a two-fold mission—to examine River and to steal valuable medicines that Mal can sell on the outer planets. In order to gain entry into the hospital, Simon dons a white coat—the symbol of his profession. The white coat empowers him to walk through the hospital as if he belongs there. While in the hospital, River instructs her brother to help a patient who is going to die. Simon is reluctant and tells her that the doctors in the hospital are the best in the core. She states in response, "Where you should be." As the patient dies, Simon finally defers to River's command and saves the patient's life. This experience provides a profound moment in which Simon is confronted with a vision of what his life could have been before he sacrificed everything for River. However, helping to save a life in the hospital "where he should be," helps him realize that medicine is not about where he is or what he knows but is actually about the people he serves.

This moment in "Ariel" marks a significant transition in Simon's progress away from the order and regiment of the Alliance and toward humanism. This transition is reflected in his costuming. After his experience in the Ariel hospital, he casts off the white coat and progressively wears more informal and casual clothing. The absence of the white coat conveys several meanings that add complexity and contradiction to his character at different times during the series. First, casting off the recognizable symbol of the medical profession is a manifestation of the fact that he has cast off the Alliance's "civilization" and has left his old life behind—like everyone else on Serenity. At times, the absence of the white coat may call into question Simon's allegiance to medicine, but this is quickly proven false by his actions. As he develops a more biopsychosocial approach, it signifies that he has divested himself of a symbol of class that can create an impersonal barrier between physician and patient. Along with the white coat, he has cast off the biomedical model in favor of a more personal, humanistic approach. Further, by rejecting the white coat, he rejects the Alliance. As Richardson and Rabb contend, by joining Mal and Serenity, Simon "is able to overcome all the socializing imposed on him by the Alliance through its school system (seen intermittently in *Serenity*) and its other means of social control (wealth, status, etc.) and to work in a self-sacrificing way to rescue his sister" (*The Existential* 149). Therefore, if conventional physician's attire represents the mandated conformity of the Alliance, then Simon demonstrates his resistance to the evil dictatorial power by not conforming. Simon gives up everything—his job, his wealth, and his status—to save River. In doing so, he abandons his acceptance by the Alliance to become a fugitive, but abandoning the Alliance allows him to transcend its opposition to the humanistic morality that Whedon espouses.

Throughout the series, Simon evolves from a mechanical physician to a humanistic one who understands the importance of physician-patient interdependence, another key aspect of the biopsychosocial model of medical practice. After Jubal Early shoots him in "Objects in Space" (1.14), Simon gives instructions to Zoë as she takes the bullet out of his leg. She tells him, "This is really not my area of expertise, Doctor. I tend to be putting these into people more than the other thing." Wash stands beside Zoë and asks Simon, "Can I mop your brow? I am at the ready with the fearsome brow mop." Zoë pulls the bullet out, and Simon lays back in the chair, exhausted with the strain. "Okay, I'm just gonna pass out for a minute, but you're doing great." This experience of the physician becoming the patient conveys a circularity of roles. This interdependence is reemphasized in the film *Serenity* when River decides to save Simon from the Reavers. He is again shot and it seems as though the crew will be overwhelmed by the onslaught of Reavers. River assesses the situation and says to her brother, "You've always taken care of me. My turn," before diving into the midst of the Reavers. From the beginning, River's well-being is Simon's primary concern. However, at this moment, he must allow her to seemingly-sacrifice herself for him and the rest of the crew. Of course, River, the perfect weapon, slaughters the Reavers, but the impact of this scene on Simon is not diminished by the outcome.

Simon begins his journey on Serenity willing to use his power as a doctor to maintain his role as River's caregiver, but now he is willing to let River go in the hope that she can save everyone else. Over the course of the series, his motivation evolves in conjunction with his approach to practicing medicine. In the beginning, the biomedical model creates distance between him and his patients, but as his valuing of the others, especially Kaylee, increases, he develops a more humanistic view of healing. The interdependence and mutual concern for one another demonstrated at the end of *Serenity* is at the heart of humanistic biopsychosocial medicine. Healing is more than fixing; it is a process that improves the whole being physically, mentally, emotionally, and socially. As Simon comes to understand this, he evolves. He is coming to understand the importance of humankind, not as bodies that need fixing but as equals in the human family. Indeed, humanism guides both Serenity and her doctor.

Notes

1. Similar to Simon's role as the medic aboard Serenity, in Whedon's *Dollhouse* (2009) Dr. Claire Saunders is the house physician employed to manage the health and wellness of the Actives and the Dolls while in their inactive state.

2. The character of Dr. Mathias is reminiscent of the scientists in *Alien: Resurrection* (1997), for which Whedon wrote the screenplay. In their attempt to clone Ripley, the scientists in this installment of the *Alien* franchise give life to a large number of clones; however, only one Ripley is naturally viable or deemed viable by the scientists. The other clones either die or are destroyed. The scientists terminate these failed attempts with no remorse. Further,

after creating the clone that is featured in the film, the scientists observe her with dispassion as if she were only the subject of an experiment rather than an actual human being. In the film, Ripley must confront the nature of her being. She is not human like the others because she is a clone. This issue is of no concern to the scientists. Thus, like Dr. Mathias, who considers River as a subject and is only concerned with her potential as a weapon for the Alliance, the scientists in *Alien: Resurrection* only consider Ripley as a subject and are only concerned with her potential for providing them with an alien. Given this example, it seems as though Whedon was concerned with the issue of humanistic health care as early as 1997.

3. Notably, films like Fritz Lang's *Metropolis* (1927) and Charlie Chaplin's *Modern Times* (1936) evoke this anxiety through metaphorical and satirical imagery.

4. This concept of mechanized medicine is also present in *Idiocracy* (2006). This sci-fi comedy is a satirical look at the future of humankind as humans get progressively less intelligent. While the idea of robotic medicine is often seriously considered in dystopian visions of the future, it is worthwhile to consider (or at least acknowledge) how the concept operates as satire in this comedic portrayal of the future.

5. This scene has striking parallels with John Ford's *Stagecoach* (1939) in which Doc Boone must deliver Lucy's baby while Dallas, the prostitute, comforts her. This western film is concerned with a group of individuals from various classes of society traveling on a stagecoach through hostile Indian territory on the American frontier. *Firefly* is concerned with a similarly motley crew traveling through hostile frontier territory. Whedon has acknowledged the influence of American film westerns in his education as a filmmaker and on *Firefly*, but the influence of *Stagecoach* is particularly clear.

6. Whedon's *Dollhouse*, in which humans are programmed like robots, provides an interesting and complex look at doctors, robots, and humanism in the physician character of Dr. Claire Saunders, although of course it is revealed that "Dr. Saunders" is yet another mechanically-constructed identity, calling into question her ability to choose her model of medical practice.

Suffering, Strength, and the Soul of the Slayer

Madeline Muntersbjorn

Buffy the Vampire Slayer is a television series about a girl with superpowers who becomes an even more powerful woman over the course of seven seasons. Buffy's story is beloved by viewers because it is not only entertaining but also empowering. We can learn how to be more human in the real world by watching our imaginary friend Buffy fight impossible monsters in a fantasy world. The Buffyverse re-imagines the human soul as neither subject nor object but as a relationship between the self, a narrative subject, and the body, an animated object. Not every animated body in this multi-verse has a soul, for it marks the distinction between the humans who have them and the vampires who do not. This rule is not universal: humans can sell their souls and, more rarely, vampires can get theirs back. Importantly, souls not only connect the material body to the literal self in an individual person but also bind people together as they suffer misery in common and nurture one another through hardship and loss. The Slayer's story challenges us to consider the connections between suffering and strength, and to distinguish between the self, as fragmentary scraps of narrative identity, and the human soul, a unifying power that binds our fragile bodies and fleeting selves in relation to one another.

Buffy Summers is strong, quick, and hardly ever sick. She is not hurt easily and heals rapidly. She repeatedly puts herself in harm's way to save others and is more often the one bringing the pain rather than the one in pain. Her body is more resilient than her sense of self. She has a martyr complex and, like many trauma survivors, has been known to dissociate. Her identity is elusive, her public persona takes years to develop, and her love life is often tragic. Even so, her sense of purpose starts out strong and grows stronger with every season. Her powers come in a package deal with an unfair burden of responsibility, thrust upon her by fate, to defend people from "the forces of darkness," broadly construed. She suffers mightily yet transforms her fate as the Chosen One into a conscious choice to use her powers for good. Given all of these supernatural factors, how can viewers relate? None of us will likely possess Buffy's super-strength or healing powers. Yet her most super power of all, her sense of personal responsibility, is something we can all acquire if we are willing to suffer in common, listen to one another, and ask, "How can I help?" This is the work of the soul, and the account of the soul presented here is compatible with spiritual and secular accounts of humanity. More importantly, imagining the human soul as a relation between our selves and our bodies has immediate consequences for how we choose to live as more responsible people in the world.

Buffy is not just a story about souls and existential suffering; it is also a story about gendered bodies and women's power and place in the world. In the first part of this essay, I consider the role audience participation plays in fulfilling the Slayer's potential as a feminist icon. One cannot be empowered by a narrative one passively consumes. We need unresolved tensions to prompt us into active construction of the Slayer's reality. In the secondary literature, Buffy's body has been discussed more extensively than her soul. Indeed it may seem anomalous that the soul should play so prominent a role in a series created by an avowed atheist. However, in the second part of the essay, I take a closer look at the secular sciences of the self. In particular, the change from "multiple personality disorder" to "dissociative identity disorder" (DID), as a diagnostic category in clinical psychology, was a progressive development. DID posits the antecedent existence of individuals who have the power to pull themselves back together after they have, for whatever reason, fallen apart. Trauma survivors, like Buffy, remind us that what we do to care for ourselves and what we do to care for others are not in conflict, for we integrate our bodies and selves most easily by being in community with others. In my view, the self is a story we make up as we go along while the body is a thing in the world; both are subject to multiple constraints. The soul is neither one without the other, but it is the enduring relations between body and self, self and others, that make lives worth living possible.

In the third part of the essay, I discuss exceptional episodes wherein Buffy does fall prey to illness—wherein her bodily integrity is compromised. She suffers everything from curses to the flu, from catatonia to paranoid delusions. These revealing episodes show that Buffy's greatest superpower is her awesome sense of personal responsibility—how she responds to suffering. Throughout the series, Buffy asks, "How can I help?" more often than she asks, "Who am I?" or "Why me?" Of course, these questions come up, for Buffy is a teenager for more than half of the series. But as she matures from fifteen to twenty-two, she realizes that finding answers to these questions is not as urgent as figuring out, "What can I do to make things better?" *Buffy* suggests that our personal wellness depends less on who we think we are and more on what we do in the world.[1] In the final section of the paper, I suggest that the human soul is neither a pre-scientific myth we ought to outgrow nor an eternal mystery never to be unraveled, but the result of a mundane commitment to being there for one another in times of grief and hardship. Our back-stories do not need to be *consistent* so long as our souls are *compassionate*. Buffy is a tough survivor who has to pull herself back together more often than most. By seeking the source of her strength we can learn to find our own. The strength of the Slayer comes into sharp focus when we join her in her suffering, for it is then that her soul sheds light on the causal connections between recovery and responsibility.

Feminist Fantasy

The basic premise of *Buffy* is a paradox. Joss Whedon avers that his goal is to tell his audience a story with a feminist moral. Rather than a dry lecture on what feminism is and why it matters, he chose instead to undermine the conventions of the horror genre by creating a new superhero out of "the little girl, the little blonde girl who goes into a dark alley and gets killed, in every horror movie. The idea of Buffy was to subvert that idea, that image, and create someone who was a hero where she had always been a victim" ("'Welcome to the Hellmouth' [1.01] Episode Commentary"). On the other hand, he puts this little blond girl through such pain and torment, viewers may fairly question whether the myth of yet another suffering sacrificial virgin, as told by some privileged white guy, genuinely nurtures a more progressive notion of "girl power."

Early on scholars praised the show's inversion of traditional gender roles, noting how the female characters have the physical, intellectual, and leadership skills (Buffy, Willow, and Cordelia) while the males provide the nurturing, decorative effect and comic relief (Giles, Angel, and Xander). As A. Susan Owen writes, "The series reconfigures some of the relations of power in the body rhetorics of horror and action by relocating narrative agency from masculine to feminine" (30). Others replied that this inversion not only reinforces the dubious view that one gender is inherently more powerful than the other but also overplays the patriarchal virtues of brawn, brains, and bravado while underplaying the awesome power of Buffy's community spirit and wisecrack wit. As Arwen Spicer observes:

> In a social context of patriarchy, it can be argued that if Xander and Giles are men coded feminine, Buffy is a woman coded masculine. This observation is

> valid. At the same time, such codings have the potential to lead to the reification of masculine gender as synonymous with power, feminine gender with weakness, a move that undoes much of the transgressive work of placing a woman in an empowered and heroic position in the first place ["Love's Bitch" par. 4].

Some question whether the intended feminist message is even compatible with a television vehicle. Even if Buffy survives this week's beating, is not her achievement undermined by the commercials that accompanied the original airing of the series, featuring comely actress Sarah Michelle Gellar batting her luscious mascara-enhanced lashes?[2] These questions are not incidental to Whedon's mission. As Elana Levine notes, a large part of *Buffy's* success as a feminist text depends upon its "embrace of ambiguity and contradiction" (173).

To object that Buffy's revealing tank tops undermine the show's feminist message is to betray anxiety about the empowered female body. As Patricia Pender wryly observes in her essay "I'm Buffy and You're ... History," in Wilcox and Lavery's *Fighting the Forces*, "If Buffy's form and Buffy's content are upheld as distinct and incompatible categories, then the inexorable logic of the binary will dictate, with awful irony, that Buffy cannot be a feminist because she has cleavage" (43). Viewers can be empowered by watching this young woman fight for her life not only because the girl in question is valiant but also because the audience can join her in resisting limiting stereotypes and arbitrary oppositions. *Buffy* understands that one might wonder what constitutes appropriate garb for a feminist action hero. In the fourth season, Buffy joins a paramilitary group in the fight against demons from hell. When asked if she wants to don the group's uniform she demurs: "I thought about it, but on me it's gonna look all Private Benjamin. Don't worry. I've patrolled in this halter many times" ("The I in Team" 4.13). Her reassurance has the power to break through the fourth wall only if the viewers on the other side embrace the possibility of a sassy sexy superhero who challenges traditional authority even as she routinely saves the day.

In an interview with Emily Nussbaum, Whedon explains that he relies on the methods and conventions of mass-market television since he wants to have a big impact on society, "If I made 'Buffy the Lesbian Separatist,' a series of lectures on PBS on why there should be feminism, no one would be coming to the party, and it would be boring. The idea of changing culture is important to me, and it can only be done in a popular medium." Several scholars point to the dialectic space created by these tensions as a critical source of the narrative's power. As Spicer notes, "These two modes of feminist discourse—one which deconstructs patriarchal hierarchy, one which retains but inverts it—need not be fully reconcilable or mutually exclusive to do valuable feminist work" ("It's Bloody Brilliant!" par. 3). The series does not articulate an account of what it must mean to be a powerful woman, but it invites us to join Buffy in her struggle to puzzle out how her superpowers connect to her conflicting identities. In my view, the overlooked piece to this puzzle is the slayer's soul, understood not as some supernatural something-or-other, but as a matter-of-fact relation between our fragmentary selves and our even more vulnerable bodies.

Psychology Today

In *The Engine of Reason, the Seat of the Soul*, Paul Churchland seeks to discredit the doctrine that humans possess an immaterial soul distinct from their bodies:

> An hypothesis that still enjoys broad acceptance throughout the world is the idea that human cognition resides in an immaterial substance: a soul or mind. This proposed nonphysical substance is held to be uniquely capable of consciousness and of rational and moral judgment. ...this familiar hypothesis is difficult to square with the emerging theory of cognitive processes and with the experimental results from the several neurosciences. The doctrine of an immaterial soul looks, to put it frankly, like just another myth, false not just at the edges, but to the core [17].

Churchland embarks on a philosophical study of the brain, the part of our bodies uniquely capable of consciousness, rationality, and moral judgment (in his view). Despite its prominence in the title, the soul is rarely mentioned in his book. Notably, Churchland invokes the soul in connection with suffering and strength. For example, when people suffer from major depression "fatigue enfolds the soul" (175); multiple sclerosis (MS), in contrast to amyotrophic lateral sclerosis (ALS), takes over slowly "allowing a strong soul some time in which to adjust" (162).

In *Rewriting the Soul*, Ian Hacking challenges the very idea that any single soul hypothesis enjoys broad acceptance throughout the world: "The idea of the soul ... is by no means a human universal. Ideas of soul, earthly or spiritual, do permeate the European background in which memoro-politics emerged. Other peoples don't have anything like the historically situated notion of the soul that I have inherited from my culture" (215). According to Hacking, Churchland is himself *myth-taken* (cf. Buffy in "A New Man" 4.12). Hacking argues that the industrial age gave birth to a fragmentary self that is a by-product of memory. The possibility of broken or damaged souls was born out of a mechanical analogy: what happens to the body in a train accident could also happen to the mind during traumatic events. Courts began to award settlements for pain and suffering; therapists began to diagnose their patients with amnesias caused by psychic trauma. According to memoro-politics, our selves can become broken by painful experiences, and these injuries to our recollected selves require compensation. *Buffy* is written within the ideological framework of memoro-politics insofar as it proposes a cause and effect relation between personal trauma and dissociativity. But, unlike Hacking's history of litigious disputes, *Buffy* is less about what victims of psychic horror might be owed in damages and more about what survivors can do to find the strength to live lives worth living.

In *Consciousness Explained*, Daniel Dennett expounds a theory of personal identity wherein the self is a real but emergent phenomenon that came into being during our evolutionary history and continues to develop during the course of our lives. Dennett's self is an after-the-fact extrapolation, rather than an antecedent fact to be explained. By nature, we are storytellers. Our selves are the "centers of narrative gravity" of the stories we tell about who we are (431ff.). After studying multiple personality disorder, he concludes that under sufficient duress a person can no longer "compute" who they are so they fragment into multiple "centers" or selves:

> These children have often been kept in such extraordinarily terrifying and confusing circumstances that I am more amazed that they survive psychologically at all than I am that they manage to preserve themselves by a desperate redrawing of their boundaries. What they do, when confronted with overwhelming conflict and pain, is this: They "leave." They create a boundary so that the horror doesn't happen to them. It either happens to no one, or to some other self, better able to sustain its organization under such an onslaught... [420].

Dennett characterizes the emergence of Multiple Personality Disorder (MPD) as a "natural experiment" in narrative self-construction gone awry. He is suspicious of the view that the self is an exception to the rule of continuity in nature wherein transitional beings and liminal forms proliferate. When it comes to the self, he rejects the view he calls, "All or Nothing and One to a Customer" (422).

Hacking does not deny that people survive horrible things, but he questions the extent to which MPD occurs outside specific social institutions, especially given the role professional therapists play in the elicitation of the diverse "personalities" that emerge in so many persons: "Is the subsequent prototypical multiple behavior one of nature's experiments? Or is it rather the way in which a certain class of adults in North America will behave when treated by therapists using certain practices, and having certain convictions?" (227). Hacking warns that psychotherapists who unreflectively subscribe to memoro-politics could generate false consciousness in their patients. Treating patients as collections of responses to past horrors, each with their own identities and memories, transforms people into products, "the end product is a thoroughly crafted person, but not a person who serves the ends for which we are persons. Not a person with self-knowledge, but a person who is the worse for having a glib patter that simulates an understanding of herself" (266). Hacking does not argue that MPD is not real. Instead, he argues that, while real enough, the disorder results less from trauma, *simpliciter*, and more from a pernicious account of what it means to be a person, namely, that we are naught but what we can recall. Significantly, there has been a recent shift in memoro-politics in our culture as people in the U.S. can no longer be diagnosed with MPD. In the American Psychological Association's *Diagnostic and Statistical Manual of Mental Disorders* (DSM), version IV from 1994, what had been MPD was renamed Dissociative Identity Disorder (DID). The new diagnosis proposes a cause-effect relationship between past trauma and the fragmentation of a person's identity. DID challenges the "All or Nothing" view of the self that Dennett rejects. However, DID reinforces the "One to a Customer" view by denying that trauma survivors or anyone else could become multiple people. In my view, DID is an improvement because it reminds caregivers that, no matter how fragmented someone's sense of self becomes, there endures one human person in each body on their watch.

In *The Myth of Sanity*, Martha Stout tells several "Tales of Multiple Personality in Everyday Life," which are grim horror stories she has heard as a therapist. Most of her patients' lives "suck beyond the telling of it" (cf. Buffy in "Earshot" 3.18). Contra Hacking, Stout argues that neurological evidence suggests that DID may be a cross-cultural phenomenon. Our most painful experiences are not easy to turn into words and are thus more difficult to integrate into our narrative selves: "the brain lays down traumatic memories differently from the way it records regular memories" (18). The degree of dissociativity a person experiences varies along a continuum and no one has a fully unified self. She questions whether there is an individuality of the behaving organism for scientists to study: "What organizes our responses, our choices? If not personality, which will fragment unpredictably under enough stress, then what is the unifying feature of a human being (besides, of course, the singularity of the biological unit itself)? Is there such a feature at all?" (208). Stout has seen people "switch" from one "alter" to another before her eyes. But Stout does not serve her patients "glib patter." Her goal is to help individuals find the strength to keep on living. Her most successful therapeutic strategy is to listen to her patients as they figure out for themselves why their lives matter:

> I listen, for example, to Marcie, she who was twice dead and twice revived by the doctors, she who is now twenty-two years old and also as old as the world. If Marcie chooses to live, it seems to me that what she will have to say about human life is prophecy, fascinating and true as any the race will ever receive [13].

To protect the privacy of her clients, Marcie is a composite character. She resembles Buffy who also dies twice before she is twenty-two and may well be said to be as old as the world. Only the strong survive—but where do they get the strength? Stout's best answer is their *souls*:

> Far from nullifying the concept of soul, as some fear it will, familiarity with dissociative identity disorder causes me, even with my scientific pretensions, to feel significantly more inclined toward the idea. Something is there—something energetic enough to shine through all the neurological compartmentalization and obfuscation of our selves, and to illuminate and guide, for better or for worse, the multiform unit we think of as "person" [*The Myth of Sanity* 208–209].

Stout's twenty years of experience as a therapist leads her to propose that there is "an astonishingly robust correlation between an individual's successful recovery on the one hand, and on the other hand, a person's preexisting conviction that she and she alone is responsible for something" (*The Myth of Sanity* 211). The robust correlation between recovery and responsibility helps us better understand why Marcie chooses to live—and why Buffy is such an empowering icon. Buffy does suffer mightily, she gets lost in her suffering, but her conviction that she is responsible for the consequences of her actions hardly ever wavers. Buffy's body is remarkable: strong, quick, hardly ever sick. But "hardly ever" is not the same as "never." When we focus on who Buffy chooses to be at her most vulnerable physiological moments, we see her soul shine all the more brightly.

Killed by Death

Buffy may be watched as a thought experiment: If you took a person's soul away, what would remain? The show's writers share Hacking's distrust of memory. When people are turned into vampires, they lose their souls, but not their memories. The writers share Churchland's fascination with the brain and consider human and monster minds alike as subject to material laws of cause and effect. But, most importantly, the writers share Stout's concern: If our souls are not our recalled selves but they are not merely processes in our brains either, what are they? In my view, the slayer's soul is strong because she embraces her sense of responsibility. Buffy integrates her discontinuous memories and her mighty yet vulnerable body into a robust relation by saving the world—a lot.

When we first meet Buffy she is torn between two identities, high school sophomore by day, vampire slayer by night. In "Witch" (1.03) Buffy imagines that cheerleading will give her a break from being the Chosen One and allow her to pass as an ordinary teenager. However, Buffy is not an ordinary teenager but someone who runs into traffic to prevent another student from getting hit by a truck. In this episode Buffy's strength is sapped by a witch's spell. The possibility of "switchers" is introduced in a plot that recalls *Freaky Friday*. Of her mother's body swap, Amy laments: "She said I was wasting my youth. So she took it." Giles reverses the witch's spells to heal Buffy who then uses a mirror to reflect the witch's killing blow back onto herself. Buffy's conscious choice to become an adult means that she must let her own youth go. However, her commitment to helping others as she becomes an adult is hardly her undoing. The courses of action Buffy must pursue to care for her own self, her family, and her community, do not conflict since they are, more often than not, one and the same course of action.

Buffy is brave and not easily scared. She patrols the night looking for trouble because she is the buffer between monsters and mortals. Nevertheless, in Season Two we learn that she dreads hospitals. In "Killed by Death" (2.18), Buffy gets the flu and must confront the awful truth about children she learned as a child: *sometimes they die*. As a child she watched her cousin convulse to death in a hospital bed. Standing helplessly at her cousin's side, no one comforted Buffy or explained what was happening. What Buffy must do to heal her inner child has everything to do with the monster lurking in the children's ward. The flu enables her to see Der Kindestod, a hideous monster that sucks the life out of children; it can only be seen by people with a fever caused by the virus. A few children draw the monster with crayons in an attempt to get the doctors to understand what is happening but, typically, their first encounter with the Child-Death monster is their last. Buffy recovers from the virus quickly, but when her mom offers to take her home, she insists on staying in the same place she fought to avoid just hours before. Healthy again, she can no longer see the monster so she breaks into the lab and doses herself with the virus. Luckily, her friend Willow does the math and protects Buffy from a lethal overdose. She gets violently ill and staggers around the hospital looking for the monster so she can defeat it before it gets any more kids. She is too late to save them all—her cousin is still dead—but she kills the monster, saves the children Der Kindestod has been stalking, and heals her past by taking a courageous risk.

What does this thought experiment episode suggest about the relation between suffering and strength? For Buffy, taking care of herself and taking care of others converge into a single course of action: *defeat Der Kindestod*. When she makes herself sick, it is not an altruistic sacrifice for she does exactly what she needs to do to heal the agony of watching her cousin die. Early in the episode, Cordelia questions whether the monster is real, "So this isn't about you being afraid of hospitals 'cause your friend died and you wanna conjure up a monster that you can fight so you can save everybody and not feel so helpless?" However tactless the question is, it is a good one. Buffy is lucky her friends ask her hard questions. The sick kids are lucky Buffy gets the flu when she does. But it is not all about chance: Buffy chooses to stay where it hurts instead of going back home. Her sense of responsibility is so strong she chooses to compromise her physical superpowers so she can more readily recognize and dispatch the demon.

In another exceptional episode, "Helpless" (3.12), Buffy is drugged, becoming so weak she cannot stop a teenage boy from harassing Cordelia without getting thrown to the ground. As before, the cause of her debilitation is a material agent, not a virus, but an "organic compound of muscle relaxants and adrenal suppressors." Unlike "Killed by Death," however, Buffy does not choose to ingest this poison. Rather, it is administered intravenously on the sly by her mentor Giles as part of a rite of passage that slayers are put through if they make it to their eighteenth birthday alive. The original gender and genre inversion of the show is inverted once again as Buffy becomes the little blond girl screaming for help, running from a vicious vampire who was a homicidal misogynist even when he (supposedly) had a human soul. The vampire snatches her red-hooded coat and uses it to get close to Buffy's mother luring her to his lair, like the wolf in the fairy tale. Betrayed and disabled, Buffy does not rush to confront the monster: she loads up on weapons first. She sets off to save her mom with no superpowers except her extraordinary sense of purpose and a literal bag of tricks. She dispatches the vampire with deception and a bottle of holy water. According to Fury and Contner's DVD commentary, some fans were displeased to discover that such an arcane religious artifact has power in the Buffyverse. This objection ignores the moral of the story: Buffy is disabled but she does not give up and she is not defeated. Giles does something truly horrible to her. The fact that she is a victim of a vicious act of betrayal and attack upon her body does not relieve her of her duty to protect her mother.

In "The Weight of the World" (5.21) Buffy suffers a bout of catatonia. Her mother has died, leaving Buffy to become her sister's guardian. Her sister needs more protection than most teens, because, until recently, she was not human but a mystical "key" with the power to unlock the barriers between parallel worlds. Some monks arbitrarily decide to transform the key into the Slayer's kid sister. Their rationale is simple: Buffy will save the world by protecting the "it" that becomes "her" little sister Dawn with her life. While catatonic, Buffy revisits two false memories over and over. In the first, her parents bring her baby sister home from the hospital and child Buffy volunteers: "I could be the one to take care of her sometimes." In the second, adult Buffy smothers her adolescent sister. Willow enters Buffy's mind and points out that the second memory never happened—Buffy does not kill her sister. The first memory is just as false but Willow does not bother to point that out. Dawn has not always been Buffy's sister, but this rupture in her memory is not keeping Buffy from pulling herself back together. Willow helps Buffy find her way out by questioning the only "real" memory in Buffy's closed loop—the recollection of the moment when, putting a book on a shelf, she let herself fantasize about the possibility that, maybe this time, the forces of darkness will win so she can just retire. Buffy feels guilty for not wanting to save the world again—and her real guilt is more debilitating than either of her false memories. Willow urges Buffy to forgive herself: "So what if you allowed yourself one moment in which you wanted the world to end." Willow's point is well taken. Buffy does not *always* embrace her sense of personal responsibility. It is good enough that she *usually* does.

In "Normal Again" (6.17), Buffy's struggle to integrate alternative identities is taken to televisual extremes as she switches between competing realities. In the dominant story arc, Buffy is stabbed by a paranoia-inducing demon. In the story arc within the episode, Buffy is a mental patient suffering from the delusion that she is some kind of "vampire slayer" with "superpowers" who must save the world from "demons." In this alternate reality, the demon's stinger is another hypodermic syringe. As an embodied being, Buffy cannot help but be bordered and, thereby, vulnerable to unwanted intrusions no matter what reality she inhabits. The commentary to this episode offered by Gutierrez and Rosenthal explains how the show's creators took pains to render both realities with the same film and filters, to avoid visually privileging one reality over another ("'Normal Again' Episode Commentary"). The audience must face the same dilemma confronting Buffy: which reality is more real? In the mental hospital reality, her mom is still alive, her parents have never divorced and Dawn was neither born nor otherwise inserted into her family. Does our hero's desire to be reunited with the family of her lost childhood make her mother appear real because of the demon toxin in her veins? Or have there never been any demons at all?

These questions are not conclusively answered. Buffy's dissociation causes things to go from bad to worse quickly in both realities. Ultimately, her mother's encouragement in hospital-reality helps Buffy find the strength she needs to survive in hellmouth-reality: "You've got a world of strength in your heart, I know you do, you just have to find it again. Believe in yourself." After thanking her mother tearfully, Buffy abandons hospital-reality and returns to the dominant story-arc to save her sister and friends (again). It is a cheer-worthy moment even as Buffy's mother, a fiction within a fiction, watches in anguish as her Buffy lapses into a stupor. As we saw in "The Weight of the World," grief and loss transcend the distinction between fact and fantasy, spilling over the arbitrary boundaries between alternative realities and connecting them in unexpected ways.

In the final season of the series, Buffy's sense of purpose is at its most clear. In "Help" (7.04) she is no longer multiple-suburban teen by day, slayer by night. Instead, she is a round-the-clock superhero and grown-up, counseling troubled teens at her sister's school: "I'm here because I want to help." Her boundaries continue to be vulnerable, but Buffy knows she cannot draw too sharp of a line between herself and the rest of the world, for saving the world is how she integrates her body and self into a resilient soul. She does not economize her efforts in the way that Dennett presumes all of us must: "If you are setting out to preserve yourself, you don't want to squander effort trying to preserve the whole world: you draw the line. You become, in a word, *selfish*" (174). Even so, Buffy continues to struggle with the question, "why bother?" She learns of a student, Cassie, who believes her death is imminent. Like her classical namesake, no one believes this Cassandra either. Buffy insists that no matter what is out to get her, Buffy can stop it. A cult of creepy boys tries to sacrifice Cassie in exchange for wealth, but Buffy defeats them and their demon with ease. A booby-trap shoots an arrow straight for Cassie's neck. Buffy catches it in midair with her bare hand and snaps it in two: "See? You can make a difference!" Cassie smiles sadly and reassures Buffy, "And you will!" before collapsing dead of congenital heart failure. Buffy is devastated: "I failed her." This time Dawn rescues Buffy from the demon of self-doubt: "Uh uh. No. You didn't 'cause you tried. You listened and you tried. She died 'cause of her heart not 'cause of you. She was my friend because of you." Dawn reminds Buffy that while she is not omnipotent, her most effective power is her willingness to listen to those who need her help and to try to make a difference in their lives.

Shiny Souls

People suffer in similar ways the world over. Perhaps because of the non-lingual neurology of suffering, there is no "outside" when it comes to the community of grief. Most people who see other people in pain can tell, whether they grew up next door or on the other side of the world.[3] Some of the humor of *Buffy the Vampire Slayer*, especially her banter and puns, has a hard time crossing cultural barriers. Yet grief transcends the Sunnydale city limits with ease. When Buffy comes home to find her mother dead on the sofa, no subtitles are necessary ("The Body" 5.16). In a fight, Buffy tends to get thrown a lot because she is smaller than most of her opponents. When monsters get a grip on her, the smart ones pitch her as far as they can. Buffy repeatedly flies through the air, hits the wall, and lands in a crumpled heap. If these were the only images of the show one ever saw, one might think the show's only purpose was to entertain psychopaths who enjoy watching little girls get tossed like so much salad. However, when Buffy gets knocked down, she gets back up and she throws down. Sometimes she is back on her feet in under a second. Sometimes it takes an episode, or even a season, before she is able to bounce back. The quick version is exhilarating, whereas the slow version is excruciating. Both encourage reflection on what it takes to recover from the inevitable pain of living in the world.

Whedonverse characters illustrate the moral Stout draws from her clinical experience: "Perhaps nothing defines unified personhood so solidly as the courage of strong commitment to personal responsibility" (*The Myth of Sanity* 156). To suppose the human soul is a relation between our bodies and our stories that is strengthened when we take responsibility for our actions is secular. But, as Riess point out, this understanding of human possibility is compatible with many religious traditions:

> There are limits to what we can do—to what we should do. Buffy has learned this lesson.... Like her, we can't take shortcuts through emotional pain or grief. Pain and consequences are instructors and have much to teach us if we have the patience to trust in the process. Karma, it turns out, is not so much a punishment as a natural law [103].

If the relationship between suffering and strength is indeed a natural law, then the account of the soul advocated here will be compatible with both scientific and spiritual accounts of humanity.

When it comes to surviving a scary world, storytellers, scientists, and theologians can agree that it is more important to ask, "what can I do to make things better?" than to construct unassailable answers to the question, "who am I?" or even "what kind of being am I?" There may not be any non-arbitrary or final answers to these abstract questions. The *Diagnostic and Statistical Manual of Mental Disorders*, like our narrative histories, is destined to endless revision. There are limits to what can be said and every prophecy, maxim, and doctrine is open to interpretation. *Buffy* distinguishes between our bodies, with their vulnerable borders; our selves, with their tendency to fragment under stress; and our souls, with their complex relations between recovery and responsibility that help us become more whole persons. The stories told throughout the Whedonverses vividly portray what Stout observes in her practice, "Just as it is more than possible to operate in the world with a single, constant identity while evincing no notion of accountability at all [i.e., most vampires], it is possible to have a deeply bewildering identity disorder that exists simultaneously with a committed sense of responsibility [i.e., most humans]" (*The Myth of Sanity* 156).

Moreover, the characters themselves illustrate Hacking's maxim, "When it comes to the language that will be used to describe ourselves, each of us is a half-breed of imagination and reality" (233). None of us will likely possess Buffy's super-strength or healing powers. But her most super power of all, her awesome sense of personal responsibility, is something we can all cultivate. In the last issue of his *Fray* comic, on the very last page, Joss Whedon describes his work: "I write stories. Mostly about girls, mostly about strength. About family, and pain, and responsibility. And the Getting of Strength." In an interview with Tasha Robinson, Whedon shares his writer's room mandate to give the audience what they *need*, not what they *want*. The audience may think they want happy endings—but what they need, if they are to join Buffy in the Getting of Strength, is for "things to go wrong, they need the tension. In my characters, there's a core of trust and love that I'm very committed to. These guys would die for each other, and it's very beautiful. But at the same time, you can't keep that safety. Things have to go wrong, bad things have to happen." As we suffer alongside Buffy and her family, and consider her continued survival as a strong feminist icon, we are invited to nurture one another through the inevitable pain that comes with being human, as Whedon has stated in his interview with Robinson: "That's sort of the point of Buffy, that I'm talking about the stuff everybody goes through. Nobody gets out of here without some trauma." However, even if trauma is inevitable, dissociative identities are not. By cultivating relations between our fragmentary selves and our fragile bodies, by recognizing the intimate connection between personal recovery and social responsibility, we strengthen our souls.

Notes

1. Richardson and Rabb make this case eloquently in their book, *The Existential Joss Whedon*.

2. Sherryl Vint contrasts how Buffy is portrayed on the show against sexualized representations of Ms. Gellar in magazines designed to appeal to the male gaze, suggesting that "the multiple and contradictory readings of *Buffy* are also a place where young women might begin to develop a critical consciousness about the construction of female identity and sexuality" (par. 22).

3. Those that do not "get it" are discussed by Stout in her book, *The Sociopath Next Door*.

Part II

Bodies, Trauma, and Recovery

"Off with their heads!—Kidding!"

The Beheading Topos in Angel*'s Pylea*

CYNTHEA MASSON

Next to a wooden stake through the heart, decapitation remains one of the few reliable methods of slaying a vampire. Thus, as one might expect of vampire narratives, both *Buffy the Vampire Slayer* and *Angel* periodically feature death by decapitation. However, the three *Angel* episodes set in the alternative dimension of Pylea at the end of Season Two are particularly notable for their persistent focus on heads and beheading outside the context of vampire slaying.[1] In Pylea, as Angel struggles to regain control of his body and the demon therein, other members of Team Angel face the prospect of bodily mutilation by decapitation: as a slave, Cordelia is forced to wear a collar designed to make her head "implode" ("Over the Rainbow" 2.20); Wesley and Gunn are locked into stocks by rebels who threaten to "put their severed heads on sticks" ("Through the Looking Glass" 2.21); Fred is nearly beheaded by a swift stroke of the *crebbil* at the *Bach'nal* ("Through the Looking Glass"); and, most significantly, Lorne is literally decapitated, his vivid green head served to Cordelia on a silver platter ("Through the Looking Glass"). Whether intact, decapitated, literal, or figurative, the heads of Pylea provide a site at which to explore yet another narrative tradition in relation to *Angel*: the beheading topos.[2] Beheading expert Regina Janes argues, "Neither essential flesh nor irreducible bone, heads are plastic. Taking meaning from the discourse in which they are inserted, heads make meanings within that discourse" (12). The heads of Pylea take meaning from a discourse of power: the power of a government to threaten its people with decapitation and the power of the people to behead a repressive regime. Individually and collectively, members of Team Angel confront literal and figurative decapitation (or threats thereof) on the path toward claiming a voice within the discourse of power and, thereby, rewriting its narrative.

To appreciate fully the significance of the Pylean heads and beheadings, one should first have in mind a basic understanding of the beheading topos, which "like the historical action itself, has a long past" (Feinstein 45). Several scholars have addressed this topic, tracing the incidents and implications of historical, biblical, and literary beheadings throughout the ages. One exceptional and relatively recent contribution is Regina Janes' book *Losing Our Heads: Beheadings in Literature and Culture*. According to Janes, "Beheading is among the most ancient, widespread, and enduring of human cultural practices" (10). As she aptly outlines through numerous, detailed examples, heads are "the body's metaphor for hierarchy and metonymy for wholeness" (178). This "metaphor of the body politic," in which the corporal head figuratively represents the corporate head, has "[s]ince the Middle Ages ... furnished an image of coherence for the representative aspects of government" (Blaine 151). Consequently, as Mary F. Godfrey explains within her discussion of the medieval poem *Sir Gawain and the Green Knight*, "Within such a tradition, in which the state is repeatedly described as a body requiring a head..., depicting decapitation becomes a shorthand for questioning the efficacy of government, as it also stands for the individual's capacity for self-rule, as the head is also part of the single body" ("*Sir Gawain*" 70). These brief excerpts purport a dual narrative purpose for heads and beheading, which is arguably reflected in the Pylea episodes of *Angel*: first, the efficacy of the Pylean government must be questioned, and, ultimately, its figurative head must be literally decapitated; second, each member of Team Angel must assert individual power (or "capacity for self-rule") to overcome threats to the literal body in order, ultimately, to cohere as a figurative body or unified team. As Frank Ardolino contends in his study of severed heads in Elizabethan drama, "Once the heads of the evil tyrants ... are cut and displayed ... people regain their identities and are free to develop their personalities within mature relationships" (170). Paradoxically, heads must roll for bodies to be whole.

Incidents of beheading earlier in *Angel*'s Season Two help establish a theme that will dominate the Pylea episodes: decapitation is a means of challenging and defeating injustice perpetrated by authority. The first episode of Season Two, "Judgment," begins with a close-up of Lorne's head—the head that will later be presented to Cordelia on a platter at the end of "Through the Looking Glass." More significantly, "Judgment" features a final conquest by decapitation when, after losing a pseudo-medieval jousting match, Angel slices off his opponent's head as a means of appealing the judges' original ruling. The end of this episode (set in Cordelia's apartment, Team Angel's temporary headquarters) features a whiteboard upon which the word "beheaded" is prominent. Beheading has saved the day in the episode and established a thematic precedent for Season Two. Angel also challenges authority through beheading when he decapitates a police officer in "The Thin Dead Line" (2.14). Though this particular officer "is the type of cop that keeps talking even after he's been decapitated," the graphic image is nonetheless one of Angel overpowering an authority figure via decollation. These scenes illustrate that prior to the Pylea episodes in which Team Angel literally and figuratively decapitates the head of authority, Angel uses decapitation to challenge authority figures. Finally, in "Belonging" (2.19), the episode that introduces the gang and the audience to Pylea, Angel offers to decapitate a particularly seedy television commercial director who, Angel believes, is exploiting Cordelia: "Do you want me to rip that guy's head off for you? Because, you know, I can really. I can just actually rip his head right off his body. I can do that." In each of these episodes (and, as will be discussed, in the Pylea episodes), "decapitation contributes to articulating the issues regarding power" (Feinstein 49).[3]

Beheading is used by those representing established power against those who threaten that power, but beheading is also used by those who successfully overturn established power. Historically, "[w]hile they may have performed the same act of violence on their victims, the warrior and the executioner occupied radically different social spaces. Only the executioner was stigmatized for serving as a professional killer" (Margaret E. Owens 171). The warrior, on the other hand, is (or certainly has the potential to be) glorified. Such is the case in the Pylea episodes where beheading is portrayed initially as a malicious act of oppression by the Pylean government and later as a welcomed act of liberation by those who overthrow the government. The human slaves or *cows*, as they are called in Pylea, are forced to wear collars that can be triggered to obliterate their heads. This practice is strikingly illustrated when Silas (the head priest) accuses Markallo (a slave) of treason; Markallo's plea of innocence is answered with a swift and brutal beheading via remote triggering of his collar ("There's No Place Like Plrtz Glrb" 2.22). In addition to the individual controls operated by slave owners, the governing priests possess a mass "killing device" designed to "[blow] their heads off"—in other words, the device is designed to kill all the slaves at once ("There's No Place Like Plrtz Glrb"). Thus the entire slave population lives under constant threat of beheading. The governing priests remain the figurative heads of state by threatening the literal heads of the people.

Of course, the use of unjust tactics by a government to control a population ironically fosters exactly the kind of political rebellion the threat was designed to preempt. Not surprisingly, in Pylea, this persistent threat of decapitation has resulted in the formation of a rebel faction (apparently comprising escaped human slaves) whose goal is to overthrow the government. Regrettably, the rebels mistake Wesley and Gunn as allies of the government and threaten to decapitate them as a means of conveying a list of demands: "Shove the list in their mouths, put their severed heads on sticks and display them outside the princess's window" ("Through the Looking Glass"). The rebels' choice of delivery method, albeit gruesome, is time-honored: "To the soldier who puts the head on a stick, the head means victory, solidarity, celebration, just triumphal rejoicing" (Janes 38). Though potentially hypocritical in that those once threatened by beheading threaten to retaliate with beheading, these identical acts have different political intentions. For example, when Silas promises, "If the princess survives the *Com-shuk, THEN* you may have her head, Barshon," he is offering a sign of power over the oppressed as a reward to a loyal subject ("Through the Looking Glass"). Similarly (though heads are not explicitly mentioned here), when Constable Narwek advises that the prisoners (Angel, Lorne, Wesley, and Gunn) be "drag[ged] … to the village square" after sentencing, his intention is to "hang their corpses as a warning"—that is, to display the absolute power of the government over the people ("Over the Rainbow"). However, when the rebel leader advises that Wesley and Gunn be executed and their heads displayed on sticks to the princess, his intention is to exhibit the democratic power of the people over the autocratic power of the government.

The juxtaposition of the government's advanced beheading technology and the comparably basic chopping-block beheading technique of the rebels is politically poignant. Immediately following the scene in which Silas beheads Markallo, Wesley and Gunn are featured in stocks, their heads encased between wooden planks, their hands tied behind their backs, about to be decapitated by an axe-wielding rebel. The government possesses the means to commit individual or mass murder without direct physical contact, whereas the rebels must physically sever enemy heads one head at a time. Later, when circumstances make it clear that Wesley and Gunn are fighting on the same side as the rebels, Sasha (the rebel leader) proudly announces: "Though their hands were tied and their necks were bared they fought with us" ("There's No Place Like Plrtz Glrb"). He then admits to Wesley and Gunn, "I'm ashamed. We nearly cut your heads off." Wesley hesitantly responds, "You were just doing your job." Though the rebel threat of beheading may be parallel to that of the rulers, the fact remains that the rebels do *not* behead Wesley and Gunn yet are ashamed of their actions, whereas the rulers *do* behead both Markallo and Lorne *and* show no remorse whatsoever. Moreover, as Wesley suggests with his comment about Sasha's "job," the rebel threat to decapitate an ally of an oppressive regime is arguably understandable as an action in a justifiable confrontation, whereas the government threat to decapitate an entire ethnic group (humans) sanctions genocide. After being freed, heads attached, both Wesley and Gunn make a conscious choice to fight for the rebel cause against the government. In this sense, as elsewhere in the Whedonverses, the Pylea episodes arguably act as political commentary in relation to the "just war" paradigm, encouraging resistance or "capacity for self-rule" against an unethical regime.[4]

Given that Lorne is the only member of Team Angel to be literally beheaded, his role is pivotal in terms of the episodes' symbolic message in relation to decapitation and political resistance. Contrary to his own advice to Angel that "[t]hings fall apart" and "[n]ot everything can be put back together no matter how much you want it" ("The Trial" 2.09), Lorne graphically illustrates that some things can indeed "be put back together" even in the most difficult circumstances. That is, Lorne is not only decapitated but subsequently *recapitated*, a distinguishing physical feature that arguably aligns him with martyrs featured in the hagiographic tradition, "wherein saints are portrayed rejoining removed heads to their abbreviated trunks, 'recapitating' and reviving the slain whole and hale" (Johnson par. 1). As Máire Johnson argues in an article about the recapitation in medieval hagiography, "the recapitated and revived are seen as members of the Church body; their restoration to life not only undoes a violent deed, but returns both the formerly slain and the body of the Christian faithful to physical integrity" (par. 2). In the process of these medieval narratives, "the recapitation *topos* comments on particular institutions ... perceived as threats to the body Christian" (Johnson par. 2). Though Lorne represents neither the Christian faithful nor the Church body, he is a member of Team Angel—of *that* figurative body; moreover, by birth and ancestry, he is a member of the Pylean social body ruled by an unjust government. Therefore, Lorne's recapitation, like that of saints in the hagiographic tradition, weakens the threat of the oppressor to silence the resistor and strengthens the figurative body of those resisting oppression.

Lorne's beheading also shares characteristics with secular beheading stories, in particular that of the Green Knight in *Sir Gawain and the Green Knight*. Not only is Lorne green, but like the Green Knight, Lorne, "although beheaded, is by no means slain" (Coomararswamy 110). As Lorne explains to Cordelia, "My people, the fun-loving Deathwok clan, you cut off our heads we just keep on ticking until you mutilate our bodies" ("There's No Place Like Plrtz Glrb"). With help from Cordelia, Groo, and Landok, Lorne's head is reunited with his body before mutilation. Thus, like the Green Knight's beheading, Lorne's beheading and, more specifically, his *re*-heading, represents a symbolic victory over the oppressor: "Heads that are re-attached, bodies made whole, a bloody trunk that defies physical laws to retrieve its own head, all confound the power of the throne, and the expected role of the royal subject" (Godfrey, "*Sir Gawain*" 82).

The expected role of the royal subject in Pylea is to obey the government and, if human, to serve as a slave: "My lord," says Markallo to Silas, "as it was ordained in the beginning our lives belong to you" ("There's No Place Like Plrtz Glrb"). Lorne illustrates otherwise—that one's life is one's own, that an individual can enact the "capacity for self-rule." Lorne's recapitation provides hope to others in Pylea, including members of Team Angel, who are fighting against the threat of decapitation in their struggle to gain empowerment.

As Godfrey contends, the Green Knight's severed head acts as "the spectacle of the mutilated, yet still-empowered body," which, through its signification of empowerment, "calls into question the fabric of all court societies: their dependence on their kings, and the positions meted out to the courtiers in attendance" ("*Sir Gawain*" 70, 69). Similarly, Lorne's head calls into question the fabric of the Pylean social hierarchy in that it defies the government's ultimate penalty for its subjects—death by decapitation. Thus, Lorne's head arguably serves as a vital signifier of resistance not only for Cordelia, who literally holds his decapitated yet animate head in her hands, but for Angel, Wesley, Gunn, Fred, and the rebels, with whom he (that is, his head) crosses paths on his way to reunite with his body. This meeting occurs in "There's No Place Like Plrtz Glrb" when Landok is captured by the rebels in the process of "transporting [his] kinsman home" in a basket. Angel says quietly to the others, "I was trying to tell you. They cut off [Lorne's] head." Momentarily, Lorne's inanimate head signifies defeat. However, when Lorne opens his eyes and speaks, startling everyone but Fred, his head ultimately represents a sign of resistance for the people. Lorne's words, spoken from his decapitated head, belie the power of the oppressor to silence him: "That the [Green] Knight can wrest the tools of execution and use them to his own ends, that his head and body still live, brings the finality of the state's use of beheading into question" (Godfrey, "*Sir Gawain*" 78). Though beheaded, Lorne retains the power to speak for himself; he thereby exemplifies the possibility that others can speak for themselves. Only after Lorne is beheaded and, though beheaded, speaks when his silence was expected does the plot move swiftly toward the figurative and literal beheading of the oppressor.

The beheading topos is historically linked to the power of speech and the silencing of dissenting voices. In a study of Chrétien de Troyes' *Lancelot, The Knight of the Cart*, Sandy Feinstein argues, "beheading serves as a complex sexual, political, and religious image representing power, particularly the power of speech" (45); she outlines the ways in which "pointed references to the head signify the relationship between it and language, or it as a container for language from which all challenges originate" (50). Those who are silenced cannot challenge their silencers. In the Pylea episodes, those in control repeatedly reprimand others for speaking. In "Over the Rainbow," Constable Narwek rebukes Angel, "You dare use your tongue in my presence!" In the same episode, Narwek commands Lorne, "You and the cow trash are not to speak." If, as Feinstein posits, the head is "the source of self-identifying speech" and signifies the "kind of power of which women were more often deprived than men: their voices" (57), then Cordelia's silencing is particularly notable. When she is first captured, Cordelia is gagged because she is too "chatty." Later, after being purchased as a slave by a Pylean woman, Cordelia attempts to voice her resistance again, stating, "I am an American, and I have rights." Unmoved by Cordelia's nationalistic plea, the Pylean woman literally shocks Cordelia (by means of the remote-controlled collar locked around Cordelia's neck) to stop her from speaking: "Cows aren't for talking. They're for doing their job" ("Over the Rainbow"). Cordelia's attempt to remove her collar is met by a swift rebuke from Fred: "if you take the collar off, things'll happen to your head—like it'll implode. So don't take the collar off, okay? 'Cause I can't talk to you if you don't have a head, okay?" ("Over the Rainbow").

Though this statement is self-evident (that is, one obviously needs a head to talk), Fred directly links the head with the voice and thus indirectly links beheading with imposed silence. Cordelia is threatened with the imposed silence of decapitation even after she is transformed from slave to princess. For example, in "Through the Looking Glass," when she asserts, "The way of things is going to change around here," Silas immediately insists Cordelia has "no authority here" and no voice in the government: "And if we tell you 'silent,' you shut your cow mouth!" He then presents her with a covered platter, lifts the lid, and reveals Lorne's severed head—an image reminiscent of John the Baptist's head, which would again align Lorne with a saint. When presented with Lorne's head, Cordelia is temporarily shocked into submission punctuated by a long, piercing scream.[5] Later, when Silas asks Markallo about Cordelia's condition, and Markallo responds "grievously distressed," Silas is pleased: "Good. We will add more heads to her collection that she might never forget who is the master here and who is the servant" ("There's No Place Like Plrz Glrb"). As with Lorne, these attempts to silence Cordelia ultimately fail, and Cordelia not only regains her voice but wields the sword that silences Silas.

Prior to finding her voice and power, Cordelia's role in Pylea is merely that of a performer. In the episode immediately preceding the Pylean trio, Cordelia dons a skimpy outfit to play a role in a television commercial, to perform as an actor ("Belonging"). In Pylea, dressed in a similarly skimpy outfit, Cordelia initially *performs* her role as princess—drawing on stereotypes of what a princess might say and do rather than understanding what she needs to do. Janet K. Halfyard discusses "Cordelia as the performer who craves the love of an adoring audience" (par. 26). "When she is sucked through the vortex into Pylea," writes Halfyard, "her dreams of being a star are suddenly realized when she is made princess and ruler, lavished with luxury and attention" (par. 26). Playing her role as princess, Cordelia condemns prisoners, staging her power with a mock pronouncement of beheading by reciting the famous line of the Red Queen from *Alice's Adventures in Wonderland*: "Off with their heads!" she decrees when Angel, Wesley, and Gunn are brought before her by the guards ("Through the Looking Glass").[6] If, as Margaret Owens contends, "mutilation and beheading are the very stuff of theatrical performance," Cordelia understands, even relishes, her role (44). However, moments later, when she realizes that the Pylean guards are about to carry out her decree, Cordelia recants, "Kidding!" ("Through the Looking Glass"). This moment is arguably transformational for Cordelia: unlike her previous acting roles, her role as Pylean princess is one in which she wields a certain degree of power. Halfyard argues that Cordelia eventually rejects performance and, thereby, "becomes more credible as an agent for the Powers that Be" (par. 29). In Pylea, Cordelia becomes more credible as an *actor*—not in the sense of a performer playing a role but in the sense of a strong woman enacting her power. Rather than *playing* with her power, rather than merely uttering the *already written* line made famous by the Red Queen, Cordelia eventually enacts her power, literally beheading the leader of Pylea's "evil regime" ("There's No Place Like Plrtz Glrb").

Cordelia's beheading of Silas can also be read as a figurative castration.[7] John Edward Damon argues, "Modern interpretations of beheading often concern decapitation as symbolic castration, and this is especially true of the story of Judith and Holofernes" (422). Godfrey similarly discusses the biblical story of Judith's beheading of Holofernes, stating "[Judith's] actions toward Holofernes have been interpreted as metaphorically, if not literally, sexual; a violation that triumphantly reverses and undoes his planned violation" ("*Beowulf*" 22). Though Silas himself did not sexually violate Cordelia, he did arrange and vehemently insist upon the "mating ritual" of the *Com-shuk* between Cordelia and the Groosalug. Consequently, Cordelia not only literally decapitates the head of the government but also figuratively castrates the man responsible for encouraging her sexual violation. Prior to her experience in Pylea, Cordelia had endured the sexual exploitation perpetrated by the television commercial director whom Angel had offered to behead. As a result of her experiences in Pylea, Cordelia wields her own sword against the exploiter, announcing "Your cow princess is tired of hearing you yak, padre" before slicing off his head ("There's No Place Like Plrtz Glrb"). The person once silenced has become the silencer. Moreover, in her new empowered role, Cordelia exploits the threat of decapitation: "I have two visions," she says to one of the other priests, "and in one of them, you get to keep your head" ("There's No Place Like Plrtz Glrb"). The priest dutifully responds, "How may I be of service, your majesty?" Though Cordelia claims that "all citizens are created equal" and though she destroys the mass killing device designed to implode the heads of all the slaves, her rise to power includes the very act of decollation she seeks to terminate. Though her action may be seen as excessively violent, it may also be seen symbolically as a necessary step in her character development from one who performs a role for others in power into one who acts for herself through her own power. For Cordelia, turning the threat of beheading into a rebellious and justified act of beheading becomes a rite of passage that transforms her from "the material girl" into an authoritative woman (Rambo par. 9).

Beheading can represent literal or figurative loss of leadership over both the self and the group: "any talk about decapitations, even metaphorical ones, also constituted a discussion about the loss of authority that a person might experience over his or her own self. Decapitation meant the loss not only of a head but also of a headship, of a headquarters, of one's nerve center" (Elwick 175). Season Two of *Angel* begins without physical headquarters, the offices of Angel Investigations having been destroyed at the end of Season One. Thus, not only does the first episode feature a literal beheading, as described earlier, but also a figurative one, both of which help to establish thematic concerns of leadership and authority in Season Two. Though a new headquarters is established within a few episodes, Angel's headship as leader of Angel Investigations gradually breaks down throughout the first ten episodes. This breakdown culminates at the end of "Reunion" (2.10) with Angel's declaration to Wesley, Gunn, and Cordelia: "You're all fired." Thus in one final assertion of leadership, Angel severs the figurative head from the figurative body, purposely separating himself from his team. Though Angel's figurative decollation may appear initially to be an inexplicable act of self-centeredness both to members of Team Angel and to the audience, his personal disclosure in Pylea implies altruistic motives for the good of the team: "[W]hen I fired you guys ... darkness was coming out in me. I didn't want you near it" ("There's No Place Like Plrtz Glrb"). Angel faced what James Elwick would call "the loss of authority" over *himself* and, consequently, over others. Through his experiences in Pylea, Angel learns not only that he has the ability to control the "darkness" within himself even at its worst but, as importantly, that Cordelia, Wesley, Gunn, and Lorne all have their own strength to overcome "darkness": that is, each member of the team survives decapitation (or the threat thereof), each illustrates his/her power, and each contributes to defeating the oppressor.

Initially, Pylea seems an ideal world for Angel—one in which, unlike in his own world, he can enjoy certain bodily pleasures, such as walking in the sunlight and admiring his reflection in a mirror. As Wesley explains to Gunn, "Angel's vampire self has been sublimated somehow by this dimension.... Only his human side has surfaced since we've been here" ("Through the Looking Glass"). Yet, paradoxically, only in Pylea does Angel's "demon-self ... totally overcome his human side"; here, the demon exists "in its purest form" ("Through the Looking Glass"). As Stacey Abbott argues, the "separation of his two sides reinforces the fact that.... Angel is the embodiment of both" ("Walking the Fine Line" par. 26). Angel's challenge in Pylea is to control his demon side, which he sees as "ten times worse" than the "darkness" he recognized in himself earlier; he worries that he "won't come back from it" ("There's No Place Like Plrtz Glrb"). His challenge for his literal body is parallel to that of his figurative body (or team): divergent parts must work together. In "Epiphany" (2.16), after reminding Angel that he lost his connection to the higher powers when "[he] fired [his] crew," Lorne advises, "there's a chance, a good chance, you won't be able to put this back together." Angel must learn, as he does both from Lorne's *re*-heading and through his own ability to control his demon during the final battle with the Groosalug, that he can "come back from" the "darkness" and that Team Angel's figurative body can be put "back together."

Faced with the prospect of beheading a literal body in Pylea, Angel takes his first symbolic step toward reunifying the figurative body of the team. Whereas in Los Angeles, Angel is advised by Lorne not to play "the-throwing-yourself-across-six-tables-and-twisting-their-heads-off-their-necks part" ("Reprise" 2.15), in Pylea Angel is encouraged by Landok and the villagers to play the executioner: "Swing the *crebbil*!" demand the Pyleans; "Sever the cow's head from its body" ("Through the Looking Glass"). With *crebbil* in hand, Angel is advised by Landok, "Strike quickly and true, Angel, then we can eat" ("Through the Looking Glass").[8] At this moment, Angel and the audience see Fred's head on the chopping block and recognize what the "great honor" of swinging the *crebbil* entails. Yet Angel chooses not to do in Pylea what he has done repeatedly in Los Angeles and what he had threatened to do to the commercial director for Cordelia: he will not separate a head from its body. Janes argues that "decapitation strikes at our identification with our bodies" (x). If Angel is the head, and Team Angel is the body, Angel must recognize the importance of reunifying the whole even if, in the process, the *whole* is reconfigured. By saving Fred from decapitation, Angel initiates the reconstruction of Team Angel with Fred as its newest member. Moreover, Angel's stand against unethical Pylean tradition serves to exemplify resistance within a society that will soon face its own social and political "reconstruction" ("There's No Place Like Plrtz Glrb").

When another priest remarks to Silas that Angel has denied "a runaway slave her rightful beheading" and, moreover, "ignores our laws and profanes our holy culture," he implies that beheading is not only a legal right but also a sacred rite in Pylea ("There's No Place Like Plrtz Glrb"). Thus, Angel's refusal to swing the *crebbil* signifies resistance to both legal and religious tradition. In response to the priest's remark, Silas acknowledges, "He does worse than that. He brings hope to the cows—for if one can be free, hope arises that *all* can be free" ("There's No Place Like Plrtz Glrb"). This hope for the people is magnified by the fact that the act of rebellion is done in the village square—the *crebbil* ceremony is public spectacle. Public beheadings serve a theatrical function. Pylea represents what Owens would describe as "a society where judicial punishment is public and spectacular," one "where it is possible to imagine a slippage between penal and theatrical scaffolds" (26).[9] The Pylean government arguably aims to scare its population into submission by staging spectacular beheadings of slaves. By obstructing the theatrical spectacle of beheading, by refusing to play his prescribed role as executioner, Angel changes the imposed script or cultural narrative.

After Angel alters the Pylean narrative by refusing to swing the *crebbil*, Fred immediately begins to narrate her own story, initially uttering a line that has since come to be associated with her: "Handsome man saved me from the monsters" ("Through the Looking Glass"). Safe but in apparent shock, she questions whether or not "[her] head came off back there," asking Angel for confirmation with regard to her embodiment: "And my head's still on?" ("Through the Looking Glass"). At first Fred cannot believe she has escaped the ultimate punishment of her oppressors and, in doing so, that she and Angel together have challenged the overarching narrative of power. Though she had previously managed to dismantle her collar and live in hiding for years, Fred had no reason to believe she would escape beheading by the *crebbil* or, indeed, escape Pylea since her attempts to create an escape portal for herself had previously failed: "I tried. For years and years—until my tongue was swollen and my head was all kaplooey" ("There's No Place Like Pltrz Glrb"). But Fred's head, along with its inherent intellect, will save both her and the others.[10] What Fred does not realize, but what Angel suspects, is that she has been opening portals without knowing their location. In response to Angel's suggestion that her attempts have indeed been successful, Fred says, "Me? I don't think so. The priests have all the power here." What Fred will learn and what her revised narrative illustrates is that she and other subjugated people do have power to escape from oppression and overcome the oppressor by using their heads.

Wesley's admission in the Pylean prison cell that he "was always horrified by those stories about the Tower of London" is particularly germane within the context of the Pylea episodes ("Over the Rainbow"). Historically "a symbol of oppression" and "the embodiment of royal power," the Tower of London gained its "reputation as a place of narrow, damp dungeons and torture chambers" (Derek Wilson 24, 146, 11). Today the Tower remains infamous not only as the site of countless beheadings but also as the grounds upon which hierarchical authority was repeatedly challenged by the people.[11] Derek Wilson completes a detailed history of the Tower by concluding, "It has ... seen more of magnificence and misery, heroism and hatred, despair and defiance than probably any other single spot on earth" (240). When Angel contends that the Tower "wasn't that bad," Wesley concurs, "Well, compared to this place I'm sure the Tower takes on a certain nostalgic glow." Though tinged with sarcasm, Wesley's statement reveals a grain of thematic truth. Pylea, like the Tower, eventually becomes a site within the *Angel*verse where, by "[c]utting off the heads of the king's officers, the rabble have re-defined themselves as the sovereign people" (Janes 71). "The lesson of the heads," contends Janes, "is that there has been a fundamental change in social hierarchies and the distribution of power" (71). Such is the lesson finally taught to the Pylean government by the rebels and Team Angel. Such is the lesson taught to the viewer.

Beheading both horrifies and fascinates: "what we witness in the early modern (and no doubt in our own) fascination with the spectacle of the dismantled body is an ambivalent mixture of desire and fear. The viewer's sense of his or her own spiritual and corporeal fragility is both excited and assuaged by witnessing an-Other suffering mutilation" (Margaret E. Owens 119–20). But what we also witness as spectators of *Angel*, watching the spectacle of beheading in Pylea, is that "the sawn-off head reminds that appetite and wrongful autonomy, the bases of the giant's evil, have been extinguished and rebuked, and *comitatus* or *societas* and its attendant control have been validated" (Cohen 176). In other words, *it is about power*; it is about the power of the people; it is about the good guys triumphing over evil. The good guys won by changing the narrative of power: by fighting back, by using the oppressors' tools against them, and by overpowering the oppressor in spite of literal and figurative blows to the head. As occurs in the narratives of L. Frank Baum's *The Wonderful Wizard of Oz* and Lewis Carroll's *Alice's Adventures in Wonderland* and *Through the Looking-Glass*, to which the Pylea episodes allude, the characters of *Angel* are immersed in adventures of another world as a means of finding and asserting their own strengths, strengths they carry back with them to their own world. "Though their hands were tied and their necks were bared," Team Angel returns home from Pylea unified in victory over the oppressor. They have not only escaped beheading but engaged in its practice to resist oppression and regain the figurative body they had lost earlier in Season Two. In *Angel*, resistance is not futile but encouraged. "There was a time," writes Janes, "when severed heads were at the center of things" (41). The implication, of course, is that such a time has long since passed. Yet as the Pylea episodes of *Angel* indicate, severed heads are still of vital concern to vampires, their associates, and the people who observe, within popular culture, signifiers for political engagement in their world.

Notes

1. The three Pylea episodes are "Over the Rainbow" (2.20), "Through the Looking Glass" (2.21), and "There's No Place Like Plrtz Glrb" (2.22).

2. To explore various literary traditions in relation to *Angel*, see *The Literary* Angel*: Essays on Influences and Traditions Reflected in the Joss Whedon Series*, edited by AmiJo Comeford and Tamy Burnett.

3. Other references to heads in Season Two include both offhand figures of speech and rather explicit verbal remarks. For example, in "Dear Boy" (2.05) Wesley suggests to the gang, "We're just going to have to put our heads together," whereas later in the same episode Angel declares to Darla, "You blew the top off my head, but you never made me happy." "The Shroud of Rahmon" (2.08) features "a body without a head"—a crime for which detectives originally question Wesley—alongside a humorous moment in which Angel asks Cordelia (in reference to her new hairstyle), "What happened? ... I mean to your head?" In "Redefinition" (2.11), having been fired by Angel, Wesley calmly suggests to Gunn and Cordelia, "Let's keep a level head, shall we?" Conversely, later in the season, Wesley harshly admonishes Angel: "[Cordelia] knows and experiences the pain in this city.... You'd have known that if you hadn't had your head firmly up your place that isn't on top of your neck" ("Ephiphany" 2.16).

4. For a detailed analysis of political engagement with the "just war" paradigm in "Why We Fight" (*Angel* 5.13) and elsewhere in the Whedonverses, see my paper "'Evil's Spreading Sir ... And It's Not Just Over There': Nazism in *Buffy* and *Angel*."

5. Cordelia's scream is comparable to the scream of the princess described in "Hush" (*Buffy* 4.10). In that episode, the scream breaks the imposed silence, restoring voices and destroying the fairytale monsters. Notably, the monsters' heads implode upon Buffy's scream at the end of the episode.

6. Years earlier, in the *Buffy* episode "Lie to Me" (2.07), Cordelia references beheading during a discussion about Marie Antoinette: "I can so relate to her.... I know the peasants were all depressed.... They were cranky. So, they're like 'Let's lose some heads!' Uh, that's fair! And Marie Antoinette cared about them. She was gonna let them have cake."

7. The association between decapitation and castration can be traced back to Freud (see Janes 136) and was later popularized by Hélène Cixous in "Castration or Decapitation?."

8. Though Landok's remark implies that the beheading is to be followed by a feast of Pylean delicacies, it arguably insinuates that the head itself will serve as the delicacy. Pylean cannibalism is broached on multiple occasions: Princess Cordelia is called the "eater of our enemies' flesh" ("Over the Rainbow"); Narwek inquires whether Cordelia wants to "dine" on the "ignoble flesh" of the prisoners ("Through the Looking Glass"); and Lorne's mother complains, "We ate the wrong son" ("Through the Looking Glass"). Margaret Owens discusses the association of beheading with cannibalism as a "sensational" means of distinguishing oneself from "the barbaric Other" (152, 159). In this context, the Pyleans could be read as "barbaric" rather than merely oppressive.

9. Cohen similarly argues, "The ritualized display of the severed head is public theatre within narrative theatre" (173).

10. Indeed, in Season Three, Fred is considered so intellectually brilliant that her head is sought by a group of demons who want to detach it from her and attach it to the body of their leader ("Provider" 3.12).

11. For details of both the beheadings and the rebellions, see Derek Wilson's *The Tower: The Tumultuous History of the Tower of London from 1078*.

Regarding Torture in *Buffy the Vampire Slayer*'s "Hush"

Erin Hollis

Can't even shout, can't even cry
The Gentlemen are coming by
Looking in windows, Knocking on doors
They need to take seven and they might take yours
Can't call to mom, Can't say a word
You're gonna die screaming, but you won't be heard.
("Hush," *Buffy* 4.10)

The somewhat frequent appearance of overt torture within the Whedonverses comes as no surprise, given that Joss Whedon-affiliated works often deal with dark subject matter and depict characters that seem to enjoy inflicting pain on one another. Because the writing team often focuses attention on those outside of normative society, the creative work regularly deals with topics that are not commonly examined, and may even be considered taboo, on typical primetime television. Whereas it is true that some primetime network shows, most notably *24*, have depicted torture, few of them deal with the subject in the nuanced and critical manner of Whedon and his creative cohorts. From scenes where Angelus tortures Giles in *Buffy* ("Becoming, Part 2" 2.22) to Niska's torture of Mal and Wash in *Firefly* ("War Stories" 1.10), the Whedonverses often focuses particular attention on the torturer's aesthetic relationship to inflicting pain; for example, both Angelus and Niska delight in the supposed "beauty" of torture, and when Faith tortures Wesley ("Five by Five," *Angel* 1.18), she invents "the five types" of torture, indicating her own aesthetic connection to the practice through describing torture as belonging to different genres. By highlighting the artistic nature of the torturer's work, these episodes within the Whedonverses create an even more dehumanized depiction of torture, as they depict the torturers as not only seeing beauty in such acts, but also deriving sadistic joy from those acts; thus, their victims become not people, but mere objects for the torturer's entertainment and aesthetic pleasure. The joy that these characters take in inflicting pain on a person's body and attempting to destroy another person's humanity by inflicting such pain is something that Whedon's narratives are particularly adept at addressing. The frequent and negative depiction of overt torture in the Whedonverse and Whedon's own response to what has been termed "torture porn" in his letter to fans on the "Whedonesque" website ("Let's Watch") encourage viewers to have an ongoing conversation about the depiction of torture and how such depictions may affect responses to actual atrocities, as Whedon's own letter to fans suggests. Additionally, because viewers are encouraged to avoid passively observing the depictions of torture in the Whedonverses and instead are encouraged to grapple actively with the ethical questions raised by such depictions, they may also struggle with their own complicity in watching such scenes of torture. However, overt depictions of torture are not the only way in which the Whedonverses address the ethical complexities raised for viewers. In particular, the oft-discussed, ground-breaking episode of *Buffy the Vampire Slayer's* "Hush" (4.10) figuratively comments on torture using subtle portrayals of what happens to both the body and the voice when one endures torture. Indeed, the use of voicelessness and subsequent attention to how the characters are embodied beings function as a metaphorical depiction of the total deconstruction of both the body and the mind of the torture victim and the subsequent dehumanization that is so often the aim of torture.

Before I discuss the episode in particular, I would like to highlight the particular approach that I am taking to Whedon's work. Whedon's famous comment to his fans to "bring your own subtext" has encouraged many critics to bring forth the subtext by looking at Whedon's own expressed opinions and attitudes toward significant issues. One such issue is gender. Whedon's oft-expressed feminist point of view is one example of a common method for critics to approach his work. Another reading of how Whedon's opinions make their way into his own creative work appears in Alyson Buckman's article, "'Go Ahead! Run Away! Say It Was Horrible!': *Dr. Horrible's Sing-Along Blog* as Resistant Text." Buckman not only reads Whedon's general feminist stance into *Dr. Horrible*, but she also interprets *Dr. Horrible* as a resistant text by pairing it with Whedon's response to both "torture porn" and the 2007 honor killing of Dua Khalil Aswad in a post on Whedonesque.com. Buckman argues, "The production, distribution, and consumption of the serial [*Dr. Horrible*] created a community that functions on the basis of mutual support and resistance to dehumanization" (par. 31). Similar to Buckman's reading of *Dr. Horrible*, I read *Buffy* Season Four's "Hush" as a resistant text as well. While the episode does not overtly depict torture, the metaphorical depiction of torture functions as commentary on and resistance to the support of acts of torture. Such a commentary is particularly highlighted through a post 9/11 reading of the episode, demonstrating the ability of Whedon's work to alter its subtext depending on the context through which it is read.

While I will be approaching "Hush" as an example of a resistant text, many scholars have addressed the commentary that "Hush" makes on communication, focusing on how at the episode's beginning, speech seems to fail each of the main characters as they go about their day. Patrick Shade, for example, discusses how communication establishes community within the framework of the series in his article "Screaming to Be Heard: Reminders and Insights on Community and Communication in 'Hush.'" Additionally, Alice Jenkins and Susan Stuart focus on how the episode "pits the authority of writing against the immediacy of speech, questioning the value of the associations the characters and audience make with each kind of interaction" (par. 2). Because the episode is unique in terms of the characters' extensive loss of speech, focusing on communication is appropriate, and even Joss Whedon noted in his commentary that the story focuses on how language constantly gets in the way of communication ("'Hush' Episode Commentary"). Yet, few have examined how the loss of voice shifts attention to the body within the episode. Bodily expression comes to the fore after the loss of voice, and through the depiction of such expression the episode comments on the effects of torture.

While "Hush" does not overtly depict literal torture, aside from the Gentleman's harvesting of hearts, the loss of voice and the subsequent actions of the characters as a result of that loss metaphorically depict how torture affects its victims both physically and emotionally. In her seminal book *The Body in Pain: The Making and Unmaking of the World*, Elaine Scarry explores the act of torture and its effects on the victim's body and voice. Scarry's theories about pain and torture have provided the foundation for much subsequent discussion of how torture is represented in literature and thus is an ideal lens through which to interpret "Hush." Scarry is particularly interested in how physical pain shatters language and removes all sense of agency from the person in pain. Pain resides in the corporeal experience of the individual and has no extension beyond the body, except when the victim expresses the feeling with his or her voice. Scarry argues that torture, in breaking the body in order to get the victim to voice a confession, deconstructs the world of the victim as the torturer takes possession of the voice, removing agency from the victim. As Scarry argues, "Intense pain is … language-destroying: as the content of one's world disintegrates, so the content of one's language disintegrates; as the self disintegrates, so that which would express and project the self is robbed of its sources and its subject" (33). Thus, the voice allows the subject the agency to widen his or her world, but the act of torture narrows that world as the torturer claims the voice as his or her own, making the victim focus entirely on the experience of the body in pain.

In her discussion of muteness in "Hush," Katy Stevens discusses how the voice is intimately connected to the materiality of the body, reflecting Scarry's examination of what happens to the voice of victims during torture. Discussing the "cloudy mist" emanating from the residents of Sunnydale as the Gentlemen steal their voices and the "visuals used earlier in the same season in the episode 'Living Conditions' (4.02) in which Buffy is seen to be having her soul stolen by a demonic college roommate," Stevens argues that these visual representations indicate how subjectivity extends beyond the body:

> This correlative pairing of images asserts the preoccupation that the voice represents something of the 'essence' of a subject, and its materiality brings to life an enigmatic element of the individual. This visualization of voice, disembodied from its source, but still "live," marks a clear appreciation for the voice as a material body in itself—a physical trace and a distinct object [83].

The connection between the voice and the subject illustrates the importance of the voice to the ability of the characters to become comfortable in their world. Thus, when the characters become voiceless, their agency immediately falls into danger as the voice represents not only the way people usually communicate with one another but also the very "essence" of who people are.

Within the episode, as the Gentlemen steal the whole town of Sunnydale's collective voice, the characters' worlds diminish. The Gentlemen not only physically torture their victims by stealing their hearts, but also metaphorically torture the town by severely limiting the town's residents' ability to project themselves into the world, an effect immediately apparent after Buffy, Willow, and Xander discover that they have lost their voices. Xander calls Buffy and Willow in an attempt to connect with someone else, but both Buffy and Xander quickly realize their inability to extend themselves into the world through the telephone. The telephone, an invention that extends the body's ability to hear from a distance, stops being an extension of the body and becomes a useless object. By taking away the voices of Sunnydale's residents, the Gentlemen remove the ability to use objects like the telephone to assert one's agency, just as torturers often take everyday objects and turn them into weapons, a process I discuss in more detail later in this essay. The effects of voicelessness are portrayed not only in these moments with the main characters of the show, but also through the extras. Throughout the episode in several scenes, groups of townspeople and students exhibit an inability to function after the loss of their voices. As Buffy and Willow walk through the town, for example, one man sits forlorn and unmoving in the middle of the street. Additionally, when Tara walks through the lobby of a school building, the other students are motionless and distraught. When one of the students drops a bottle, the shattering sound within the silence startles everyone and also reinforces their voicelessness. After the characters lose their voices, none of them are comfortable within their own bodies. Scarry asserts that the loss of voice highlights how people are alienated from their own bodies, arguing that "only in silence do the edges of the self become coterminous with the edges of the body it will die with" (33). By creating an episode in which all of the characters lose their voices, Whedon highlights not only the embodied nature of each of his characters, but also the power associated with having a voice. The torturer's desire to control the voice of the victim is a desire to dehumanize that victim and silence his or her agency. The difficulty the town of Sunnydale has in its voiceless state mimics this loss of agency at the hands of the Gentlemen who indeed do torture residents by removing their hearts after also taking their voices.

After the Sunnydale community loses its voice in "Hush," what Scarry describes as "artifacts of civilization" (39) quickly become opportunities for the Gentleman to exploit the helplessness of the community and to turn such artifacts into weapons. Scarry highlights how those who torture often transform everyday, domestic objects, "artifacts of civilization," into weapons. Even the rooms in which the torture takes place are converted into weapons:

> In torture, the world is reduced to a single room or set of rooms. Called 'guest rooms' in Greece and 'safe houses' in the Philippines, the torture rooms are often given names that acknowledge and call attention to the generous, civilizing impulse normally present in the human shelter. They call attention to this impulse only as a prelude to announcing its annihilation. The torture room is not just the setting in which the torture occurs; it is not just the space that happens to house the various instruments used for beating and burning and producing electric shock. It is itself literally converted into another weapon, into an agent of pain [40].

Scarry further describes the shelters and objects that civilization has built up around itself as extensions of the body. The impulse to create a chair, for example, is inspired by the desire to relieve the weight of the body, just as the walls of a house protect the body from extreme temperatures. Torturers take these items of comfort and turn them into weapons, which, in effect, is an attack on the body. Even a victim's body can become a weapon, as a torturer recognizes the smallest levels of humanity and exploits them to wound the victim. The artifacts of civilization work to make the body less noticeable so that, as Scarry argues, "consciousness develops other objects" (39). Using these artifacts to wound instead of comfort the body reverts all attention back to the body, and all extensions of the body that people have created in order to live more comfortably in the world disappear, removing agency from the victim and shifting the victim's focus to the body in pain.

Whedon cleverly transforms such mundane moments and places, Scarry's "artifacts of civilization," into opportunities for the Gentlemen to wreak havoc on Sunnydale, mirroring the way in which torturers often convert items meant for comforting the body into weapons that will wound the body and break the voice of the victim. In many ways, the town of Sunnydale itself functions as a metaphorical tortured body throughout the episode as it is depicted as falling apart after the entire community loses its collective voice. As Buffy and Willow make their way through its main street, the bank is closed, the liquor store remains open, many in despair are gathering in religious worship, and one man capitalizes on the event by selling whiteboards at an inflated price. It is clear from how Buffy and Willow hold hands as they walk down the street that the town, a function of civilization meant to make people more comfortable and to provide a community, is no longer a protective element but a potential weapon, just as torture victims' bodies become weapons used against them. Although throughout the series people are constantly in danger in Sunnydale, since it sits atop a Hellmouth, the town mostly maintains it normalcy until this loss of voice. Most of the residents of Sunnydale, after all, seem to have no idea of the constant danger, explaining away vampire and demon attacks as accidents with "barbeque forks" as Joyce does after she is attacked by Darla in the Season One episode, "Angel," (1.07) and as "gangs on PCP" as Principal Snyder does after Spike and his minions attack Sunnydale High in the Season Two episode "School Hard" (2.03). But society falters when it can no longer extend itself beyond its corporeal reality. Later in the episode, as Riley and Buffy are patrolling the town in order to keep order, the town seems even further destroyed. Riley breaks up a fight and a car has crashed into a fire hydrant, leaving it spouting water everywhere. The Gentlemen's act of removing the voices of the entire town risks destroying it, and such destruction acts as a weapon for the Gentlemen as most of the townspeople are too busy paying attention to the increasing chaos in the town to worry about what the Gentlemen are doing. That is, the town works against itself much in the same way a torture victim's own body becomes a weapon against itself; the Gentlemen cleverly allow the town to act upon itself instead of actually inflicting torture. And, similar to acts of torture in which the victims' bodies are used against them, the town turns on itself, allowing the Gentlemen to move around freely as Sunnydale threatens to devolve into chaos.

Additional artifacts of civilization also function in the episode as weapons for the Gentlemen. As Scarry argues, rooms act as an extension of the body as they provide shelter so that people do not have to worry about the vulnerability of their bodies to outside elements (40). In particular, when the Gentlemen attack one of their victims in his dorm room, the victim's room is turned into a weapon against him. Rooms generally make their inhabitants feel safe and protected. The Gentlemen's victim illustrates this trust as he sleeps peacefully and answers the Gentlemen's knock without question. His room, which a moment before had allowed him to sleep uninterrupted, is now a weapon as no one can hear him or see him suffering as the Gentlemen cut out his heart. The Gentlemen use the protective privacy of the room to their advantage; that is, since no one can see or hear the assault that is taking place, the room aids the Gentlemen in going about their torture without interruption, converting the privacy afforded by the room into a weapon against the victim. Even the victim's bed, something that is meant to make it easier for the body to forget itself in sleep, acts as a weapon as the Footmen use the bed as a buttress to their restraint.

As the episode continues, the residents of Sunnydale increasingly realize just how unsafe they are. When Tara runs from the Gentlemen, knocking on doors crying out for help, no one answers, as they fear who will be on the other side. This breakdown of society and destruction of the artifacts of civilization isolate Tara so that she has nowhere to turn. That rooms are no longer safe is even further emphasized when Tara knocks on a door and one of the Gentlemen answers, bloody heart in hand. She desperately searches for an enclosed space of safety, only to discover that such safety is no longer assured. Only through her connection with Willow is she able to find a safe space that had yet to be converted into a weapon against her.

In addition to using artifacts of civilization as weapons, the Gentlemen mimic the common practice in torture of using medical practices, which should focus on health and healing, by carrying medical bags and using scalpels as weapons. Scarry provides a long list of a variety of historical and cultural examples of medicine being used as a form of torture, including an instance in Portugal where "doctors studied photographs of maimed prisoners as well as the prisoners themselves in order to further the design of the torture procedure" (42). She further discusses how torturers convert medical practices into weapons that intend to wound (42). The Gentlemen act as metaphors of the conversion of medical practices into torture devices. In the scene where they cut the heart out of their victim, the mere sound of the scalpel entering the body highlights how a tool once meant as an aid to healing transforms into a weapon meant for wounding and killing. Moreover, the Gentlemen make their way calmly through the town like doctors making house calls, reflecting once again how the

Gentlemen convert everyday occurrences into weapons. By using the metaphor of a house call, which most viewers would recognize as old fashioned, Whedon further perverts the common by taking something from an apparently "friendlier" time and rendering it ominous.

In addition to taking mundane events and objects and converting them into weapons or places of danger, Joss Whedon's focus throughout the episode on the characters' hands replaces the agency usually provided by voices in daily interaction, highlighting the very part of the body that can both wound and heal, both destroy and create.[1] In the commentary for the episode, Whedon mentions that the actors that played the Gentlemen were mimes, who were better able to embody Whedon's intentions for the characters. The Gentlemen are constantly characterized in the episode by how they use their hands. Because they seem so distant from their own embodied nature—they do not walk, but float; their facial expressions remain frozen in a creepy grin; and they never speak—their hands do the majority of the speaking for them. Their hands communicate an artistic sensibility towards the acts that they are committing, reflecting other episodes of *Buffy* and *Angel* in which overt torturers are depicted as enjoying the aesthetic nature of torture.[2] Among the first camera shots of one of the Gentlemen is one that focuses on his hands placing a box on a table and delicately opening that box in order to collect the voices of Sunnydale's residents. Further, in the appearance of one of the Gentlemen in Buffy's dream, there is an explicit focus on his hand, as Riley touches Buffy's shoulder, and she turns around to see the Gentleman, hand outstretched towards her. As the episode continues, this focus on the Gentlemen's hands continues. They float through the halls of the dormitory picking a room to attack, gesturing delicately and emphatically in order to express themselves. In one notable shot, a Gentleman's hand is the focus as he makes his way into a house in order to harvest a heart. Whedon comments that for that particular moment he asked the actor to "give me Nosferatu on the hand" and "up it came, curled like a spider" ("'Hush' Episode Commentary"). The expressiveness of the movement of the hand in this shot clearly depicts the agency and subjectivity of the Gentlemen demonstrating how they wrestle control and agency from the town. Furthermore, after harvesting the heart from their victim in the dorm, the Gentlemen express their approval with a light "golf clap," speaking again through their hands ("'Hush' Episode Script"). If the removal of voices causes a subsequent removal of agency, the Gentlemen exhibit their agency through their hands, speaking with their hands in a manner unavailable to the citizens of Sunnydale. They are the most expressive characters in terms of hands in the episode, indicating that, for the moment at least, they have all of the power in the Sunnydale community and thus are free to torture their victims, turning them into objects that the

Gentlemen subject to their attacks. They maintain their power as torturers by their expression of agency through their clear control of their hands. They are comfortable in their voiceless state in contrast to most of the residents of Sunnydale who awkwardly seek to express themselves through body language.

That the Scoobies are less able to express themselves merely with their hands than are the Gentlemen is indicated throughout the voiceless portion of the episode. In the scene in which Giles provides the exposition of the Gentlemen, for example, the Scoobies constantly misunderstand each other's gestures. When Willow points at her chest, indicating that what the Gentlemen are gathering is hearts, Xander misinterprets the gesture as her meaning breasts, and when Buffy makes a staking motion with her hand, everyone thinks she is making a masturbatory gesture. Further, towards the end of the episode, when Buffy realizes that the box from her dream is in front of her, she gestures at Riley to destroy the box. He misunderstands her hands and breaks another item, so Buffy must clarify her gesture by miming a box opening. All of these instances demonstrate how clumsy the characters can be at using their hands to express themselves, which exacerbates their powerlessness and lack of agency since they have neither the use of their voices nor the adept use of their hands to aid them.

Yet, the characters do learn during the episode that their hands can provide them agency and an ability to express their subjectivity in the same way that their voices previously had as they become less clumsy using their hands. During his presentation to the group about the Gentlemen's background, Giles uses his hands to create authority, pointing his fingers when something is important. Anya, Xander, and Spike also clearly express themselves with their hands. Spike makes a rude gesture at Xander; Anya makes a sexual gesture at Xander; and Xander snaps to get people's attention. Each of these gestures embodies the personality of the character, indicating the agency available in using the hands to express oneself. Anya, especially, seems to excel at using her hands to communicate, perhaps because she so often simply says what she means rather than engaging in witty banter. Further, Buffy and Willow's clasped hands as they walk down the street indicates their desire for connection. Whedon emphasizes this in his script when he describes the scene: "The girls walk hand in hand, needing the feel of each other's presence" ("'Hush' Episode Script"). Their joined hands provide comfort to one another, replacing the comfort of supportive language that they might use in a similar situation. Giles also becomes incredibly expressive with his hands, and his role as a father figure seems to determine his gestures. When Buffy and Willow enter his home, he immediately comforts Buffy by placing his hand on her shoulder, which she in turn touches in a gesture of shared concern. And, in response to Willow's written greeting, "Hi Giles," on her whiteboard, he reaches out with his hands and gives her a paternal hug. Such increasing expressiveness mimics how torture victims begin to build up resistance to their torturers as they speak to one another through messages left on walls or inscribed in books.

Perhaps the strongest example of the potential for hands to provide agency to the characters is when Tara and Willow are fleeing from the Gentlemen. As they find a momentarily safe space behind a locked door, Willow, with Tara's help, tries to move a vending machine to block the door. They quickly realize they cannot physically move it, and Willow slouches in dejection before trying to teleport it magically. As Tara realizes what Willow is trying to do, she reaches her hand towards Willow's hand. They join hands, look in unison at the machine, and successfully and forcefully move it to block the door, saving themselves from the Gentlemen. Their clasped hands empower them to fight back against the Gentlemen, acting as a metaphorical replacement for the power that the voice can sometimes provide in response to torture. Tara and Willow's connection allows them agency through a return of the community that the Gentlemen removed from Sunnydale as they removed everyone's voice. Much like torture victims find strength through the community provided with connection to other victims, Tara and Willow's connection creates agency through a re-iterated sense of community.

The agency provided by Willow and Tara's joined hands in this scene is repeated when Buffy's voice returns and her scream literally explodes the Gentlemen. Scarry describes the hope that is sometimes provided by a solitary human voice within the midst of the silencing of torture:

> In this closed world where conversation is displaced by interrogation, where human speech is broken off in confession and disintegrates into human cries, where even those cries can be broken off to become one more weapon against the person himself or against a friend, in this world of broken and severed voices, it is not surprising that the most powerful and healing moment is often that in which a human voice, though still severed, floating free, somehow reaches the person whose sole reality had become his own unthinkable isolation, his deep corporeal engulfment. The prisoner who, alone in long solitary confinement and repeatedly tortured, found within a loaf of bread a matchbox containing a small piece of paper that had written in it the single, whispered word "Corragio!," "Take courage" [50].

Buffy's scream acts as a figurative "take courage" moment that represents the healing process of using language to create connections and to express atrocities. While Buffy literally explodes the Gentlemen, and victims of torture can only metaphorically do so, this scene demonstrates the power of the lone voice to return agency to those from whom it had been removed. Scarry further argues that as "torture consists of acts that magnify the way in which pain destroys a person's world, self, and voice, so these other acts that restore voice become not only a denunciation of the pain but almost a diminution of the pain, a partial reversal of the process of torture itself" (50). As the entire town regains its voice, Buffy's solitary scream—her reclamation of voice and therefore the agency she can exert through her body—begins the healing process.

By subtly depicting metaphorical torture throughout the episode and illustrating its effects and how victims might regain their agency through community and connection, Whedon encourages viewers, both through this episode and his letter to fans on Whedonesque about Dua Khalil Aswad, to confront their own complicity either through failing to protest torture or through viewing scenes of torture for entertainment. In her book, *Regarding the Pain of Others*, Susan Sontag writes specifically about the effects of looking at the atrocities often depicted in war photographs. Beginning her book with a discussion of Virginia Woolf's response to war in *Three Guineas*, Sontag explores how the advent of war photography changed civilians' response to war, arguing that "photographs of the victims of war are themselves a species of rhetoric. They reiterate. They simplify. They agitate. They create the illusion of consensus" (6). Sontag further argues that when viewers look at representations of cruelty that "[n]o moral charge attaches to the representation of these cruelties. Just the provocation: can you look at this? There is the satisfaction of being able to look at the image without flinching. There is the pleasure of flinching" (41). In discussing the conflicting emotions that may surface when a viewer looks at war photographs, Sontag uncovers the similar response many viewers have to what critics, including David Edelstein, describe as "torture porn." Movies such as *Captivity*, *Hostel*, and the six movies that comprise the *Saw* series invite moviegoers to experience both the provocation and the pleasure that Sontag discusses in *Regarding the Pain of Others*. While there is definitely a difference between looking at fictional images of violence and torture and viewing actual pictures of violence, the parallel that can be drawn here is to the pleasure that the viewer may take in looking at violence. The very act of covering the eyes when watching a horror movie reveals the twinned responses of repulsion and pleasure so commonly experienced in response to horror films. Viewers cover their eyes in a desire not to see, but peak through their fingers at the same time as they desire also to see what repulses them. Viewers are thus both attracted and repelled by the images, enjoying, in many ways, the feeling of being repulsed.

It is this response that disturbed Joss Whedon in relation to the movie *Captivity* and the so-called "honor killing" of Dua Khalil Aswad. In the previously mentioned letter posted on Whedonesque.com on 20 May 2007, Whedon explicitly addresses the relationship between fictional depictions of torture and the occurrence of actual torture. Commenting on the brutal torture and murder of Dua Khalil Aswad and the fact that the event was captured on video by several of the spectators who chose to be passive observers rather than take action to intervene against the violence, Whedon highlights the complicity of not only the bystanders of the murder but also of CNN and, perhaps, of CNN's viewers:

> That she was torturously murdered for this [being seen in the company of a Sunni Muslim] is not, in fact, a particularly uncommon story. But now you can watch the action up close on CNN. Because as the girl was on the ground trying to get up, her face nothing but red, the few in the group of more than twenty men who were not busy kicking her and hurling stones at her were filming the event with their camera-phones.
>
> There were security officers standing outside the area doing nothing, but the footage of the murder was taken—by more than one phone—from the front row. Which means whoever shot it did so not to record the horror of the event, but to commemorate it. To share it. Because it was cool ["Let's Watch"].

That CNN chose to show this footage in some ways implicates them in the horror of those who chose to commemorate the event by filming it. Because the bystanders' intentions were not to show the world the horrific nature of the event but to celebrate the event, the dissemination of those images allows that celebration to be extended into the world. Later in the letter, Whedon draws a comparison between this event and the trailer for the movie *Captivity*: "The trailer resembles nothing so much as the CNN story on Dua Khalil. Pretty much all you learn is that Elisha Cuthbert is beautiful, then kidnapped, inventively, repeatedly and horrifically tortured, and that the first thing she screams is 'I'm sorry'" ("Let's Watch"). Thus, Whedon connects fictional images to real images, arguing that the persistent view of women as inferior to men is responsible for both the fiction and the reality. And he recognizes the pleasure that people might take in both sets of images, saying that the video of Dua Khalil Aswad and the movie *Captivity* are "both available for your viewing pleasure" ("Let's Watch"). Whedon's recognition of the pleasure that people take in such horrific images mirrors Sontag's discussion of the process of being confronted with horrific images of war.

That Whedon is aware of the effects of regarding violent images alters how a viewer might approach an episode like "Hush." In the episode, he does not seek to provide the viewer with pleasure as a result of flinching in response to violent images; rather, he uses suspense and usually chooses not to depict overly violent images (he does not show anyone's heart being cut out, for example), choosing a nuanced approach to horror rather than resorting to "torture porn." By doing this, he provides a commentary on torture and on depictions of violence in general that allows the attentive viewer critically to approach the act of torture and the twinned acts of depicting and watching torture (whether fictional or real) by making that viewer aware of the common effects of torture. Whedon never lets his viewers become comfortable with what they are watching as he encourages them persistently to bring their own point of view to bear on his creations by inviting them to "bring their own subtext"; one such subtext for "Hush" is an underlying criticism of the act of torture and of becoming complicit in torture by watching and taking pleasure in it. Because Whedon does not overtly depict any act of torture in the episode, viewers move beyond a mere desire to see what repulses them and begin to question why they might want to see such images in the first place. Whedon also gives the voiceless characters of Sunnydale the power to overcome the torture of the Gentlemen, pushing against depictions of characters being tortured in other films or television series. Instead of having his characters say "I'm sorry" as Elisha Cuthbert does in response to torture in *Captivity*, Whedon allows the characters their own agency as they figure out how to defeat the Gentlemen. Buffy never apologizes when she has lost her voice; instead, she proactively asks Giles how she can get her voice back. By giving his characters strength in response to the Gentlemen's metaphoric torture, Whedon reflects the moments when victims of torture find a way to speak to and comfort one another in spite of the torturer's attempts to remove such connections. An interpretation of the episode as what Buckman would call a "resistant" text encourages viewers to find their own voices in response to the atrocities in the world ("Go Ahead!" par. 1).

At the end of his letter regarding Dua Khalil Aswad, Whedon makes a call to action to his fans:

> All I ask is this: Do something. Try something. Speaking out, showing up, writing a letter, a check, a strongly worded e-mail. Pick a cause—there are few unworthy ones. And nudge yourself past the brink of tacit support to action. Once a month, once a year, or just once. If you can't think of what to do, there is this handy link. Even just learning enough about a subject so you can speak against an opponent eloquently makes you an unusual personage. Start with that. Any one of you would have cried out, would have intervened, had you been in that crowd in Bashiqa. Well thanks to digital technology, you're all in it now ["Let's Watch"].

His urging to action highlights how important it is to object to atrocities such as torture, no matter the circumstances used to justify them. Whedon also recognizes that people have been so persistently bombarded with violent images that they may have become apathetic toward taking action. As Sontag argues, "[M]aking suffering loom larger, by globalizing it, may spur people to feel they ought to 'care' more. It also invites them to feel that the sufferings and misfortunes are too vast, too irrevocable, too epic to be much changed by any local political intervention" (*Regarding the Pain* 79). Whedon pushes back against this hopelessness as he highlights the responsibility of viewers to cry out and intervene when confronted with brutality. "Hush" provides a subtle commentary on the process of torture that also encourages an active response from the viewer. Within the episode, the metaphorical depiction of the process of torture, with its destruction of language and the victims' worlds, as well as the depiction of discovering the possible agency of the body and the power of the voice held up against torture, guides the viewer towards taking action. Of course, when someone steals one's voice, it is distressing and the world seems smaller and the body feels helpless, but, the episode argues, "take courage" (Scarry 50) and find ways to effect change and fight back against those who would seek to cause pain and destruction.

Notes

1. This discussion of hands in "Hush" is indebted to and inspired by Rhonda Wilcox's comment in her essay "Fear: The Princess Screamed Once" that "one could do an entire essay on hands in 'Hush'" (*Why Buffy Matters* 157).

2. Notably, Angelus enjoys torturing Giles in "Becoming II" (*Buffy* 2.22) and Faith enjoys torturing Wesley in "Five by Five" (*Angel* 1.18).

"You're the one who sees everything!"

Xander's Eye Patch and Visible Disability in Buffy the Vampire Slayer

Brian Cogan

One of the neglected areas in *Buffy* studies is the issue of disability and disability studies. This is strange, as *Buffy* has had no lack of characters that are marked by different aspects of illness, injury, and other supposed afflictions, both symbolic and literal. Examples include Buffy's death (on two different occasions), Angel's curse, Joyce's illness and subsequent death, and serious injuries that befall most of the characters at one point or another. Although many of the characters in the show appear to be perfect stereotypical (white/cis/heterosexual/middle class/able-bodied) inhabitants of a small, untroubled town in California, there is much more below the surface than it appears. Even a cursory examination of the core group proves fertile ground for an analysis based on disability studies. Within the Scooby Gang, there are numerous apparent depictions of supernatural disability, including Anya's demon past, Spike's vampirism, and Willow's growing addiction to magic. What is fascinating about these perceived disabilities is that their origins are grounded in the supernatural. Most of these characters, created by heavy use of make-up and prosthetics, are marked as demonic or evil in various ways, and we are clearly meant to interpret them as obvious outsiders, marked by their difference. After all, as many scholars have pointed out, mediated representations of disability are often symbolic as well as literal.

In terms of the way in which disability is represented in mainstream media, it is typical (at least for most of the history of television and film) that the imagery used resembles both literary tropes, as well as the kinds of images that tend to reinforce the status quo. As Barnes and Mercer note, this has always existed to some extent and has always been part of constructing hierarchies of power based on constructed ideas of normalcy. As they write, "historically disabling imagery has reinforced the social exclusion and repression of disabled people" (109; edition 2001). This is not a recent phenomenon, but has been a consistent part of literature for as long as stories have been told. Stereotypes from such iconic figures such as Captain Ahab and Richard III contain large amounts of what could be called "an enduring association with the 'grotesque' and supernatural" (Snyder and Mitchell, "Re-engaging the Body" 70). In order to properly let the audience know that a character is the antagonist, an easy mechanism has been a physical deformity or obvious perceived disability. As Snyder and Mitchell also emphasize, "The most prevalent image in films and especially television has been the maladjusted disabled, grotesque and supernatural" ("Re-engaging the Body" 70). Even in *Buffy*, these images are prevalent, with grotesque looking demons being the norm, but perhaps for different reasons than in most mass media representations. For the most part, many media texts have traditionally used these representations because of the way in which the audience is unconsciously trained to read disabled characters as villains or marginalized victims.

This imagery of the disabled as grotesque other is not just the practice of lazy storytellers, filmmakers, and television producers, but also represents the way in which society marginalizes the disabled socially and politically. Unfortunately, many readers/viewers look no deeper than that surface association between disability and othering. In order to understand how images and representations of the disabled often function as "accurate" information for many consumers of mass media, we also need to understand the prevalent social and political factors involved in creating the environment in which disability itself is discussed and defined. According to McColl and Brickenbach, "What this means is that the expression of disability cannot be properly understood in isolation from the social and physical world that contributes to, and sometimes creates, the limitations that a person with disabilities experiences" (8). Disability itself is a condition where those considered disabled by the dominant society have "problems not caused by their impairments, but rather because society is organized in a way that does not take their needs into account" (Tregaskis 10). In other words, a "disability" is only that because society reinforces "normal" ability as that which the majority shares and privileges.

In the first two episodes of the series, Buffy, embarrassed by her past as a vampire slayer, tries to fit in. She finds that although she is physically able to pass for "normal," her actions (and her past) mark her as an outcast, one akin to Xander and Willow, who are outcasts by virtue of not being at the top of the high school social hierarchy Even though Buffy herself can pass Cordelia's "interview" to hang with the cool kids, it is no longer within her nature to ally herself with the dominant clique. Her past as a vampire slayer has marked her as an outsider as well, one symbolically disabled in the Sunnydale hierarchy because she cannot change her nature. How can one be a cheerleader when patrolling the cemetery at night takes precedence? Erving Goffman, in his work on the way in which society and media representations stigmatize the disabled, notes that appearance is not the only indicator of what symbolic state or societal position one is placed in by one's peers, but relates directly to societal constructions of reality. According to Goffman, "The special situation of the stigmatized is that society tells him he is a member of the wider group, which means that he is a normal human being, but that he is also 'different' in some degree and that it would be foolish to deny this difference" (123). While Goffman wrote this over four decades ago, many of the issues he addressed still exist in mediated representations of reality in the present.

However, as the series develops, Buffy and the Scoobies' primary world shrinks from the "normal" Sunnydale to their daily fight against the supernatural. It is here that various representations of difference again suggest both alignment with the supernatural and disability (i.e., slayer Buffy, vampire Angel and later Spike). However, the narrative quickly undermines such a simplistic reading of these characters' different abilities, positioning those with supernatural ability as the majority in the supernatural realm. In a world where the norm for the core group is different ability rooted in the supernatural, we must ask if being "normal" is then the true disability. Often under-examined across the spectrum of analytical works on *Buffy* is the character of Xander Harris, the most "normal" of the gang, by virtue of not having supernatural abilities.

From his introduction in "Welcome to the Hellmouth" (1.01), it is immediately apparent that both Xander and Willow are symbolic outsiders in the town of Sunnydale. Sunnydale, in many ways is the prototypical white, upper-class high school, where all divisions (the ugly, disabled, minorities, etc.) are largely absent, both symbolically and literally. Xander is clearly an outsider in Sunnydale High School, which like most American high schools is largely clique driven. Unlike Cordelia's color-coordinated group of cool kids, who have the power to disarm any geek's approach with a withering stare and a sarcastic comment, Xander is marked by his outsiderness. He comes across as geeky and awkward, masking his insecurity with a constant barrage of nervous jokes. Xander, with his trove of pop culture references and comic book trivia, is marked as one of the key types consistently bullied in high school: the geek. Notably, Xander even refers to himself early on in the series as "the king of cretins" (Golden and Holder 28), the comic relief to the main team members. During the first few seasons of *Buffy*, it seems clear that Xander knew early on that, even in as diverse a group as the Scooby gang, he could tell he was the most different. Even though Xander has a few friends and rides a skateboard, he does not fit in anywhere. As Michael McKeon pointed out, "Xander's callow recklessness is hinted at early in the series. Introduced as a youth literally out of control, Xander precariously weaves and winds his way between students on his skateboard as he makes his way to Sunnydale High" (132). Literally knocked off his feet (and skateboard) by the sight of Buffy, Xander clearly will never fit into the "popular" clique of Sunnydale, a power Buffy possesses because of her appearance. This does not stop Xander from trying, and even going so far as to try and date Buffy, a "new girl" who by her appearance was defined by the rigid rules of high school hierarchy as out of his league. Xander possesses the self-confidence of the true geek and starts hitting on Buffy immediately and maintains an obvious crush on her for most of the first two seasons. As Morris writes, "He wants what the pecking order says he should not have and however consistently he is punished for reaching too high, he continues to reach" (51). He can never fit in with the "cool" kids as epitomized by Cordelia (although he can eventually date Cordelia, and even hurt her feelings by cheating on her with Willow), but that does not stop him from trying and failing. It seems clear early on in the series that the character of Xander Harris will always be symbolically ostracized. But appearances can be deceiving. The evolution of Xander from a "callow youth" to a formidable soldier is one of the great narrative arcs of the television series, as explored in the following passage:

> Xander is a fascinating paradox. To many viewers, he was simply comic relief to the "stronger" characters, but Xander was far more than mere sidekick. Indeed, Xander is the only member of Buffy's gang with no special abilities, yet upon closer examination, the one character the Scoobies can always count on when the battle explodes, no matter how dire the situation. Eventually, Angel, Cordelia, Oz and Giles all leave town. Spike and Anya flirt with their evil, demonic ways and when Willow turns evil, she almost destroys the world all by herself. But Xander remains in Sunnydale ready to help Buffy take on whatever threat comes next [Camron par. 17].

Despite (or perhaps because of?) a lack of super powers, magic, or any kind of advanced technology, Xander is the most consistent character in the Buffyverse. Xander is hiding nothing below the surface; he is what he is, a bit of a nerd, and as normal as anyone in Sunnydale can possibly be. Xander is aware of his position in Sunnydale and uses humor as a defense mechanism, even to the point of self-deprecation. In a group that initially included a Watcher, a budding witch, a vampire, and a vampire slayer, Xander's powerlessness marked him as the king of the geeks. And unlike Willow, a fellow geek with actual abilities (scholastic and technological prowess), Xander is a geek without any actual obvious powers or abilities. This lack of powers positions him as "disabled" in comparison to his supernaturally-enabled friends.

Whereas the character of Xander Harris is always integral to *Buffy*, Xander finally comes into his own as a fully realized character, one who can finally contribute equally to the Scooby gang *and* be comfortably marked by his outsider status as symbolically disabled in the episode "The Zeppo" (3.13). In this episode, his lack of power is addressed in a way that both parodies the conventions of a typical *Buffy* episode, but also allows for his symbolic disability to be addressed head on for the first time. "The Zeppo" is considered by many *Buffy* scholars to be one of the most important episodes in the series, and it is certainly the one that most fully explores Xander's character and his ongoing transformation at that point in the series. To Romesburg, "the episode dramatizes Xander's transformation from boy to man as he passes through several typical rites of manhood and assumes some of the more distinctive qualities of masculinity" (91). Romesburg, who used the episode as a teaching tool in his classroom, noted distinct changes in how students not only looked at Xander after watching the episode, but were also able to look at themselves in terms of their conceptions of masculinity. He notes that this episode helped students "sharpen what they defined a man to be by what Xander is not" (91). In "The Zeppo," Xander's inherent difference is even apparent when among zombies on a joyride. As Lorna Jowett observed, "Of course Xander is not 'part of the group' [of zombies] because he is not like them. This difference of masculinity is articulated as a physical difference. Xander is not dead." (*Sex and the Slayer* 101). Even amongst zombies, Xander can only play at masculinity since the dead of Sunnydale are seemingly more masculine and, therefore, more powerful than Xander. Xander is excluded from both the Scooby gang and from the zombie gang because he is still seemingly powerless and thus the consummate outsider. As Camron noted about the episode, "Before the opening theme song plays, we see Xander as the weakling of the group; the first one out of the battle and the only one who needs help getting up at the end. When he tries to assert himself, he is verbally castrated by one of the slayers" (par. 6). Trying to reassert some dignity, Xander jokingly explains his important contribution to the battle, asking, "Who at a crucial moment distracted the lead demon by allowing her to pummel him about the head?" Naturally Faith cannot help but take him down a peg, noting that "Yeah, that was real manly, how you shrieked and all."

Whereas many read the episode primarily in terms of masculinity and the passage to manhood, another equally valid interpretation is to analyze the episode as Xander coming to terms with the constructed "limitations" through which his symbolic disability has been used by the other Scooby gang members (and the rest of Sunnydale) to define him. As Xander became more symbolically disabled/powerless in early episodes, he was confined in the constructed identity forced upon him by the others in the Scooby gang, an object of comic relief, and sometimes even pity. This is of course ironic, as Xander is literally the outsider in the outsider group, fighting alongside those much more powerful than him, demonstrating great courage. This symbolic definition by others is nothing new in the disabled community and as Laurence Kriegel has noted, "The world of the crippled and disabled is the creature who has been deprived of his ability to create a self ... he must accept definition from outside the boundaries of his own existence" (33). While Xander is certainly brave—"from the beginning, Xander is gung ho about confronting force far above his ability" (Morris 51)—he is also from the start of the series marked in the hierarchy of both Sunnydale and in the Scooby gang as an outsider. This is intentional in terms of making Xander not just a character that viewers can see as a proxy, but also as the butt of jokes and mockery. When Xander tries to explain how important he is to the group in "The Zeppo," Cordelia responds with a smirk, "Integral part of the group? Xander, you're the ... the useless part of the group. You're the Zeppo." As Morris notes, "Whedon cements Xander's low status as a member of the grouping in this episode" (52). Xander is considered useless, but when forced to work on his own, he starts to come to terms with his status and identity. Morris further observes, "While the gang is researching Sunnydale's latest apocalypse, Xander becomes virtually useless. He goes out on his own, encounters, befriends and ultimately defeats a gang of zombie hoodlums intent on blowing up Sunnydale High. At the end of the episode his friends tell him all about the excitement he missed. Xander reacts with quiet humility grounded in the realization that he has no prowess" (Morris 52). Morris' reading is not the only way to read Xander's actions at the end of the episode, however. Camron suggests an alternative understanding: "He does not need to tell his friends that he is the real hero of the night, that he saved them all. He does not need to brag to reinforce his masculinity. Externally, Xander remains the same, but internally the character is finally comfortable with who he is" (par. 14).

Xander has not just been transformed by his encounter with the zombies; he has also passed through another symbolic rite, losing his virginity to Faith. Although Faith has only used him because of his convenient presence, Xander does gain confidence in his abilities, thanks to Faith's attentions. After having sex with Faith (even though she shrugs it off as no big deal as soon as they are done) and becoming symbolically more masculine, Xander begins to take control of his destiny. As Camron noted, "Though his masculinity is not yet fully realized—he still wants Buffy to dispatch the evil for him—the act of searching for the villains on his own is a huge step" (par. 12). This, however, reinforces the characterization of Xander not just as becoming symbolically more masculine, but also in terms of coming to terms with the way in which the others see him and define him. The powerless/disabled Xander is no longer defined by the perceived limitations that Buffy and the others unwittingly impose upon him. Xander was always struggling not because he was less powerful, but because of his tacit *acceptance* of the limitations that the rest of the Scooby gang saw. As Camron writes, "To be perfectly fair, Xander was never one to shy away from a fight. The character always manages to work through his fear and face the evil of the week. But the new and improved Xander (now with 100% less virginity) isn't just along for the ride; he actively seeks out the danger and faces it alone without magic and super-strength at his side" (par. 13).

Although Xander is arguably the weakest, he is in a state of constant evolution. "The Zeppo" is not the first or only time that Xander is transformed. He is possessed by a hyena spirit in "The Pack" (1.6), he joins essences with Buffy, Willow, and Giles—notably contributing the heart—to defeat Season Four's Adam ("Primeval" 4.21), and is split into two different Xanders in "The Replacement" (5.03). In "The Replacement," the splitting of Xander in two leads to contrasting aspects of the same person, emphasizing perceived ability and disability. In this episode, one Xander is symbolically the "weaker" of the two parts of Xander's personality and another the stronger and more confident. Rod Romeburg notes that students who observe Xander's split into positive and negative sides see it as "unlike 'real' Xander, who the regular *Buffy* audience knows is almost always one step behind the rest of the Scooby gang and seems nearer to the qualities my students connect to adolescence, this twin has the successful emerging adult character most students want to emulate" (89). Although Romeburg looks at this in terms of maturity and growth, I again suggest this episode can be read as exploration of a character who is symbolically disabled and who refuses to be marginalized or labeled by outsiders. Although Xander has not yet fully realized his potential by the early fifth season, clearly he has been making strides towards acceptance of what others see as his limitations and realizations about what his powers actually are or can be. Xander, who had long struggled with his sense of self, can now fully evolve into an integral part of the Scooby gang.

Nonetheless, Xander's lack of power or magic is still the most common way in which the others in the group primarily view him. In a group of friends defined by their powers, Xander can easily be read as the "disabled" one. In this framework, Xander must learn to adapt to being differently-abled, and indeed he successfully turns his "disability" into "ability," becoming the one who can actually "see," who can make sense of the world around him and his friends. This final transformation occurs in the last season and a half, especially after the departure of Giles, Buffy's Watcher. Without Giles, the Scoobies must grow into their roles, taking more ownership and accepting more responsibility, resulting in a more cohesive team. As Giles intended, in the absence of "adult" authority, all of the characters are forced to become more self-reliant, especially Xander. This is especially true in the last season, when following Giles' and Willow's departure for England, Xander must step up to be Buffy's equal and primary source of support. Xander's unique position as an outsider among outsiders, and "powerless" among the powerful, (his presumed disability) forces him to adapt to survive and thrive in the supernatural world, and he develops a distinct advantage over the others in learning how to step back from the magical world and "see" what is really going on around him, to be a (the?) voice of wisdom. Ironically, it is this very ability that results in Xander's transition from symbolically disabled to literally disabled.

In the seventh season, Xander's adapted ability is threatened in one of the most disturbing parts of the last season of *Buffy*, when the evil defrocked priest Caleb makes an unusually vicious attack on Xander ("Dirty Girls" 7.18). After handily defeating and wounding or killing several of Buffy's army of potential slayers, Caleb turns his attention to Xander, sizing him up and then telling him, "You're the one who sees everything, aren't you? Well, let's see what we can't do about that." Caleb then viciously gouges Xander's left eye out. Caleb's attack is not as random as it initially appears. For a "normal" person, losing an eye is a disabling injury; for Xander this attack on his physical vision is intended to disable his extra-normal vision and weaken the combined power of the Scoobies by removing his abilities from the group. Caleb has noticed Xander's presumed disability, his normalness, which gives him a unique distinction as a symbolic outsider and an ability that the others do not possess, the ability to step back and truly assess the situation. Without any real powers, Xander possesses the perspective of a character without the supernatural or technological means to solve problems.

However, this injury empowers Xander as opposed to making him symbolically weaker. The older, wiser Xander of the seventh season understands that he has always had the abilities needed to be an integral part of the Scooby gang. As Golden and Holder noted, Xander contributes not from being powerful or combat ready, but from his "loyalty to Buffy and the others and his willingness to do what ever is necessary to help out…" (29). Because he cannot fight, use computers or magic powers, he actually has to consider the consequences of his actions, to deliberate, and, as seen later in the comic series become a successful general because of his well-honed analytic abilities. Xander's response to a (presumably disabling) injury is key in understanding the way in which the disabled community re-imagines the idea of perceived disability and taking control of an issue that has been used to marginalize them for years. Barton makes a key point, noting that in "subverting the negative into positive, disabled people are thus involved in varying degrees of intensity and effectiveness in a struggle or naming difference itself" (11). Xander, who has always been disabled symbolically (being non-supernatural in a supernatural world), becomes more fully actualized when he is literally disabled.

In gouging his eye out, Caleb also changes the group dynamic, but not in the way he had intended. Xander is physically changed. As a result of this attack, Xander wears an eye patch for the rest of the final season and his character continues to wear one in the comic book sequel seasons. The eye patch gives Xander a literal way to articulate his difference and sets him apart from the others in a unique way—first as a source of pity, then later as a full-fledged and respected member of the team at last. He is marked by his disability as someone as symbolically powerful as the others in the Scooby gang—just as Spike's vamp face, Willow's ever magically-induced hair color changes, and Buffy's extraordinary speed and strength physically mark them as differently-abled. Losing his eye gave Xander literal insight instead and allowed the character to be fully realized, perhaps disabled by "normal" standards, but finally equally as powerful as the rest of the gang.

While this process is apparent after the events of "The Zeppo" in numerous episodes in Seasons Three through Seven, it is most apparent after the episode "Dirty Girls" where Xander loses an eye and gains both strength and wisdom at the same time. Nothing is the same after the events of "Dirty Girls," and even Buffy's unquestioned leadership is challenged and the traditional order is upended. In the trade of an eye for knowledge, Xander Harris not only changes as a character, but is (intentionally) also connected to classical folklore via the story of the transformation of the Norse god Odin, who traded his eye for wisdom.

Whedon and his writing team had used classical mythology in terms of the overall structure of Buffy, but examining the growth of Xander through Norse Mythology provides insight into Xander's late blooming maturity and his alignment with perceived disability. In Norse mythology, Odin trades one of his eyes to Mimir, a nature spirit who was also the guardian for the well of all knowledge, situated below the world tree, Yggdrasil. Although the leader of the Norse pantheon, Odin was not omnipotent and wanted to know all there was to know about the world. According to Daly, "Odin became the one eyed god by giving an eye to Mimir to put in the well. The loss of one eye was the price Odin paid for the wisdom and foresight for which he was famous" (69). This idea of sacrifice and voluntary disability is a well-known motif in myth and legend and not restricted to Norse legends alone. Alby Stone noted in an issue of *Folklore* that the legend of Odin's acquisition of knowledge via loss is also mirrored not only in Irish mythology and the grail legends, but "is reminiscent of Asiatic Shamanic lore" (33). John Carey makes a similar assertion that the theme of losing an eye in exchange for wisdom, healing, or a gift is thematically present in the legends of many cultures, even going so far as to question whether it is connected to the New Testament story of Jesus curing the leper, along "with similar stories in Buddhist and Jania legends" (215). In numerous legends, one must sacrifice in order to gain wisdom, and Xander is only the most recent example of the resonance of the mythical idea of trading literal "sight" for symbolic "sight," and, therefore, fully realizing Caleb's cogent analysis of Xander as the "one who sees everything."

Thematically, the eye-patch has of course long been associated with disability, with numerous pirates, villains, and shady characters in fiction marked by their eye-patch and connoted as "sinister." The eye-patch has held many negative connotations to those unaware of either its mythic connections or its re-evaluation in modern disability studies, as Connor and Benjoian demonstrated in an exercise they used in class. They observe that in the exercise, they "have students draw representations of their understanding of how incarnations of good and bad look. Many will portray 'bad' as having a physical disability—a hunched back, a hook, wooden leg, an eye-patch, an 'ugly' face, or an animal-like monstrous appearance" (6). Even to modern students, whose most common vision of "pirate" is the two-eyed Jack Sparrow, the eye-patch is still a visual representation of the perceived grotesque. Although born of guilt, the fact that at first Willow and Buffy can barely stand to look at Xander's eye, reinforces this association with the grotesque. This is made apparent when Xander is in the hospital following the attack and attempts to be his old, comic-relief self. Seeing how upset Willow and Buffy (who has fled the room) are, Xander exclaims that, "I might need a parrot," elaborating in response to Willow's confused look, "Well, to go with the eye patch to really complete the look I think I still have that [pirate] costume from [Season Six's] Halloween." Xander even jokes to Willow about gaining literal powers from Caleb's attack, saying, "I can't taste anything right now anyway. I keep waiting for my other senses to improve 50%. Yeah, they should kick in any day now." As a newly disabled person, Xander is taking on the baggage here that so many suddenly-disabled people do—attempting to prove they are still the same person to those in their life who are traumatized by their new disability. However, ultimately, both the Scoobies and the audience come to see that Xander's eye patch symbolizes not only his defeat in battle, but also his newfound maturity and wisdom.

In the last episodes of the seventh season of *Buffy*, and when Xander was reconfigured for the comic book series of *Buffy the Vampire Slayer: Season Eight*, he was not only shown as more powerful in the hierarchy of the slayer army, but also was meant to evoke a classic Marvel comic character: Nick Fury. Although Whedon's turn helming the Marvel Cinematic University (MCU) and writing Nick Fury was yet to come, Xander's resemblance to Fury, both in Fury's appearance as leader of the "Howling Commandoes" during World War II and as an agent of S.H.I.E.L.D., is seemingly deliberate. In the comic book continuation of Buffy (and generally recognized as canon), Xander's abilities to train and lead the slayers are much more evident, and he functions as a literal general in Buffy's army. Many of the *Buffy* comic serial covers are humorous re-imaginations of earlier comic book covers, and issue twenty-nine actually depicts Xander as Nick Fury[1] leading a team of heavily-armed Slayers into battle. The character of Nick Fury is another example of how a perceived disability is actually a comic book characterization of both hidden strength and symbolic otherness; as a savvy commander, Fury is a literal representation of the myth of Odin and the acquisition of knowledge through sacrifice. He is also more powerful and a better leader thanks to his perceived disability, which for both Fury and Xander is meant to represent a "battle scar" and the strength of the character's ability instead of a limitation.[2]

Apparently, this role for Xander had also been planned for early on in the last televised season. In the DVD commentary for the episode "Dirty Girls," episode writer Drew Goddard and actor Nicholas Brendon discussed Xander's importance as the "center" of the show and how Caleb, by disabling Xander, effected the collapse of the stability of the *Buffy* universe ("'Dirty Girls' Episode Commentary"). Brendon noted that there had been talk of killing off Xander's character and having him come back as the First (the enemy, or "Big Bad" in Season Seven who could take the form of any character that had previously died on the show). However, Goddard explained why they could not kill off a character as important to the chemistry of the show as Xander, noting that, "we just felt like, you know what, we're going out on this season. Xander is too important to the show.... It's important that he's injured because we want the group to fracture, but at the end we want the group to come back together.... Xander has always been there, and he's never wavered." In *Buffy*, although the show was ostensibly about the role of the Slayer, it was also a strong ensemble show where the chemistry between the core group of characters was just as important as the lead. In having Xander lose an eye rather than having him killed, the writers played upon the emotional investment that fans had with the character, as well as solidifying his role as central to the group dynamic. By disabling Xander, he is made not weaker but stronger and more integral to the group. On the DVD commentary for "Dirty Girls," Drew Goddard and Nicholas Brendon also discuss Xander's new re-imagination as Nick Fury. Goddard explains, "We wanted to see Xander standing strong at the end because it's so important." Brendon responds by agreeing and adding, "And still taking charge." Goddard then makes the reference clearer by stating, "And still taking charge. Just looking kick ass. I mean, Nick Fury.... I mean seriously, the eye patch is always tough" ("'Dirty Girls' Episode Commentary"). With the loss of his eye, Xander transforms into Nick Fury, albeit with an army of potential slayers instead of Howling Commandos, but still "standing strong," finally a realized character comfortable with his powers and his role in the Buffyverse. In the Season Eight comics, Xander is clearly the field general of a vast army of slayers who respect him, obeying his order without question. Whereas many fans initially used Xander as an entry point into the show, perceiving him as a representative of the average fan, Xander proved himself to be far from average. Like many *Buffy* fans, he grew and changed in the course of the seven years of the show and in the comic book sequel of Season Eight. While analyzing Xander through the lenses of gender studies or as a reinvention of masculinity are certainly worthwhile interpretations, Xander's transformation is also largely one about not just the way in which disability is represented, but also in the way in which disability is redefined by members of the disabled community itself. Xander's journey, highlighted in the early seasons via "The Zeppo," is one of gradual discovery and acceptance of his true strengths and abilities. When Xander is forced to finally take charge in Season Seven, he proves that he will not be defined by the limitations others try to impose upon him. Xander has lost an eye and his eye-patch presents his perceived disability in a way that others cannot ignore.

Whatever critical stance one takes in analyzing the *Buffy* canon, it is clear that Xander is one of the fullest and most evocative characters in *Buffy*. To new fans, Xander can be read in multiple ways—as the audience's proxy, as a gender studies example, or in terms of the classical hero's journey—but one thing is certain. Xander's growth contains multiple references to the ways in which disability studies have helped to change public perception about the lack of representation and stereotypical portrayals of the disabled community in media. In the Whedonverses, misconceptions of many sorts are addressed and Xander's eye-patch proves that sometimes an eye-patch is not just a symbol of lost ability, but a mechanism for fully realizing a character's potential. From losing an eye and seeing less, to becoming the general he had been training for since the Slayers were activated, Xander demonstrates that although most media portrayals of disability are clichéd and stereotypical, in the right hands, a disability can be shown as truly empowering within the context of the disabled individual. In losing an eye, Xander becomes fully actualized and abled.

Notes

1. Most likely *Sgt. Fury and His Howling Commandoes* #13.

2. On Nick Fury, originally a nineteen sixties Marvel comic about a gung-ho group of U.S. commandoes fighting behind enemy lines during world War II, comic book writer Stan

Lee moved the character twenty years into the present and recreated him as a master spy, inspired by the *Man from UNCLE* television series. Apparently after much success in World War II, Fury had moved into espionage, along with several of the other Howling Commandoes and had lost his left eye in a battle that was initially not specified. According to Stan Lee, the genesis of the character was based on the popularity of spy movies and television shows during the sixties, with the intention that "we were going to out-Bond-Bond…and out UNCLE-UNCLE!" (Goulart 270). While this Stan Lee quote is filled with the usual "Stan talk" of the nineteen sixties, it does illustrate a valid point about what the comic was trying to achieve in depicting Fury as a master spy, not a man with a disability.

British Vampire, "American Disease"

William the Bloody as Victorian Neurasthenic

J. Bowers

"Some of your hurts you have cured,
And the sharpest you still have survived,
But what torments of grief you endured.
From the evil which never arrived."
—Ralph Waldo Emerson, *May Day and Other Pieces*

"William the Bloody awful poet,
skipping down the lane … good boy,
bad boy, all the sodding same.
You like it? Wrote that one myself."
—Spike, "Beneath You" Original Script (*Buffy* 7.02)[1]

Beginning with his first on-screen swagger in "School Hard" (2.03), fan-favorite Spike was presented to Buffy viewers as a 1970s punk, even though his early admission that he killed a Slayer during the Boxer Rebellion (1898–1901) reveals that he is much older than his appearance might suggest. We do not learn much more about the character's backstory until Season Five's "Fool for Love" (5.07), in which flashbacks to Spike's Victorian "childhood" clue the audience in on something that Buffy and the rest of the Scooby Gang never discover: long before he was "Spike," he was "William," a nebbish, sexually-inert Victorian gentleman who happily doted on his invalid mother until the predatory, hyper-sexualized Drusilla transformed him into a vampire in 1880.

Considerable critical attention has been paid to William's self-conscious construction of "Spike" as a counterbalance for his less-than-macho Victorian past, as well as the highly gendered nature of the character's evolution from effeminate human dandy into self-consciously hyper-masculine vampire. As Rhonda Wilcox argues, "the whole Spike persona seems a highly masculinized compensation for the relatively feminized poet William," right down to the phallic nickname he selects for himself ("Every Night" par. 5). While this is certainly true from a Freudian perspective, reading William/Spike through a *pre*-Freudian lens, as appropriate given the timing of William's transformation into Spike, yields a new take on the character.

Christine Lloyd, a.k.a. "Shadowkat's" self-published essay "Spike and Willow: Unleashing the Monster to Hide the Geek," first appeared on her personal website in 2002. In this piece, Lloyd briefly mentions the possibility that Spike's pre-vampire human persona, William (the Bloody Awful Poet), is a prime example of "a certain recognizable historical character type from the late 19th century. The neurasthenic male." Indeed, the main thrust of Lloyd's argument—that both Willow and Spike developed aggressive personalities to hide their bookish pasts—is valid. However, her casual reference linking a long-obsolete nineteenth-century mental health diagnosis to a twentieth-century television character is flawed, and how viewers understand William's psyche deserves further investigation. The discourse of neurasthenia, the most common mental health diagnosis of the late nineteenth century, offers a compelling view of William's metamorphosis into Spike, and, to some extent *back again*, as a narrative of illness and recovery.

A diagnosis of "neurasthenia" covered a baffling array of mental disorders in the late nineteenth and early twentieth centuries. The term "was used to characterize practically every nonspecific emotional disorder short of outright insanity, from simple stress to severe neuroses" (Gosling 9). But despite its omnipresence at the turn of the century, "neurasthenia" rapidly fell out of fashion following World War I. Case studies of the disease have been out of print since the 1920s, coinciding with the rise of Freudian psychoanalysis, and neurasthenia is no longer included in the American Psychiatric Association's *Diagnostic and Statistical Manual of Mental Disorders* (Lutz 23). However, in 1880, the year in which Drusilla sired William, neurasthenia was still a buzzword in the London medical community, and the disease's "popularity" had lasting side effects on popular culture. The neurasthenic male—bespectacled, socially and physically impotent with the opposite sex, and preoccupied by intellectual "brain-work"—was a common trope in nineteenth-century literature, and it remained a stock character in portrayals of the nineteenth century throughout the twentieth.[2] This enduring stereotype almost certainly influenced the writers of *Buffy* while they were inventing Spike's Victorian past—if not directly, then subconsciously, as the late nineteenth-century discourse surrounding neurasthenia seems to be at the root of the modern "geek" or "nerd" stock character frequently seen in television and film. Just as classical Greek drama and sixteenth-century Italian *commedia dell'arte* relied on basic "types" to instantly familiarize audiences with characters on stage, serial television has always referenced visual cues and personality traits originally ascribed to Victorian neurasthenics when portraying "geeky" characters, perhaps trusting that viewers' collective cultural memory will make the connection. Bad vision requiring thick glasses, stammering speech, ineptitude with the opposite sex, intense interest in study and introspection—all traits originally used to diagnose neurasthenia in the nineteenth century—are familiar visual cues used to distinguish "nerds" on sitcoms, cartoons, and serial dramedies like *Buffy*.[3]

At this point, a certain *caveat lector* is necessary—I am about to undertake the dubious task of diagnosing a fictional character with an imaginary disease. To do so, I have taken a cultural-historical approach, poring over a Giles-ian assortment of crumbling, leather-bound nineteenth-century American and British medical treatises, then reading them alongside James Marsters' portrayal of William/Spike in *Buffy the Vampire Slayer*. I have relied primarily on the episodes "Fool for Love" and "Lies My Parents Told Me" (7.17) for insight into the patient's mental state immediately prior to his transformation into a vampire—a transformation that I read as a fortuitous "cure" for his neurasthenia.

The Diagnosis

If William the Bloody had gone to his family doctor in 1880 complaining of social phobia, impotence, stammering, a lack of success with his poetry, and general feelings of alienation, he may have been upset to learn that he suffered from neurasthenia, but he certainly would not have been surprised. Neurasthenia, or "nerve weakness," was a common diagnosis during the last few decades of the nineteenth century, a period marked by rapid urbanization, commodification, and industrialization on both sides of the Atlantic. First described in 1869 by George Miller Beard, a neurologist from Connecticut, neurasthenia was also colloquially known as "the American disease," or "Americanitis," due to its supposed prevalence in the United States, the nation believed to be hurtling most rapidly toward modernity—but Londoners, like William, were not immune. Indeed, the spread of neurasthenia to Europe, argued Beard, was evidence that humanity, as a whole, was hurtling too fast into the post-industrial age ("A Practical Treatise" vii).

Attacks of neurasthenia were especially concentrated in urban areas, where constant exposure to such nerve-wracking modern inventions as the telegraph, the railroad, and the popular press was unavoidable. Bright, bold advertisements assaulted the eyes, painted and pasted on the walls of buildings. Manufactured goods were spectacularly displayed in shop windows, providing a dizzying array of consumer choices. Cheap, plentiful amusements, such as "music halls, cinemas, and short-story magazines" coerced careless urbanites to crave "a change of interest every few minutes," as well as the physical stimulation of the nerves that these new pastimes were believed to provide (Briggs 29). Neurologists argued that all of these modern conveniences and entertainments produced in most men an "inability [...] to apply themselves steadfastly to any one set of ideas" (29). Attention spans were shortening at an alarming rate, preventing the sustained attention that seemed necessary to succeed in business and social interactions. Nostalgia for the simpler, pre-industrial lifestyle of the eighteenth century was widespread, even in medical textbooks. "In bygone days the world was a peaceful place in which our forefathers were denied the chance of combining exercise with amusement dodging murderous taxis; knew not the blessings of 'Bile Beans,' nor the biliousness they blessed either; they did not fall victims to 'advert-diseases,'" wrote neurologist Isaac G. Briggs in 1892, arguing that "painful nerve wounds" were the inevitable, unavoidable result of city life (27).

The prevalence of neurasthenia in the late-nineteenth century illustrates the widespread Victorian belief that the unnaturally stimulating environment of the modern city forcibly attacked the human body and mind. In his influential 1903 essay on the urban milieu, "The Metropolis and Mental Life," theorist and social critic Georg Simmel mourned the "blasé attitude" that seemingly resulted from "rapidly changing and closely compressed contrasting stimulations of the nerves" (54). Turn-of-the-century city dwellers, Simmel argued, experienced heretofore unprecedented stimuli, thanks to their rapid movement between private and public spheres, between the cluttered Victorian parlor and the "threatening currents and discrepancies of his external environment" (52).

On *Buffy*, William's status as a product of this late nineteenth-century urban landscape is emphasized by the set design, costuming, and lighting selected for his flashbacks. Unlike the more open, occasionally even rural environments of the Liam and Angelus-centric flashbacks that appear throughout *Buffy* and *Angel*, William's Victorian world is claustrophobic and insistently urban. Shadows and low-key lighting dominate the Spike-centric flashbacks in "Fool for Love," "Lies My Parents Told Me," and "Destiny" (*Angel* 5.08), long before William is transformed into a vampire, suggesting that the polluted streets of London are just outside. The cluttered *mise-en-scène* of his mother's apartment reminds us that nineteenth-century London provides ready access to manufactured goods, transportation, and a complex social life—a system that the habitually nervous, emotionally immature William cannot access.

The excess of exterior stimuli experienced in a turn-of-the-century metropolis like London was said to be particularly damaging to members of the upper class, a belief that transformed neurasthenia into a fashionable diagnosis that, like consumption, spoke to a rarefied sensitivity of character.[4] Using a flawed, early application of Darwin's theory of evolution, neurologists like Briggs and Beard argued that upper-class men would naturally be those who were most afflicted, as generations of engaging in mentally taxing "brain-work," such as writing, finance, law, and politics would have given the upper class more sensitive nerves than their coarse, working-class counterparts. This "scientific" association with society's elite made neurasthenia a fashionable diagnosis. A British medical pamphlet dated 1894 defines the disorder as "a disease which is identified with civilization, prevailing, in fact, wherever the struggle for existence is intense and the rivalry of fashion, luxury, and follies exists ... widely prevalent among the upper and affluent classes, and among those who think too much as well as among those who think too little" (Gorton 2). There was an "epidemic of neurasthenia among cultural producers" at the turn of the century (Lutz 19). Many artists and writers (the occupation to which William aspired) were diagnosed with neurasthenia as an explanation for their introspective, sensitive temperaments.

This special sensitivity was, physicians argued, a double-edged sword—it allowed their upper-class patients to enjoy rarefied sensual pleasures inaccessible to the poor, such as fine art and literature, but it also rendered them more susceptible to severe nervous shock. Lacking reliable knowledge about the relationship between mind and body, physicians dabbling in the new specialty of neurology blamed neurasthenia for a host of complaints registered by their wealthy patients. Judging by the case studies printed in period medical texts, before Freud and the advent of modern psychology, the conditions now diagnosed as stress, depression, anxiety, sexual addiction, hypochondria, social phobia, agoraphobia, borderline personality disorder, erectile dysfunction, obsessive compulsive disorder, and post-traumatic stress disorder, among others, were all frequently viewed as signs of an overtaxed or depleted nervous system, instead of mental illnesses with specific symptoms, requiring specific courses of treatment and therapy. Masturbation also came under fire, as it was thought to deplete one's supply of "nervous energy," a commodity both mysterious and finite.

Because it was often viewed as the male variant of the historically-feminine disorder hysteria, neurasthenia was thought to feminize afflicted young men, rendering them more sensitive and emotional than their mentally healthy peers (Showalter 294). Mitchell, resorting to the typically chauvinistic rhetoric of the day, wrote that he had often "seen soldiers who had ridden boldly with Sheridan or fought gallantly with Grant become, under the influence of painful nerve-wounds, as irritable and hysterically emotional as the veriest girl" ("Fat and Blood" 39). Thus, a diagnosis of neurasthenia was, in a social sense, a form of castration. It meant "a rejection of fundamental manly virtues—achievement, ambition, dominance, independence" in favor of traits that were viewed as innately feminine, including "vulnerability, dependence, passivity, and invalidism" (Rotundo 191).

Neurasthenia was also, in some cases, a socially acceptable way for a man to excuse himself from the responsibilities of career and family. As Elaine Showalter notes in "Hysteria, Feminism, and Gender," "for some male intellectuals, the neurasthenia diagnosis relieved anxiety about lapses from conventional masculine sexuality by classifying them under the manly heading of overwork" (296). In addition to feminizing male sufferers, a diagnosis of neurasthenia could represent a return to the comforting irresponsibility of childhood and infancy. When a neurasthenic man returned to the family home to rest and be nursed back to health (or, in William's case, never left), he was unconsciously "repeating the boyhood experience of nurture and dependence in a place sheltered from the world" (Rotundo 192).

Unsurprisingly, given neurasthenia's alleged power to feminize and infantilize robust young men, sufferers received gender-specific treatment. Women who were allegedly debilitated by "nerve weakness," including figures such as Edith Wharton and Charlotte Perkins Gilman, were urged to take "rest cures" like that described in Gilman's 1892 short story "The Yellow Wallpaper," cutting themselves off from family and social duties, solid food, and other potentially anxiety-producing stimuli, essentially infantilizing themselves for months at a time (Lutz 221). By contrast, male neurasthenics—a demographic that allegedly included Theodore Roosevelt, Marcel Proust, Charles Darwin, Henry James, and William Dean Howells—were encouraged to engage in travel, hunting, fishing, horseback riding, boxing, and other outdoor activities thought to provide gentle stimulation to frayed nerves, or a healthy outlet for primitive, masculine impulses unnaturally stifled by modern urban living. As E. Anthony Rotundo has noted, cures like these allowed the neurasthenic man to re-immerse himself "in certain classic values of boy culture: play, the rejection of care and responsibility, the pursuit of pleasure" (192).

Though multitudes of symptoms were detected and recorded in case studies of real-life neurasthenics, only a few are measurable in a television vampire. Still, from viewers' first glimpse of William, a number of the symptoms of neurasthenia are immediately apparent. William's glasses highlight the "defective vision, astigmatism and other structural defects of the eyes," believed to be common physical indicators of neurasthenia (Gorton 10). In marked contrast to the self-assured physicality of Spike, William exhibits physical weakness. In "Fool for Love," he chooses to sit down while the other men at the Victorian society party stand. He leans, kneels, and rests his head in his mother's lap throughout "Lies My Parents Told Me." When offered a tray of *hors d'oeuvres*, he waves them away, suggesting that he may suffer from the digestive complaints frequently seen in neurasthenics.

Beyond the few physical symptoms either observed or conjectured, William also clearly exhibits the neurasthenic temperament described by physicians of his era. "The neurasthenic," wrote Charles L. Dana, Professor of Diseases of the Mind and Nervous System in the New York Post-Graduate Medical School in 1890, "loses interest in his work, dreads to undertake any responsibility, has morbid fears regarding his business, his sexual functions, his general health, his future, or some trivial subject" (qtd. in Gosling 81). Indeed, William's infantilized position in his family prevents him from assuming the occupational and social responsibilities typically held by a man of his age. Anxieties about his romantic prospects appear to occupy all of his mental faculties, and he seems in no hurry to advance his career—all traits commonly cited in period case studies of neurasthenic men.

Writing in 1894, David Allyn Gorton, M.D., noted that the male neurasthenic's "memory of words is impaired, as also the coordination of speech" (5), a symptom illustrated by William's famous inability to remember "another word for gleaming," and his stammering speech as he clumsily attempts to negotiate a social gathering with his high society peers in "Fool for Love." The neurasthenic's propensity to be "easily vexed and annoyed" (5) is also on display here, as William experiences sudden and acute frustration with his lack of wit, declaring himself to be "the very spirit of vexation" ("Fool for Love"). He is "easily discouraged, timid, and vacillating" (Briggs 30) in his dealings with Cecily, automatically accepting her rejection. Exhibiting "a marked lack of interest in men and things" (30), another trait frequently seen in neurasthenics, William curtly informs his male peers that he has no opinion about what amounts to a city-wide murder spree—preferring instead to loudly proclaim his interest in "creating things of beauty," in an attempt to turn the conversation back to his favorite subject: himself. This preoccupation with self is echoed in William Taylor Marrs' 1908 autobiography *Confessions of a Neurasthenic*: "Often I entertained the effeminate notion that people were talking about me, when I ought to have known that they could easily find some more interesting topic of conversation" (27).

Moreover, Isaac G. Briggs in *Epilepsy, Hysteria, and Neurasthenia* (1921) elaborated on the narcissistic temperament of the male neurasthenic, with a description that aptly applies to William the Bloody—and, for that matter, to his later persona as Spike in his dealings with Buffy. Merely substitute "Buffy" for the "observers" and "others" mentioned in this passage describing a typical neurasthenic's social interactions:

> Extremely self-conscious, he thinks himself the observed of all observers. If others are indifferent toward him, he is depressed; if interested, they have some deep motive; if grave, he has annoyed them; if gay, they are laughing at him; the truth, that they are minding their own business, never occurs to him, and if it did, the thought that other people were not interested in him, would only vex him [35].

Spike sees himself as the center of Buffy's universe—he lives in a delusional world where he believes that he is "the Big Bad" (a title he never really holds)—and claims that everything unpleasant that happens to him has somehow been orchestrated or indirectly caused by Buffy. He views her as the source of all his problems. But what *was* the root cause of *William's* habitual vexation? Most period case studies of neurasthenia blame the disorder on major life events, including bereavement, "disappointment," "loss of friends or property," "Society Life," and "humiliation," events that a modern therapist would identify as "stressors" (Briggs 27).

We know from the events of "Fool for Love" and "Lies My Parents Told Me" that William frequently experienced disappointment and humiliation, from his peers as well as would-be publishers. The fact that his father's whereabouts are never mentioned in the canon suggests bereavement as a possibility. In William's case, given the hyper-sexualization of his later vampire persona, I contend that much of the blame can be placed on another leading cause of neurasthenia in young men—sexual repression coupled with excessive "self-abuse," or masturbation. Indeed, sexual neurasthenia, the branch of the disorder that most often affected young men like William, was frequently diagnosed after observing an unhealthy tendency to turn the sex drive inward, instead of exercising it via "healthy" sexual activity with a wife. "Erections and emissions are frequent, first at night with amorous dreams, then in the day as a result of sexual thoughts; weakness and pain in the back follow," cautioned Briggs, outlining the nerve-weakening—and, therefore, potentially feminizing—effects of "self-abuse" (38).

As Rhonda V. Wilcox astutely points out, "the living William qualifies as an exemplar of repression of the Id" ("Every Night" par. 4), a psychological problem that pre–Freudian neurologists, desperate to find a physical cause for mental complaints, would have characterized as evidence that the pressures of urban life had somehow compromised the fluids in his nerves and genitalia. Most case studies of male neurasthenics recorded by Beard featured some element of sexual dysfunction, either in the form of excessive masturbation, impotence, or both. William's obvious virginity prior to being vamped and his Oedipal fascination with his ailing mother are both characteristics that can be read as evidence of the sexual repression inherent in his pre-vampire persona—a reading reinforced by the depiction of his vampire "birth" in "Fool for Love" as a sexual awakening. There is also William's genuine fear that Drusilla will "get his purse." His word choice here seems strangely anachronistic, since wallets, not purses, were in fashion for English gentlemen by the 1880s. William Shakespeare frequently used the word "purse" as a euphemism for the human scrotum, a pun that underlined the connection between money and masculine potency. According to the Oxford English Dictionary, this meaning persisted well into the late nineteenth century. The word's use as a euphemism for female genitalia appears to have been a twentieth-century development. Thus, the writers' word choice here is a double entendre, playing on both Victorian and modern sexual connotations of "purse," simultaneously feminizing William's virginity *and* revealing his fear of castration/emasculation.

William's sexual frustration would have doubtlessly been exacerbated by the social expectation (reinforced by his mother's assertion that he needs "a woman in his life") that he should continue the family line in his conspicuously-absent father's stead. The danger posed by the effete, impotent neurasthenic male to the established patriarchy seems to have been a source of considerable anxiety to the British upper and middle classes at the turn of the century, as the entailment system meant that a male heir was necessary to inherit the family's estate, lest it be lost. Novels from the period, including Henry James' *The Spoils of Poynton* and E.M. Forster's *Howards End* anxiously equate the loss of ancestral homes with the dissolution of social power and the troubling rise of a growing lower-middle class. In "Fool for Love," this anxiety is brought into clearer focus with Cecily's declaration that the neurasthenic William is "beneath" her. He may suffer from a disorder traditionally associated with the upper class, but he himself is not a member.

In addition to the social pressure she placed on her son, William's mother's chronic illness was also a potentially potent contributor to his neurasthenia. In both "Fool for Love" and "Lies My Parents Told Me," nursing his mother effectively prevented twenty-something William from pursuing a life outside the home. No mention is made of a job outside his (apparently unpublished) poetry, and William's invalid mother seems to be wholly dependent upon him for company and daily care. After her transformation into a vampire, William's mother accuses him of "slithering from her like a parasite" ("Lies My Parents Told Me"), but in reality, she had their relationship backwards—a pre–Freudian neurologist would have read William's mother as a form of psychic vampire, draining her son's nervous reserves. Writing in 1893, Silas Weir Mitchell, infamous proponent of the "rest cure," reached for rather gothic rhetoric to describe how an ailing relative could lead to neurasthenia-by-proxy: "On the parasitic relationship between the sick and the well: By slow but sure degrees the healthy life is absorbed by the sick life, in a manner more or less injurious to both, until, sometimes too late for remedy, the growth of the evil is seen by others" ("Fat and Blood" 31). Elsewhere, Mitchell elaborates on this metaphor with characteristic misogyny, denouncing the neurasthenic woman as a "… vampire, sucking slowly the blood of every healthy, helpful creature within reach of her demands" ("Wear and Tear" 30).

Notably, these examples are far from the only instances in late nineteenth and early twentieth-century medical literature where neurasthenia is equated with vampirism, anemia, or an imbalance in the circulatory system. A need for large quantities of more vital blood is a frequent theme in discussions of the disorder, as neurasthenic veins were thought to coagulate into what George Miller Beard calls a "fixed, passive congestion, through which the blood flows slowly, like the water in our Southern lagoons" ("Sexual Neurasthenia" 39). In the early twentieth century, the Italian neurologist Angelo Mosso published influential studies on neurasthenia that "proved" that fatigue physically altered the composition of the blood. By injecting the blood of fatigued laboratory animals into the veins of a resting animal, Mosso believed he had shown that the symptoms of neurasthenia could be transferred, just as the infusion of vampire blood in the Buffyverse transfers vampirism to a drained victim (Gosling 89).

Paging Dr. Dru

Though a host of bodily organs and systems were allegedly affected by neurasthenia, neurologists generally agreed that the disorder's cause—and ultimate cure—must lie in the blood that sustains the whole body. "If an adequate stream of pure blood, of blood made pure by the efficient cooperation of organs of low degree, be necessary for the life of the muscle, in order that the working capital may be rapidly renewed and the harmful products rapidly washed away, equally true, perhaps even more true, is that of the brain," warned physiologist Sir Michael Foster in 1894, speaking to an assembly of medical students at the University of Cambridge, England (qtd. in Love 541). S. Weir Mitchell's treatment recommendations for neurasthenics included isolation and the force-feeding of pureed raw meat, a substance thought to help replenish fatigued cells, and "fatten and redden" the blood. He echoed Foster's advice in his ominously-titled 1893 study *Fat and Blood: An Essay on the Treatment of Certain Forms of Neurasthenia and Hysteria*, claiming, "If I succeed in first altering the moral atmosphere which has been to the patient like the very breathing of evil, and if I can add largely to the weight, and fill the vessels with red blood, I am usually sure of giving general relief" (41).

It is, coincidentally, through the "filling of the vessels with red blood" that William the Bloody (Awful Poet) receives a temporary respite from his crippling neurasthenia. By re-presenting the über-masculine Spike to viewers in "Fool for Love" as a textbook example of a Victorian man feminized by neurasthenia, the writers of *Buffy the Vampire Slayer* seem to suggest that only the masculine, penetrative force of vampirism can cure what ails him—in an intriguing inversion of the traditional vampirism-as-disease paradigm.

When Drusilla impulsively decides to turn William into a vampire, she does more than create an undead mate for herself—she cures him of his crippling neurasthenia. While describing his death to Buffy in "Fool for Love," Spike describes becoming a vampire as "new strength coursing through me," a turn of phrase suggesting that the transformation process, like the most popular cures suggested for neurasthenia in the nineteenth century, began in the blood. Though we know little about how vampire physiology works in the Buffyverse, a few details are certain. Of course, vampires on *Buffy* and *Angel* require regular infusions of blood to sustain "life." Therefore, becoming a vampire allows human William to perpetually supply his weakened nerves with fresh blood "donated" by his non-neurasthenic victims.

We also know, from "Darla" (*Angel* 2.07), that becoming a vampire instantly cures physical maladies, such as syphilis. The change in William's physicality after his transformation is immediately noticeable. In "Lies My Parents Told Me," instead of kneeling by his mother's side, resting his head on her lap, leaning on furniture, and otherwise exhibiting signs of physical weakness as his human-self did, vampire William dominates his mother's parlor. His glasses are gone—and never seen again—suggesting that vampirism corrected his defective vision. His halting stammer disappears. Formerly retiring and shy, William now expresses a strong desire to go out dancing and visit the theater with his mother and Drusilla, rejoicing at the thought of attending (and most likely, violently disrupting) public events. It appears that his social phobia has been replaced by genuinely anti-social tendencies. And in newly-turned William's pelvis-first swagger and exaggerated, sensual mouth movements, we see the first (canonical) appearance of many of the cocksure mannerisms that James Marsters habitually employs in his portrayal of Spike.

In addition to the immediate beneficial physiological and psychological effects that vampirism had on William, his new lifestyle as a member of Angelus' globetrotting vampire family fortuitously resembles the course of treatment prescribed by turn-of-the-century authorities on neurasthenia, who were opposed to the "rest cure." In order to achieve a lasting cure, Mitchell wrote, the neurasthenic must "disentangle … from the meshes of old habits" and be removed from contact "with those who have been the willing slaves of their caprices" ("Fat and Blood" 36). In this sense, William's decision to stake his mother and leave her London flat behind for good is an important step in his "cure." In Moses Allen Starr's 1907 *Organic and Functional Nervous Diseases,* Mitchell declares:

> Mental rest is not secured by an absence of mental activity, but by directing the mind into new channels and calling into play new departments of the organism, thus incidentally leaving those previously acting and now exhausted, to recuperate. This is the secret of the success of travel, diversion, and novel employment in the treatment of neurasthenia [287].

We know from later flashbacks in *Buffy* and *Angel* that Spike traveled extensively after becoming a vampire, claiming victims (including two slayers) in a century-long rampage through Paris, Prague, China, Rome, New York City, Woodstock, and many other exotic locations—a far cry from his mother's cozy gas-lit parlor. As a vampire, William replaces his old neurasthenic mental preoccupations—his poetry, his mother, and Cecily—with new, physical obsessions. Throughout the series, Spike is portrayed as a violence addict, often using fighting as a form of therapy or self-soothing. He also exhibits an insatiable libido and a reputation as a ladies' man, charming Drusilla, Harmony, Buffy, and her mother. And his most enduring obsession—his single-minded mission to slay (and later, seduce) the Slayer—is a purely physical pursuit, far removed from the intellectual pastimes he enjoyed as a neurasthenic human. William's fascination with literature—an interest common among neurasthenics—is replaced by an addiction to television, punk rock, and video games, popular twentieth-century entertainments that seem a far cry from the Victorian drawing room.

Although vampirism was (for obvious reasons) not recommended as therapy for neurasthenics by Victorian physicians, for William, the physical and emotional benefits of being turned into a vampire seem to have served many of the same functions as medically-sanctioned treatments for neurasthenia. But Spike's "cure" is, as we will see, only a temporary fix for his symptoms, which resurface at various points throughout Seasons Four, Five, Six, and most tellingly because of his returned soul, Seven (and again in Season Five of *Angel*). As we learned from Darla in "The Prodigal" (*Angel* 1.15), when it comes to vampires, "what we were informs all that we have become." Accordingly, there are moments in the series where Spike experiences what might be read as a mild attack of neurasthenic symptoms: notably, during his convalescence in a wheelchair in Season Two; in "Lovers Walk" (3.08), because Drusilla has dumped him; and after the installation of his Initiative chip in Season Four. In all of these instances, Spike is plunged into extreme depression as a result of having one of his addictions (Dru, violence) unceremoniously taken away from him, and he responds by awkwardly attempting to interact with the Scooby Gang.

It could be argued that Spike seeks out the Scoobies only because his personal goals mesh fortuitously with theirs, especially early on. He ostensibly sides with Buffy against Angelus in Season Two to win back Dru and so the world and its sensual pleasures will continue to exist. In "Lovers Walk," the Scoobies would like Spike to reunite with Drusilla so that he will leave Sunnydale; in Season Four, the Scoobies' status as the town's premiere demon-magnets makes them obvious companions for a violence-addicted vampire who can now only fight demons. Yet beyond these pragmatic excuses for bringing Spike into the Scooby fold, his misguided desire for human contact—so strong that it overrides his vampiric instinct to hunt and kill humans—can be read as an echo of William the neurasthenic poet's desperate need to connect with others, despite his social ineptitude.

Spike also experiences a partial resurgence of his neurasthenic symptoms whenever his masculinity is repressed or threatened. Angelus' (implied) seduction of Drusilla in Season Two, and her decision to leave Spike for a chaos demon shortly thereafter function as a direct attack on his sexuality, as the woman who (literally and figuratively) took his virginity has finally forsaken him. In Season Four, Spike's chip prevents him from indulging in the violence that, for him, has been a physical outlet for anxiety on a par with the boxing and outdoor sports that physicians recommended to male neurasthenics at the turn of the century. After his chip is installed, Buffy and other characters—including Spike himself—begin describing him with impotence rhetoric or as "neutered," a term that directly attacks his masculinity, just as the symbolic castration of neurasthenia feminized him while he was alive. Whenever Spike is stripped of the coping mechanisms that have been central to his recovery from neurasthenia (sex, violence, travel), he reverts to his old neurasthenic ways.

His behavior in these situations is a strange and terrifying amalgam of William's social ineptitude and Spike's evil impulsiveness. Echoing William, Spike shares his innermost emotions with the Scooby Gang, a social group that, like his Victorian peers, does not acknowledge his hurt feelings, or even his capacity to *have* his feelings hurt—a parallel reinforced when Buffy echoes Cecily's cruel words, "You're beneath me" to Spike ("Fool for Love"). He also instinctively seeks out maternal figures, like Buffy, Joyce, and Willow—a habit suggesting that his Oedipal fascination with his mother is still partially intact. When depressed, he cries, babbles nonsensically to himself, and drinks heavily, visibly frustrated that his (in his mind) invincible Spike persona is being forced to experience the failure and rejection that plagued William daily. It seems no coincidence that after the installation of his chip, the series' most obvious euphemism for impotence, Spike is outed as a daytime TV fanatic, begging to watch *Passions* while in captivity at Giles' apartment and talking to the television while *Dawson's Creek* is on. Spike's obsession with soap operas, a modern iteration of the sentimental serial literature popular among Victorian women, is played to comedic effect whenever it is brought up, for obvious reasons. However, in Season Five's "Checkpoint," after the reveal of William the poet in "Fool for Love," viewers can read Spike's willingness to watch *Passions* with Joyce as an implicit link to his relationship with his late mother. In fact, traces of Spike's neurasthenic human persona are always evident when he is around Buffy's mom. She comes to view him as a sensitive, harmless young man who feels right at home discussing the art world ("Crush" 5.14), or his dismal love life ("Lovers Walk"), and he eulogizes her as a "decent" lady who "always had a cuppa" for him ("Forever" 5.17), obviously a substitute for his long lost "mum."

However, these regressions to his neurasthenic ways are mild in comparison to the attack that grips Spike at the beginning of Season Seven, following the restoration of his human soul. During Spike's tenure as a squatter in the Sunnydale High School basement, visual cues in his costuming and makeup invite viewers to associate this new incarnation of Spike with his Victorian past. His hair is long and disheveled, as it was when he was William, and he has not bleached or cut it in quite some time. His usual armor of coat, t-shirt, and combat boots has been replaced by random, drab clothing. He stammers uncharacteristic dialogue that obviously refers to his earlier life as a nineteenth-century neurasthenic, lamenting that he "dropped (his) board in the water and the chalk all ran," wondering about "another word for glowing," and calling for his "mum" in "Lessons" (7.01). At this point in the series, even his affected North London working class accent gives way to the mannered diction that William used. It is as though the return of Spike's soul temporarily "resets" him to his human self, forcing him to spend the first part of the seventh season reintegrating his two personas. "It's just the three of us," he mutters in "Lessons," perhaps referencing his human self, his vampire self, and the First Evil. The process naturally brings his neurasthenic symptoms to the surface, particularly in the episode "Beneath You" (7.02), as Spike/William attempts to reenter Buffy's life. This episode's title serves as an intentional, self-referential double entendre, referencing both the First's imminent attack on Sunnydale and eerie warning "From Beneath You, It Devours" *and* the Buffy/Cecily parallel established via similar words during the third act of "Fool for Love."

Alone in the basement, Spike cringes, slouches, and mutters to himself about "manners, breeding, and lack of etiquette," all concerns that point toward the anxiety about socializing with the upper class that he experienced as a neurasthenic human. His fractured speech patterns match those that Briggs noted in the neurasthenic male, as "his ideas are restive, continuous thought is impossible, and when talking he has to be 'brought back to the point' many times. Memory and attention flag, and he listens to a long conversation … without grasping its import" (29). But now, more than a century after his rejection by his Victorian peers, the "upper class" that William seeks to join is the Scooby Gang. His behavior at this point is William performing "Spike." Longing to show Buffy that he has changed, he bleaches and cuts his hair before donning his "costume"—an uncharacteristically bright blue shirt. Then he heads to her house for a scene that parallels his unsuccessful attempt to negotiate upper-class society in "Fool for Love."

Just as William tried to get Cecily alone at the party so that he could confess his feelings, Spike/William is not content until he convinces Buffy to speak to him in private, away from her friends. She rejects him flatly, telling him that everything about him is "wrong." Still reeling from Spike's attempted rape in "Seeing Red" (6.19), Buffy understandably does not welcome him back immediately into her social circle, but he accompanies her on patrol anyway, struggling to make conversation and find the right words to apologize, exhibiting the lack of control over language noted in his neurasthenic human persona. Spike/William repeatedly insists that he has "changed" and helpfully examines a crime scene. In this portion of the episode, he is leaning toward his William persona, self-consciously performing what his souled-self thinks a "hero" should be.

At the Bronze, when Anyanka recognizes the human soul within Spike, he responds by reverting to the villainous persona we remember from his first appearance in "School Hard." He sexually harasses Buffy, asking her if she is ready for "another round in the balcony," one of the many places where the two of them have had sex—a taunt that emphasizes the hyperactive sexuality of the Spike persona. The swaggering, sneering Spike we see here is almost a caricature of his former self, complete with a punk rock soundtrack. This facet of his persona remains at the forefront until, having accidentally impaled an unfortunate human victim on a piece of rebar, Spike/William's neurasthenic symptoms resurface with a vengeance. "Too much, too much, too much, too much," he babbles, clutching at his head and chiding himself for making the "wrong maneuver." His attempt to socialize with Buffy by helping her fight evil has backfired, causing her to stare at him with disgust—just like his long-dead Victorian peers.

In the infamous church confession that ends the episode, Spike exhibits even stronger neurasthenic symptoms. He rejects his costume, lamenting his inability to "hide" behind his vampiric persona. His expenditure of nervous energy has weakened him yet again. He leans on the church's architecture and collapses on the floor instead of supporting himself. He stammers and repeats words, unable to articulate. And most tellingly, he makes an overt reference to masturbation, asking Buffy, "Did you make me weak, thinking of you, holding myself, and spilling useless buckets of salt over your [pause] ending?"

Prognosis

The connection between the neurasthenic William and the Spike/William hybrid we see in "Beneath You" is writ even larger in the episode's shooting script, which reveals that a few references to Spike's past as William were excised during filming. In the original version of Spike's church confession to Buffy, he refers to himself directly as "William the Bloody awful poet," literally asking viewers to recall the neurasthenic coward seen in "Fool for Love," and tries to integrate his human self with this new, ensouled version of Spike ("'Beneath You' Church Scene"). Interestingly, the choice of metaphor that writer Douglas Petrie initially made for this scene compared Spike's soul to a "rusty switchboard," emitting "sharp shocks" ("'Beneath You' Church Scene"), language that suggestively evokes electroshock therapy, which would be first introduced in 1938. Petrie, who also wrote "Fool for Love," was clearly thinking of William as he conceived of Spike's post-soul persona, a fact that seems to verify the power that the stereotype of the neurasthenic Victorian man still holds in popular culture.

While viewers have no reason to believe that Petrie and the other writers responsible were aware that they were creating a textbook illustration of Victorian neurasthenic manhood when they created Spike's backstory, the fact that the symptoms of neurasthenia can be identified in a postmodern television vampire speaks volumes about the hold that the neurasthenic archetype still has on our collective cultural memory. Though neurasthenia now only persists as a pseudoscientific curiosity, on the same level as phrenology and physiognomy, the neurasthenic man is, along with the cowboy, one of the most enduring male archetypes of the 1800s, so recognizable as a stock character type of that era that many of us giggled with recognition when we first saw William the Bloody (Awful Poet).

Notes

1. See "'Beneath You' Church Scene—Original vs. Produced Version."
2. See Mr. Woodhouse in Jane Austen's *Emma* (1815), William Taylor Marrs' *Confessions of a Neurasthenic* (1908), O. Henry's *Let Me Feel Your Pulse, Or Adventures in Neurasthenia*

(1910), Tibby Schlegel in E.M. Forster's *Howards End* (1910), Marcel Proust's *In Search of Lost Time* (1913–1927).

3. See Dobie Gillis on *The Many Loves of Dobie Gillis* (1959–1963), Paul Pfeiffer on *The Wonder Years* (1998–1993), Steve Urkel on *Family Matters* (1989–1998), Brian Krakow on *My So-Called Life* (1994–1995), Ross Geller on *Friends* (1994–2004), Leonard Hofstadter and Sheldon Cooper on *The Big Bang Theory* (2007–2019), and naturally, *Angel*'s (1999–2004) Wesley Wyndam-Price (first introduced on *Buffy*) and Fred Burkle, among many others.

4. It is worth noting here that William's mother appears to be a victim of "consumption," a.k.a. tuberculosis, coughing blood into her handkerchief. Though tuberculosis was widespread among the lower classes during the nineteenth century, it was frequently viewed as an upper-class disease due to its association with the fragile genius of writers, musicians, and visual artists. William may have viewed his mother's illness as a mark of distinction—biological proof that he was destined for literary fame.

Trauma, Technology, and the Affective Body in *Firefly* and *Dollhouse*

EMILY JAMES HANSEN *and* KATHERYN WRIGHT

"Pain reveals who we really are."
—Adelle DeWitt in "Stop-Loss" (*Dollhouse* 2.09)

The ways we can connect with our world and each other is increasing exponentially and, while technology has the potential to foster an exchange of ideas and information, it also has the power to disrupt and destroy lives. Social networking, for example, can encourage deep connections between individuals, but there comes a price with that openness that is allowed through technology. In the television series *Firefly* (including its feature film sequel *Serenity*[1]) and *Dollhouse*, technology enables River and Echo, respectively, to experience the feeling of complete openness of what we call the affective body, though this openness results from disabling trauma. Using Baruch Spinoza's definition of "affect" in his seventeenth-century philosophical treatise *Ethics* as a starting point to examine what it means to be made to feel, we navigate through the experience of being an affective body in *Dollhouse* and *Firefly*, examining how trauma and technology shape how we connect with others, how connection has the power to restore Echo's and River's humanity and, through them, illustrate how technology can also re-connect viewers to those around them.

Affect and the Whedonverse

Although *affect* may seem like a cumbersome concept, think of it as a kind of gut feeling people have that they can't really explain, but it nonetheless exists. Gut feelings are important; they help make us who we are as individuals. Spinoza asserts, "He who conceives, that he affects others with pleasure or pain, will, by that very fact, himself be affected with pleasure or pain" (Part III, Proposition 30). Working with Spinoza's definition of affect, Gilles Deleuze discovers a concept that signifies thought without representation (1). Affect is a felt intensity that extends beyond the individual body. To affect others, to be affected by others—this description indicates a reciprocal connection between two or more human bodies, or more provocatively, between the body and environment. Teresa Brennan in *The Transmission of Affect* explains, "The transmission of affect means, that we are not self-contained in terms of our energies. There is no secure distinction between the 'individual' and the 'environment'" (6). The "individual" represents a relational process with a broader community environment composed of both human and non-human (especially in the Whedonverses!) agents.

It is here, in the capacity of affect to facilitate emotional connections with each other, where our use of the concept extends previous scholarship that focuses on the significance of chosen families in the Whedonverses. As a nontraditional family structure, chosen families bond through common interests and commitments between each member (see Battis, *Blood Relations*). The Scooby Gang in *Buffy the Vampire Slayer* is a chosen family that forms through shared experiences like fighting vampires, thwarting apocalypses, and surviving Sunnydale High. The chosen family offers protection for its members while biological relations (like Joyce, Dawn, and Connor) are more often than not liabilities—an ironic twist in a narrative world filled with blood-sucking vampires. A chosen family is the group of people to whom you're closest; they know when you're in pain, or they are the people you care about enough to lie to. After the Scoobies resurrect Buffy in Season Six, the series arc involves a struggle between her chosen family and Buffy coming to terms with living, even though she wants to protect her friends from the knowledge that when they resurrected her they actually expelled her from heaven.

There is a similar chosen family in *Firefly,* and like the Scoobies, Mal and his crew connect through a shared experience. As Battis explains in "Captain Tightpants: *Firefly* and the Science Fiction Canon," Mal, Zoë, Wash, Inara, Kaylee, Jayne, Book, Simon, and River initially come together because they're all running away from something: war, poverty, or the Alliance; but the family they forge becomes "more powerful and more enduring than their biological families at home" (2). It's hard to view Adelle, Echo, Ballard, Sierra, Victor, Topher, and company as a chosen family in *Dollhouse* until we see the group living with each other at the farm and fighting together against the Rossum Corporation in "Epitaph Two: Return" (2.13).

These families grow to trust and protect each other as they fight together to save the world.

When *affect* enters into this conversation about the chosen family, however, it offers another way to think about how characters in these 'verses make emotional connections with each other beyond shared experiences. During Mal's flashback in "Out of Gas" (1.08) where he and Zoë meet Wash for the first time, Zoë's intuition about her future husband gets the best of her. She tells Mal, "Something about him bothers me." Even though this scene plays as a joke for viewers who know the couple ends up together, it offers a brief example of two characters affectively connecting without context. Her gut feeling she has with him ("he bothers me") progresses into a deep relationship. This brief moment in *Firefly* underscores a tension between the family chosen through shared experience and the myriad of other ways humans connect with each other, including affectively. What happens to the individual when the emotional intimacy of a chosen family is extended to hundreds, thousands, millions of people, or when the knowledge of shared experiences becomes secondary to the affective relations people have with each other?

Both individual storylines and larger narrative arcs within the Whedonverses explore the human costs of connection without context. The *Buffy the Vampire Slayer* episode "Grave" (6.22) begins with Giles returning to Sunnydale with borrowed power from a coven in order to help Willow, to stop her free fall down the spiraling path of murderous revenge and destruction. As she tortures Giles, Willow drains that energy from him—"a little pick-me-up"—and when she does, she falls back in a dizzying head rush. "Wow. It's incredible.... It's like I'm connected to everything. I can feel, it feels like, I can feel. Everyone. Oh. Oh my god. Oh my, all the emotion. I, the pain. No, it's too much. It's just too much." The ability to feel everyone simultaneously, to connect with everyone, is dangerous, and, of course, this is illustrated by Willow's attempt to destroy the world in response to the affectively shared pain. The "yellow crayon" exchange with Xander reaffirms the power of the chosen family over the collective expression of pain.

Buffy has her own experience of psychic openness in "Earshot" (3.18) when she comes in contact with demon blood and can hear the thoughts of her classmates. The primary difference between Willow at the end of Season Six and Buffy in this episode is that, while Willow feels pain, Buffy hears thoughts. Reading the conscious thoughts of others doesn't necessarily necessitate affective connection. Buffy's experience is debilitating, but it isn't disabling. However, Giles' explanation that if Buffy's psychic abilities are not removed, she will lose her sanity suggests her experience would have reached a similar level to Willow's given time. This does not necessarily mean she would have also tried to end the world to stop her pain as Willow does; regardless, the two examples offer an interesting parallel on this topic

Firefly and *Serenity* introduce a new twist to the affective experience of connection without context. The Alliance engineers River's body into what can only be described as an affective war machine, where River's ability to "read" people directly ties into her psychosis. River attempts to explain her condition in the series finale "Objects in Space" (1.14): "She [River] understands, but she doesn't comprehend ... it's getting very, very crowded." River is engineered into what we call an *affective body*, a body that is made to feel. She cannot help but to connect with others without context. River must process a thousand gut feelings felt by others, but lived through her individuated body. The opposite of River's affective body is Echo's seemingly unaffected one in *Dollhouse*. Caroline is, quite literally, disconnected from everyone when the Rossum Corporation transforms her into Echo. As a counterexample to River's psychosis, Echo is numb. As her name suggests, she is an echo of others. The Alliance in *Firefly* and the Rossum Corporation in *Dollhouse* manipulated the physical bodies of both River and Echo to maintain their power, to the detriment of both women (and ultimately, these larger entities themselves). The next section focuses on how River and Echo have been transformed through trauma, exploring the ethical consequences of their bodily transformations.

Traumatizing the Body Through Technology

While all bodies have the capacity to affect and be affected, the affective body represents complete openness—the ability, as Echo from *Dollhouse* explains, to "feel them all" without any previous contact. When the Alliance hacks into River's brain, they transform her into an affective body. *Serenity* explains how River's psychosis is rooted in her capacity to feel the collective pain of the Reavers. She cannot control her empathetic connection with the Reavers; their agony lives on through River's body. On the other side of the equation is Echo who, as Caroline, is basically anesthetized. She is made numb by the Rossum Corporation who, as the audience discovers in the series finale, hijacks Caroline's body (transforming her into Echo) because of its biological giftedness. Ironically, Echo's "awakening" results from her special physiological ability to "feel" all of the imprints inside her. She transforms into an affective body, which gives her the ability to manipulate the dystopian world she finds herself in and to take down the organization that stole Caroline's humanity. The comfort of the chosen family is lost in the production of the affective individual body, and the strength of that familial connection—an essential feature of the Whedonverses—is lost in the production of the unaffected self. For both characters, the affective body is created through a series of traumatic events they must overcome in order to be an impactful member of their chosen family. Both River and Echo are transformed into affective bodies through bodily trauma. In so doing, these two characters push the body's capacity to affect and be affected to its breaking point, which results in behavior that is destructive and debilitating for those around them.[2]

There are various forms of trauma, ranging from individual trauma to collective, societal trauma (one such example is the emotional reaction and collective trauma Americans felt on September 11, 2001). Each traumatic experience, both individually and collectively, yields similar symptoms, though each individual may handle them differently. Trauma can be physical or psychological and these two types can occur simultaneously or in concert with one another. Neurologist Robert Scaer writes in *The Trauma Spectrum: Hidden Wounds and Human Resiliency* that "trauma itself exists on a continuum and ... many events that ordinarily would not be considered life-threatening can be traumatic depending on their meaning within the context of the victim's prior life experiences" (205). He sees a brain/mind/body continuum, in which all three connect, react, and respond to one another. As Gina Ross notes in her book *Beyond the Trauma Vortex*, "[w]hen people are traumatized, their internal system remains aroused and this arousal sends signals of threat. Always on edge, unable to relax, they are constantly aware of a pervading sense of danger and suspicious of everything and everyone. Failing to grasp the source and reason for their discomfort, their fear escalates. This, in turn, amplifies a need to identify the source of the threat, which they project outside of themselves" (65). Trauma, therefore, can manifest itself in physical, emotional, and psychological ways.

River's Trauma

Firefly's River was sent to an Alliance academy when she was a teenager where the Alliance experimented on and traumatized her. In "The Train Job" (1.02), River dreams she is still strapped to a chair, while the Alliance sticks needles into her brain. She wakes, screaming. In the next episode her brother, Simon, tells Inara that River "still won't talk about what it was that they did to her at the academy" ("Bushwacked," 1.03). River is afraid to, or unable to, speak about her trauma. When she does talk about it, she speaks in a jumble of nonsensical phrases. Eventually, we learn that River is unique. Because of her affective body, she is able to hear and feel things that no one else can. She can sense everything. After Simon sneaks her into a hospital in "Ariel" (1.09), a brain scan reveals that the Alliance has stripped her amygdala, the part of the brain that regulates emotional responses. As Simon explains to Jayne, she can feel everything and it is against her will. Simon tells Jayne that the Alliance doctors "opened up her skull. That's a scalpel scar. They opened up her skull and they cut into her brain.... They stripped her amygdala.... It's like a filter in your brain that keeps your feelings in check. She feels everything. She can't not." This physical tampering with her brain leaves River unable to control her emotions, and she often has physical and emotional outbursts: in "Ariel," she picks up a knife in the kitchen, calmly walks over to Jayne, and slices his chest open. Her only explanation: "He looks better in red." To the crew, this is a violent, unexplainable act. With the virtue of hindsight, audiences realize after the episode that River was reacting to Jayne's intention to betray her and Simon to the Alliance. Her reaction seems inappropriate, but it ultimately parallels Mal's equally violent end-of-episode threat to blow Jayne into space should he betray any of the crew again.

The "R. Tam, Session 416" in the Bonus Features of the *Serenity* Collector's edition DVD offers glimpses into the extent of River's trauma. The five clips are shown out of order but they reveal the gradual trauma River experiences as she becomes more and more agitated. She is no longer lively or coherent, and she stabs the counselor interviewing her. The emotions that River feels are a direct result of being physically and emotionally traumatized. She is unable to reciprocate the pain and fear she feels, and the Alliance, for its part, does not feel her pain. The more they try to bend her will to theirs, the more withdrawn and traumatized she appears, culminating in her lashing out at both an Alliance doctor (in "R. Tam, Session 416") and Jayne (in "Ariel" 1.09). Ironically, River's traumatic experience leaves her unable to connect emotionally to the others onboard Serenity in traditional ways. The film goes even further in clarifying the nature of her affective body. When she warns the crew that the Reavers are coming in the opening sequence, River experiences quick flashes to corpses and Reavers. As the crew begins to explore the formerly lost planet of Miranda, River begins to melt down. "They're everywhere. They're all inside me. They're saying nothing. Please get out." A dolly shot circles around River, revealing that she is surrounded by Miranda's dead; she is connecting to that emptiness. Her psychosis derives from her affective connection to the Reavers who are also victims of the Alliance's quest to control bodies through technology.

Echo's Trauma

Dollhouse contains a bevy of social commentary along with the trauma. What happens to the "Dolls" or "Actives" is very much like human trafficking and prostitution—and other consent victimizations. The Rossum Corporation loans out Echo, and Boyd, her handler, acts as her pimp. Every successful engagement, or satisfied client, results in payment for Boyd (both as Boyd the employee and as the executive behind Rossum). He keeps her "safe" so he can continue to victimize and prostitute her. Echo, for her part, has fallen into a sort of unconscious Stockholm syndrome because of her devotion to her handler, a devotion that is manufactured when she becomes an affective body. In "Getting Closer" (2.11), we realize who Boyd really is, essentially the "Man" who has affected Echo/Caroline, and who, under the guise of being her handler and protector, ensures that the body remains affective. In "The Hollow Men" (2.12), Boyd promises he will protect Echo, but only so that he can harvest her spinal fluid. He protects the affective body, not the person. He refers to Caroline as Echo but, by doing so, Boyd acknowledges that she is no longer a whole person, but the victimized form. Not using her real name further victimizes her by not acknowledging who she really is. At this point she is Caroline once more (her original personality has been restored), and Boyd knows this. Boyd reminds Echo/Caroline that he has protected her—playing into the guilt she might feel as a victim. She tells him, "I loved you."

In the premiere episode of *Dollhouse*, Adelle DeWitt tells Caroline, "What we do helps people. If you become a part of that, it can help you" (1.01). Topher, the programmer at the Los Angeles Dollhouse, makes Caroline/Echo a victim to help victims: a powerful, opening statement and precursor of the trauma and rehabilitation to come. Echo is imprinted with a memory of a victim who was kidnapped by the same man who kidnapped her client's daughter. Though she is not an actual kidnap victim, she is made to believe she is one via the imprint. As she experiences the emotions of a survivor, becoming an affective body traumatizes her. In "Meet Jane Doe" (2.07), Echo refers to herself as a "people person," which is a pun regarding the thirty-plus personalities in her head simultaneously. Echo can seamlessly switch from personality to personality and uses this ability to train so that she can take the Dollhouse down from the inside. Later in "Meet Jane Doe" (2.07), Echo tells Ballard "I've been saving this body for her [Caroline], but I'm not her" and later emphasizes "I'm *not* her. My name is Echo." She acknowledges that her life will never return to what it was and, instead of fighting that notion, Echo embraces it. Her passion to do the right thing is, as Michael Marano suggests, her "inner capacity, a latent inborn talent" (42). Like River, Echo doesn't stay traumatized or victimized by her affective body; rather, she uses it as an ability.

Technological Interventions

River's and Echo's transformations illustrate how two different institutions of power, the Alliance and Rossum Corporation, impose their own agendas onto their physical bodies. With River, the chance for the government to manufacture an assassin was too hard to pass up. Echo, like all of the other dolls, finds herself a part of a very expensive prostitution ring that uses her anesthetized body to make a lot of money with the hopes of taking over the world. The affective body is, either from the outset in the case of River or as the narrative evolves in the case of Echo, a byproduct of that traumatic intervention by these institutions. The affective body is also a byproduct of technological interventions on the brain. While River's giftedness made her an ideal test subject for the Alliance, she was created through a series of brain operations alongside years of behavioral conditioning. As trauma to the brain so often does, this surgery permanently and fundamentally alters who River is. Her body, explored in both the series and film, represents a mixture of good genes illustrated by her exceptional abilities and technological innovation intended to exploit those abilities. The visual image of the teacher sticking a pencil into River's head that cuts to doctors forcing a needle into her brain at the beginning of the movie iterates the violence of this integration between the body and technology.

The technological interventions transform River's body into a weapon. In "River Tam and the Weaponized Women of the Whedonverse," Michael Marano notes, "The idea of a woman as created by a weapon-maker within Patriarchal contexts is a recurring motif in the worlds imagined by Joss Whedon, the so-called 'Whedonverse.' It's a motif, perhaps better defined as 'the woman as weapon,' that reaches its apotheosis with the developmental journey of River in *Firefly* and *Serenity*" (37–8).[3] Marano sets up the discussion of River-as-weapon by situating her position within the context of other weaponized women in the Whedonverses, starting with Ripley from *Alien: Resurrection* (for which Whedon wrote the script) and moving through other well-known residents of the Whedonverses: Buffy, Anya, Darla, and Dawn. He comes to the conclusion that "River's talent, her remarkableness, her spirit, is a necessary component of her weaponization" (42). Her gifts, spirit, and intuitive nature are valuable to the Alliance, and they use this "latent inborn talent" as the basis for her weaponization (42). River, however, is more than a weapon. Her affective body is a byproduct of this process of weaponization, which becomes a liability for the Alliance. The Alliance makes her into a self that can feel without any limitations. Patricia Clough argues, "The technoscientific experimentation with affect … inserts the technical into felt vitality, the felt aliveness given in the preindividual bodily capacities to act, engage, and connect—to affect and be affected" (Clough 2). According to Clough, bodies feel through technology. It is precisely this capacity that the Alliance taps into, but cannot control.

Like River, Echo is transformed through technology. Rather than intellectual giftedness, Echo's uniqueness exists in her biochemical makeup. The integration of the "Active architecture" into her brain exposes her genetic potential. Echo migrates between an anesthetic state of existence as a Doll and her special ability to feel all of her imprints simultaneously, essentially placing her bodily affective capacities in overdrive.[4] The creation of a Doll is a painful process beginning when the recruit must sign away five years in exchange for a life without conscious consequences. Using a technological interface of his own creation, Topher Brink wipes and then stores the Doll's original memory on a portable hard drive called a wedge. For each subsequent engagement, Topher designs an imprint that fulfills the parameters of the given assignment. These imprints piece together memories, affects, specialized knowledge, language, and can even trigger glandular responses as illustrated when Echo is imprinted with the persona of a mother who can breastfeed ("Instinct" 2.02). While not on an engagement, their doll-like existence consists of polite generalities, simple art classes, Tai Chi, massages, and pre-established scripts like, "I try to be my best." However, events in the unfolding narrative of the series reveal the affective capacities of the Doll's body. In the episode "True Believer" (1.05), Topher and Dr. Saunders discover the Doll Victor is extra-consciously attracted to Sierra (something thought impossible while in the doll state).

Echo begins to experience a sort of residual, sensory feedback even after the imprints from her engagements have been wiped. As the narrative arc unfolds across the course of two seasons, Echo begins to retain emotional triggers from her engagements even after her brain has been wiped of specific memories. She carves pieces of information onto the back of the glass screen that covers her while she sleeps at the Dollhouse, has "urges" to continue incomplete engagements like in "Man on the Street" (1.06), and eventually gains control over the multiple memory downloads in "Meet Jane Doe" (2.07). Echo explains to her handler Paul, "I remember everything. Sometimes I'm someone else and then I come back, but I still feel them. All of them. I've been many people. I can hear them, sometimes suddenly. I'm all of them, but none of them is me" (2.01). Echo's ability to feel "all of them" indicates a degree of bodily awareness thought impossible after someone is wiped, but the body that is coming alive is not Caroline Farrell, the body's original identity.

Echo's affective body is an unintended consequence of the technology that transforms her into a Doll. Similar to River, the capacity to perceive the feelings of everyone as opposed to their own individuated emotions (even as those feelings are not associated with a particular memory or lived experience) make Echo something other than the detective, prostitute, mother, or friend she transforms into throughout the course of the series. Echo's original persona, Caroline, becomes one of the many. Rather than breaking down into a mess of psychosis like River, Echo learns to embrace her unrequited emotional connections with the personalities in her head.

The Affective Body: Disability or Enhancement?

The integration of the body with technology enables River and Echo to transcend the physical limitations of ordinary people, like the Six Million Dollar Man or Bionic Woman. In *Firefly*, River's body works more efficiently and effectively than everyone else around her. River becomes a weapon, as does Echo, but in a different kind of way since Dolls can be whatever the clients want them to be. The transcendent power of technological intervention in both of these series, its ability to make humans into something better, mirrors the general tenants of transhumanism as outlined by the "Transhumanist Declaration" written in 1998.[5] Transhumanists "believe that humanity's potential is still mostly unrealized. There are possible scenarios that lead to wonderful and exceedingly worthwhile enhanced human conditions" (2). River and Echo represent "enhanced human conditions" of the transhumanist paradigm where trauma extends the use of their mere (albeit gifted) bodies. River, just like the Reavers, illustrates the latest of several attempts by the Alliance to make people "better" (*Serenity*). Similarly, the plan for Rossum goes well beyond making money; the bad guys work to escape the earthly boundaries of their bodies and live forever while exploiting entire populations of people in the process. Echo represents the beginning of a trajectory that ends when the world comes under the control of Rossum. Both women illustrate attempts to make bodies better, but neither the Alliance nor Rossum can contain the emotional connections the women have with others.

The affective body is an unintended consequence of the Alliance and Rossum's attempts to enhance the human condition for their own means. Its production is a torturous, traumatic process that disables its victim by opening their bodies to the pain of the world. Returning to Spinoza's definition of affect in *Ethics*, "He who conceives, that he affects others [...] will [...] himself be affected" (Part III, Proposition 30). Because the complete openness that River and Echo experience cannot be reciprocated, they are psychologically disabled, which wasn't according to plan. Neither the Reavers nor the crew, not even her own brother, can feel what River feels. The personalities echoing in Echo's mind presumably cannot appreciate what it feels like to be Echo. They remain individuated identities, even as they all are collected within the same body. Not only are River and Echo unable to express the pain of their victimization to others, they cannot ever enter into any kind of reciprocal relationship with any of the personalities in their head. Even Echo's attempt to keep Paul alive in her head after his body dies in "Epitaph Two" (2.13) is based on their prior experience as two separate people who come together through a shared attraction. As such, the affective body in *Firefly* and *Dollhouse* represents a type of disability in the Whedonverses.

Though the empathetic connections that resonate through the affective body are unrequited, and hence disabling to both River and Echo, they are the keys that lead to the downfall of Rossum and the diminished power of the Alliance to operate without accountability. In each series, the government or corporation sees people as information, products, and sites of exploitation. Both entities miscalculate the power of empathy, of the very human experience of affective connection. Humans feel, and the enhanced bodies of River and Echo feel even more. Although the affective body functions as a disability because River and Echo cannot reciprocate the pain they experience, it exposes a fundamental flaw behind the attempts by the Alliance and Rossum to transcend human nature. To love, to hate, the ability to connect with each other in very powerful and often inexplicable ways, is what defines us as individuals and members of a community. The affective body is an extreme version of those very qualities that make us human.

As a disability, the affective body is what empowers both River and Echo in their inevitable attempts to destroy the very infrastructures that attempted to make them into something better. It's the monkey wrench in the machine that inevitably interrupts attempts by the Alliance and Rossum to control the world as efficiently as possible. However, the affective body is effective in this role only because of their relationships to their chosen families; indeed the affective connection that creates power out of River's and Echo's affective disability in their respective series is the chosen family. Even though River and Echo play key roles in bringing down the bad guys, the chosen family is still what gets things done. The chosen family provides more than just connection; it's a commitment that these characters make to a group of people. This commitment and reattachment to the chosen family, rather than the rawness of an affective relationship, allows their disability to become an ability. This reattachment helps heal the trauma of the affective body. It's Mal, Zoë, Wash, Ballard, Topher, Adelle—members of the crews at the heart of both of these shows—who give each other strength and empowerment in a way the biological connection may or may not do.

Recovery and Rehabilitation

"The human body can undergo many changes, and nevertheless retain impressions, or traces, of the objects ... and consequently, the same images of things" (Part III, Postulate 2). There are traces or echoes, as Spinoza says, of what was there before. The same can be said for *Firefly* and *Dollhouse*. Summer Glau, the actress who plays River, is but one physical bridge between the two shows. River becomes agitated during the "R. Tam Sessions" and claims that she cut up her mattress to find a pea that was hurting her spine, echoing the fable "The Princess and the Pea." River is as sensitive as the princess because she can feel *everything* since she has been affected. In "The Hollow Men" (2.12), Echo is strapped to a table in a lab so that her spinal fluid can be drained. She tries to protect her spine from Boyd, but he still manages to stick her with needles. The damage to River's amygdala resonates when Dollhouse programmer Bennett Halverson (also played by Summer Glau) remarks to her friend Caroline in a flashback that she would love to see her [Caroline's] amygdala. These echoes speak to the connections between these two characters. Both are victims of trauma and, to a degree, overcome that trauma. Their chosen families, those beloved characters that stick together through everything, give River and Echo the chance at rehabilitation. River and Echo demonstrate an incredible resilience in terms of their physical and psychological trauma, and not only do they find ways to heal, but they also work toward helping others.

Although the bioengineering of River and Echo permanently scar them, they both come to terms with their trauma and bring about social change with the help of those people who have become family: the motley crew of the ship Serenity and the survivors of the Dollhouse. River, along with the crew of the ship Serenity, are able to weaken the Alliance. Rhonda Wilcox reads the scene in *Serenity* where River throws up on Miranda after the crew discovers the truth behind the Reavers as physical release of her trauma, a way to regain control of her mind and body (Wilcox, "I Do Not Hold" 161). The truth, quite literally, sets her free from the pain of others. Echo's gradual journey of self-awareness from anesthetized Doll Echo to multi-dimensional Echo who has integrated many personalities into one helps her heal. River's release, both physically and emotionally, contrasts Echo's acceptance of who she is and what she can become. The disability that makes Echo different becomes her greatest asset in the fight against the Rossum Corporation. As a victim, Echo serves a larger purpose of helping other victims. It reveals a human understanding rooted in the body's capacity to connect affectively with others, even if that connection is mediated through technological interventions.

Friend Me, Please!

Now more than ever, people establish and maintain personal connections through the Internet. The rise of social networking over the past decade and its infiltration in all things popular culture, from online distribution and viral marketing to Twitter feeds taking center stage on the local news, provides a new forum of information exchange through a technological interface where being connected is a value in and of itself. The affective bodies of River and Echo, coupled with other examples from the Whedonverses, offer a compelling framework to think about the nature of connection, what one gives up and what one gains in the process. Connection is not something that is ever taken for granted, from the emotional support offered through the strength of the chosen family to the disabling figure of the affective body. Yet, the ability of River and Echo to overcome the trauma of the affective body and recognize the power of the chosen family is what makes them all the more human in their attempt to save the world. Again.

Notes

1. In this essay we will use *Firefly* to denote the television series and the story arc as it continues in the feature film, *Serenity*.
2. In addition to River and Echo, Alpha in *Dollhouse* may also be considered an "affective body" and, like River, is driven mad by his own openness.
3. Marano acknowledges the possibility for more Whedon "apotheosis-y" explorations in the future, as the essay was published in 2007 and *Dollhouse* aired two years later.
4. Alpha, too, experiences a similar sense of being in "overdrive": after Topher dumps multiple imprints into Alpha, he switches back and forth at random without maintaining the sense of control over the personalities the way Echo can. This is especially evident in "Omega" (1.12).
5. For more on Transhumanism and the Whedonverses, see also Perdigao, Dunway, and Calvert *Being Bionic* and "The AI."

The Token Fatty

Three Whedon Series in Search of a "Normal-Sized" Woman[1]

Sherry Ginn

An avowed feminist and creator of some of the most popular female characters of the late twentieth century and early twenty-first century, Joss Whedon's female characters illustrate the type of woman that many male and female fans admire. Able to take care of themselves and their friends and families, the women of *Buffy the Vampire Slayer* (*Buffy*) and *Firefly/Serenity* are anything but helpless damsels-in-distress. As a matter of fact, Buffy is easily considered a hero (Cornillon), as are most of Whedon's other female characters. Even the female Dolls of *Dollhouse*, although repeatedly de- and reprogrammed depending upon the dictates of their clients, are trained to take care of themselves should the need arise (e.g., "The Target," "Gray Hour"). Nevertheless, few of his female actors were similar in terms of physicality to the average American woman, and it is puzzling as to why the characters in these series would be so physically dissimilar to this average American female size. Significantly, many fans have reacted to the physical size of the recurring characters, and perhaps this is why Whedon's various series have included one token "fatty" in the character list. The purpose of this essay is to examine these tokens in three of Whedon's series: *Buffy*, *Firefly/Serenity*, and *Dollhouse*.

Review of the Literature[2]

The 26 January 2007 cover of *People* magazine[3] fanned the flames of the continuing debate over the size of women in the entertainment industry (Tyra Banks). Tyra Banks looked stunning in a red one-piece swimsuit and asked, "You call this fat?" The model and television host was reacting to the furor over the news that she had gained 30 pounds. This was a timely issue for me as I was at a point in one of my Developmental Psychology courses where we could talk about health and well-being, body image and body satisfaction, and self-esteem. As we discussed the importance of these issues in women's lives, the students calculated Ms. Banks' Body Mass Index (BMI), a statistic used to determine the fat content of the body based upon height and weight. Standing 5' 10" in height and weighing 161 pounds, Ms. Banks's BMI was 23.1, which is considered healthy.

Although BMI measurements can actually overestimate body fat content in athletes and other people with muscular builds, the United States Department of Health and Human Services considers it to be an important indicator of health. A BMI greater than 25.0 indicates a person is overweight, and one greater than 30.0 indicates obesity. Being overweight or obese is correlated with an increased risk of health problems, including hypertension, heart disease, and diabetes.[4] Just as dangerous is being underweight, defined as a BMI below 18.5. Women who are underweight may stop menstruating (amenorrhea), lose body hair, develop osteoporosis (brittle bones) and anemia, and increase their risks of infections since the immune system needs calories in order to work efficiently (Guinea Piggy).

Nevertheless, many women risk the dangers resulting from being underweight, including dangers beyond the physical. Self-esteem is related to weight in contemporary Western society, and many women compare themselves to other women as they attempt to determine the preferred weight, body shape, and body size. Unfortunately, overweight women suffer a loss of self-esteem when they compare themselves to both under- and overweight models (Smeesters, Mussweiler, and Mandel), with the opposite effect reported in underweight women. Such results confirm many reports that indicate the deleterious effects of media exposure to both heavy and thin models, although the effect is generally seen in white as opposed to black women (Schooler, Ward, Merriwether, and Caruthers). Watching mainstream television predicted poorer body image for white women but not for black women. Watching black-oriented television actually predicted a healthier body image for black women. However, Jefferson and Stake reported that both African American and European American women expressed more body dissatisfaction if they had internalized Western beauty ideals.

Cross-cultural studies find virtually the same results. For example, Australian school girls perceive themselves as overweight even when their BMI indicates that they are underweight (Tiggemann and Pickering). These girls reported high levels of body dissatisfaction, which was correlated with television viewing. The more hours spent watching soap operas, serials, and movies, the more likely the girls were to experience body dissatisfaction.

Hours spent watching music videos were correlated with a drive for thinness. The effects of various media can be seen in girls as young as six (Dohnt and Tiggemann) as well as those in the ten- to thirteen-year-old age range (Clark and Tiggemann).

Levine and Murnen note that many people cloud the issue by placing the blame on various media as the *causal* agents in the negative body image that many women possess. Instead they argue that emphasis should be placed on the *impact* that media have on women and increasingly men as well. Given that people of all ages use media for a variety of reasons, including the development of identity, sexuality, and gender roles, it should come as no surprise that media influence their behavior. The proposition that "thin is normative and attractive" derives from the actors performing in television, film, magazines, the internet, etc. (Levine summarizing his own research, cited in Levine and Murnen 15). American girls and women are becoming increasingly heavy, but the body ideal to which they are exposed is unrealistically thin. For example, the average American woman is 5'4" tall and weighs 140 pounds. She wears a size 14 dress.[5] The "ideal"—defined by most runway and magazine models, Miss America, and Barbie—is 5'7" tall, weighs 100 pounds, and wears a size 8 dress. About one-third of women wear a size 16 or larger (Lacey). However, even though the average woman wears a size 14, this is the size least likely to sell, indicating perhaps unwillingness on the part of those average women to admit being that "large" ("Size 14").

Dozens of research reports indicate that the more television adolescent girls watch the more likely they are to be dissatisfied with their bodies, internalize and strive for the thin ideal, and display eating disordered behavior, both anorexia and bulimia (see for example, Grabe, Ward and Shibley Hyde; Hargreaves and Tiggemann; Levine and Murnen). As if those effects were not serious enough, exposure to thin models can also lead to depression, stress, guilt, shame, unhappiness, insecurity, and lowered self-esteem (Stice and Shaw). Research also indicates that body satisfaction of adult women and men is negatively influenced by media exposure (Green and Pritchard). These undesirable physical and psychological effects are so serious that the UK's Royal College of Psychiatrists has called "for an 'editorial code' to encourage media to stop its 'damaging' portrayal of unhealthy body images" (Streeting, Lehane, Allison, and Drake; "Experts" 6).[6] Sigman notes that a similar call was made in 2000, but things have only gotten worse since that time.

Given Joss Whedon's avowed feminism it is puzzling as to why he would seem to be in the mainstream of media representation in perpetuating physical stereotypes in his female characters. The empowered women he envisions in his television series *Buffy the Vampire Slayer, Angel,* and *Firefly* belie any reliance on traditional feminine stereotypes. As a matter of fact, Whedon would be classified as a Third-Wave feminist (see Pender's book *I'm Buffy and You're ... History*). The precursor to the third-wave, second-wave, or liberal feminism, places feminism firmly within the bounds of political liberalism (Tong). These feminists believe that women should be given equal access with men to educational and vocational opportunities. In addition, liberal feminists recognize that sex and gender are not synonymous, and that traditional gender roles are stultifying for men as well as women. Thus, liberal feminists would advocate that men and women become more androgynous. Third-wave feminism builds upon the foundation of liberal feminism, but recognizes that liberal feminism did not address issues relevant to women of color and women who were not heterosexual. Third-wave feminism attempts to be more inclusive, embracing the uniqueness of every woman (Dicker and Piepmeier), and yet, though Whedon in many ways fits into the third-wave feminism, he has not embraced women of size in his various series, with a few exceptions, these notably being Tara, Kaylee, and Mellie/November on *Buffy*, *Firefly*, and *Dollhouse*, respectively.[7]

Measurements for most of the actresses portraying the major characters in the Whedonverses are readily available on the Internet. These data are presented in Table 1. Three of these, Buffy, Willow, and Echo, are barely at the light end of the ideal weight[8] for their height, and Inara and River are below the light end. Tara, Cordelia, and Fred are slightly above the light end, whereas Mellie is about midway. Using the available heights and weights for each actress we can also calculate their BMI. Willow, Anya, Tara, Cordelia, Zoë, Echo, and Mellie would all be considered healthy, which is defined as a BMI of 18.5–24.9, as would Buffy if her weight were 108 pounds. However, if Buffy's BMI were calculated using the lowest weight in her range (97 pounds) then she would be classified as unhealthy, which is a BMI < 18.5. This is also true of Fred and Inara. River's BMI places her in the underweight category as well.

Keeping Up with the Boneses[9]

Buffy the Vampire Slayer (*Buffy*) had several female characters over its seven season run. These included Buffy Summers, Willow Rosenberg, Cordelia Chase (through Season Three), Anya (starting in Season Four), Dawn Summers (starting in Season Five), and Tara Maclay (Seasons Four–Six). Only Tara would be considered remotely "oversize," and I contend that it was because that is the way her character was meant to be portrayed. Buffy was small and needed to be in order to provide the necessary contrast with her strength: who would expect such a little girl to be such a bad-ass? Cordelia never appeared too thin to me. Dawn was small as would be expected of a barely pubescent young woman. It appeared that the writers were playing around with the notion that Dawn was a budding anorexic or bulimic in several episodes (e.g., "Flooded" and "Gone") when she would not eat at home. However, considering her other problems, like kleptomania and a general whininess, perhaps they knew the fans would react negatively if Dawn became even more problematized. Anya seemed incredibly thin, yet she is roughly the same height as Willow, and weighs more. Despite appearances, each of these women, with the exception of Sarah Michelle Gellar (and then only at her smallest), are well within the healthy range of BMI.[10]

Tara, portrayed by Amber Benson, appeared much larger than any of the other female characters on *Buffy*. Earlier episodes of *Buffy* emphasize her face, and her wardrobe could almost be described as frumpy, or plain and unfashionable. Tara dresses for comfort, with long skirts and bulky sweaters that hide any hint of her figure. In the few scenes where we see her in slacks, they generally fit loosely, unlike Willow's or Buffy's, and they are not cut in such a way as to flatter her figure. Nevertheless, on occasion she would wear a midriff top with her slacks and the viewer could see that Tara possessed a flat stomach, which is not what one would necessarily expect in a woman who dresses like her. In short, Tara's wardrobe suggests that she is much larger than she is, as if she is wearing clothes that will hide bodily flaws, like a large abdomen, hips, and thighs. Indeed, women frequently buy magazines that contain articles about how to dress to hide such flaws. Several television programs (such as *How to Look Good Naked* and *What Not to Wear*) are specifically designed to help women dress to accent their assets and hide what women perceive to be their flaws.

One of the most compelling visual scenes in seven seasons of *Buffy* occurred in the episode "The Body" (5.16). Buffy is sitting in the waiting room of the local hospital, preparing to talk with her mother's doctor, after her mother's death. Beside her on the couch is Tara. This very shy young woman wishes to comfort Buffy but is unsure of how to do so. Eventually Tara tells Buffy of her own mother's death, which occurred when she was seventeen years old. To Buffy's question about the death, Tara replies that the death of a parent "is never easy," regardless of whether or not it is sudden. As the two young women talk, the discrepancy between their sizes is glaringly apparent.[11] Buffy is small and lithe, her smallness hiding the reality of her Slayer strength. Tara on the other hand is large. She is by no means fat or overweight in any normal universe, but compared to the Slayer some viewers may perceive her as a Hulk. Even compared to her lover, Willow Rosenberg, Tara is presented as a large, comforting presence. When compared to the three primary female characters in *Buffy*—Buffy, Willow, and Anya—Tara would be considered a plus-size girl.

One might argue that Tara is hiding her physicality because of the brainwashing she received at the hands of her family, specifically her father. As mentioned earlier, Tara's mother died when she was seventeen. She is now roughly twenty and away from her family for the first time. Shy and sweet, Tara has joined a Wiccan group on campus, where she meets Willow, but she lacks many close friends. On her twentieth birthday Tara's father, brother, and cousin come to Sunnydale to take her home ("Family" 5.06). They tell Tara and those around her that they, as her family, must protect everyone from her, from what she is—a demon. In this episode viewers begin to understand some of Tara's earlier actions (e.g., hiding the accouterments of spells when working with Willow). Because she believes that she is a demon, she has tried to dampen her femininity. At the end of the episode, in a climatic confrontation between Tara's male-dominated family and the Scoobies, Spike effectively demonstrates to Tara and the others that Tara is not a demon; the men in her family have used that lie and the fear the lie generated to control the women in their family. By the episode's end, Tara breaks free of her family's control and stays in Sunnydale with Willow. Although we do not subsequently see a dramatic change in Tara's physical appearance, we do occasionally see her dress in more stylish, even sexy clothing. One notable example occurs in the episode "Once More, With Feeling" (6.07), when Tara wears a very flattering bustier with a long flowing skirt. She is with Willow, and as the two women walk across campus, two young men gaze appreciatively at them. Willow indicates to Tara that the men are watching her, that she is beautiful. Yet Tara does not consider herself to be beautiful even though Willow repeatedly tells her that she is.

As presented in Table 1, Amber Benson's weight lies at the low end of the normal range for her height. Her BMI also lies close to the end point of normal. These data indicate that she is not overweight. However, that did not stop many fans from bashing her about her weight on various fan message boards when she joined the cast of *Buffy*. Some fans[12] were apparently rather hateful in their remarks, calling both the actor and the character fat and ugly, leading the actor to eventually respond. Ms. Benson's remarks are reproduced in Nikki Stafford's *Bite Me!* One wonders if the fans' bitter remarks were made in response to her size (when compared to the other female cast members), to her character's sexuality, or to the fact that Willow chose Tara over Oz. Any or all of those probably contributed to the bitter and harmful comments.

Whedon can hardly be unaware of the intense pressure placed on female actors to adhere to the unrealistic physical standards demanded by Hollywood.[13] When casting the role of Kaylee in *Firefly*, Whedon supposedly told Jewel Staite to gain twenty pounds,[14] which Staite verified in several interviews (e.g., Lee). A careful reading of these interviews, however, reveals a number of discrepancies about why he wanted her to gain weight, how much weight she actually did gain, and how much of an argument she employed against the suggested weight gain (for example, see Mo Pie). Interestingly, Ms. Staite lost the weight after the series ended, but Whedon did not require her to regain the lost weight prior to the start of cinematography for *Serenity*. One could question Whedon's decision to have Kaylee larger than normal for the original series. For one, she does not look larger than normal on the series, unless she is compared to River Tam, who is extremely thin, and River's thinness is to be expected. After all, she just spent several years in a government facility where Alliance scientists experimented on her brain. Such torture should leave physical as well as mental scars.

Moreover, Kaylee does not look larger than normal when compared to the other two female characters, Inara Serra and Zoë Warren Washburne, either. Inara is a Companion, what we would consider a very high-class prostitute, a combination Geisha and Greek Hetaera (Aberdein; Davidson). Although not necessarily required for her profession, Inara is physically beautiful. She wears clothing that is richly colorful and flattering to her figure and is always made-up, even when not entertaining clients. Her dark coloring and dramatic make-up render her exotic and lush and this disguises the fact that she is also thinner than normal, slightly below or just at a normal BMI, as indicated in Table 1. Compared to Kaylee, she is sophisticated and glamorous, and this distracts the viewer from any notion that she might be thinner than usual as well. Zoë is taller than average, the tallest of all of Whedon's female actors, and she weighs more than any of the other female actors, with the exception of Mellie/November on *Dollhouse*. Zoë can also be described as lush in the sense of having a curvy body with the more typical measurements for an hour-glass figure. Her clothes fit her body very well and do nothing to detract from her physical form. Zoë is also a warrior woman and her size reinforces that fact—she is as big as many men and not afraid of a fight, having demonstrated her courage in the War for Independence. In contrast to Kaylee, Zoë is more than capable of taking care of herself, her husband, and her crew.

However, one might also expect Kaylee to be thin as a means of stressing the marginal existence "enjoyed" by Serenity's crew. The crew does not always have access to fresh food and sometimes food is scarce ("Serenity" 1.01). As a matter of fact, having a crew with a "powerful need to eat" leads Captain Reynolds to engage in questionable activity on occasion (*Serenity*). Although she is the ship's engineer, Kaylee is also the heart of the crew (Burns): she gets along with them all, including Jayne, and is always sweet and kind. It is obvious that she is a tomboy, but she also asserts her femininity, often wearing "flowered shirts or cute, frilly kinds of stuff" (*Firefly: The Official Companion*, Volume One 114). Kaylee is a woman who enjoys sex and is not ashamed to admit it (*Firefly: The Official Companion*, Volume Two 146), which makes Jubal Early's threat of rape all the more terrifying for her (and us as well) in "Objects in Space" (1.14). All of these traits suggest that Kaylee is a model for the new woman, the woman who can have it all, as envisioned by third-wave feminism (Beadling); nevertheless, Kaylee's physical status as a larger-than-"normal" woman is questionable. If Whedon wanted to present a character more typical of the average viewer, then he did not succeed with Kaylee.

However, the character Mellie—whose Doll designation is November—was presented as a plus-size character on *Dollhouse*.[15] Although not the main character in the series, Mellie played an important role in the series' first season as she served to distract FBI Special Agent Paul Ballard from discovering the exact location and secret agenda of the Dollhouse. Mellie is planted in Ballard's apartment building and programmed to fall in love with him. She is to keep him occupied and, if possible, make him fall in love with her. She is clearly enamored of him when we first meet her in the series. We almost feel sorry for a woman who appears to lurk at the door of her apartment waiting for her neighbor to come home. Mellie and Paul do become friends and eventually become lovers ("Man on the Street" 1.06). Mellie frequently makes comments about her physical appearance, indicating that she believes in the social stereotypes about plus-sized women and, as such, is too large to be pretty. Paul tells her not to worry about it, that she is not too big, that she is beautiful (much like Willow reassuring Tara on *Buffy*). He is attracted to her, and when they become sexually active, her response is very vocal. It is only later in the season that we learn Mellie is not only an Active, but she is also a sleeper agent, an Active who can be triggered to engage a particular mission without endangering her primary imprint. Thus, we do not know if her physical reaction to Paul's lovemaking is because he is a good lover, or she is a good Active and has been programmed to react to him that way. At least until we learn that she is an Active, we can celebrate the fact that she is presented as a larger than normal woman, who generates sexual desire in an attractive man, and enjoys sexual activity.[16] We can presume that Tara was the same: larger than normal, capable of generating sexual desire in both men and women, and capable of enjoying sexual activity as well.

Of particular significance to the discussion of the relationship between sexual attractiveness and size is that the Dollhouses' ostensible reasons for being were primarily to cater to the sexual desires of male and female clients. People with enough money could hire any Active for any type of encounter; most encounters included sexual relations, and Actives could be programmed to be passive or active, hetero- or homosexual, or any other type requested by the client. It is to be wondered why none of the Dolls, other than November, could be considered plus-size, given that some people are sexually attracted to large men and women (they are called fat fetishists). One would assume that some of them are rich and could afford the Dollhouse's prices, but this issue is never brought up in the series.

Conclusion

If one wishes to view television with an eye to celebrating diversity, then the typical American program is not likely to allow the viewer to do so. The typical program is cast with predominately Caucasian actors, and the female actors are likely to be thinner than the average woman. Indeed, television programs that are geared toward a minority audience, and cast with minority actors, will at least be more reflective of a physically diverse ethnic population. Joss Whedon's programs are not reflective of the diversity of the American population with respect to the ethnic status of his actors, casting only five ethnic minorities[17] for major roles in his television programs. In addition, as this essay has indicated, only one of his female actors would be considered close to the size of the average American woman (Mellie). Much has been made about Whedon's work with respect to his celebration of female power and his attempts to educate the general public about matters relevant to women throughout the world. His insistence upon addressing violence against women in these programs, and his portrayals of female sexuality in all of its permutations are also to be applauded. However, while these efforts are laudable, a greater attempt to celebrate the diversity of the American population with respect to body size is needed. Joss Whedon commands a great deal of respect, and he has a legion of fans willing to support him in all of his creative, political, and philanthropic endeavors. "We have done the impossible. And that makes us mighty," says Joss Whedon of *Serenity*, the sequel motion picture he succeeded in making after *Firefly*'s short-lived run on television. Doing the impossible with respect to body size and appearance may not make us mighty, but it would be a start.

Table 1. Height, Weight and BMI of Major Female Characters Compared to Ideal

Character	Height	Weight	Ideal Weight for Height[10]	BMI[3]
Buffy	5' 2.5"	97–108	108–143	17.8–19.8
Willow	5' 5"	116	117–155	19.3
Anya	5' 5"	128	117–155	21.3
Tara	5'4"	118	114–151	20.3
Cordelia	5'7"	125	123–164	19.6

Character	Height	Weight	Ideal Weight for Height[10]	BMI[3]
Fred	5'8"	120–132	126–164	18.2–20.1
Kaylee	5' 5"	Unknown	117–155	Unable to Calculate
Zoë	5'10.5"	140	132–174	19.8
Inara	5'7.5"	114–120	123–164	17.6–18.5
River	5'6.5"	112	120–159	17.8
Echo	5' 6"	120	120–159	19.4
Mellie	5' 9"	145	129–170	21.5
Sierra	5'7.5"	Unknown	123–164	Unable to Calculate

Notes

1. I am certainly not trying to insult anyone with my choice of a title. It is entirely sarcastic. I used to be as light as Amber Benson (we are the same height), but that was many years and many pounds ago. However, even though I proudly proclaim myself a feminist, I still find myself a slave to the scales. All of that conditioning is difficult to counter. I would like to thank the people who posted replies to a blog by Mo Pie about "Dollhouse, Fat Willow and Joss Whedon." Most did call Whedon to task for choosing actors who wear a size 0 and then throwing in the "token," who is generally a size 4 or so. No way is a size 4 "fat."

2. References used in this essay were those current during the run of Joss Whedon-created series (1997–2010). As such, the research results would have been available to the public, not just the academic community. Unfortunately more recent research data show that people—and not only white American women—are still dieting, still starving, still undergoing surgical alteration, and still seeking an unrealistic body size. For a summary of research on this issue, see Grogan.

3. The cover can be accessed using any search engine. I used Google and simply typed in "Tyra Banks *People* cover." Not only will you get the picture of her, you will find her comments on the topic, as well as many responses to her, and the media hype.

4. There is a lot of misinformation about BMI and obesity on the internet. Useful information can be found at the National Institutes of Health and WebMD websites, two reputable and monitored sites. See "Assessing Your Weight and Health Risk" and DerSarkissian.

5. The average woman may be a size 14, but the Centers for Disease Control contends that she is also 20 pounds overweight (Bowers).

6. Replies were printed in the Reflections column of *Nursing Standard*'s 31 March 2010 issue. Respondents were in favor of the code, although each had specific responses to the call ranging from not tough enough to stop the airbrushing or at least let the public know when it occurs.

7. Neither of the female characters on *Angel* would be, or could be, considered plus-size. Cordelia has always struck me as a good size, and Fred is extremely thin. A running joke throughout Season Three has Gunn referring to Fred's "scrawny self." Given that Fred spent several years living in a cave and scrounging for food, it is logical that she would be very thin. The joke about her size is usually contrasted with the amount of food she eats, as if she is making up for her starvation. This behavior most probably reflects the aftereffects of the trauma she sustained from being kidnapped, thrust into a demon-world, and then hunted as a "cow." Much of Fred's behavior would indicate post-traumatic stress disorder (PTSD).

8. The ideal weight ranges presented in Table 1 were obtained by comparing height and

weight charts from 3 different sources available on the internet: Disabled World, Weight Watchers, and Metropolitan Life. The Metropolitan Life charts listed weights depending upon whether one has a small, medium, or large frame. The other two did not. Hence the Met Life charts had a much larger range than the other two, with a heavier end point.

9. I wish that I could claim this, but the author was Aric Sigman. See Works Cited, for the complete citation.

10. I used Google to search for the heights and weights for each actress. As might be expected there was some discrepancy. For example, Alyson Hannigan was listed as being anywhere from 5'4" to 5'9". Five inches would make a significant difference as far as BMI calculations are concerned. Thus, her BMI could range from 17.2 to 20; 20 is healthy, but 17.2 is not. Another problem with this search is that the information was obtained from sites with 2010–2011 dates. Each actress might have weighed less (or more) when *Buffy* was on the air. Indeed, Emma Caulfield does admit to losing weight prior to *Buffy* and one would assume that she is heavier now. If that is in fact the case then it supports my contention that she was very thin when the show was on air. I was unable to calculate Kaylee's BMI as I could not find Jewel Staite's weight listed anywhere on the internet; likewise with Dichen Lachman. I used a standard calculator for the BMI determinations; there are many such calculators available on the Internet. For Sarah Michelle Gellar/Buffy, Morena Baccarin/Inara, and Amy Acker/Fred, I used the lowest weight and the highest weight to achieve the range listed. Of the actors listed in Table 1, I have seen Anya, Tara, and Cordelia in person and have met Fred, Kaylee, Zoë, River, Echo, Mellie, and Sierra at various "cons" in the years since these series aired. None of them, including Mellie, are overweight.

11. Rhonda Wilcox discusses this episode in *Why Buffy Matters* and defies anyone to find glamour in the scene. Buffy looks unkempt with "hair that looks flat and a bit greasy; her skin is pale; there are shadows under her eyes." On the other hand, Tara's "more or less average body size has always presented resistance to Hollywood standards" (179).

12. Amber Benson responded frequently to comments about her size while on *Buffy* and since then. See Kregloe, as well as Tarnoff, for her remarks about fans' reactions to her on *Buffy* as well as her comments, in general, about the size of female actors. Bashing plus-size stars, or stars that viewers think are plus-size, continues, as evidenced by the uproar over a blogger's remarks about *Mike & Molly* on *Marie Claire's* Facebook page. The magazine invited readers to respond to the question "Would you be uncomfortable watching overweight people make out on television?" The response to the blogger's negative comments—she would be "grossed out"—was swift and severe. Any Google search of the words "Marie Claire Mike and Molly" will yield dozens of sites with commentary, including an apology by the Editor of *Marie Claire*.

13. It is interesting that no one will actually say who makes the rules as far as the preferred physical type. Directors blame producers, who blame sponsors, who blame the people who buy their products. They say they only give us what we want, and we want thin models generally with big breasts.

14. Jewel Staite is certainly not the first actor to gain weight for a role, nor will she likely be the last. The days when plus-size actors were celebrated have gone. See Haslam and Haslam for a review of this issue.

15. I am not the only person who notes that Mellie is not a plus-size woman, and that Joss Whedon does not choose "normal" sized women to act in his series. Consider for example the "Dollhouse, Fat Willow and Joss Whedon" blog by Mo Pie and responses to it, not only about Mellie but also about the original Willow (Riff Regan).

16. Mellie loses Paul to Echo in the end and that might indicate that a "fatty" cannot keep a man, always losing out to the thinner woman. Only one of the three token "fatties" in the Whedonverses gets her true love: Tara is killed, Mellie loses Paul to Echo, but Kaylee gets Simon.

17. These five are J. August Richards as Charles Gunn on *Angel*; Gina Torres as Zoë Warren Washburne on *Firefly* (and Jasmine on *Angel*); Ron Glass as Shepherd Book on *Firefly*; and, Dichen Lachman as Sierra and Harry Lennix as Boyd Langton on *Dollhouse*.

"It's about power"

New Bodies, Connection, and Healing in Seasons Six and Seven of Buffy the Vampire Slayer

Kelly L. Richardson

> "Write your self. Your body must be heard. Only then will the immense resources of the unconscious spring forth."
> —Hélène Cixous, *The Laugh of the Medusa*

As Cixous reminds us, the physical body intersects with the construction of identity, and that assumption certainly has permeated much of Joss Whedon's work. Throughout his canon, Whedon has consistently focused on the body as a metaphorical vehicle to explore narrative. Despite his continued use of this technique in other TV series and films, *Buffy the Vampire Slayer* remains perhaps his most relevant and significant representation of female power, in large part because of the series' longevity. Unlike *Angel* or *Firefly*, its seven-season run allowed the writers to explore female characters over a period of time. As the characters evolved, so too did their understanding of strength and responsibility; consequently, the show's final two seasons provide some of the series' most compelling—because they are so complex—representations of female power.

From its very first season, *Buffy the Vampire Slayer*, in almost Hawthorne-like fashion, repeatedly featured characters whose physical, public selves house secret, private identities. This approach clearly allowed the writers to explore identity through the metaphorical use of the monster; however, beyond the vampires and demons are also transformations of the ordinary individual through such storytelling devices as invisibility, possession, animalism, and spiritual imprisonment as seen with Marcie in "Out of Sight, Out of Mind" (1.11), Amy in "Witch" (1.03), the high school students as hyenas in "The Pack" (1.06), and Sid the dummy in "The Puppet Show" (1.09). This range of physical transformations with humans works well symbolically during the high school era of the show as it speaks to the anxieties of identity. As the seasons continue, these transformations become less about individual identity and more about constructions of evil with villains whose physicality defines them: the Mayor experiences both not being able to be harmed physically and the "ascension" into a giant snake-demon; Adam is a Frankenstein-collection of body parts; and Glory is an imprisoned god who body-shifts with the human Ben. However, in the show's final two seasons, the storylines return to focusing more distinctly on how physical transformation reflects transformation into adulthood as the characters explore their strengths through new challenges, and they come to understand their changed bodies in different ways. As Rhonda V. Wilcox has observed, characters in Season Six and Seven repeatedly refer to "power" as being a primary subject of concern (*Why Buffy Matters* 91).[1] This treatment of power intersects with the treatment of physicality, particularly through the storylines of Buffy and Willow.

Whereas all of the main characters in these seasons experience some physical trial or transformation (Dawn's temporary possession, Xander's loss of an eye, Anya's shift from human to demon and back again, Giles' primary role from Watcher to warrior, Spike's restoration of his soul), Buffy and Willow are distinctive as their narratives share important parallels that have long-reaching implications not only for them individually but also the other characters. First, they both experience traumatic events so painful that their sense of self becomes disrupted. Buffy is "ripped" from heaven, while Tara is "ripped" from Willow when Warren murders Tara. Second, not only does the trauma become experienced physically as Buffy returns to life and Willow is splattered with blood, but this physicality extends to the creation of actual new physical bodies for both Buffy, as her body reforms during her resurrection, and Willow, as her body cannot separate itself from the magic she channels into it. Third, the characters' responses to these events lead them to emotional places hitherto unexplored in part because the "rules" have changed. No longer are the "white hats" and the "black hats" clearly defined, leaving Buffy and Willow to process this moral ambiguity and pain. Finally, instead of a tidy resolution, both storylines feature a protracted, and thus more authentic, dramatization of the healing process; an essential element to both women's healing is their choice to reclaim their power and to integrate their new bodies with these new senses of self.

This process of integration is a difficult one for the characters; however, it creates one of the most significant narrative arcs of the series as these women seek to heal themselves, an important message of the show. As Michele Byers argues, "The show's feminist impulse says that women should be able to protect themselves and their loved ones, to be respected for their intellectual and physical capabilities, to insist on their right to emotional and bodily integrity, and to desire to be nurtured as well as to nurture" (172).[2] Part of expressing this "feminist impulse" is to dramatize not only the heroics of a supernatural battle but also the heroics of surviving and healing from a traumatic event and to restore, as Byers says, "emotional integrity"—something *Buffy* clearly does with its two main female characters in these seasons. Moreover, studying these stories in conjunction with each other and analyzing how these characters come to terms with their new bodies and rehabilitate themselves emotionally provides viewers with complex representations of power from both an individual and collective perspective.

"Wrecked": Trauma and Altered Bodies in Seasons Six and Seven

"That was intense. That's gotta change you."
(Willow, "After Life" 6.03)

Joss Whedon describes Season Six as "the dark of the woods, the darkest part of the path" ("Life Is the Big Bad"), and this quality can clearly be observed right from the beginning with Buffy's resurrection. Gregory Erickson and Jennifer Lemberg explain that Season Six introduces us to

> a different world—one where Buffy and her friends will suffer and inflict extreme violence and terror—and these extreme experiences are often expressed and negotiated through the idea of the body. Seasons Six and Seven develop the idea of the body as cultural text, rewriting it through acts of (re)appropriation, misappropriation, passing, imitation, doubling, and resignification [115].

Erickson and Lemberg continue to examine how the final two seasons "use the body as a site and metaphor of rupture, insecurity, and destabilization" (115). Using criteria for post-traumatic stress disorder from the American Psychiatric Association, they describe Buffy's resurrection as traumatic, as it is an event "'outside the range of usual human experience'" (119). Likewise, Laurie Vickroy explains trauma as "a response to events so overwhelmingly intense that they impair normal emotional and cognitive responses and bring lasting psychological disruption" (ix). Citing the work of Bessel Van der Kolk and Onno Van der Hart, she explains that traumatic events, whether a single event or a repeated one,[3] lead victims to feel a sense of "helplessness" over their lives (13). Vickroy notes Judith Lewis Herman's research that explains how people often "separate or dissociate themselves from physical and emotional self-awareness to avoid pain," but warns "this capacity can create defensive self-restrictions, which can become ingrained, prolonging expectations of punishment or failure, instigating debilitating depression, and precluding relationships outside the captive situation" (13).

Buffy and Willow both have experiences and exhibit behavior that match these descriptions. While Buffy's story certainly takes more center stage—she is the Slayer after all—analyzing the parallels between the stories creates a context for each. This context reminds viewers not only to consider their stories in relation to their community but also to consider what Fran H. Norris and Martie P. Thompson explain as "community psychology's ecological perspective" to traumatic experiences, the view that "includes the assumption that people and their environments mutually influence one another and cannot be understood alone; people are part of an interconnected whole and not isolated entities" (51). In other words, while physical pain is experienced individually, the emotional implications of trauma often affect more than the individual; healing may then be enhanced by an understanding of the communal impact as well as the individual pain.

The trauma for each occurs at different points of time—Buffy at the beginning of Season Six, Willow at the end. As Erickson and Lemberg observe, Buffy's trauma occurs in her resurrection ("Bargaining" 6.01) (119) at the beginning of Season Six after sacrificing herself to save Dawn and the world from the impending apocalypse at the conclusion of Season Five. This arc at the end of Season Five concluded the traditional story line for the heroine, and a sense of finality, of her being "finished," permeated the scene.[4] After being dead for 147 days ("After Life" 6.03), Buffy is resurrected in her coffin due to a spell cast by her friends Willow, Xander, Anya, and Tara. Confused and clearly terrified, she claws her way to the surface. Walking the streets of Sunnydale, she observes even more horrific scenes as a motorcycle gang of demons loots the town, sets fires, and, in one of the most disturbing scenes of the series, rips apart the Buffybot, her mirror image, in what viewers know to be robotic form but that the newly resurrected Buffy seems incapable of recognizing as such yet. Buffy returns to the tower—the place of her death—replaying the scene and understandably asking her sister Dawn, "Is this hell?" Buffy has observed death, caused death, and been revived before, but this situation is different: we find out in "After Life" (6.03) that she has been in heaven, not the hell dimension that her friends assumed. Because they also—somewhat surprisingly—do not think to exhume the body before the ritual, Buffy's trauma is compounded by the experience of escaping her coffin and grave.[5]

Willow's major trauma occurs in the devastating scene of Tara's murder. Having been separated because of Willow's increasing use of magic, their reunion is short-lived as Warren's bullets—intended for Buffy—come through the window and hit Tara in the chest, splattering Willow and her white shirt with Tara's blood ("Seeing Red" 6.19).[6] The random and sudden event would affect anyone deeply, but especially someone like Willow, who has cultivated a sense of being the one in control, who can handle "it," whatever that "it" is. Season Six is an important one in her development as the season opened with her assuming responsibility as the leader of the group, unlike in previous seasons where she refers to herself as a "sidekick" ("Buffy vs. Dracula" 5.01). Willow also has shared her feelings of insecurity more freely at different times throughout this season. She describes herself to Tara as a "spaz at fifteen" ("All the Way" 6.06), and refers to her "stupid, mousy ways" ("Two to Go" 6.21); she also tells Buffy how the magic made her different, a "super" version of herself ("Wrecked" 6.10). After Willow and Tara broke up because of Willow's abuse of magic, her isolation intensified. Having had it restored only to have it "ripped away" through Tara's sudden death confronts Willow with a situation where not only does she lose Tara but she also loses the person who made her feel special. Without Tara, she loses a sense of self. Typical of Willow, she turns first to magic, to the same powers that resurrected Buffy. Denied, however, because this has been a natural and not a mystical death, Willow turns to her other standby option of research; however, this time, she will use the books in a much different way.

Both Buffy's loss of heavenly reward in death and Willow's loss of Tara show the characters taken by surprise, removing their control over the scene and confronting them with incidents that do not fit into the plans they have for themselves. Certainly, these scenes metaphorically capture the challenges of growing older and facing the difficulties of unexpected pain (one of Season Six's primary themes). More so, though, how these characters respond to these events—physically, intellectually, and emotionally—provides viewers with provocative portrayals of the difficulties and processes involved with healing.

"As You Were": Physical Revisions and Emotional Consequences for Buffy and Willow

"There's a thing about magic. There's always consequences. Always!" (Spike, "After Life" 6.03)

Despite the contrasting nature of the traumas—one restoring Buffy's life, one removing Tara's—both result in the creation of new bodies for Buffy and Willow. For Buffy, it is a literal new body as, at the end of the first part of "Bargaining" (6.01), we get a view of her from the side in her coffin showing her skeletal remains before the camera moves to a position above her as magic restores her flesh into the recognizable heroine. This graphic physical restoration fits with the shocking nature of the episode. Roaming the streets, her sight and hearing have been affected and take some time to restore themselves; she at first observes the world around her through a kind of tunnel vision with muffled sound. Given the depressed nature of her senses and her disoriented state, one may worry that she will be more vulnerable to the motorcycle gang; however, when she is struck by Razor and her friends are threatened, Buffy fights. When Razor hits her and her lip bleeds, her injury and the physicality of her body it represents make her retaliate. Using demons rather than vampires as the primary danger in the episode certainly adds to the hellish look of the scene, but it is also true that vampires would involve a less physical confrontation; these demons demand a different physical attention in order to defeat them. Buffy's body remembers its strength, a sign that, while Anya may worry she is "broken," Buffy's identity as the Slayer—whose physicality defines her—is still intact. Indeed, Xander sees her fighting and exclaims, "She's Buffy. She's herself again" ("Bargaining" 6.02).

In Season Six, Buffy's physical strength remains part of her identity, no matter what is happening externally. In "Tabula Rasa" (6.08), she loses her memory because of a botched spell of Willow's; however, she is happy about her physical strength, exclaiming, "I'm like a superhero or something," after she kills a vampire. In "Flooded" (6.04), she acts more like herself after a fight with a demon at a bank, assertively standing over the loan officer instead of cowering before him as she did before the altercation. Although one's essence is separate from the body in the Buffy universe, bodies nevertheless give the characters information about who they are. Frances Early notes: "Regardless of context, Buffy's body is wedded to her sense of self and is always relevant to the action at hand" and that it "has an essentialist attribute: she is stronger than others because she is the Chosen One" (59). While observing that Buffy's body is also "a powerful and fluid open image" (59), Early's article nevertheless reminds us that Buffy is different because of her physicality, not her social or cultural conditioning.

In contrast, Willow's new body is sourced from an external object: magic books. The entire situation is not the normal scenario for a *Buffy* episode. Warren is neither demon, nor god, nor vampire, nor snake monster; he is human, albeit one who has done a terrible thing. Willow wants to make him suffer, and she does not care about moral consequences. She is pragmatic in her pursuit of this goal; less concerned with issues of right and wrong, she is looking for power and looking for it quickly. Wilcox refers to Willow as a "shadow and foil for Buffy" (*Why Buffy Matters* 49), and we can see this relationship by comparing Willow's appropriation of knowledge with Buffy's naturally-given power. Wilcox explains that Willow has shown "a dangerous desire for control repeated and emphasized over the years" (*Why Buffy Matters* 49), and viewers witness her follow this need for control in one of the series' more provocative visual sequences, in which she enters the Magic Box, pulls the books off the shelves with her magical powers, sinks her hands into the books, and literally pulls the words into her ("Villains" 6.20). As the text travels up her body, we observe her new physical self with dark hair, dark eyes, and lowered voice. From this point, Willow "is the magics," and her merging with the primal forces creates a physical body that contains a new and awesome sense of power. When Warren axes her in the back, for example, it does not harm her ("Villains" 6.20). She also can manipulate and move through space as she does with Buffy and Dawn when she transports them from Rack's to the Magic Box ("Two to Go" 6.21). Willow's choice to alter her physical body by absorbing unearned power quickly has devastating consequences for her and her friends.

Both women next undergo a profound period of personal change, and both characters share important similarities in their physical, intellectual, and emotional reactions to that change. Physically, Buffy and Willow house a strength unique to them. Intellectually, they are able to retain the ability to make strategic decisions and effectively analyze their situations. However, their moral differences allow viewers to understand the intellect differently. Understanding the consequences of taking life in a different way from the others because of her Slayer experience, Buffy maintains objectivity, in part because she knows that she will be the one asked to carry out the plans in physical ways that will often result in death.[7] She remains mindful that supernatural powers do not authorize one to kill humans. Despite her emotional turmoil, she chooses to remain aware of the consequences of her actions, thus strengthening a positive sense of self.

Like Buffy, Willow can distance herself from emotion to make strategic decisions; however, unlike Buffy, her choices are problematic because, rather than strengthening her, Willow's cold intellect leads her further away from healing because her decisions reflect no sense of morality, only vengeance. Some of these strategic actions, despite their emotional cost, include how she activates effective spells such as increasing her physical strength to fight Buffy ("Two to Go" 6.21) and using her shirt that is stained with Tara's blood in a spell to locate Warren ("Villains" 6.20). In her confrontation with Warren, we see a decisive Willow who understands his motives and misogyny. Willow's dark power removes the limits that she normally places on herself to articulate her understanding of others. Elsewhere in the series, Spike is the one who voices this kind of analysis, but here the magical power has led Willow to use her understanding against others, rather than fostering forgiveness. Willow knows that Buffy will try to prevent her from attacking the Trio. As such, she must carry out the revenge herself with a certainty that leads her to destroy Warren in an extremely body-conscious way: flaying ("Villains" 6.20).

Despite these different moral compasses, Buffy's and Willow's similarities appear again as each experiences emotional alienation from herself and her friends. Previously to this season, Buffy has not always expressed her feelings to her friends. As Elyce Rae Helford asserts, the series does not always allow for women's expression of anger, with Buffy typically avoiding confrontation with others and channeling her anger through humor (23). The trauma of resurrection exacerbates this tendency toward isolation as, throughout most of Season Six, Buffy feels completely out-of-character as "Buffy"; in the Scoobies' attempt to help their friend, they have inadvertently disrupted her physical, emotional, and spiritual sense of self. As Whedon explains, "Buffy was the centered person who had herself to rely on and she lost that. Coming back from the dead will do that to you. She really questioned why she was back, why she was there, and questioned her power" ("Life Is the Big Bad"). Her emotional recovery will necessitate not only re-establishing the "rules" for her Slayer work, but also her connections with her friends and her sense of self as "Buffy."

Buffy has generally always felt some separation from the others because of her Slayer identity, but that separation has been balanced by her love for them. These bonds are so strong that she willingly gives her life for Dawn's in Season Five's final episode. Over several episodes in Season Six, we observe Buffy struggle to return to this place of connection. At first, she lies to her friends by thanking them for bringing her back, believing her lie to be protective. We do see her attempt to talk to the group—especially in "Smashed" (6.09) and "Tabula Rasa" (6.08)—but these attempts are stopped by magical interruptions such as the reveal of Amy being "de-ratted" in the former and the loss of memory in the latter.

The most significant communicative relationship she has is with Spike.[8] She can reveal the truth to him, perhaps because he was not involved with the resurrection spell. Also, Spike has experienced physical and corresponding emotional trauma as well, both because he has died and crawled out of his own grave when he awoke as a vampire and because of the government implanting the behavior modification computer chip that causes him pain when he attacks a human. Buffy feels close to Spike while simultaneously disconnected from the others and herself, and the result of such contradictory emotions is that she enters into a sexual relationship with him. While the chemistry between the two characters certainly makes for compelling television, Buffy's choice to be with him further isolates her as she moves away from her sense of morality—not "Slayer" morality, necessarily, but "Buffy" morality. For Buffy, to use Spike solely in this way without an emotional attachment is wrong for her, but the intensity of her pain leads her to be with him repeatedly. Spike understands that her involvement with him is a result of the pain she feels in relation to her friends, and he also seeks to isolate her from the others—telling her, for example, in "Smashed" (6.09), "I'm the only one here for you pet! You've got no one else!" As Drew Z. Greenberg explains in his commentary to the episode, Buffy and Spike can hurt each other because they are physically different from the others—they are, indeed, "superheroes" ("'Smashed' Episode Commentary"). For the first time, though, Buffy is starting to see similarity with Spike not in her physical strength but her moral and emotional choices. She is behaving more like Spike and less like Buffy before the resurrection. As she sings in "Once More, With Feeling," "I was always brave, and kind of righteous, now I'm wavering." Buffy uses their physical similarities to forget about the emotional pain, but she realizes that to acknowledge Spike as a potential emotional equal would remove her further from her Buffy sense of self, so she does not accept the possibility.

Because Buffy's identity is so connected with her physicality and because the body can provide her with information, Buffy is upset when she realizes that Spike—who should not be able to hit a human (but who can hit non-humans)—can strike her without pain. Concerned that she came back "wrong," she asks Tara to check the spell. Tara is her choice as she knows the others would judge her for being with Spike. Tara explains in "Dead Things" (6.13) that Buffy is "different" in that the ritual "altered [her body] on a basic molecular level," a change that affects the chip; however, she reassures Buffy it is just "surfacey" stuff, and that she is still human. This new information makes Buffy realize that her relationship with Spike has more to do with her own choices than any physical misfiring. Taking responsibility for her feelings is part of her healing because it moves her away from a place of denial and isolation to one where she acknowledges the reality of the situation. As Wilcox argues, "Buffy *wants* to see her body as monstrous in order to justify her connection to Spike and her own violent sexual predilections—both of which help her feel" ("Set on This Earth" 98). Buffy, as Wilcox explains elsewhere, must "forgive herself[,] … Spike, and the side of herself represented by him" (*Why Buffy Matters* 86). This self-forgiveness is key to helping her move beyond her emotional state that looks for punishment and judgment.

Also part of Buffy's healing is that she realizes her neglect of Dawn. At first overwhelmed by her return to life, Buffy does not have the perspective to be vigilant of Dawn's care. She leaves her sister often on her own or with friends, and she relies on Giles for direction about Dawn in "Life Serial" (6.05) and "All the Way" (6.06). Only the threat of losing custody of Dawn forces her to recognize the consequences of her continued isolation. Moreover, the revelation of Dawn's stealing in "Older and Far Away" (6.14) dramatizes to Buffy the extent of Dawn's own pain. Buffy realizes her role as Dawn's mentor when they fight together for the first time in the season's final episode. Their crawling out of the grave together, as opposed to Buffy's solitary climb that opened the season, metaphorically captures this healed relationship. Buffy learns that part of her power is being a mentor and a sister. Her choice to be a mentor at the end of Season Six reflects her restored sense of agency as Buffy and the Slayer. Moreover, by accepting Dawn—a creature made from Buffy's own physical body—she accepts that external forces sometimes wield more control than we plan for or expect.

Just as Buffy's pain causes her alienation from the group, so too does Willow feel estranged. In part, this is consistent with Willow's largely independent study of magic. While gifted in terms of intelligence and ability, Willow develops her power primarily by study on her own. Giles does not train her as he trains Buffy, and without a strong mentor figure, Willow develops her skills without real supervision or interaction with other witches, with the exception of the often-equally inexperienced Amy and Tara. After Buffy's death, Willow assumes the leadership role in the group, a position that seems to necessitate some distancing from the others. She feels personally responsible for bringing Buffy back. This responsibility leads to a pragmatic sense of morality and secrecy.[9] For instance, Willow sacrifices a baby deer for the resurrection spell and keeps information about the dangers of the ritual away from the others. She even lies to Tara when she tells her that she does not understand the words of the "possessed" Buffy that reveal information about the sacrifice ("After Life" 6.03). Associating "good stuff" with what is necessary moves Willow away from a paradigm of good and evil and toward one based on means, such as ruthlessly extracting energy from others around her when she needs more "juice," in "Two to Go" (6.21) and, later, in Season Seven in "Get It Done" (7.15).

Like Buffy, Willow's isolation from the others is strengthened because her choices about her new power separate her from them. Even while they do the resurrection spell together, it is Willow who is the supernatural focal point—the slashes appear on her arms, the bugs move in her body, the light shimmers around her, the snake emerges from her mouth. The success leads Willow to minimize the danger and to focus on her achievement. Giles angrily tells her that he thought she "would respect the forces of nature," but Willow has clearly moved beyond a sense of balanced power to one that is prideful, telling him that "I did what no one else could do.... I was amazing" ("Flooded" 6.04).[10] Achieving such power without a clear sense of boundary or responsibility[11] leads Willow to see others and the world as objects to be manipulated through magic, even though she does not seem to understand that she is imposing her will for selfish reasons. Wilcox explains:

> Her ability to control the physical and the solid with her mind and spirit leads her to feel a greater and greater distance from the physical; rather than feeling herself connected to the world, she sees herself as able to manipulate it as a

> possession. This relationship to the physical world is yet another attitude often associated with the traditional patriarchal dominion over the earth.... As Season Six proceeds, Buffy immerses herself in the physical while Willow, exerting control over it, distances herself from it ["Set on This Earth" 99].

Such willful domination, instead of being a heroic action to avenge her friend, is damaging not only to Willow but to the entire Scooby Gang. She thinks she can handle the power, but without a moral center, Willow places herself in jeopardy.

Willow's abuse of power is her response to the pain caused by the trauma of Buffy's death and her inability to have saved her. Instead of understanding that problems need to be worked through and not suppressed, Willow wants to make the negative energy go away, denying the issue by denying the energy. This approach is seen most clearly in "Tabula Rasa" (6.08) in which she manipulates Buffy's and Tara's minds into forgetting their sad feelings. Another example occurs in her fight with Giles when Willow denies the importance of the physical by waving a hand over her bleeding face, healing it immediately while saying "This is nothing. It's all nothing" ("Grave" 6.22); however, the physical is clearly something as she is willing to sacrifice the world to rid it and her of any physicality at all. Without a paradigm to process emotional and physical pain, she is overwhelmed. Instead of isolating herself and destroying what she does not want to feel, Willow must, like Buffy, re-connect with her community in order to start the healing process. This time, it is Xander who appeals to her sense of humanity and reaches her through her pain, refuses to leave her, and holds her as she breaks down. The turn to healing begins with a restoration of her previous physical state. Her hair and eyes lighten, and Willow Rosenberg is recognizable once more.

For both Buffy and Willow, although they have strength in the power they wield over the physical world—Buffy through her physical strength and Willow through her magical ability—they still must take another step in order to heal fully from their respective trauma: their recovery necessitates reconnection to themselves and others, a process that captures the often gradual and complex nature of healing in a contextualized way.

"Lessons": The Restoration of Buffy and Willow

"Let yourself live already." (Spike, "Normal Again" 6.17)

The gradual nature of healing is taken up in Season Seven after the intense damage of Season Six. Tellingly, Season Seven's "Big Bad" is not an enemy that can be physically hit and located in a specific lair; rather this season's "Big Bad" is the First Evil, an entity without physical form that exerts power by manipulating others. Its incorporeal nature makes its power one of psychological influence, and its Protean manifestations allow it to interact with all of the characters, evoking emotional responses. Characters may intellectually know they are not seeing their loved ones, but the illusion of the physical reappearance prompts painful, though honest, reactions. Both Buffy and Willow must risk emotional experiences with The First in order to heal fully.

By the end of Season Six, Buffy has been reunited with her sense of purpose and returns to a place of leadership, something that strengthens her Slayer identity and creates a transition point for her reintegration into the group.[12] As the others continue to get used to this new, yet original, "Buffy," they still understand her role as the Slayer. However, this initial step at emotional healing—her return to leadership—also forces her to confront and understand the burden of responsibility she has always felt as the Slayer. In a number of ways, this feeling of obligation—the fact that she is the Slayer—is what makes her feel disconnected from her friends throughout the series, a fact that is particularly brought to light in the final two seasons. In "Conversations with Dead People" (7.07), she reveals her complicated feelings to her former school mate, Holden Webster: she does feel superior to her friends, though at the same time she feels profoundly undeserving of their devotion and love. Throughout Season Seven, she perseveres, however, in repairing the relationships, and she uses this healed state to help others. This process is illustrated most directly in her role as school counselor, where she listens to the problems of high school students, and as mentor to the Potentials. Both situations create opportunities for healing as Buffy returns to her place as a leader, reconciles with others emotionally and shares her strength rather than isolating herself.

Willow, likewise, undergoes a significant period of healing before she can learn how to wield her power constructively. Season Seven is structured in such a way so that we see Willow's return to emotional health occurring through processing some important emotional issues in four sets of relationships—with Giles, her friends, Kennedy, and the Potentials. At the beginning of the season, viewers see that Giles, along with the coven, has been serving as a mentor to Willow in England. Willow understands that her new body, while still being Willow, nevertheless contains a supernatural force that must be understood and trained in order to control it. She also learns that "everything is connected" and that along with the beautiful, the earth has "deep, deep black" ("Lessons" 7.01). In order to fully heal, she must integrate her knowledge of both the connection and the darkness.

Returning to Sunnydale, Willow is understandably afraid of seeing her friends ("Same Time, Same Place" 7.03). Her fear is so intense that it actually alters the group's perception of reality as Xander and Buffy cannot see

Willow and vice versa, a fact that almost results in Willow being eaten by the demon Gnarl. Once she understands that they do indeed miss her, the friends are able see each other again. The episode is yet another reminder of the importance of healing and connective conversation in order to perceive others accurately. The episode ends with Buffy choosing to share strength with Willow as Willow heals herself magically, a scene that bodes well for their continued work together and for Willow using magic and companionship for rehabilitation rather than destruction.

Receiving the forgiveness of her friends allows Willow to take an important step in her recovery—pursuing another romantic relationship after the loss of Tara; however, her relationship with Kennedy confronts her with yet another key piece of the recovery process. Because Willow feels guilty about being with Kennedy instead of seeing this new relationship as an important part of her renewal, she transforms into Warren due to a spell that curses Willow to choose her own punishment ("The Killer in Me" 7.13). Physically turning into Warren metaphorically captures her guilt about moving on as well as confronts her directly with her crime. Her negotiation of her guilt and her movement toward acceptance dramatizes the costs of taking power that has not been earned as well as the necessary role of self-forgiveness in healing.

Most notable in Season Seven is how these episodes lead Willow to her final spell of transforming the other Potentials into Slayers ("Chosen" 7.22). Given that it is the last episode of the series, viewers might easily assume that Buffy and her group will be successful and thus undermine the real risk that Willow is taking. Her attempts at spells have often had serious consequences, and in the final season alone, they have conjured up physical manifestations of Dark Willow with a change in hair and eye color as seen in the episodes at the fraternity house ("Selfless" 7.05), the return of Buffy from the Shadow Men ("Get It Done" 7.15), and a simple locator spell in which the First possesses her ("Bring on the Night" 7.10). Indeed, during this final spell Kennedy is physically beside Willow in case she turns dark again. Willow risks her physical and spiritual life, as heroically as the Potentials, because she understands that she is the only one who can affect such a magical diffusion of energy. Her power must be used, and her motive to empower rather than to dominate others illustrates that power can heal. This healing and redemption is made physically visible as light infuses the scene, and she temporarily has white hair. This physical alteration suggests that she has integrated the dark and has healed herself through connection to others.

Susan Bordo argues that when analyzing power systems, a method is needed to "describe a power whose central mechanisms are not repressive, but *constitutive*" (92). Understanding representations of trauma and healing can be a part of these reformed understandings about female power.

Buffy's and Willow's storylines metaphorically capture the changing understanding women have of themselves as they age, as their bodies and circumstances change, including enduring and healing from emotional and physical trauma. Understanding these new bodies and realities often involves confrontations with emotion and self-perception. Moreover, the stories indicate how emotional scars cannot be dismissed or denied, but need community and time to heal, prescriptions that allow for the "constitutive" force that Bordo calls for.

Moreover, this idea that community can be a "constitutive" force connects with Whedon's remarks about the interplay between Season Six and Seven during an Academy of Television Arts and Sciences Panel Discussion. He speaks of "earning" back both Buffy's return from the dead and Willow's experiences with dark magic in Season Six, and, in Season Seven, returning the show to its original mission of the "joy of female power, of having it, using it, sharing it" ("Academy of Television"). Given this purpose, it is no wonder that Whedon included such a close attention to the connection between the physical and emotional spheres of identity, and in the process of healing these fractured components, showed that female power does not have to exist in isolation but can be developed and affirmed by the healing power of community. This choice indeed "earns" both storylines and the mission of the series overall.

Notes

1. Wilcox notes the following uses of the word: Dark Willow's "It's about the power," at the end of Season Six; Amy's "This is about power" in "The Killer in Me" (7.13); Buffy telling Dawn "It's about power" at the beginning of "Lessons" (7.01); and the First Evil's statement "It's about power" at the end of "Lessons" (7.01) (*Why Buffy Matters* 91).

2. Byers notes how *Buffy* has received some criticism because, while it endorses female empowerment, the stories are told using actors that reinforce conventional definitions of beauty. Byers suggests these reactions "can be traced to 'the body problem,'" drawing on Bordo's point that "the body is 'a powerful symbolic form' as well as a 'site of struggle'" (174).

3. Sanchez-Hucles and Gamble differentiate between Type I Trauma—"sudden, brief, unexpected, and devastating" events—and Type II traumas, which "involve chronic and repeated exposure" (104).

4. Sara Crosby, in comparing Buffy's sacrificial ending in "The Gift" with *Xena* and *Dark Angel*, says that Buffy's story differs from these others in its final emphasis on community, asserting "The series finale in 2003 sees them succeed as the episode creates this space for a permanent feminist community and heroic female identity" (176).

5. It is interesting that it is Xander and not the usually more astute Willow who discerns this, suggesting how Willow's guilt over Buffy's death can and has affected her perception.

6. Tara's body is left at the house to be found by Dawn and then to be taken away by the coroner and buried. Tara's graphic death is unusual as characters typically do not have to deal with bodies as vampires go to dust once staked or supernatural energies dissipate once defeated; however, with Tara, as with Joyce in "The Body" (5.16), the physical loss of a human is presented in a concrete way.

7. At the end of Season Five, for instance, when they are debating how to defeat Glory,

Buffy yells at Giles in frustration: "Tell me to kill my sister!" ("The Gift" 5.22). However he "reasons" with her about the solution, he is asking her to murder Dawn. That it is Dawn intensifies the emotion, yet it still indicates that Buffy understands whatever is the plan, she will be the agent of the action. The consequences will be hers to bear, and so, she takes her role seriously—perhaps a reason why Giles kills Ben in that same episode and does not ask her—because he knows she would refuse.

8. The role Spike takes in Buffy's recovery is nodded to in "As You Were" (6.15) when he goes by the codename "The Doctor."

9. Buffy has kept things from the others as well—Angel's return in Season Three and Dawn's true identity, for example. However, she usually is trying to protect others from knowledge rather than Willow who does not want to reveal the "unpleasantness" sometimes associated with her choices.

10. Willow will shift pronouns between "we" and "I" in talking about the resurrection spell, indicating slips in how she perceives responsibility and her sense of identity. See "Bargaining" (6.01) and "Tabula Rasa" (6.08).

11. Buffy has learned that just because one has power to do something does not mean one should. See, for example, episodes from the third season with Faith such as "Bad Girls" (3.14) and "Consequences" (3.15).

12. Turning points include when she becomes afraid that she is really going to disappear after being shot by the Trio's invisibility gun ("Gone" 6.11), when she chooses to return to what may be her Sunnydale "mental construction" in "Normal Again" rather than kill her friends in order "to get healthy" (6.17), when she ends her relationship with Spike ("As You Were" 6.15), and when she fights Willow ("Two to Go" 6.21 and "Grave" 6.22).

"Sweetie, your epidermis is showing"

Theorizing Skin in and Through Joss Whedon's Buffy the Vampire Slayer[1]

FRANCES SPROUT

A year or so before writing this, I began noticing increased interdisciplinary attention to skin,[2] and, with either of Joss Whedon's *Buffy the Vampire Slayer* or *Angel* fairly continuously looping at the end of my long teaching days, I began to notice that skin imagery and tropes permeated both shows. Whedon, I would argue, uses such imagery to question identity and examine inter-subjectivity, to explore morality and the limits of individual and collective responsibility in a world marked by relativity rather than by absolutes. Perhaps most obviously, skin works as a way to consider the boundary between humanity and monstrosity, a boundary declared permeable by the atrocities of the twentieth century. Yet while interested in this overall deployment of skin imagery and tropes, I was particularly fascinated by a trio of images from *Buffy*: (1) Willow, full of grief and rage at her lover, Tara's, death, appropriating the letters of the "black arts" books through her skin; (2) Willow flaying alive her lover's murderer, Warren; and (3) the skin-eating Gnarl demon peeling and eating strips off a captive, paralyzed Willow. Collectively, I argue, these scenes not only suggest a confrontation of the Foucauldian with the Bakhtinian body, but they also point beyond the dichotomy that such a confrontation stages. That is, they do not simplistically favor the carnivalesque conception of a porous, open body enmeshed with the world around it—called Bakhtinian after the cultural theorist Mikhail Bakhtin who sketched out this historical paradigm. Nor do they reductively condemn those systems of classification and order of the monadic, bourgeois body identified with another cultural theorist, Michel Foucault. Instead, collectively these three scenes imply the possibility for a different, and intersubjective, inscription of the body, and this possibility shadows a more general movement within *Buffy* from a patriarchal, hierarchical system of classification and regulation to a feminist, egalitarian system of fluid, contingent knowledge. This political shift is signaled and effected by one person, Willow Rosenberg, and it occurs through her, first, giving full rein to the monstrous within her skin, and second, being fully vulnerable to rejection by her friends and, instead, beginning to heal through accepting the inter-subjective nature of her identity.

Before looking more closely at these three scenes, though, let me first establish the persistent deployment of skin imagery throughout the series. As a marker of monstrosity in *Buffy* and *Angel*, for example, skin's unreliability hints at the series' complexity. Certainly, a myriad of evil demons are distinguished in part by their bumpy or scaly or fissured or otherwise non-human dermal covering. However, numerous exceptions render apparently monstrous skin an untrustworthy guide to its inhabitant's character: Clem, for example, whose bumpy skin, long droopy ears (and, admittedly, appetite for kittens) are at seeming odds with his sweet, helpful nature. Less likeable, perhaps, but relatively benign and occasionally helpful, if mercenary, is *Angel*'s informant demon, Merl. Both Buffy (along with her helpers, the Scoobies) and Angel (with his team of investigators) are alert to, and governed by, these moral nuances among the apparently monstrous. On both shows, however, other forces base their supposed war against evil strictly on the (generally visible) distinction between human and demon. The Initiative, even in the more amenable form of Buffy's boyfriend, Riley, is paralleled in *Angel* by his investigator Charles Gunn's former "crew"; although the two groups are very differently constituted, they are equally unable to see past superficial difference—manifest especially in an individual's skin—to judge humans and demons alike by their behavior rather than their looks.[3]

Besides the many demons whose skin immediately signals their difference and raises questions about their worth and their moral code, numerous demons assume human skin for nefarious purposes and cannot easily be recognized for what they are. The demon that Angel tracks at a singles bar ("Lonely Heart" 1.02) exemplifies this group: apparently just another lonely seeker of romance or sex, this demon, in bed with its unsuspecting "date," abandons the skin it has exhausted to occupy a new human, leaving behind a trail of eviscerated bodies. When Angel figures out its *modus operandi* and tracks it to its current and newly found home in the bartender, the beast's exposure and disintegration is displayed through the distasteful images of skin peeling away in ugly large flapping sections.

Besides demons temporarily occupying human skin, many who appear human only signal their demon identities when their skin changes: vampires are the most obvious instance, with their normal, if pale, skin transformed to bumpy foreheads. But Angel's sidekick and erstwhile guide

Doyle, with little to no inclination toward violence, might be a fairer example of a demon who passes easily for human until, with a sneeze, his face erupts in prickles fit for a hedgehog. Another example is Anya whose appearance through several seasons reflects her accidentally (and, at least initially, reluctantly) resumed humanity; as a vengeance demon, however, her skin is transformed drastically with patterns in relief decorating face and body. As this range of examples suggest, changeability of skin does not reliably indicate goodness or evil, anymore than does consistent smoothness or bumpiness.

Skin does seem to warn, however, if too late, of dangerous intentions in the case of the major contenders, although these Big Bad opponents are able to appear convincingly human for sustained periods: *Buffy*'s Mayor and Glory, and, in *Angel*, Jasmine. Even before the Mayor transforms himself into a giant snake, for instance, his skin demonstrates his demon nature through the invincibility he has engineered, re-sealing itself mystically after each attempted wounding. Glory's situation, skin-wise, is more complicated, with both Glory and Ben occupying the same body, Ben's body having been created solely as a vessel to contain Glorificus' godly energy. Or rather, as Glory describes it, they share the same "meatsack" ("The Weight of the World" 5. 21), but the body changes dramatically across gender, the skin visually morphing in the process; Ben, for example, returns to his body to find it encased in Glory's red dress ("Spiral" 5.20).

Skin-wise, though, most interesting of these three Big Bad bodies is that of Jasmine, who appears to have "normal" human skin (mocha-colored, Angel and Connor dreamily agree in "Shiny Happy People" [4.18], enthralled with her radiant beauty) until destruction of a magic charm unveils devotees' eyes to reveal maggots writhing beneath it. And before that, when only Angel and his team recognize Jasmine's true nature, an interesting scene in "Sacrifice" shows her skin opened by slashes to her followers' bodies, but also shows the slashes mystically closing (4.20), reminiscent of the Mayor's invincibility as displayed in "Graduation Day, Part One" (*Buffy* 3.21). Once Jasmine's true name has been released into this world, her skin appears pustular and ugly, a closer reflection, supposedly, of her real nature. Indeed, in their iconography of skin, the Jasmine episodes not only point to the Western cultural tradition's tendency to "revil[e] and denigrat[e]" the "(Bakhtinian) grotesque body" for its "loss of control" while proffering higher status on the "(Foucauldian) disciplined, regulated and regimented docile body" (Holliday and Hassard 9), but in some ways appear to reinforce it. The world presided over by the beautiful, smooth-skinned, sunny-tempered Jasmine is a peaceful, ordered, coherent world; the exposure of her dermatological challenges accompanies a descent into chaos, violence, and fear.

This brief reading of Jasmine's skin suggests that the Buffy/Angelverse entrenches or relies on the widely held assumption that any "true self" can be found beneath the skin. Support for such an argument might also be found in the numerous instances of doubled and/or changed selves in both *Buffy* and *Angel*, doublings or changes that mark a contradiction between exterior and interior. The Buffy[ro]bot's skin can be peeled back, for example, to show her workings ("Intervention" 5.18); Giles' eyes shine through his magically-imposed demon skin ("A New Man" 4.12); and decoy [robot] Warren's eye pops mechanically from its socket ("Villains" 6.20). These examples from *Buffy* are similar to *Angel*'s Jasmine episodes in their evocation of all those expressions which mark a divergence between the expectations raised by our body's surface and that which that surface encloses, those idioms emphasizing the illusory potential of skin—that "Beauty is only skin deep," for example, or that something really gets under our skin. Claudia Benthien has collected a wealth of such expressions, primarily in German, but also in other European languages including English, and they reflect convincingly a common and influential conception of skin.

At the same time, however, I would argue that the over determination of doubling throughout both *Buffy* and *Angel*—it would be difficult to find a major character whose body has not been borrowed or changed or copied in some way—points to an unwillingness to accept this opposition of superficiality and depth as a truism. Rather than trying to hammer home a distrust of potentially illusory surfaces, the redundant doubling points to an exploration of identity, a desire to understand in what it inheres and an insistence on that understanding being embodied. Benthien presents a second group of sayings, generally older and much less circulated currently, which equate skin and subjectivity. In these idioms, she observes, "the essence does not lie beneath the skin, hidden inside. Rather it is the skin itself, which stands metonymically for the whole human being" (17). That two such contradictory groups of expressions could each represent a common construction about skin testifies to a longstanding ambivalence in our perception of this bodily envelope, an ambivalence built into our language at a rather fundamental level.[4]

Thus while many of the doubling episodes in *Buffy* and *Angel* appear, as in the case of Jasmine, to reinforce a sense of the skin as an untrustworthy indicator of what it encloses, several of the doublings have a less clear message. In the case of Willow and her evil vampire double, both versions, superficially identical, are equally authentic in their respective dimensions ("Doppelgangland" 3.16); when Xander is split into two versions, an ill-groomed, more adolescent-behaving self and a polished, ambitious, and better-dressed young man, the Scoobies determine that these are simply different aspects of the "real" Xander ("The Replacement" 5.3).

Both Angel and Angelus, although they argue about whose claim to the body is legitimate, equally attest to their continued co-existence beneath shared skin (among many episodes, perhaps the best example of this can be found in "Orpheus" 4.15). Whether cases that reveal an imposter beneath the skin, however, or those that present simultaneous doubles each claiming authenticity, these episodes, which we might gather under the heading—One Self/Two Skins—prompt some serious meditation about identity. If we summarize their plots as "It looks like her, but it is not" OR "It is him, but it does not look like him," we have a chiasmatically-complicated relationship between skin, doubles, and identity that mirrors the paradox Benthien reveals in the perception of skin for centuries.

This "duality of thinking about skin [both] as covering [and] as self," Benthien asserts, corresponds to "two models of the so-called body-soul relationship that still predominate today" (36). Of much longer standing is the "conception of the skin as a house ... in which the subject lies hidden" (36). Benthien traces the analogy between skin and house—with "the other senses seen as locked gates or windows capable of being closed ... the skin itself ... a static and impermeable boundary between the self and the world" (28)—as having only "replaced that of the body as dress" in the last two hundred years, although "both body images were already known from antiquity and Christianity as spatial ideas about the in-dwelling of the soul" (24). This notion of body-skin as an impregnable shell for an autonomous soul achieved dominance with the Enlightenment's liberal humanist emphasis on the individual.[5]

With modern psychoanalysis, however, skin was recognized as the primary organ by which the body senses itself and the world. In contrast to the Enlightenment-favored view of skin sealing off the soul from the world ("diametrically opposed," says Benthien) is "the perception of skin as a felt boundary that can be experienced through the sensory perceptions of pain and pleasure and thus forms, in the early childhood process of individuation, the precondition for all object relationships later in life" (36). Freud begins what Benthien terms the "rehabilitat[ion]" of the skin as an "organ of perception" (36) by emphasizing its role in developing the ego. Marc LaFrance traces this rehabilitation in psychoanalytic history, beginning at Freud, moving through Donald Winnicot and Wilfrid Bion, then pausing to emphasize Didier Anzieu's important role in naming and outlining the "ego-skin." LaFrance's particular interest is in the Anglo-American psychoanalysts Esther Bick and Thomas Ogden whose focus is on the self, but whom LaFrance reads for their understanding of the skin's relationship to that self. Generally, what all these psychoanalysts agree on is that our egos develop by touching and being touched. What LaFrance's Anglo-Americans outline, more specifically, are four important points: (1)

the mind (or soul) only becomes coherent and learns the world through the body; (2) the self's body and mind are not only constituted by but also constitutive of the other's body and mind; (3) much of what we assume is innate in the self is actually acquired; and (4) a secure sense of physical and mental containment is one of the self's most significant and vital achievements (19). In all of these points, it is the skin—our tactile system—that mediates the body's interaction with the world.

Keeping in mind this notion of the skin as the primary organ through and by which the body develops a coherent sense of self in relationship to others, it is time to turn to the three scenes featuring Willow and skin imagery. It is worth pausing just a bit longer, however, to consider Willow and why her skin-ego might be particularly apt for an exploration of the relationship between skin and identity. Certainly, when we first meet Willow Rosenberg in "Welcome to the Hellmouth" (1.01) there's little indication of the condition of her skin, other than that she keeps it very well covered. Identified to Buffy by Cordelia as one of the "losers" to avoid, Willow presents herself as very friendly, although well aware of her low social status—she assures Buffy that Buffy need not let herself be seen sitting with Willow. But the Slayer pulls Willow into the small circle that eventually becomes the Scoobies, gradually lending Willow the confidence to "seize the day" (albeit with risks of fatalities).[6] Equally gradually, we see Willow's dress change from "the softer side of Sears" ("Welcome to the Hellmouth" 1.01), as Cordelia so unkindly describes it, to clothing choices more expressive of her engagement with her friends and her newfound sense of purpose.[7]

What remains consistent is that Willow continues to rely on her scholarly abilities to demonstrate her worth. In the first moments we see her in relationship with someone else—Xander, on whom she has long had a serious crush—we see her eagerly agreeing to help with math homework. Not much later, Buffy explains her willingness to ignore Cordelia's advice (against befriending Willow) by her ambition to do well in school and thus needing Willow's help—not really a flattering explanation, but one Willow appears to accept quite happily. Conversely, in "The Harvest" (1.02), Willow uses her "brainy student" knowledge to wreak an unsuspected revenge on Cordelia and her cohort, tutoring them to complete their Computer Science assignment with the command "Deliver"—the correct meaning of the "Del" button being, of course, "Delete."

Numerous critics have written about the significance of Willow's role in *Buffy*. Matthew Pateman writes about her "disappearing Jewishness" and comments that her identity is performative, in keeping with the series' prevailing mode of identity. Rebecca Beirne primarily concerns herself with the series' portrayal of lesbianism, lamenting its tendency either to normalize it (in a loving couple, Tara and Willow) or to associate it with magic, and she finds Willow's performance of her sexuality inauthentic, at least until her relationship with Kennedy. I am more interested in Beirne's labeling of Willow as the "most flexible character in *Buffy*." Here she echoes Jes Battis' study articulating Willow's hybridity, the study most relevant to reading my trilogy of images. Battis focuses on Willow's liminality and hybridity to demonstrate the Bakhtinian aspect of *Buffy* found in "its characters' status as incomplete, becoming, and [their capability for] wild transgression" ("She's Not All Grown" par. 1). Battis convincingly demonstrates that Willow's "state of evolution" ("She's Not All Grown" par. 2) is more pronounced than other characters because she is the one least sure of her own identity, the one who most relies on others to define her.

Battis speaks of Willow's fluid identity in terms of her corporeality, or rather lack of it ("She's Not All Grown" par. 16), and in doing so recalls those psychoanalytic theories which insist that our egos develop through our bodies, particularly through the sensations of touching, and being touched by, others. When Battis claims that Willow "fails to maintain her own body without making the radical foreclosures needed to satisfy her friends' expectations" ("She's Not All Grown" par. 16), he calls to mind LaFrance's summary of psychoanalytic work regarding the role of skin in early development of the ego. Both Bick and Ogden, as LaFrance reads them, trace an inability to internalize the experience of skin as a container to the lack, in infancy, of "an enduring experience of epidermal envelopment"; an infant, that is, only learns to recognize its own skin as the limit of itself and the boundary between self and meaningful others through "regular and reliable experiences of skin-to-skin contact with its caregiver" (9). Without such skin-to-skin contact during infancy, an individual will develop either a "perforated" mental skin or none at all, resulting in considerable and enduring anxiety about leaking, non-cohesion, and/or falling apart.

To counteract or cope with this anxiety, subjects with an insecure sense of embodiment will develop what Bick and others term a "second skin" which takes the form of repetitive behaviors or postures designed to hold the individual together, to create a reassuring sensation of discrete, autonomic cohesion. Of fascinating pertinence to Willow's insecure embodiment is LaFrance's comment that "according to Bick [precocious speech] can be understood as a container substitute … or 'skin of words' when the body is experienced as insecure" (10–11). Might it not be possible to extend this understanding to include Willow's enveloping herself in knowledge? Whereas her speech may or may not have been precocious, and is, when we meet her, more stammering than fluent, she associates herself throughout with books and their contemporary counterpart, computers—arguably, a "skin of words."[8]

If knowledge, represented by books and the written word, has been central to Willow's intersubjectivity, the "skin" through which she not only defines and contains her own identity but through which she also maintains relationships with others, the access this knowledge provides her to magic—her knowledge *of* magic—challenges that identity and those relationships. This psychic skin, formed of magic and knowledge, takes a back seat to her physical, tactile skin's negotiation of intersubjectivity as Willow's sexuality is awakened in her relationship with Oz (and her physical infatuation and flirtation with Xander). However, when Oz's werewolf self (indeed, a second skin of his own) leads him into infidelity with Veruca, Willow turns to her growing knowledge of magic to hold herself together, conjuring a spell to wreak disastrous revenge on the pair. Although she does not complete the spell, is instead interrupted and threatened with death by Veruca and then rescued by Oz, the reliance on magic to defend herself against the world's griefs foreshadows what will happen after Tara dies.

Indeed, while Willow resists using magic to inflict vengeance on Oz and Veruca, she turns to it when her friends fail, in her perception, to fill the gap Oz leaves, to hold her together as she grieves his loss. Although Tara soon fills this void for Willow, providing her a new identity as lesbian girlfriend, and although both share appreciation for and proficiency in magic, Willow not only soon outstrips Tara's skill, but she relies on magic to supply more and more of her needs, to Tara's growing concern and disapproval.

Even during their relationship, Willow uses magic to guard against the vicissitudes which accompany love and life. Although her growing facility with these arts is primarily used to fight Evil alongside the Scoobies, this is not the case when she lends her knowledge, surreptitiously, to Dawn. Falling apart at the death of Buffy's mother, Willow desperately seeks just the right sweater—arguably a skin substitute, an enveloping reinforcement of internal cohesion (*Buffy*, "The Body" 5.16). Failing to maintain boundaries, her leaky or "perforated" skin-ego, allows her to experience Dawn's grief so intensely that she expedites Dawn's disastrous efforts to re-animate her mother ("Forever" 5.17). While the other Scoobies also grieve Joyce's death and try to comfort Dawn, even Spike recognizes what a horrible mistake will result from any attempt to retrieve Joyce from the grave. Yet Willow has a history of inscribing her relationship with others through her knowledge; rather than refuse Dawn sympathetically but firmly, as Tara does, she is shaped by the pressure of Dawn's grief into the "second skin" of the accommodating tutor.

Even before Willow surrenders to her growing dependence on magic, though, there are indications she still fears "that her constructed identity may have no substance beneath it" (Battis, "She's Not All Grown" par. 21). This is Battis' convincing reading of Willow's dream in "Restless" (4.22).

Battis notes that within this dream, Willow's "corporeality is as fluid as her dream world" and that "the only talismanic character traits that she brings to her own dream ... are the ones with which she has been most keenly inscribed by her friends" ("She's Not All Grown" par. 20). Most interestingly, in light of what transpires after Tara's death, Willow dreams herself "painting Greek characters on Tara's naked back ... invo[king] Aphrodite [not to inflict] pain and care" ("She's Not All Grown" par. 19). Battis finds this invocation "oracular" given that the combination of Willow's love for Tara and her love of magic will "drive the conflict that precipitates her addiction and subsequent flight from reality" ("She's Not All Grown" par. 19). To Battis' connection of this scene with Willow's eventual darkness, I would add that both scenes involve skin covered with letters in a context of love and pain (the latter only potential in the dream).

In fact, although the dream image is of Willow painting characters on Tara's back and the letters called forth later from the "black arts" books cover Willow's body, an argument might be made that Tara's skin, by the role it plays in inscribing Willow's identity through the tactility of their shared sexuality, is also Willow's skin. It is when the borders of their respective skins meet that Willow feels most sure of who she is, and losing Tara's skin (as she tries to guard against, in her dream), means losing her own sense of cohesion, the skin that holds her together *as* Willow. Perhaps this is what is also symbolized in Willow's dreamed transformation at the hands of the First Slayer. In the dream she shares with Xander, Giles, and Buffy after helping channel the power of the Slayer lineage to defeat Adam ("Primeval" 4.21), Willow's fears of her "true self" being revealed culminate in a classroom. Here, she stands in front of mocking and indifferent classmates, in her most bookish, immature form. Attacked by the First Slayer, as her portion of the dream ends, Willow's "*skin* becomes yellowish, almost reptilian" (Battis, "She's Not All Grown" par. 22, emphasis added). While the other characters are mauled or have organs removed in their portions of the dream, Willow's injuries are manifest at the level of her skin, that which holds her body and identity together.

If we see Tara's skin as shared by Willow, as inscribing her with a sense of (conditional, contingent) self, we can understand that its removal through Tara's "abrupt and shocking" death (Battis, "She's Not All Grown" par. 30) triggers Willow's almost-immediate recourse to magic. As Battis says, "Tara's death ... fragments Willow's already-compromised identity beyond repair, causing her to become wholly subsumed and *embodied* by magic" ("She's Not All Grown" par. 33, emphasis added). This embodiment by magic is manifest in the blackening of Willow's eyes and hair as she rages against Osiris, defying his refusal to return her beloved to life. However, the transformation of her identity from the most knowledgeable Scooby and Tara's girlfriend to grief-enraged witch is most explicit when Willow declares, "I *am* the magic," in the first of the three pivotal scenes featuring Willow and skin ("Villains").

In this scene at the Magic Box, Willow ignores Anya's attempts at intervention as well as her protestations that the sequestered "black arts" books must remain out of bounds. Instead, rather than search the books in any orderly fashion, she pulls them, using magic, into a jumbled pile on a table and proceeds to empty them. As the black printed words leave their pages, they stream toward Willow, forming a column that divides to spiral symmetrically around each of Willow's arms toward her trunk, over her body, and up across her face. They form, in other words, a skin, providing a strong visual image of the enveloping cohesion they provide Willow, before they are integrated into her embodied self. In this visuality, the words represent not only the magic which is Willow's most recent recourse for a "second skin," but also the facility with books which inscribed her identity before magic. As a visual metaphor, they certainly evoke Bick's "skin of words" (qtd. in LaFrance 11). While Battis' reading of this scene has already made the point that Willow "allow[s] [magic] to embody her," this embodiment is even more productively understood by noting that it happens at the level of the skin. Such attention, I believe, leads to a more powerful apprehension of Willow's next move, her revenge on Warren, as well as of her subsequent treatment by the Gnarl demon.

Because, of course, visualizing these words as magic and book-knowledge enveloping and lending cohesion to Willow—seeing them, in other words, as skin—offers symmetry to the second pivotal scene, that in which Willow flays Warren alive ("Villains"). Doing so, removing the dermal boundary which maintains Warren's body as separate while containing his monstrosity, Willow's own monstrous act collapses the distinction between them. When Amy's spell later has Willow assume Warren's physical appearance in "The Killer in Me" (7.13), it merely concretizes a truth that flaying Warren reveals about Willow: their shared reliance on knowledge—whether of science or of magic—not only for their identities but also for the power it confers, as well as their shared disregard for communal law when that law thwarts their perceived needs or desires. Willow's need for a second skin woven of magic and words is mirrored in Warren's horrifically exposed and vulnerable flayed torso. And if Warren's torso, in eliciting our horrified response (as it does that of Buffy, Xander, and Anya) also elicits our grudging acknowledgment of his humanity, the act of flaying peels back Willow's humanity to reveal the monster capable of such an act. The relationship between the two W's, if not of similarities then of reversals, is also potentially visible when (prior to the flaying) Willow magically sews Warren's skin closed at its major opening, his lips, an act which arguably projects Willow's sense that she will not be heard in her grief, no matter how loudly she cries out her loss.[9]

Juxtaposing the flaying with Willow's skin-enhancing disruption and expropriation of the "black arts" books also evokes the contrast between Bakhtinian and Foucauldian systems of order and conceptions of the body. While, in its grotesquerie, Warren's torso recalls Bakhtinian disorder with its abundance of horrific corporal punishment, it also recalls those anatomy-text images which led to the classified and controlled human body and the concomitant perception of the autonomous, discrete, bourgeois individual. As Benthien informs us, flaying "represents a synthesis of the most extreme form of capital punishment (torture) and the medical production of knowledge" pointing to the belaboring, in the "visual arts of the sixteenth and seventeenth centures" of flaying as a scene (62). She offers reproductions of many works from this period, both those that depict flaying as a cruel and horrifyingly painful punishment with the victim in an agonized position as well as anatomical illustrations which show the *écorché* (flayed subject) as co-operating with, even participating in, the removal of his skin, peeling it back to expedite dissection or visual exploration. Benthien notes that the pictorial representations of flaying as punishment (and of the myths or legends that inspired them) represent a society in which "the flaying of one man at the hands of others seeks to restore the existing order symbolically through the use of the most extreme means" (72). Further, she notes, in taking from the transgressors "the boundary of their bodies," flaying "deprives [them] of their identity along with their lives; in extinguishing the skin, it obliterates the person" (72).

During the eighteenth century, however, flaying as punishment "disappears as a pictorial subject as suddenly as it had burst on the scene in the sixteenth century" (81). Benthien attributes this to the "humanization of punishment that occurs with the disappearance of penal torture," citing Foucault's work in *Discipline and Punish*. This humanization "causes the body of the perpetrator to vanish from public view" (Benthien 81). Even more, perhaps, it reflects "the change in mentality that substituted the perception of the body as porous, open, and at the same time interwoven with the world in a grotesque way with one that viewed it as an individuated, monadic, and bourgeois vessel that the subject was considered to inhabit" (37). Following Benthien's reading of Bakhtin, Warren's flayed torso, effected by a witch who has overturned a system of classification and order, returns us from the bourgeois (Foucauldian) body with its closed, linear boundaries to the grotesque body whose "very boundary … reveals [its] intermingling with the world" (38). That is, Warren's flaying is clearly a Bakhtinian scene, and it appears to represent a triumphant eruption of that earlier paradigm within the infinitely more controlled Foucauldian system that has prevailed since the Enlightenment.

The Foucauldian classification systems, I would argue, and those institutions linking knowledge with power, are represented, in *Buffy*, by Giles' positioning in a school library by the Watchers Council. The Council's rigid reliance on bureaucratic and patriarchal classifications and regulations is, sadly, thus associated with the books pored over by the Scoobies, books whose battered leather covers reflect centuries of sequestered and guarded knowledge. Over the course of the series, Buffy defies the Council, Giles is fired, the school is burned, and the Scoobies eventually move their operational base to the Magic Box—even through all these changes, the books they consult must be approached with care. The "black arts" books, in particular, symbolize knowledge whose power can either support or overturn the *status quo*. It is this dangerous and subversive knowledge that Willow releases to form the skin of her new identity, and while we cheer Buffy's rejection of the Council's control, Willow's dis-ordering of dangerous knowledge returns us too frighteningly to the pre–Foucauldian.

Because, however, many celebratory aspects of the Bakhtinian can be found in both *Buffy* and *Angel*,[10] the return to the grotesque in punishment is clearly not presented as laudatory. If the horror on her friends' faces at Warren's flaying does not sufficiently convince us of this, Willow's willingness, in her gargantuan (i.e., Bakhtinian) rage, to destroy the world surely will. Although we may desire a body more enmeshed in the world than that of the Foucauldian bourgeois monad, we nonetheless want one more protected by law than that of the Bakhtinian grotesque. To begin to imagine such a body, we must follow Willow's exploration of skin's boundaries through one more disturbingly graphic scene, that of Willow and the Gnarl demon in "Same Time, Same Place" (7.03); indeed, this scene earned the Parents Television Council rating as one of "TV's worst clips" for 2001–2004 ("Playing Worst Clips"). And while most fans discussing it online at a Whedonesque bulletin board are incensed by the PTC's attempts at censorship, several also acknowledge that the scene is tough to watch: Andarcel said, "someone helpless with her skin being peeled off and eaten … needlessly grotesque"; Angela posted, "Gnarl creeps me out. That whole scene gives me the wiggins"; batmarlowe hates the PTC's sanctimonious approach but admits that the Gnarl "[s]lowly peeling off Willow's skin and having the blood sucked and licked up was sickening for me" and remembers feeling, the first time the episode aired, that it was atypical for *Buffy* in the way it draws out pain. Pixxelpuss similarly comments on this scene being atypical, more disturbing than other violence in the series, and she attributes that to its being "graphic … well-lit and slow" ("Whedonesque Commentary").

I would agree that much of this scene's power resides in its insistence—through its length, close-ups, and lighting—that we watch. Earlier in this episode, Xander says of a skinned body that it is "[t]ough to look at," and Buffy replies, "And yet my eyes refuse to look away. Stupid eyes" ("Same Time, Same Place" 7.03). This perversely scopophilic fascination, combined with revulsion, characterizes the Kristevan abject: "The fascinated start that leads me toward and separates me from them," with "them" being those "improper" and "unclean" items that are "radically excluded and [draw us] toward the place where meaning collapses" (Kristeva 2), that confound, in other words, the boundaries by which we make sense of our world. And even more than a flayed torso, which, while horrifyingly exposed nonetheless has a certain integrity, the pieces of skin that Gnarl peels off Willow and slowly feeds into his mouth are no longer Willow, yet they are; surely they are not food, yet if Gnarl is eating them, they obviously are. Willow, Gnarl mocks her, is inside him. We wish our stupid eyes might look away, but revolted, fascinated, we continue to stare.

Amplifying this scene's saturation with the abject is Willow's shame and self-loathing. Her deep-seated fear that her heinous crime of flaying Warren is unforgivable triggers a spell which isolates her from her friends. When Gnarl captures her, then, his assault on her skin merely materializes an abject that was already there, embodies her shame at the boundary of her physical self. The pieces of skin, the blood-licking, the revolting sounds Gnarl makes as he savors his meal, all manifest those elements of ourselves that we "permanently thrust aside in order to live" (Kristeva 3). Food loathing, Kristeva says, and she uses "*skin* on the surface of milk" (2, emphasis added) to exemplify it, is perhaps the most elementary and most archaic form of abjection. Combining this loathing of food with a loathing of bodily waste—turning the bodily waste *into* the loathed food, directs flashing arrows at Willow's shame.

Beyond the fascinated revulsion, what intrigues me about this scene is the way it rewrites a longstanding metaphor for change, that of the new skin. Benthien writes of this "topos of flaying as a process of cleansing and growth, as the peeling out from inauthentic forms and identities," a topos which she attributes to "a euphemistic reinterpretation and metaphorization of the gruesome flaying ritual. The act of radical self-alienation is stylized into a moment of self-becoming" (83).[11] Whedon clearly eschews euphemism in the skin-peeling scene, although he does reinterpret the "flaying ritual" ("Same Time, Same Place"). He also modifies the self-alienation, so that it becomes not only a peeling away of self from self, but, through Willow's spell, a separation from friends as well by literally displacing Willow so that she and her friends exist in the same space/time without awareness of each other. And he extends the refusal of euphemism to the scene in which

Willow, rescued by her friends and ensconced at home, works to regrow new skin—a process that is emphasized as painful and exhausting. Perhaps most importantly, this scene emphasizes "a moment of self-becoming" as, rather, a lengthy (not momentary) process of self-becoming in/through others and, even more, in/through others while connected to the earth.

Surely, it is not just coincidental that this connection, occasioned by and materialized over/through skin, takes place in the last televised season of *Buffy*, a season asserting Willow's pivotal role in overturning the ancient patriarchal governance of Slayers. In his cultural history of skin, Steven Connor sketches the perception of it as, first, a screen, then a membrane, stating that it has now become "a place of minglings, a mingling of places" (26). This characterization is Connor's rendering of Michel Serres' term, "milieu," and Connor explains the special place skin occupies in Serres' philosophy of the sense. The "ground against which the other senses figure," these other senses themselves "milieu, or midplaces where inside and outside meet and meld," skin, Connor says, is "the milieu of … milieu" (27). His assertion that "skin mediates the world by mingling with it" (29) is as apt a description as one could want of what Willow does, meditating on her bed, holding Buffy's hand, drawing—as the Coven has taught her to—on the power of the earth's connectedness to and with all things, to heal herself. Mingling with the world, with her friend, through her skin, Willow re-covers (from) her shame and abjection.

This painful, yet paradoxically loving, gentle, reconfiguring of the metaphor of skin renewal encapsulates *Buffy*'s overall politics. Whereas the show's carnivalesque mix of comedy, violence, fleshiness, and the grotesque often works to subvert the Foucauldian order it signals through libraries, schools, the military, and the Watchers Council, it does not, finally, hold up Bakhtinian disorder as a realistic sustained response. Although such disorder—as represented both by Willow flaying Warren *and* by her own skin being peeled away by Gnarl—serves a worthy political purpose, the trio of skin imagery involving Willow models a move back to order. Yet this order is differently negotiated, particularly in terms of gender. Benthien points out that the image of renewal through the replacement of skin has rarely, if ever, pertained to women, and she argues that this is because removing the "concealing veil" of a woman's skin "would fundamentally destroy the myth of her being other" (86). When Gnarl chows down on Willow's skin, then, not only does she reconstitute her subjectivity in relationship with her friends as she renews her skin, but she also destroys the mythology which allows the patriarchal Watchers Council to control Slayers for millennia. Willow's dermal experiences lead directly to the changed order which culminates in her releasing the power of the Potentials from the patriarchal control imposed by Watchers from time immemorial.

Buffy and *Angel* abound with images, conversations, and even entire plots organized around skin, so much so that digressions continually threatened to distort the shape of this paper. Focusing on the three chosen scenes, however, emphatically demonstrates the importance of skin as a milieu that demands to be investigated. With so much still to explore for the shows to make significant contributions to the burgeoning field of skin studies *and* reciprocally, for skin studies to illuminate readings of *Buffy and Angel*, it is time, as a certain hero once said, to go to work.

NOTES

1. This quotation, from *Angel* episode "You're Welcome" (5.02) was suggested to me as a possible title by my friend and colleague, Cynthea Masson. *Angel* offers abundant possibilities for another essay developing the rich implications of Whedon's skin imagery. Besides Lindsey's runic tattoos worn as protection against the Senior Partners ("You're Welcome" 5.12), there is the symbol inscribed on Cordelia's hand that maddens her with grief at the world's pain ("To Shanshu in L.A." 1.22); the desiccation of skin that almost claims Winifred Burkle in "The Price" (3.19); and, of course, the eventual transformation of Fred's skin after her death as her body is claimed by Illyria.

2. Claudia Benthien, whose book *Skin: On the Cultural Border Between Self and the World* is itself an example of this increased attention, catalogues "a large number of events with the human skin as their theme" as well as architectural theory's focus on the "skin" of buildings" (viii). Her list is not limited to Germany, but includes events in Tokyo and New York. In *The Book of Skin*, Steven Connor similarly claims that skin "has never been so much in evidence as it seems to be today. . . not only in critical and cultural theory but also in contemporary life," and he cites as evidence its "pervasive(ness)" in cinema and photography as well as the prevalence of cosmetics and plastic surgery (9).

3. Cordelia, a member both of the Scoobies *and* of Angel's investigators, initially judges worth by visual appearance, including skin, as is particularly manifest in her relationship to Doyle. Doyle fears that any revelation of his hybrid identity will destroy his chances of pursuing Cordelia romantically, based on comments she makes, responses she evinces, particularly notable in "Bachelor Party" (*Angel* 1.07). However, Cordelia overcomes any revulsion she might feel to Doyle's demonic aspects when she confronts these as part of his whole identity in the moving episode "Hero" (*Angel* 1.09). Her changed attitude toward Doyle demonstrates a laudable ability to move beyond rigid understandings of good and evil, human and demon. This understanding culminates in Cordelia's acceptance of her own transformation into a demon, supposedly to accommodate the visions that threaten to kill her (*Angel*, "Birthday" 3.11).

4. Steven Connor goes back even further to consider the language of skin in early Egypt as well as Classical Greece and Rome. He indicates several Greek and Latin words: *derma* (the Greek for "hide") and *chros* (also Greek, common name for "skin" but with numerous other uses reflecting various aspects of skin, color, proximity, whole body); *cutis* (Latin for living skin) and *pellis* (Latin for dead, flayed skin, a word that "evokes disgust") (10–11). Connor argues that the duality these words reflect is manifest even today in a "certain unsteadiness in the ways in which skin is referred to in medical language," pointing to the way that the "science of the skin is called 'dermatology,' but early hospitals ... would more commonly refer to 'cutaneous' diseases" (11).

5. This conception of skin, best exemplified in *Angel* by Illyria's hollowing-out, and appropriation of, Fred's body, is very common throughout both series.

6. In "Welcome to the Hellmouth," the first episode of *Buffy*, the Slayer advises Willow to "seize the moment" because "tomorrow you might be dead," with the unfortunate result that

Willow leaves the Bronze, unwittingly, with a vampire. She is, of course, rescued by Buffy, so that she is able to return the favour, in "Surprise" (2.13), reminding Buffy of the Slayer's own recommendation, carpe diem, nudging her toward consummating her physical relationship with Angel.

7. In, "'That Was Nifty': Willow Rosenberg Saves the World in *Buffy the Vampire Slayer,*" Matthew Pateman connects Willow's change in dress to her "ontological disruptions" (76) and links it to her changed physical appearance in her transformation, after Tara's death, to "irrational, world-destroying, über-witch" (76). I find this characterization somewhat extreme, seeing development rather than disruption at such an essential level as "ontological" implies.

8. Willow's tendency to babble when she is nervous or excited might be read as an adult extension of precocious speech. Certainly, this tendency emphasizes her words as a point of contact between herself and others, thus emphasizing the similarity between skin and words, the construction of a skin out of words.

9. This might explain why Willow, in contrast to Xander's immediate 911 calls when Buffy is shot, instead immediately invokes Osiris. Perhaps Tara's body is more demonstrably beyond help, but we might recall that Buffy's response, in the shock of discovering her mother's body, was to call Giles.

10. Yael Sherman's article usefully outlines Bakhtinian elements throughout the series.

11. Interestingly, Benthien adds that the trope has historically "transferred metaphorically to human beings" a biological "process of cyclical regeneration that occurs in the reptile world" (83), reminding me that Willow's skin, in her dream encounter with the First Slayer, turns "almost reptilian" (Battis, "She's Not All Grown" par. 22).

"I've got these evil hand issues"

Amputation, Identity, and Agency in Angel

Tamy Burnett

One of the most commonly quoted lines from *Angel* comes from the pivotal episode "Epiphany" (2.16) when the titular hero expresses the idea that has come to be something of an unofficial motto for the show: "If nothing we do matters, then all that matters is what we do." As a show about a vampire with a soul, the storylines in *Angel* regularly focus on the title character's quest for redemption for past acts. Although the show's emphasis is on the metaphysical soul as the marker of Angel's alignment with good or evil, Angel's journey toward redemption is regularly intertwined with metaphors of physicality. In the show's mythology, the ultimate signifier of redemption is the Shanshu, a prophesized mystical transformation in which a souled vampire becomes human. Team Angel sees this possible outcome as a cosmic reward, signifying Angel's redemption from past sins. However, the show repeatedly undermines the accuracy of prophecy and instead emphasizes action absent reward, encouraging characters to commit selfless, helpful acts—both to make up for past harm and because it is the right thing to do.

Ultimately, this positioning is unsurprising for a show steeped in existential philosophy (a topic many Whedonverse shows engage with). Indeed, several scholars have explored in depth questions of existentialist philosophy in relation to *Angel* and the other shows examined in this collection. Most notable are the commentaries offered by J. Michael Richardson and J. Douglas Rabb (*The Existential Joss Whedon*), K. Dale Koontz (*Faith and Choice in the Works of Joss Whedon*), Cynthea Masson ("What the Hell?"), and Dean A. Kowalski and S. Evan Kreider (*The Philosophy of Joss Whedon*). The majority of scholarship to focus on existentialist philosophies does so from a spiritual or metaphysical perspective, as an existentialist ethos for one's actions—and rightly so, as the writers of these narratives are often concerned with the *why* of character motivation and narrative.

However, given that these stories are told via a visual medium, it comes as no surprise that in addition to the metaphysical considerations of existentialism, these television 'verses are often also concerned with questions of physicality, both the physical action of carrying out one's choices and the physical costs of taking action. This is especially true in *Angel*, a series where, as Stacey Abbott argues in *Angel: TV Milestones*, "each of the main characters undergoes some form of violent bodily attack that serves to explore anxieties about the nature of the 'self' as it is reshaped and redefined" (56). Abbott offers several detailed examples of such attacks in her chapter on *Angel* as TV horror. In addition, as Abbott notes, each major character "carries the burden of his or her own past, insecurities, personal failings, and transgressions, and is, like Angel, looking for some form of redemption" (4).

In a variation on these co-joined themes of bodily transformation and redemption, two other major characters—Lindsey McDonald and Spike—share a specific challenge to their bodily integrity: the trauma of involuntary hand amputation and subsequent transplantation/reattachment. Although metaphors about hands and agency abound throughout popular culture and the Whedonverses in particular,[1] Lindsey's and Spike's hand-related storylines offer an especially rich point of comparison because they provide significant insight into the development of the show's larger themes about redemption, heroic identity, and personal agency—while also exploring response to and recovery from physical trauma.

Emphasis on the corporeal body, especially when individual body parts metaphorically represent metaphysical concepts, is a long tradition in Western storytelling, and audiences automatically recognize key metaphors housed in bodies/body parts, such as the head representing reason or the heart signifying one's emotional center. Of all body parts with strong symbolic meaning, hands represent agency and one's ability to act. According to Bruce Rybarczyk and Jay Behel in "Limb Loss and Body Image," although each person responds to limb loss differently, "The loss of a hand or arm, because of its highly symbolic and multifunctional nature, is known to be more traumatic than the loss of a leg" (24). As such, the amputation and replacement of a character's hand/hands offers an especially rich point of inquiry into *Angel*'s investment in questions of physicality and chosen action. This is all the more true in light of who the two major characters to experience involuntary hand amputation in the series are.

Both Lindsey and Spike struggle throughout their tenure in the *Buffy/Angel*-verse to understand themselves and their motivations, especially in relation to the heroic model represented by Angel himself. In fact, the two serve parallel narrative purposes in relation to the series' central character. They are what Roz Kaveney terms "shadow doubles" of Angel (64). More than that, though—for the series is littered with doubles—Lindsey and Spike are doubles of each other as well as of Angel. Both are positioned as on-again/off-again antagonists to Angel and as equally on-again/off-again protégées of Angel's, seeking his help and following his model of heroic identity. Lindsey's and Spike's storylines, then, are especially resonant for the ways that they mirror each other, intersect, and reinforce several of the show's primary themes, as well as because of how the trajectories of these amputee characters further resonate with the title character's journey.

The primary themes of the series *Angel* are epitomized by the character Angel, the 250-plus-year-old vampire with a soul, who seeks atonement for his history as a violent, sadistic monster. Throughout the series, Angel struggles to balance his two natures: the caged demon who revels in causing pain and the souled champion dedicated to protecting the innocent from monsters like he once was. Ultimately, the vampire's understanding of the Shanshu's promise and his own place in the world shifts; Angel comes to recognize that he must undertake actions because they need to be done, not to balance the cosmic scales or for the promise of reward. In fact, he signs away his chance of Shanshu near the end of the series. This act demonstrates recognition and embrace of an ethos of heroism in which one takes action simply because it is the right thing to do; likewise, this ethos demands that one accept the consequences of one's actions, whether good or bad.

Perhaps unsurprisingly, given the reversion of Angel to Angelus and the series' focus on characters occupying liminal spaces, villainous or antagonist characters on *Angel* also often grapple with questions of redemption, how to exercise agency, and duality of identity. Of all the show's villains and Angel's personal antagonists, this parallel is especially significant for the (often evil) lawyer Lindsey McDonald and for the vampire Spike. When Angel shifts from hero to villain or even somewhere in between, his body bears little outward evidence (excepting, of course, his affinity for leather pants when evil). In Lindsey's case, however, his struggles are embodied in his amputated hand, the prosthetic that replaces it, and finally the transplanted hand he receives. So, too, does Spike experience a similar, if condensed, trajectory in relation to the loss and return of his hands.

Hands, of course, symbolize a person's agency and ability to act. Phrases and sayings reinforcing this symbolic meaning litter the English language, from the nautical "all hands on deck" or the political "right-hand (wo)man," in which "hand" stands in for an individual person acting under another's direction, to phrases like "idle hands are the devil's playground" or the action of "washing one's hands of" a situation, wherein the "hands" represent agency or action. Further, several idioms evoke the image of hands in a specific state to symbolize a larger concept: "caught red-handed" implies guilt by evoking the image of a murderer with blood marking his hands, and "[winning] hands down" comes from horse racing where a jockey winning by a comfortable margin can hold her hands in a relaxed, lowered posture, rather than using them to urge her mount on.

Historically, of course, the symbolic importance of hands is not limited to English-speaking, or even Western cultures. In his book, *A History of Limb Amputation*, John Kirkup traces examples of hand amputations through recorded history and around the globe, focusing on ones that served a legal or judicial purpose. He follows the historical practice of punitive hand amputation through several examples, ranging from a punishment for physicians whose patients died in ancient Babylon, to a writer and his publisher who lost their hands in late sixteenth-century England for producing a pamphlet questioning Queen Elizabeth I's "marital ambitions" (39), to Indian civilians captured by an anti–British prince in the late eighteenth century and punished for serving the East India Trading Company (39), to women found guilty of infidelity on islands off West Africa in the mid-nineteenth century (40), to an Afghan prisoner of the Taliban in 1999 (39).

This prevalence through time, geography, and culture of the symbolic nature of hands and of hand amputation as a punitive measure means that, as a narrative element, hand amputation carries clear and universal connotations. In *Angel*, the amputation of Lindsey's and Spike's hands clearly signifies their use of agency to act in a manner harmful to others, to use their hands for purposes deserving of punishment. Within the context of a show whose primary themes are redemption and agency, how Lindsey and Spike respond to their amputation and subsequent transplant or reattachment offers significant insight into the ethos that "all that matters is what we do."

Lindsey McDonald is the logical starting place for considering hand amputation in *Angel*—after all, about one-third of Lindsey's total screen time as a frequently reoccurring character involves the narrative of his amputated hand. Further, Angel is the one who amputates Lindsey's hand and the transplantation of a new hand becomes a central point upon which Lindsey's narrative trajectory and understanding of agency pivots.

Lindsey begins the series as a modern Horatio Alger protagonist, a young lawyer who has transcended his poor, rural roots and is now on the fast track to promotion at the evil law firm Wolfram & Hart. Due to Wolfram & Hart's status as the series' overarching Big Bad, Lindsey crosses paths with Angel quite often. Their frequent intersections mean that when, towards the end of the first season, Lindsey has moral reservations about one of the firm's plans (exploiting blind children), he turns to Angel for help in "Blind Date" (1.21), claiming a desire to be free of employment at Wolfram & Hart. In the following episode, however, Lindsey's position with the law firm has been reestablished; in fact, he has been promoted to junior partner, or as Cordelia says, he "sold [his soul] for a six-figure salary and full benefits package" ("To Shanshu in L.A." 5.22). This rapid shift in Lindsey's allegiances, and the pull he feels between his desire for success and his own, somewhat murky ethical code, represent his larger characterization throughout the series. He often allows the ends to justify the means, especially when the end directly benefits him. Further, he regularly fails to look too closely at his own actions or take responsibility for them.

These aspects of his character are highlighted in the scene in which he initially loses his hand, which soon follows his promotion and occurs in the subsequent episode, "To Shanshu in L.A." (5.22). This episode is particularly illuminating in terms of Lindsey and Angel's characterizations and interactions. Wolfram & Hart has launched a psychic attack on Angel's friend and colleague, Cordelia. He finds and kills the demon who is responsible. However, Angel must also recover information on a scroll to fully cure Cordelia. During the confrontation, Lindsey ends up in possession of the scroll; he refuses to give it to Angel claiming that "I'm seeing things more clearly now. I see that what happened here tonight was foretold.... I see that you are either the one with the power or you're powerless."

Angel is unmoved by the power of the prophecy Lindsey references, and the vampire responds to Lindsey's grandiose claims of insight by asking, "You see what I'm going to do to you if you don't give me the scroll?" Lindsey, misjudging the amount of power that possessing the scroll actually affords him smugly replies, "You need the [scroll] to cure your friend. She's your connection to The Powers That Be. And since it's foretold that we sever all your connections, well..." as he moves the scroll over open flames, clearly intending to destroy it. Before the scroll can catch fire, Angel throws a scythe, severing Lindsey's right hand and preventing the scroll from burning.[2] As the music swells, Angel ends the confrontation with one last piece of advice before turning and walking away: "Don't believe everything you're foretold."

Although Lindsey and Angel often trade barbs and smug rejoinders, Angel's parting words to Lindsey are delivered without the self-satisfaction one might expect. Instead, the matter-of-fact way that Angel offers this advice suggests that he took no pleasure in severing Lindsey's hand. The juxtaposition of these two uses of the idea of severing in conjunction with the fact that Angel's actions allow him to save Cordelia clearly position him and his actions as being on the side of good and his corporeal punishment of Lindsey as warranted and just. This scene is also significant because Lindsey's attempts to justify his action here as fulfilling destiny suggest a lack of agency or at least individual responsibility for his actions. Angel's final words, and the swelling musical score, capture the series' ultimate philosophy—that "destiny" can be circumvented, that each individual is the master of their own fate. More than once in the episode Angel verbally makes clear that Lindsey is responsible for his own choices, that if he chooses to align himself with Wolfram & Hart or other agents of evil, he must be prepared to accept the consequences of those actions. Equally true is that if Lindsey truly wishes to escape his entanglement with the law firm, Angel will readily help him, regardless of their antagonistic past.

The idea of Lindsey losing a hand as a result of how he exercises his agency is reiterated several episodes later in "Epiphany" (2.16), when his same hand is symbolically re-amputated. In the episode, Lindsey attacks Angel, angry and jealous that Angel slept with Darla, a vampire/woman Lindsey is in love with.[3] The confrontation concludes with Angel shattering Lindsey's prosthetic hand with a sledgehammer. Although the amputation is more symbolic the second time around, the message remains the same: Lindsey once again loses his hand—the symbolic representation of his agency—because of his choices.

Lindsey's narrative arc takes a dramatic turn at the end of Season Two in the episode "Dead End" (2.18). The episode opens with a sequence of images emphasizing Lindsey's frustrations with the loss of agency and ability his lost hand represents. We see him wake up and struggle through a morning routine of shaving one-handed, choosing his necktie from a selection of pre-knotted ties as he dresses, and pausing to look longingly at the guitar he can no longer play. The scene highlights Lindsey's growing frustration with his lot in life—a lot to which he still largely ignores his own contributions.

However, when he arrives at work, his boss unexpectedly sends him to have a new hand transplanted onto his arm. When Lindsey wakes from surgery, the thin pink scar around his wrist is the only sign of the transplant. In addition to the personal sense of wholeness and agency the transplant returns to Lindsey, the fact that his employer arranged for the expensive mystical-medical procedure is an obvious sign that he, and not his colleague Lilah, will receive the promotion promised to one of them while the other will be terminated—likely both from their job and from life.

The promise of promotion and the restoration of Lindsey's body via transplant is a short-lived joy, however. In his first client meeting post-surgery, Lindsey looks down at his notepad to realize that his new hand, of its own accord, has been writing "kill" over and over, prompting Lindsey to ask it "who are you?" His question echoes fears long expressed in literature, film, and other artistic endeavors about the promise and threat of organ transplantation, blood transfusion, etc.—namely that the personality, identity, social station, and all accompanying non-tangible characteristics of the donor would supersede the recipient's, that the transplant/

transfusion recipient would be subject to the vices and other "undesirable" qualities of the donor.

Stories about the promise and threat of transplant procedures date back to antiquity. In more modern history, the stories tend to express fears of the advancement of science, industrialization, and rationality, situating organ and tissue transplantation in the context of horror. Among the most famous of these examples are Mary Shelley's 1818 gothic novel *Frankenstein* and H.G. Wells' 1896 science-fiction classic *The Island of Doctor Moreau*. In *Flesh and Blood: Organ Transplantation and Blood Transfusion in Twentieth-Century America*, Susan E. Lederer explains that, as medical technology progressed towards the possibility of viable transplantation in the twentieth century, "novels, plays, and popular films of the early twentieth century explored the darker side of what came to be called 'spare parts surgery.' [...] Many of these productions pressed the issue of the transmission of more than body parts or fluids; in the novels and films, when the surgeon transfers the hand of a murderer, the hand retains its desire to kill" (5).

Literature, film, and popular culture of this time period likewise grappled with the implications of shared body components and the possibilities connected to racial, ethnic, religious, gender, etc., identification, usually, though not exclusively, through the expression of xenophobic fears. Focusing on blood transfusions—which were practiced long before the first successful organ transplant in 1954—Lederer traces examples ranging from *The Hospital Baby*, a 1912 silent film, to Frank Kinsella's 1899 *The Degeneration of Dorothy: A Novel*. At one end of the spectrum is a romanticization of blood transfusion, such as found in *The Hospital Baby*, in which an infant girl receives a blood transfusion from a student doctor, whom she later grows up to marry. At the other end of the spectrum are narratives like Kinsella's heavy-handed novel, in which the transfusion recipient—a beautiful, young, proper English woman—is changed by receiving blood from a donor of a different ethnic background, in this case, Spanish. She is so changed that she, of course, goes crazy and dies from the "disturbing, vile-germed life fluid" (qtd. in Lederer 110). And, of course, myths and stories about vampires echo these same fears about the power a donor may exert over a recipient via "transplanted" blood, as foregrounded in such seminal vampire texts as Joseph Sheridan Le Fanu's *Carmilla* (1872) and the more famous Bram Stoker's *Dracula* (1897). Given how much of *Angel*'s narrative is constructed around the fear of being turned into a vampire—or the promise for Angel of being returned from that condition to a mortal state as human—the parallel storylines about hand amputation and transplantation take on new depth.

In the episode "Dead End," when Lindsey realizes that he may have gotten more than intended with his new hand, he turns to Angel for help. The series lives up to its genre roots in horror when the two discover the origins of Lindsey's new appendage, and Lindsey is faced with the most significant moral crisis yet. The two uncover Wolfram & Hart's spare parts warehouse, a horrifying lab full of medical equipment and suspended animation chambers filled with naked young male and female bodies missing various limbs and organs. One chamber holds little more than a torso, missing both arms, both legs, and the head, while in another the torso cavity is held open, suggesting that more than limbs are available to Wolfram & Hart's clientele. The camera pans across several such chambers before zeroing in on one male body missing its right hand, before panning up to the man's face, covered by a medical breathing mask. Lindsey recognizes him as Brad, someone who started with Wolfram & Hart about the same time as Lindsey—suggesting their fates could have easily been reversed.

"Kill," the otherwise motionless Brad pleads, and Lindsey asks, "Kill who? Huh? Who do you want to kill?" presumably working on the assumption that knowing who Brad wishes to kill will give Lindsey an outlet for their hand's murderous impulses. However, Brad's response is anything but what Lindsey expects or what the myths about transplanted tissue would have us believe. "Kill ... [pause] me," Brad pleads.

Two important things happen in this scene. First, Lindsey is faced with the harsh reality of the social abuses in which his employers are willing to engage. Wolfram & Hart's spare part warehouse chillingly echoes the early history of transplant medicine, especially in the exploitative ways the powerful historically obtained "donations." Indeed, as Stuart J. Youngner notes in *Organ Transplantation: Meanings and Realities*:

> The legacy of [historical fears of organ transplant and real-life stories of organ theft and grave robbing] [...] are very much alive in our collective consciousness. Stimulated by the steady diet of upbeat news stories, sermons, and public service announcements about transplantation and the need for more organs, fears that people will actually be killed for organs find free reign in popular culture. Horror books and movies tell tales of powerful and maniacal physicians (either functioning independently or as agents of even more powerful scoundrels) who take advantage of patients or other, weaker persons to obtain their organs [39–40].

Wolfram & Hart and their mystical demon healers certainly qualify as such.

Second, Lindsey turns to Angel, deferring to the vampire's frequent positioning as the voice of moral authority, and asks, "What am I supposed to do here?" Angel flat out refuses to give Lindsey directions. "I know what I'd do," the vampire says. "This is your deal." By refusing to answer, Angel forces Lindsey to acknowledge and own up to any actions he chooses to take—including unplugging the chamber in which his donor is being held, thereby euthanizing the man whose hand Lindsey now uses. This moment serves as a turning point for Lindsey. The following day, when his promotion is announced, Lindsey walks away from his life at Wolfram & Hart. Significantly, though, his manner of exit reveals that although he has learned some, he has not fully internalized Angel's lessons about heroic agency. Kaveney suggests that this is "redemption without all that much in the way of repentance, penance, or even a firm purpose of amendment; it [is] by some criteria no redemption at all" (66).

The scene begins with Lindsey, Lilah, and several Wolfram & Hart employees gathered around a conference table. Nathan, Lindsey and Lilah's boss, begins to announce which of the two young attorneys will be promoted. When it becomes clear it will be Lindsey and not Lilah who will receive the promotion, Lilah reaches for the gun in her handbag. Lindsey stills her hands with his transplanted right hand and says, "They chose me. I'm clearly the guy. […] You could've had it. But you didn't have what it takes." He then quickly raises his right hand between them, causing Lilah to jump and scream briefly as he wiggles his fingers and explains what Lilah does not have: "an evil hand." Lindsey rises from the table and demands of Nathan, "You know you gave me an evil hand, right? I've been writing 'kill, kill, kill' on everything. It's crazy. Anything could happen." Lindsey then demonstrates how anything could happen with his evil hand. He uses it to grab the security guard's gun, shoot the guard in the foot, and then wave the gun around the room at the other employees while he mock protests, "Stop it, evil hand, stop it." He fires off several more shots around the room, especially in Nathan's direction before shrugging, "I just can't control my evil hand."

Lindsey's performance of "an evil hand" is obviously a calculated move, designed to make his boss think that pursuing him will be too costly an endeavor for the firm. Yet, Lindsey clearly also uses the moment to indulge in some self-gratifying actions, like grabbing Lilah's backside on his way out. And that blend of performance and taking advantage of the situation reveals a central tenant of Lindsey's character—that he is not prepared to accept full responsibility for and control over his actions. His hand may not be evil, but he revels in the "excuse" of lost agency.[4]

As previously discussed, throughout the series, Angel is usually set up as the voice of moral authority. However, during this same second season, he struggles with parallel questions about agency and desire to use his power in selfish ways, before ultimately returning to the heroic path. Lindsey's exit from a life of overt selfishness and service to evil is more a model of necessity. The contrast between the two characters makes clear that in a world where "all that matters is what we do," Angel is invested in using his agency wisely and in the service of helping others, while Lindsey continually reverts to exercising his agency in self-serving ways, except in the most extreme circumstances.

With the addition of Spike to the regular cast in Season Five and specifically with Spike's own amputation storyline, we see another version of this story arc that offers a different model of response to and recovery from amputation. Spike's hand amputation occurs midway through Season Five of *Angel*. By that point, he is well-experienced with attacks on his bodily integrity. Spike is first introduced in *Buffy*'s Season Two episode "School Hard" (2.03) as a vampire who was part of Angelus' vampire family in the late nineteenth century. Although the various flashbacks to Spike's past indicate that his violence is often driven by a desire to belong or a vengeful reaction to not belonging, in contrast to Angelus' pure sadism, both series make clear that Spike's history is littered with violence, including seeking out and murdering two previous vampire slayers. He is often positioned as a counterpoint to Angel/us: enjoying life where Angel/us is brooding; quick-witted and sarcastic where Angel/us is serious; and an ally to Buffy against Angelus or when Angel is not able to be one.

Throughout his combined seven seasons across *Buffy* and *Angel*, Spike's bodily integrity is attacked over and over, from his broken back and stint confined to a wheelchair in *Buffy*'s second season, to the behavior-therapy microchip implanted in his brain by the Initiative in *Buffy*'s fourth season (a metaphoric amputation of his fangs), to his return from his death in the *Buffy* finale as a ghost without any bodily integrity whatsoever in *Angel*'s fifth season. This history is significant because it highlights Spike's familiarity with adjusting to changes in his physical abilities, which have prepared him more so than Lindsey to move past the initial horror of amputation, as well as his progression towards accepting ownership of his agency and responsibility for his actions

The show *Angel* plays with the idea of doubling in contrasting Angel and Spike quite often, especially in the fifth season when both have shared so much similar and parallel history and are now in direct competition for the starring role in the Shanshu prophecy. As K. Dale Koontz observes, the two "[seem] to be eternally locked in a binary relationship" (*Faith and Choice*, 27). However, a less obvious, but no less significant doubling occurs with Spike and Lindsey, and this doubling is made visible through the repetition of Lindsey's hand amputation storyline, albeit in a condensed format.

In the episode "Damage" (5.11), Spike and Angel seek to help a mentally ill young Slayer, Dana (Navi Rawat). In addition to being haunted by memories of past abuse at the hands of a man who kidnapped and tortured her as a child, Dana's mental state is under assault from psychic dreams of past slayers' fights with demons and monsters, exacerbating her condition. Dana captures Spike and alternately confuses herself with the two slayers he killed and confuses him with the man who tormented her as a child. She drugs Spike and cuts off his hands, explaining "[you] can't touch me anymore." She has taken away his agency—and the agency of the man who hurt her—in the only way she knows how. By the episode's end, though, Angel and team rescue Spike and use Wolfram & Hart's resources to reattach his hands.

Before Spike's capture by Dana, Angel attempts to talk him out of going after her, arguing that because of her visions of past Slayers, he and Spike are the last two who should confront her. Spike, with his usual forthrightness asks, "What do you want me to do? Go all boo hoo because she got tortured and driven out of her gourd? Not like we haven't done worse, back in the day." Angel, ever the model of redemption agrees sorrowfully, "Yeah, and it's something I'm still paying for." Spike's reply at this point is telling. He flippantly says, "And you should let it go, mate. It's starting to make you look old." The key difference here is Angel's recognition that the path to true redemption requires one to accept responsibility for one's actions and to act consciously in service of good; although Angel's curse does require a degree of brooding, Angel's relationship with guilt was well-established long before he learned of his curse's happiness clause. In contrast, Spike is positioned as doing good now, but being less concerned with past sins, though there is plenty of previous evidence elsewhere in *Angel* and *Buffy* to suggest that Spike is fully cognizant of his past evil and takes responsibility for it. He is not abdicating his guilt; rather his performance of identity is a mechanism through which he is able to function rather than following Angel's model of wallowing in guilt for a century before setting out to do good works. In other words, he and Angel simply deal with the weights of their souls differently. However, aside from the verbal jab about Angel looking old—a form of sparring that is *de rigueur* for the two vampires—this exchange seeks to highlight the transformation Spike will undergo in the episode, as it directly contrasts with Spike and Angel's conversation post-amputation and post-reattachment of his own hands.

At the end of "Damage," Angel visits Spike, who is recovering in a Wolfram & Hart medical facility and inquires about whether Spike is in "a lot of pain." Spike's semi-snarky reply of "More than I'd like. But not as much as you would. Just what I deserve" sparks a deeper conversation. Angel protests, "I didn't say that" and Spike fully takes responsibility, where throughout the episode he has been abdicating responsibility, either through his earlier admonition to Angel to "let it go," or his protests to Dana that he was not the specific man who tortured her. Spike tells Angel, "The lass thought I killed her family. And I'm supposed to what, complain because hers wasn't one of the hundreds of families I did kill?" Spike then asks Angel about Dana's future, what will happen to her. Angel shares that she has been claimed by Buffy's team. Spike laments that, "she's too far gone to help. She's one of us now. She's a monster." Angel protests: "She's an innocent victim," and Spike counters that, "So were we [pause] once upon a time." Angel echoes Spike's final words in agreement, "Once upon a time." This co-opting of the classic opening words of fairy tales in Western culture is an inversion where being an innocent victim once upon a time leads to a dark path as agent of evil. However, as Spike and Angel demonstrate, it also can be seen as a starting point for another narrative, one that continues beyond evil acts and onto a path towards redemption.

Notably during this entire exchange Spike's hands remain motionless at his sides on top of the blankets of his hospital bed. This absence of movement is significant. James Marsters' portrayal of Spike is as an extremely physical individual. Spike's hands are always in motion, emphasizing the character's physical presence and agency in the world, starting with his very first appearance in *Buffy*'s "School Hard." From his anecdote about his Woodstock experience—"I fed off a flowerperson, and I spent the next six hours watchin' my hand move"—to his first meeting with Buffy and his mocking slow clap applause of her slaying ability, to the provocative way he rubs his hand down his chest to draw the viewer's eye to his groin when he explains that he likes weapons because "they make me feel all manly," Spike's hands are an integral part of his kinetic personality—the mannerisms that define how he lives and moves within his body. As Cynthea Masson and Marni Stanley note in their essay on Spike's use of camp aesthetics, much of the vampire's actions are a performance designed to emphasize a particular point through theatricality. The absence of any such movement in this scene is a stark contrast to Spike's usual state of being and drives home the seriousness of his verbal contributions to the scene. Here, stripped of his ability to use his hands to construct the theatrical elements of identity that regularly clothe him, we are directed to read Spike's verbal comments as completely genuine.

Spike's articulated recognition of the responsibility he bears for his past actions is demonstrated through his direct statement about the hundreds of families he has killed and through his correction of Angel's assessment of Dana as an innocent victim. His comment that he and Angel were innocent victims, too, once upon a time, is a pointed acknowledgment. Matt Hills and Rebecca Williams read this exchange as representing "an abject collapse of the distinction [...] between monster and victim" (213). The scene also intentionally evokes the genre of fairy tales, reinforcing that life is not a fairy tale, and regardless of who they once might have been, Spike and Angel are responsible for the actions of their soulless selves. The series' clear message about redemption then, is not concerned with the degree of evilness or the direct blood on one's hands. Rather, it is concerned with one's willingness and ability to take responsibility for past evils and selflessly work to do better in the future.

This is the point at which Spike and Lindsey's parallel narrative positioning diverges. Although Spike's journey from villain to hero has been a long and winding road and the experience of hand amputation is not solely responsible for his final transformation, the fact that the series uses this particular narrative to serve as a final definitive moment in Spike's redemption and understanding of agency puts him in direct contrast with Lindsey, who has also returned in the fifth season.[5]

In that final season, Angel is running Wolfram & Hart, trying to turn its resources to better uses. Lindsey returns and begins a campaign against the firm and, by extension, Angel. However, Lindsey's journey ends in defeat. In the series' finale, Lorne (Andy Hallett) assassinates Lindsey on Angel's orders, telling him, "You're not part of the solution, Lindsey. You never will be" ("Not Fade Away" 5.22). These words are especially powerful, coming from a character who both avoids violence when at all possible and who has psychic senses that allow him to see into the hearts and futures of those around him. Lorne and Angel understand that Lindsey never will learn to accept responsibility for his agency and the actions he undertakes. That Lindsey is perhaps incapable of change, or at the least unwilling to change, is made clear by Lindsey's dying protestation that he has been killed by "a flunky" rather than Angel. As Jennifer Hamilton notes, "For Lindsey, this is a most dissatisfying death. […] In Lindsey's estimation dying at the hands of the hero is his fitting end" (51). Lindsey's reaction to death is a focus on himself—selfish anger not over being killed, but over being killed by a "flunky," rather than anything altruistic or even remorse for his past sins.

Lindsey allows his anger and sense of victimization to cloud his perception, refusing to fully recognize the power of his own agency—in short, Lindsey never learns. In contrast, Spike is willing and able to take responsibility for his past actions. The nature of that divergence is why the shared storyline of hand amputation and transplant/reattachment is so fitting for these two figures. Loss of limb can have serious psychological impacts for the amputee. In addition to obvious issues related to ability and self-image that accompany loss of limb, Rybarczyk and Behel argue in "Limb Loss and Body Image" that "Among health professionals working with individuals with amputations, body image changes are cited as a critical issue in adjustment to limb loss and prosthesis acceptance. […] Although many people manage this intricate transformation of self-concept with only mild, transient distress, some individuals […] develop lasting negative attitudes about themselves" (23). Additionally, the authors suggest that "one's sense of one's body in motion, performing activities both routine and extraordinary, also is an essential aspect of body image. This kinetic aspect of body image, while frequently overlooked, is central to the rehabilitation process" (24). Or, said another way, one's sense of self derived from one's physicality and attached to one's agency is key for rehabilitation—or, in *Angel* terms, redemption. Equally significant is what Rybarczyk and Behel have to say about the relationship between amputation and the construction of one's narrative of amputation—especially in regards to traumatic amputations: "The cause of a disability can also have a substantial impact on the individual's response to and ultimate ability to cope with the disability and attendant changes in body image" (24). Specifically, if one views one's traumatic amputation as "random, unnecessary, and[/or] unfair," this perception can cause the amputee to "creat[e] a personal narrative with a theme of tragedy, victimization, and overwhelming loss" (24). This certainly seems to be the case for Lindsey, who continually allows his anger at Angel to define his sense of self. Had Lindsey been able to accept his amputation differently, to acknowledge his own contributions to the outcome of the confrontations in which he lost his hand, his story may have ended differently. Because Spike is able to accept and acknowledge the actions committed by the hands he loses, he is able to recover and genuinely seek redemption, becoming the hero Lindsey fancies himself but fails to become.

To be fair, Spike must not live with his loss as long as Lindsey, having his hands reattached a few hours after they are severed. However, Spike's shame in the scene following his reattachment and his past history suggest that he would have adapted to the loss better and not have been as likely to let the amputation derail his desire for heroic identity. As detailed previously, Spike's history contains several attacks on his physical body that have impacted his sense of self, including one previous (metaphorical) amputation—of his fangs when he is chipped by the Initiative.[6] Although he still physically has his fangs and learns he can fight against demons, his loss of ability to directly harm humans does not translate into an extended strategy game as it likely would have with Lindsey. Spike could have been off starting fires or cutting brake lines or building bombs. Instead, he ends up joining the Scoobies. Indeed, the chip almost functions as a prosthetic soul—an imperfect prosthesis to be sure, but one nonetheless.[7] Following the chip comes the actual soul, and following that comes his resurrection as a ghost where, essentially, his entire body has been amputated. In all of these cases, Spike adapts to his circumstances. He experiences anger, and his sense of self is clearly shaken, yet without this history he may not have been able to make the final shift in identity to fully heroic champion that he does as a result of his hand amputation. Each time he is presented with a loss of physicality and accompanying agency equivalent to limb amputation, he adjusts his self-image and finds a way forward, continuing on the path that ultimately leads him from villain to hero.

This is the key difference. Lindsey cannot accept responsibility for his own agency. Spike can and does. Narratively, both orbit Angel in parallel ways throughout the series, and in response to his heroic model, Lindsey and Spike grapple with questions of self-identity specifically related to their perceptions of self as villainous or heroic. Following hand amputation and the attendant symbolic removal of agency and change in self-perception, it is only by embracing Angel's motto that "All that matters is what we do" (and taking responsibility for the consequences of one's actions) that Spike—and not Lindsey—is able to fully shift from villain to hero.

Notes

1. In *Buffy* these references range from the Glove of Myhengon, a mystical metal glove that grants the wearer significant destructive power ("Revelations" 3.07), to Buffy serving as the Hand of the being the Scoobies create through a spell combining their strengths ("Primeval" 4.21). *Firefly*, of course, features the villainous Alliance agents who River describes as, "two by two, hands of blue" ("The Train Job" 1.02). In *Dollhouse*, Bennett loses use of her left arm—and hand—while helping Caroline sabotage the evil corporation Rossum ("The Left Hand" 2.06). In *Doctor Horrible's Sing-Along Blog*, examples range from the title character who sings that "all that matters is taking matters into your own hands," to Captain Hammer explaining that his hands are "not the hammer. […] The hammer is my penis" when taunting Doctor Horrible about his sexual conquest of Penny. Even in *Angel*, a pre-occupation with hands shows up at various points ranging from the stalker who could psychically detach limbs, including his hands, to harass his victim in "I Fall to Pieces" (1.04), to Cordelia's vision of a world in which she had not joined Angel Investigations upon moving to L.A., in which Wesley has lost his left arm fighting demons ("Birthday" 3.11).

2. There are possible readings related to the fact that Lindsey loses his right hand worth considering. Historically across ancient cultures, the right hand is aligned with goodness while the left is aligned with evil. However, it is also worth noting that Christian Kane is right handed, and the removal of the actor/character's dominate hand presents more challenges to function and emphasizes the impact of the loss. In fact, in multiple interviews, Kane has commented about how challenging he found it to accomplish everyday tasks like eating lunch while in costume with the prosthetic hand. For example, see Eramo or "Interviews—Christian Kane."

3. The relationships between Angel and Darla, Lindsey and Darla, and Angel and Lindsey in relation to Darla are extremely complicated and intricate and they echo the equally complex "love triangle" that is Angel/Buffy/Spike. The relationships between Lindsey and Angel and Spike and Angel are both characterized by an undercurrent of Eve Sedgwick's triangle of homoerotic desire, as noted by Kaveney and discussed at length by Alyson Buckman in "Triangulated Desire in *Buffy* and *Angel*." Indeed, there are several Freudian readings and castration analogies we could employ in discussing Lindsey's loss of hand and agency, especially in light of Angel's role in removing that agency and the homoerotic undercurrents to Lindsey and Angel's interactions.

4. This excuse of lost agency is an extension of Lindsey's experience at Wolfram & Hart, where his accountability has only been to the firm's goals, not to any outside morality. Additionally, in contrast to Lindsey's "evil" hand here are Lilah's hands which uncharacteristically fail her in the scene. As Sharon Sutherland and Sarah Swan have noted, our first introduction to Lilah in the series emphasizes her positioning as a femme fatale, and her hands are integral to this imagery. They explain, "Lilah is a dark-haired beauty, with pale skin and red lips, seated at a dimly lit bar. Her hand movements are important: we notice her twirling a finger around a glass of red wine and later swirling a glass of scotch. […] These visual cues […]

clearly announce that Lilah is a dangerous woman" (55). And indeed, throughout the series she proves just how dangerous she is again and again, repeatedly earning the compliment Cordelia pays her when she calls the lawyer a "vicious bitch" ("Billy" 3.06). Yet, in this scene, Lilah's hands fail her and although she comes out on top it is through no action of her own, only through Lindsey's defection from Wolfram & Hart. Lilah's hands fumble in her bag for a gun that we know will do little to aid her before Lindsey covers her hands with his transplanted one, taking control of the situation. When he releases her hands, they fly up to cover her face and continue to flutter nervously throughout the scene, around her face and neck or wrapping around her body in a futile attempt to protect herself. She does not know what to do in this moment and her hands betray that ignorance.

5. The contrast is something the show plays with as well, given Lindsey's impersonation of Doyle and attempt to set up Spike in the role Angel occupied during the first season, as a "hero of the people" ("Damage" 5.11). No doubt Lindsey's motives here have more to do with antagonizing Angel than true altruism.

6. In fact, this is implicitly acknowledged as an amputation when Spike describes his chipped condition by saying "Spike had a little trip to the vet and now he doesn't chase the other puppies anymore," equating his loss of ability to kill with neutering a dog, most commonly accomplished through the amputation of the testicles ("Pangs" *Buffy* 4.08).

7. It is important to note when considering the ways the chip might function as a prosthetic soul of sorts that, although Spike's actions are on the side of good, his motivations are far from selfless. In many ways, his actions are as clunky (in motivation terms) as Lindsey's are in terms of ability when he functions with his plastic, prosthetic hand. I am indebted to Samira Nadkarni for this observation.

Episode Guide

Buffy the Vampire Slayer, Season One (Network: WB)

Episode	Title	Writer(s)	Director	Air Date
1.01	Welcome to the Hellmouth	Joss Whedon	Charles Martin Smith	10 Mar 1997
1.02	The Harvest	Joss Whedon	John T. Kretchmer	10 Mar 1997
1.03	Witch	Dana Reston	Stephen Cragg	17 Mar 1997
1.04	Teacher's Pet	David Greenwalt	Bruce Seth Green	24 Mar 1997
1.05	Never Kill a Boy on the First Date	Rob Des Hotel & Dean Batali	David Semel	31 Mar 1997
1.06	The Pack	Matt Kiene & Joe Reinkemeyer	Bruce Seth Green	07 Apr 1997
1.07	Angel	David Greenwalt	Scott Brazil	14 Apr 1997
1.08	I Robot.... You, Jane	Ashley Gable & Thomas A. Swyden	Stephen Posey	28 Apr 1997
1.09	The Puppet Show	Rob Des Hotel & Dean Batali	Ellen S. Pressman	05 May 1997

Episode	Title	Writer(s)	Director	Air Date
1.10	Nightmares	Joss Whedon (Story) & David Greenwalt (Teleplay)	Bruce Seth Green	12 May 1997
1.11	Out of Mind, Out of Sight	Joss Whedon (Story) & Ashley Gable (Teleplay) & Thomas A. Swyden (Teleplay)	Reza Badiyi	19 May 1997
1.12	Prophecy Girl	Joss Whedon	Joss Whedon	02 June 1997

Buffy the Vampire Slayer, Season Two (Network: WB)

Episode	Title	Writer	Director	Air Date
2.01	When She Was Bad	Joss Whedon	Joss Whedon	15 Sept 1997
2.02	Some Assembly Required	Ty King	Bruce Seth Green	22 Sept 1997
2.03	School Hard	Joss Whedon (Story) & David Greenwalt (Story & Teleplay)	John T. Kretchmer	29 Sept 1997
2.04	Inca Mummy Girl	Matt Kiene & Joe Reinkemeyer	Ellen S. Pressman	06 Oct 1997
2.05	Reptile Boy	David Greenwalt	David Greenwalt	13 Oct 1997
2.06	Halloween	Carl Ellsworth	Bruce Seth Green	27 Oct 1997
2.07	Lie to Me	Joss Whedon	Joss Whedon	03 Nov 1997

Episode	Title	Writer	Director	Air Date
2.08	The Dark Age	Dean Batali & Rob Des Hotel	Bruce Seth Green	10 Nov 1997
2.09	What's My Line, Part 1	Howard Gordon & Marti Noxon	David Solomon	17 Nov 1997
2.10	What's My Line, Part 2	Marti Noxon	David Semel	24 Nov 1997
2.11	Ted	David Greenwalt & Joss Whedon	Bruce Seth Green	08 Dec 1997
2.12	Bad Eggs	Marti Noxon	David Greenwalt	12 Jan 1998
2.13	Surprise	Marti Noxon	Michael Lange	19 Jan 1998
2.14	Innocence	Joss Whedon	Joss Whedon	20 Jan 1998
2.15	Phases	Rob Des Hotel & Dean Batali	Bruce Seth Green	27 Jan 1998
2.16	Bewitched, Bothered and Bewildered	Marti Noxon	James A. Contner	10 Feb 1998
2.17	Passion	Ty King	Michael Gershman	24 Feb 1998
2.18	Killed by Death	Rob Des Hotel & Dean Batali	Deran Sarafian	03 Mar 1998
2.19	I Only Have Eyes for You	Marti Noxon	James Whitmore, Jr.	28 Apr 1998
2.20	Go Fish	David Fury & Elin Hampton	David Semel	05 May 1998

Episode	Title	Writer	Director	Air Date
2.21	Becoming, Part 1	Joss Whedon	Joss Whedon	12 May 1998
2.22	Becoming, Part 2	Joss Whedon	Joss Whedon	19 May 1998

Buffy the Vampire Slayer, Season Three (Network: WB)

Episode	Title	Writer	Director	Air Date
3.01	Anne	Joss Whedon	Joss Whedon	29 Sept 1998
3.02	Dead Man's Party	Marti Noxon	James Whitmore, Jr.	06 Oct 1998
3.03	Faith, Hope & Trick	David Greenwalt	James A. Contner	13 Oct 1998
3.04	Beauty and the Beasts	Marti Noxon	James Whitmore, Jr.	20 Oct 1998
3.05	Homecoming	David Greenwalt	David Greenwalt	03 Nov 1998
3.06	Band Candy	Jane Espenson	Michael Lange	10 Nov 1998
3.07	Revelations	Douglas Petrie	James A. Contner	17 Nov 1998
3.08	Lovers Walk	Dan Vebber	David Semel	24 Nov 1998
3.09	The Wish	Marti Noxon	David Greenwalt	08 Dec 1998
3.10	Amends	Joss Whedon	Joss Whedon	15 Dec 1998
3.11	Gingerbread	Thania St. John (Story) & Jane Espenson (Story & Teleplay)	James Whitmore, Jr.	12 Jan 1999

Episode	Title	Writer	Director	Air Date
3.12	Helpless	David Fury	James A. Contner	19 Jan 1999
3.13	The Zeppo	Dan Vebber	James Whitmore, Jr.	26 Jan 1999
3.14	Bad Girls	Douglas Petrie	Michael Lange	09 Feb 1999
3.15	Consequences	Marti Noxon	Michael Gershman	16 Feb 1999
3.16	Doppelgangland	Joss Whedon	Joss Whedon	23 Feb 1999
3.17	Enemies	Douglas Petrie	David Grossman	16 Mar 1999
3.18	Earshot*	Jane Espenson	Regis Kimble	21 Sept 1999
3.19	Choices	David Fury	James A. Contner	04 May 1999
3.20	The Prom	Marti Noxon	David Solomon	11 May 1999
3.21	Graduation Day, Part 1	Joss Whedon	Joss Whedon	18 May 1999
3.22	Graduation Day, Part 2	Joss Whedon	Joss Whedon	13 July 1999

Buffy the Vampire Slayer, Season Four (Network: WB)

Episode	Title	Writer	Director	Air Date
4.01	The Freshman	Joss Whedon	Joss Whedon	05 Oct 1999
4.02	Living Conditions	Marti Noxon	David Grossman	12 Oct 1999
4.03	The Harsh Light of Day	Jane Espenson	James A. Contner	19 Oct 1999

"Earshot," an episode about a potential school shooting, was not aired during the originally intended week in response to the Columbine High School shooting on 20 April 1999 in Columbine, Colorado.

Episode	Title	Writer	Director	Air Date
4.04	Fear, Itself	David Fury	Tucker Gates	26 Oct 1999
4.05	Beer Bad	Tracey Forbes	David Solomon	02 Nov 1999
4.06	Wild at Heart	Marti Noxon	David Grossman	09 Nov 1999
4.07	The Initiative	Douglas Petrie	James A. Contner	16 Nov 1999
4.08	Pangs	Jane Espenson	Michael Lange	23 Nov 1999
4.09	Something Blue	Tracey Forbes	Nick Marck	30 Nov 1999
4.10	Hush	Joss Whedon	Joss Whedon	14 Dec 1999
4.11	Doomed	Marti Noxon, David Fury, and Jane Espenson	James A. Contner	18 Jan 2000
4.12	A New Man	Jane Espenson	Michael Gershman	25 Jan 2000
4.13	The I in Team	David Fury	James A. Contner	08 Feb 2000
4.14	Goodbye Iowa	Marti Noxon	David Solomon	15 Feb 2000
4.15	This Year's Girl	Douglas Petrie	Michael Gershman	22 Feb 2000
4.16	Who Are You	Joss Whedon	Joss Whedon	29 Feb 2000
4.17	Superstar	Jane Espenson	David Grossman	04 Apr 2000

Episode	Title	Writer	Director	Air Date
4.18	Where the Wild Things Are	Tracey Forbes	David Solomon	25 Apr 2000
4.19	New Moon Rising	Marti Noxon	James A. Contner	02 May 2000
4.20	The Yoko Factor	Douglas Petrie	David Grossman	09 May 2000
4.21	Primeval	David Fury	James A. Contner	16 May 2000
4.22	Restless	Joss Whedon	Joss Whedon	23 May 2000

Buffy the Vampire Slayer, Season Five (Network: WB)

Episode	Title	Writer	Director	Air Date
5.01	Buffy vs. Dracula	Marti Noxon	David Solomon	26 Sept 2000
5.02	Real Me	David Fury	David Grossman	03 Oct 2000
5.03	The Replacement	Jane Espenson	James A. Contner	10 Oct 2000
5.04	Out of My Mind	Rebecca Rand Kirshner	David Grossman	17 Oct 2000
5.05	No Place Like Home	Douglas Petrie	David Solomon	24 Oct 2000
5.06	Family	Joss Whedon	Joss Whedon	07 Nov 2000
5.07	Fool for Love	Douglas Petrie	Nick Marck	14 Nov 2000
5.08	Shadow	David Fury	Dan Attias	21 Nov 2000
5.09	Listening to Fear	Rebecca Rand Kirshner	David Solomon	28 Nov 2000
5.10	Into the Woods	Marti Noxon	Marti Noxon	19 Dec 2000

Episode	Title	Writer	Director	Air Date
5.11	Triangle	Jane Espenson	Christopher Hibler	09 Jan 2001
5.12	Checkpoint	Douglas Petrie & Jane Espenson	Nick Marck	23 Jan 2001
5.13	Blood Ties	Steven S. DeKnight	Michael Gershman	06 Feb 2001
5.14	Crush	David Fury	Dan Attias	13 Feb 2001
5.15	I Was Made to Love You	Jane Espenson	James A. Contner	20 Feb 2001
5.16	The Body	Joss Whedon	Joss Whedon	27 Feb 2001
5.17	Forever	Marti Noxon	Marti Noxon	17 Apr 2001
5.18	Intervention	Jane Espenson	Michael Gershman	24 Apr 2001
5.19	Tough Love	Rebecca Rand Kirshner	David Grossman	1 May 2001
5.20	Spiral	Steven S. DeKnight	James A. Contner	08 May 2001
5.21	The Weight of the World	Douglas Petrie	David Solomon	15 May 2001
5.22	The Gift	Joss Whedon	Joss Whedon	22 May 2001

Buffy the Vampire Slayer, Season Six (Network: UPN)

Episode	Title	Writer	Director	Air Date
6.01	Bargaining, Part 1	Marti Noxon	David Grossman	02 Oct 2001
6.02	Bargaining, Part 2	David Fury	David Grossman	02 Oct 2001

Episode	Title	Writer	Director	Air Date
6.03	After Life	Jane Espenson	David Solomon	09 Oct 2001
6.04	Flooded	Jane Espenson & Douglas Petrie	Douglas Petrie	16 Oct 2001
6.05	Life Serial	David Fury & Jane Espenson	Nick Marck	23 Oct 2001
6.06	All the Way	Steven S. DeKnight	David Solomon	30 Oct 2001
6.07	Once More, with Feeling	Joss Whedon	Joss Whedon	06 Nov 2001
6.08	Tabula Rasa	Rebecca Rand Kirshner	David Grossman	13 Nov 2001
6.09	Smashed	Drew Z. Greenberg	Turi Meyer	20 Nov 2001
6.10	Wrecked	Marti Noxon	David Solomon	27 Nov 2001
6.11	Gone	David Fury	David Fury	08 Jan 2002
6.12	Doublemeat Palace	Jane Espenson	Nick Marck	29 Jan 2002
6.13	Dead Things	Steven S. DeKnight	James A. Contner	05 Feb 2002
6.14	Older and Far Away	Drew Z. Greenberg	Michael Gershman	12 Feb 2002
6.15	As You Were	Douglas Petrie	Douglas Petrie	26 Feb 2002
6.16	Hell's Bells	Rebecca Rand Kirshner	David Solomon	05 Mar 2002

Episode	Title	Writer	Director	Air Date
6.17	Normal Again	Diego Guiterrez	Rick Rosenthal	12 Mar 2002
6.18	Entropy	Drew Z. Greenberg	James A. Contner	30 Apr 2002
6.19	Seeing Red	Steven S. DeKnight	Michael Gershman	07 May 2002
6.20	Villains	Marti Noxon	David Solomon	14 May 2002
6.21	Two to Go	Douglas Petrie	Bill L. Norton	21 May 2002
6.22	Grave	David Fury	James A. Contner	21 May 2002

Buffy the Vampire Slayer, Season Seven (Network: UPN)

Episode	Title	Writer	Director	Air Date
7.01	Lessons	Joss Whedon	David Solomon	24 Sept 2002
7.02	Beneath You	Douglas Petrie	Nick Marck	01 Oct 2002
7.03	Same Time, Same Place	Jane Espenson	James A. Contner	08 Oct 2002
7.04	Help	Rebecca Rand Kirshner	Rick Rosenthal	15 Oct 2002
7.05	Selfless	Drew Goddard	David Solomon	22 Oct 2002
7.06	Him	Drew Z. Greenberg	Michael Gershman	05 Nov 2002
7.07	Conversations with Dead People	Jane Espenson & Drew Goddard	Nick Marck	12 Nov 2002
7.08	Sleeper	David Fury & Jane Espenson	Alan J. Levi	19 Nov 2002
7.09	Never Leave M	Drew Goddard	David Solomon	26 Nov 2002

Episode	Title	Writer	Director	Air Date
7.10	Bring on the Night	Marti Noxon & Douglas Petrie	David Grossman	17 Dec 2002
7.11	Showtime	David Fury	Michael Grossman	07 Jan 2003
7.12	Potential	Rebecca Rand Kirshner	James A. Contner	21 Jan 2003
7.13	The Killer in Me	Drew Z. Greenberg	David Solomon	04 Feb 2003
7.14	First Date	Jane Espenson	David Grossman	11 Feb 2003
7.15	Get It Done	Douglas Petrie	Douglas Petrie	18 Feb 2003
7.16	Storyteller	Jane Espenson	Marita Grabiak	25 Feb 2003
7.17	Lies My Parents Told Me	David Fury & Drew Goddard	David Fury	25 Mar 2003
7.18	Dirty Girls	Drew Goddard	Michael Gershman	15 Apr 2003
7.19	Empty Places	Drew Z. Greenberg	James A. Contner	29 Apr 2003
7.20	Touched	Rebecca Rand Kirshner	David Solomon	06 May 2003
7.21	End of Days	Douglas Petrie & Jane Espenson	Marita Grabiak	13 May 2003
7.22	Chosen	Joss Whedon	Joss Whedon	20 May 2003

Angel, Season One (Network: WB)

Episode	Title	Writer	Director	Air Date
1.01	City Of	Joss Whedon & David Greenwalt	Joss Whedon	05 Oct 1999

Episode	Title	Writer	Director	Air Date
1.02	Lonely Heart	David Fury	James A. Contner	12 Oct 1999
1.03	In the Dark	Douglas Petrie	Bruce Seth Green	19 Oct 1999
1.04	I Fall to Pieces	Joss Whedon (Story) & David Greenwalt (Story & Teleplay)	Vern Gillum	26 Oct 1999
1.05	Rm w/a Vu	David Greenwalt (Story) & Jane Espenson (Story & Teleplay)	Scott McGinnis	02 Nov 1999
1.06	Sense & Sensitivity	Tim Minear	James A. Contner	09 Nov 1999
1.07	Bachelor Party	Tracey Stern	David Straiton	16 Nov 1999
1.08	I Will Remember You	David Greenwalt & Jeannine Renshaw	David Grossman	23 Nov 1999
1.09	Hero	Howard Gordon & Tim Minear	Tucker Gates	30 Nov 1999
1.10	Parting Gifts	David Fury & Jeannine Renshaw	James A. Contner	14 Dec 1999
1.11	Somnambulist	Tim Minear	Winrich Kolbe	18 Jan 2000
1.12	Expecting	Howard Gordon	David Semel	25 Jan 2000
1.13	She	David Greenwalt & Marti Noxon	David Greenwalt	08 Feb 2000

Episode	Title	Writer	Director	Air Date
1.14	I've Got You Under My Skin	David Greenwalt (Story) & Jeannine Renshaw (Story & Teleplay)	R.D. Price	15 Feb 2000
1.15	The Prodigal	Tim Minear	Bruce Seth Green	22 Feb 2000
1.16	The Ring	Howard Gordon	Nick Marck	29 Feb 2000
1.17	Eternity	Tracey Stern	Regis B. Kimble	04 Apr 2000
1.18	Five by Five	Jim Kouf	James A. Contner	25 Apr 2000
1.19	Sanctuary	Tim Minear & Joss Whedon	Michael Lange	02 May 2000
1.20	War Zone	Garry Campbell	David Straiton	09 May 2000
1.21	Blind Date	Jeannine Renshaw	Thomas J. Wright	16 May 2000
1.22	To Shanshu in L.A.	David Greenwalt	David Greenwalt	23 May 2000

Angel, Season Two (Network: WB)

Episode	Title	Writer	Director	Air Date
2.01	Judgement	Joss Whedon (Story) & David Greenwalt (Story & Teleplay)	Michael Lange	26 Sept 2000

Episode	Title	Writer	Director	Air Date
2.02	Are You now or Have You Ever Been	Tim Minear	David Semel	03 Oct 2000
2.03	First Impressions	Shawn Ryan	James A. Contner	10 Oct 2000
2.04	Untouched	Mere Smith	Joss Whedon	17 Oct 2000
2.05	Dear Boy	David Greenwalt	David Greenwalt	24 Oct 2000
2.06	Guise Will Be Guise	Jane Espenson	Krishna Rao	07 Nov 2000
2.07	Darla	Tim Minear	Tim Minear	14 Nov 2000
2.08	The Shroud of Rahmon	Jim Kouf	David Grossman	21 Nov 2000
2.09	The Trial	David Greenwalt (Story) & Douglas Petrie (Teleplay) & Tim Minear (Teleplay)	Bruce Seth Green	28 Nov 2000
2.10	Reunion	Tim Minear & Shawn Ryan	James A. Contner	19 Dec 2000
2.11	Redefinition	Mere Smith	Michael Grossman	16 Jan 2001
2.12	Blood Money	Shawn Ryan & Mere Smith	R.D. Price	23 Jan 2001
2.13	Happy Anniversary	Joss Whedon (Story) & David Greenwalt (Story & Teleplay)	Bill L. Norton	06 Feb 2001
2.14	The Thin Dead Line	Jim Kouf & Shawn Ryan	Scott McGinnis	13 Feb 2001

Episode	Title	Writer	Director	Air Date
2.15	Reprise	Tim Minear	James Whitmore, Jr.	20 Feb 2001
2.16	Epiphany	Tim Minear	Thomas J. Wright	27 Feb 2001
2.17	Disharmony	David Fury	Fred Keller	17 Apr 2001
2.18	Dead End	David Greenwalt	James A. Contner	24 Apr 2001
2.19	Belonging	Shawn Ryan	Turi Meyer	01 May 2001
2.20	Over the Rainbow	Mere Smith	Fred Keller	08 May 2001
2.21	Through the Looking Glass	Tim Minear	Tim Minear	15 May 2001
2.22	There's No Place Like Plrtz Glrb	David Greenwalt	David Greenwalt	22 May 2001

Angel, Season Three (Network: WB)

Episode	Title	Writer	Director	Air Date
3.01	Heartthrob	David Greenwalt	David Greenwalt	24 Sept 2001
3.02	That Vision Thing	Jeffrey Bell	Bill L. Norton	01 Oct 2001
3.03	That Old Gang of Mine	Tim Minear	Fred Keller	08 Oct 2001
3.04	Carpe Noctem	Scott Murphy	James A. Contner	15 Oct 2001
3.05	Fredless	Mere Smith	Marita Grabiak	22 Oct 2001
3.06	Billy	Tim Minear & Jeffrey bell	David Grossman	29 Oct 2001
3.07	Offspring	David Greenwalt	Turi Meyer	05 Nov 2001
3.08	Quickening	Jeffrey bell	Skip Schoolnik	12 Nov 2001
3.09	Lullaby	Tim Minear	Tim Minear	19 Nov 2001

Episode	Title	Writer	Director	Air Date
3.10	Dad	David H. Goodman	Fred Keller	10 Dec 2001
3.11	Birthday	Mere Smith	Michael Grossman	14 Jan 2002
3.12	Provider	Scott Murphy	Bill L. Norton	21 Jan 2002
3.13	Waiting in the Wings	Joss Whedon	Joss Whedon	04 Feb 2002
3.14	Couplet	Tim Minear & Jeffrey bell	Tim Minear	18 Feb 2002
3.15	Loyalty	Mere Smith	James A. Contner	25 Feb 2002
3.16	Sleep Tight	David Greenwalt	Terrence O'Hara	04 Mar 2002
3.17	Forgiving	Jeffrey bell	Turi Meyer	15 Apr 2002
3.18	Double or Nothing	David H. Goodman	David Grossman	22 Apr 2002
3.19	The Price	David Fury	Marita Grabiak	29 Apr 2002
3.20	A New World	Jeffrey Bell	Tim Minear	06 May 2002
3.21	Benediction	Tim Minear	Tim Minear	13 May 2002
3.22	Tomorrow	David Greenwalt	David Greenwalt	20 May 2002

Angel, Season Four (Network: WB)

Episode	Title	Writer	Director	Air Date
4.01	Deep Down	Steven S. DeKnight	Terrence O'Hara	06 Oct 2002
4.02	Ground State	Mere Smith	Michael Grossman	13 Oct 2002
4.03	The House Always Wins	David Fury	Marita Grabiak	20 Oct 2002
4.04	Slouching Toward Bethlehem	Jeffrey Bell	Skip Schoolnik	27 Oct 2002

Episode	Title	Writer	Director	Air Date
4.05	Supersymmetry	Elizabeth Craft & Sarah Fain	Bill L. Norton	03 Nov 2002
4.06	Spin the Bottle	Joss Whedon	Joss Whedon	10 Nov 2002
4.07	Apocalypse, Nowish	Steven S. DeKnight	Vern Gillum	17 Nov 2002
4.08	Habeas Corpses	Jeffrey Bell	Skip Schoolnik	15 Jan 2003
4.09	Long Day's Journey	Mere Smith	Terrence O'Hara	22 Jan 2003
4.10	Awakening	David Fury & Steven S. DeKnight	James A. Contner	29 Jan 2003
4.11	Soulless	Elizabeth Craft & Sarah Fain	Sean Astin	05 Feb 2003
4.12	Calvary	Jeffrey bell, Steven S. DeKnight, & Mere Smith	Bill L. Norton	12 Feb 2003
4.13	Salvage	David Fury	Jefferson Kibbee	05 Mar 2003
4.14	Release	Steven S. DeKnight, Elizabeth Craft, & Sarah Fain	James A. Contner	12 Mar 2003
4.15	Orpheus	Mere Smith	Terrence O'Hara	19 Mar 2003
4.16	Players	Jeffrey bell, Elizabeth Craft, & Sarah Fain	Michael Grossman	26 Mar 2003
4.17	Inside Out	Steven S. DeKnight	Steven S. DeKnight	02 Apr 2003
4.18	Shiny Happy People	Elizabeth Craft & Sarah Fain	Marita Grabiak	09 Apr 2003

Episode	Title	Writer	Director	Air Date
4.19	The Magic Bullet	Jeffrey Bell	Jeffrey Bell	16 Apr 2003
4.20	Sacrifice	Ben Edlund	David Straiton	23 Apr 2003
4.21	Peace Out	David Fury	Jefferson Kibbee	30 Apr 2003
4.22	Home	Tim Minear	Tim Minear	07 May 2003

Angel, Season Five (Network: WB)

Episode	Title	Writer	Director	Air Date
5.01	Conviction	Joss Whedon	Joss Whedon	01 Oct 2003
5.02	Just Rewards	David Fury (Story & Teleplay) & Ben Edlund (Teleplay)	James A. Contner	08 Oct 2003
5.03	Unleashed	Sarah Fain & Elizabeth Craft	Marita Grabiak	15 Oct 2003
5.04	Hell Bound	Steven S. DeKnight	Steven S. DeKnight	22 Oct 2003
5.05	Life of the Party	Ben Edlund	Bill L. Norton	29 Oct 2003
5.06	The Cautionary Tale of Numero Cinco	Jeffrey Bell	Jeffrey Bell	05 Nov 2003
5.07	Lineage	Drew Goddard	Jefferson Kibbee	12 Nov 2003
5.08	Destiny	David Fury & Steven S. DeKnight	Skip Schoolnik	19 Nov 2003
5.09	Harm's Way	Elizabeth Craft & Sarah Fain	Vern Gillum	14 Jan 2004
5.10	Soul Purpose	Brent Fletcher	David Boreanaz	21 Jan 2004

Episode	Title	Writer	Director	Air Date
5.11	Damage	Steven S. DeKnight & Drew Goddard	Jefferson Kibbee	28 Jan 2004
5.12	You're Welcome	David Fury	David Fury	04 Feb 2004
5.13	Why We Fight	Drew Goddard & Steven S. DeKnight	Terrence O'Hara	11 Feb 2004
5.14	Smile Time	Joss Whedon (Story) & Ben Edlund (Story & Teleplay)	Ben Edlund	18 Feb 2004
5.15	A Hole in the World	Joss Whedon	Joss Whedon	25 Feb 2004
5.16	Shells	Steven S. DeKnight	Steven S. DeKnight	03 Mar 2004
5.17	Underneath	Elizabeth Craft & Sarah Fain	Skip Schoolnik	14 Apr 2004
5.18	Origin	Drew Goddard	Terrence O'Hara	21 Apr 2004
5.19	Time Bomb	Ben Edlund	Vern Gillum	28 Apr 2004
5.20	The Girl in Question	Steven S. DeKnight & Drew Goddard	David Greenwalt	05 May 2004
5.21	Power Play	David Fury	James A. Contner	12 May 2004
5.22	Not Fade Away	Jeffrey Bell & Joss Whedon	Jeffrey Bell	19 May 2004

Firefly (Network: FOX)†

Episode	Title	Writer(s)	Director	Air Date
1.01	Serenity	Joss Whedon	Joss Whedon	20 Dec 2002

†*Episodes of* Firefly *are ordered here per the DVD release order, not the order of original airing, reflecting Whedon's intentions.*

Episode	Title	Writer(s)	Director	Air Date
1.02	The Train Job	Joss Whedon & Tim Minear	Joss Whedon	20 Sept 2002
1.03	Bushwacked	Tim Minear	Tim Minear	27 Sept 2002
1.04	Shindig	Jane Espenson	Vern Gillum	01 Nov 2002
1.05	Safe	Drew Z. Greenberg	Michael Grossman	08 Nov 2002
1.06	Our Mrs. Reynolds	Joss Whedon	Vondie Curtis Hall	04 Oct 2002
1.07	Jaynestown	Ben Edlund	Marita Grabiak	18 Oct 2002
1.08	Out of Gas	Tim Minear	David Solomon	25 Oct 2002
1.09	Ariel	Jose Molina	Allan Kroeker	15 Nov 2002
1.10	War Stories	Cheryl Cain	James A. Contner	06 Dec 2002
1.11	Trash	Ben Edlund & Jose Molina	Vern Gillum	21 July 2003
1.12	The Message	Joss Whedon & Time Minear	Tim Minear	Unaired in U.S.
1.13	Heart of Gold	Brett Matthews	Thomas J. Wright	Unaired in U.S.
1.14	Objects in Space	Joss Whedon	Joss Whedon	Unaired in U.S.

Dollhouse, Season One (Network: FOX)

Episode	Title	Writer(s)	Director	Air Date
0.00	Echo	Joss Whedon	Joss Whedon	Unaired
1.01	Ghost	Joss Whedon	Joss Whedon	13 Feb 2009
1.02	The Target	Steven S. DeKnight	Steven S. DeKnight	20 Feb 2009
1.03	Stage Fright	Maurissa Tancharoen & Jed Whedon	David Solomon	27 Feb 2009
1.04	Gray Hour	Sarah Fain & Elizabeth Craft	Rod Hardy	06 Mar 2009

Episode	Title	Writer(s)	Director	Air Date
1.05	True Believer	Tim Minear	Allan Kroeker	13 Mar 2009
1.06	Man on the Street	Joss Whedon	David Straiton	20 Mar 2009
1.07	Echoes	Elizabeth Craft & Sarah Fain	James A. Contner	27 Mar 2009
1.08	Needs	Tracy Bellomo	Felix Alcalá	03 Apr 2009
1.09	A Spy in the House of Love	Andrew Chambliss	David Solomon	10 Apr 2009
1.10	Haunted	Janes Espenson, Maurissa Tancharoen, & Jed Whedon	Elodie Keene	24 Apr 2009
1.11	Briar Rose	Jane Espenson	Dwight Little	01 May 2009
1.12	Omega	Tim Minear	Tim Minear	08 May 2009
1.13	Epitaph One	Joss Whedon (Story) & Maurissa Tancharoen (Teleplay) & Jed Whedon (Teleplay)	David Solomon	Unaired

Dollhouse, Season Two (Network: FOX)

Episode	Title	Writer	Director	Air Date
2.01	Vows	Joss Whedon	Joss Whedon	25 Sept 2009
2.02	Instinct	Michele Fazekas & Tara Butters	Marita Grabiak	02 Oct 2009
2.03	Belle Chose	Tim Minear	David Solomon	09 Oct 2009
2.04	Belonging	Maurissa Tancharoen & Jed Whedon	Jonathan Frakes	23 Oct 2009

Episode	Title	Writer	Director	Air Date
2.05	The Public Eye	Andrew Chambliss	David Solomon	04 Dec 2009
2.06	The Left Hand	Tracy Bellomo	Wendey Stanzler	04 Dec 2009
2.07	Meet Jane Doe	Maurissa Tancharoen, Jed Whedon, & Andrew Chambliss	Dwight Little	11 Dec 2009
2.08	A Love Supreme	Jenny DeArmitt	David Straiton	11 Dec 2009
2.09	Stop-Loss	Andrew Chambliss	Felix Alcalá	18 Dec 2009
2.10	The Attic	Maurissa Tancharoen & Jed Whedon	John Cassaday	18 Dec 2009
2.11	Getting Closer	Tim Minear	Tim Minear	08 Jan 2010
2.12	The Hollow Men	Michele Fazekas, Tara Butters, & Tracy bellomo	Terrence O'Hara	15 Jan 2010
2.13	Epitaph Two: Return	Maurissa Tancharoen, Jed Whedon, & Andrew Chambliss	David Solomon	29 Jan 2010

Works Cited

Abbott, Stacey. *Angel.* TV Milestones, Wayne State University Press, 2009.

______. "Kicking Ass and Singing 'Mandy': A Vampire in LA." *Reading* Angel: *The Spinoff With a Soul,* edited by Stacey Abbott, I.B. Tauris, 2005, pp. 1–13.

______. "'Nobody Scream... Or Touch My Arms': The Comic Stylings of Wesley Wyndam-Pryce." *Reading Angel,* edited by Stacey Abbott, I. B. Tauris, 2005, pp. 189–202.

______. "Walking the Fine Line Between Angel and Angelus." *Slayage: The Journal of the Whedon Studies Association,* vol. 3, no. 1, 2003.

Aberdein, Andrew. "The Companions and Socrates: Is Inara a Hetaera?" *Investigating* Firefly *and* Serenity: *Science Fiction on the Frontier,* edited by Rhonda V. Wilcox and Tanya R. Cochran, I. B. Taurus, 2008, pp. 63–75.

"Academy of Television Arts and Sciences Panel Discussion." *Buffy the Vampire Slayer: The Complete Sixth Season DVD Collection,* 20th Century Fox, 2004.

Agents of S.H.I.E.L.D. Creators Maurissa Tancharoen, Jed Whedon, and Joss Whedon, ABC, 2013–2020.

Alien: Resurrection. Writer Joss Whedon, Director Jean-Pierre Jeunet, 20th Century Fox, 1997.

Allen, Ruth and Raymond G. Nairn. "Media Depictions of Mental Illness: An Analysis of the Use of Dangerousness." *Australian and New Zealand Journal of Psychiatry,* vol. 31, no. 3, June 1997, pp. 375–81.

American Psychiatric Association. *Diagnostic and Statistical Manual of Mental Disorders (DSM-5),* 5th ed., American Psychiatric Association Publishing, 2013.

______. *Diagnostic and Statistical Manual of Mental Disorders,* 4th ed., American Psychiatric Association Publishing, 1994.

Americans with Disabilities Act (1990) and Amendments (2008). Pub. L., 110–325.

Angel. Created by David Greenwalt and Joss Whedon, The WB, 1999–2004.

Anna_Palindrome. "We're Not Looking for Pity: The Trouble With Poster Children." *Bitch Magazine,* 4 December 2009.

Annaham. "Liberal Ableism." *Disabled Feminists,* 28 August 2010, https://disabledfeminists.com/2010/08/28/liberal-ableism/, Accessed 20 Feb. 2011.

"Any Anxiety Disorder." National Institute of Mental Health, 2010, http://www.nimh.nih.gov/statistics/1ANYDIS_ADULT.shtml, Accessed 4 Feb. 2011.

Ardolino, Frank. "Severed and Brazen Heads: Headhunting in Elizabethan Drama." *Journal of Evolutionary Psychology,* vol. 4, no. 3–4, 1983, pp. 169–81.

Arrowsmith. Director John Ford, John Ford Productions and Samuel Goldwyn Co., 1931.

"Assessing Your Weight and Health Risk." *National Heart, Lung, and Blood Institute,* http://www.nhlbi.nih.gov/health/public/heart/obesity/lose_wt/risk.htm, Accessed 29 Jan. 2011.

Austen, Jane. *Emma.* John Murray, 1815.

Banks, Samuel A. "The Doctor's Dilemma: Social Sciences and Emerging Needs in Medical Education." *Nourishing the Humanistic in Medicine: Interactions with the Social Sciences,* edited by William R. Rogers and David Barnard, University of Pittsburgh Press, 1979, pp. 277- 96.

Banks, Tyra. "You Call This Fat?" *People*, 26 January 2007, cover.
Barbour, Allen B. *Caring for Patients: A Critique of the Medical Model*. Stanford University Press, 1995.
Barnes, Colin and Geof Mercer. *Disability: Key Concepts*. Polity Press, 2001.
Barnes, Colin, Michael Oliver, and Len Barton. "Introduction." *Disability Studies Today*, edited by Colin Barnes, Michael Oliver, and Len Barton, Polity Press, 2002.
Barton, Len. "Sociology and Disability: Some Emerging Issues." *Disability and Society: Emerging Issues and Insights*, edited by Len Barton, Longman, 1996.
Battis, Jes. *Blood Relations: Chosen Families in* Buffy the Vampire Slayer *and* Angel. McFarland, 2005.
_____. "Captain Tightpants: *Firefly* and the Science Fiction Canon." *Slayage: The Journal of the Whedon Studies Association*, vol. 7, no. 1, 2008.
_____. "'She's Not All Grown Yet': Willow as Hybrid/Hero in *Buffy the Vampire Slayer*." *Slayage: The Journal of the Whedon Studies Association*, vol. 2, no. 4, 2003.
Baum, L. Frank. *The Wonderful Wizard of Oz*. George M. Hill, 1900.
Beadling, Laura L. "The Threat of the 'Good Wife': Feminism, Postfeminism, and Third-Wave Feminism in *Firefly*." *Investigating* Firefly *and* Serenity: *Science Fiction on the Frontier*, edited by Rhonda V. Wilcox and Tanya R. Cochran, I. B. Taurus, 2008, pp. 53–62.
Beard, George Miller. *A Practical Treatise on Nervous Exhaustion (Neurasthenia): Its Symptoms, Nature, Sequences, Treatment*. New York: E.B. Treat, 1894.
_____. *Sexual Neurasthenia (Nervous Exhaustion): Its Hygiene, Causes, Symptoms, and Treatment; with a Chapter on Diet for the Nervous*. New York: E.B. Treat, 1884.
Beirne, Rebecca. "Queering the Slayer Text: Reading Possibilities in *Buffy the Vampire Slayer*." *Refractory: A Journal of Entertainment Media*, 03 Feb. 2004, Accessed 27 Jan. 2011.
Bellin, Joshua David. *Framing Monsters*. Southern Illinois University Press, 2005.
"'Beneath You' Church Scene—Original vs. Produced Version." www.buffy-boards.com Discussion Board, 31 July 2010, https://buffy-boards.com/threads/beneath-you-church-scene-original-vs-produced-version.50172/.
Benthien, Claudia. *Skin: On the Cultural Border Between Self and the World*. Translated by Thomas Dunlop, edited by Lawrence D. Kritzman, Columbia University Press, 2002.
Berube, Michael. "Equality, Freedom, and/or Justice for All: A Response to Martha Nussbaum." *Cognitive Disability and its Challenge to Moral Philosophy*, edited by Eva Kittay and Licia Carlson, Wiley-Blackwell, 2010, pp. 97–109.
The Big Bang Theory. Creators Chuck Lorre and Bill Prady, Warner Bros., 2007–2019.
Blade Runner. Director Ridley Scott, Warner Bros., 1982.
Blaine, Marlin E. "The Representative Body, the Severed Head, and the Rump: Figurations of the English State, 1640–1662." *1650–1850: Ideas Aesthetics and Inquiries in the Early Modern Era*, vol. 16, 2009, pp. 151–67.
Blatt, Burton. *Christmas in Purgatory: A Photographic Essay on Mental Retardation*. Allyn and Bacon, 1969.
Bordo, Susan. "The Body and the Reproduction of Femininity." *Writing on the Body: Female Embodiment and Feminist Theory*, edited by Katie Conboy, Nadia Medina, and Sarah Stanbury, Columbia University Press, 1997, pp. 90–110.
Bowers, Katherine. "Can You Be Healthy at Any Size?" *Women's Health*, 29 Mar. 2010, https://www.womenshealthmag.com/health/a19899286/fat-acceptance/, Accessed 29 Jan. 2011.
Brennan, Teresa. *The Transmission of Affect*. Cornell University Press, 2003.
Briggs, Isaac G. *Epilepsy, Hysteria, and Neurasthenia*. London: Methuen & Co, 1921.
Brockett, L. P. "Idiots and Efforts for Their Improvement." 1856. *The History of Mental Retardation: Collected Papers*, edited by Marvin Rosen, Gerald R. Clark, and Marvin Kivitz, vol. 1, University Park, 1976, pp. 71–86.
Brown, Jeffrey A. "Gender, Sexuality and Toughness: The Bad Girls of Action Film and Comic Books." *Action Chicks: New Images of Tough Women in Popular Culture*, edited by Sherrie Inness, Palgrave, 2004, pp. 47–74.
Buck, Pearl S. *The Child Who Never Grew*. John Day, 1950.
Buckman, Alyson R. "'Go Ahead! Run Away! Say It Was Horrible!': *Dr. Horrible's Sing-Along Blog* as Resistant Text." *Slayage: The Journal of the Whedon Studies Association*, vol. 8, no. 1, 2010.

_____. "'Much Madness is Divinest Sense': *Firefly's* 'Big Damn Heroes' and Little Witches." *Investigating Firefly and Serenity: Science Fiction on the Frontier*, edited by Tanya R. Cochran and Rhonda V. Wilcox, I.B. Tauris, 2008, pp. 41–50.

_____. "Triangulated Desire in *Angel* and *Buffy*." *Sexual Rhetoric in the Works of Joss Whedon: New Essays*, edited by Erin B. Waggoner, McFarland, 2010, pp. 48–92.

_____. "'We Are Not Who We Are': Joss Whedon and the Practice of Inter-auteurial Casting." *Cleaning an Actual Slate: Joss Whedon, Intra-auteurial Casting, and the Whedonverse*, series editor Sherry Ginn, McFarland, forthcoming.

_____, Katherine Troyer, and Juliette Kitches, eds. *Trauma, Memory, and Disability in the Whedonverse* [tentative title], series editor Sherry Ginn, McFarland, forthcoming.

Buffy, the Vampire Slayer. Created by Joss Whedon, The WB/UPN, 1997–2001/2001–2003.

Burns, Maggie. "Mars Needs Women: How a Dress, a Cake, and a Goofy Hat Will Save Science Fiction." *Serenity Found: More Unauthorized Essays on Joss Whedon's* Firefly *Universe*, edited by Jane Espenson, BenBella, 2007, pp. 15–25.

Bussolini, Jeffrey. "Television Intertextuality After *Buffy*: Intertextuality of Casting and Constitutive Intertextuality." *Slayage: The Journal of the Whedon Studies Association*, vol. 10, no. 1, 2013.

Butler, Jeremy R., and Steven E. Hyler. "Hollywood Portrayals of Child and Adolescent Mental Health Treatment: Implications for Clinical Practice." *Child and Adolescent Psychiatric Clinics of North America*, vol. 14, 2005, pp. 509–22.

ButYouDontLookSick.com, www.butyoudontlooksick.com, Accessed 30 Apr. 2021.

Byers, Michele. "*Buffy the Vampire Slayer*: The Next Generation of Television." *Catching a Wave: Reclaiming Feminism for the 21st Century*, edited by Rory Dicker and Alison Piepmeier, Northeastern University Press, 2003, pp. 171–87.

Byrne, Peter. "Stigma of Mental Illness and Ways of Diminishing It." *Advances in Psychiatric Treatment*, vol. 6, no. 1, Jan. 2000, pp. 65–72.

The Cabin in the Woods. Directed by Drew Goddard, Written by Drew Goddard and Joss Whedon, Lionsgate, 2012.

Call, Lewis. "'That Weird, Unbearable Delight': Representations of Alternative Sexualities in Joss Whedon's *Astonishing X-Men* Comics." *Slayage: The Journal of the Whedon Studies Association*, vol. 12, no. 2/vol. 13, no. 1., 2014–2015.

Calvert, Bronwen. "The AI and the Looking Glass: Embodiment, Virtuality, and Power in *Agents of S.H.I.E.L.D.*, Season 4." *Slayage: The Journal of the Whedon Studies Association*, combined vol. 17, no. 1, 2019.

_____. *Being Bionic: The World of TV Cyborgs*, IB Tauris, 2017.

_____. "Inside Out: Motherhood as Demonic Possession." *Slayage: The Journal of the Whedon Studies Association*, combined vol. 12, no. 2/vol. 13, no. 1, 2014/2015.

_____. "Mind, Body, Imprint: Cyberpunk Echoes in the Dollhouse." *Fantasy Is Not Their Purpose: Joss Whedon's* Dollhouse, edited by Cynthea Masson and Rhonda V. Wilcox, special issue of *Slayage: The Journal of the Whedon Studies Association*, vol. 8, nos. 2–3, 2010.

_____. "'The Shell I'm In': Monstrous Embodiment and the Case of Illyria in *Angel*." *Joss Whedon: The Complete Companion: The TV Series, the Movies, the Comic Books and More*, edited by PopMatters.com, 2nd revised and updated edition, Titan Books, 2015, pp. 181–190. Also presented in earlier form as "'The Shell I'm In': Monstrous Embodiment and the Case of Illyria in *Angel*" at *Buffy Hereafter: From the Whedonverse to the Whedonesque: an Interdisciplinary Conference on the Work of Joss Whedon and its Aftereffects*, Istanbul, Turkey, 17–19 October 2007.

Camp, Mary, et al. "The Joker: A Dark Night for Depictions of Mental Illness." *Academic Psychiatry*, vol. 34, no. 2, March 2010, pp. 145–149.

Camron, Marc. "The Importance of Being the Zeppo: Xander, Gender Identity and Hybridity in *Buffy the Vampire Slayer*." *Slayage: The Journal of the Whedon Studies Association*, vol. 6, no. 3, 2009.

Cantor, Norman L. *Making Medical Decisions for the Profoundly Mentally Disabled*. MIT Press, 2005.

Captivity. Director Roland Joffé, Captivity Productions, 2007.

Carey, Allison C. *On the Margins of Citizenship: Intellectual Disability and Civil Rights in Twentieth-Century America*. Temple University Press, 2009.

Carey, John. "Irish Parallels to the Myth of Odin's Eye." *Folklore*, vol. 94, no. 2, 1983, pp. 214–218.
Carlson, Licia. *The Faces of Intellectual Disability: Philosophical Reflections*. Indiana University Press, 2009.
Carroll, Lewis (aka Charles Lutwidge Dodgson). *Alice's Adventures in Wonderland*. Macmillian, 1865.
_____. *Through the Looking-Glass, and What Alice Found There*. Macmillian, 1871.
Churchland, Paul M. *The Engine of Reason, the Seat of the Soul: A Philosophical Journey into the Brain*. MIT Press, 1995.
Cixous, Hélène. "Castration or Decapitation?" Translator Annette Kuhn, *Signs*, vol. 7, no. 1, 1981), pp. 41–55.
_____. "The Laugh of the Medusa." *Feminisms Redux: An Anthology of Literary Theory and Criticism*, edited by Robyn Warhol-Down and Diane Price Herndl, Rutgers University Press, 2009, pp. 416–431.
Clark, Levina, and Marika Tiggemann. "Sociocultural and Individual Psychological Predictors of Body Image in Young Girls: A Prospective Study." *Developmental Psychology*, vol. 44, no. 4, 2008, pp. 1124–1134.
Clogston, John S. "Disability in Coverage in American Newspapers." *The Disabled, the Media, and the Information Age*, edited by Jack Adolph Nelson, Greenwood Publishing, 1994, pp. 45–58.
Clough, Patricia Ticineto, and Jean Halley, editors. *The Affective Turn: Theorizing the Social*. First ed., Duke University Press Books, 2007.
Cohen, Jeffrey Jerome. "Decapitation and Coming of Age: Constructing Masculinity and the Monsters." *Arthurian Yearbook 3*, edited by Keith Busby, Garland, 1993, pp. 173–92.
Coleridge, Peter. *Disability, Liberation, and Development*. Oxfam Publishing, 1993.
Comeford, AmiJo, and Tamy Burnett. *The Literary Angel: Essays on Influences and Traditions Reflected in the Joss Whedon Series*. McFarland, 2010.
Connor, David, and Bejoian, Lynne "Crippling School Curricula: 20 Ways to Re-Teach Disability." *The Review of Disability Studies: An International Journal*, vol 3, no. 3, 2007, pp. 3–12.
Connor, Steven. *The Book of Skin*. Reaktion, 2004.
Coomaraswamy, Ananda K. "*Sir Gawain and the Green Knight*: Indra and Namuci." *Speculum* vol 19, no. 1, 1944, pp. 104–25.
Cornillon, Susan K. *Images of Women in Fiction: Feminist Perspectives*. Bowling Green University Popular Press, 1972.
Corrigan, Patrick W. "How Clinical Diagnosis Might Exacerbate the Stigma of Mental Illness." *Social Work*, vol. 52, no. 1, Jan. 2007, pp. 31–39.
Creed, Barbara. *The Monstrous Feminine: Film, Feminism, Psychoanalysis*. Routledge, 1993.
Crosby, Sara. "The Cruelest Season: Female Heroes Snapped into Sacrificial Heroines." *Action Chicks: New Images of Tough Women in Popular Culture*, edited by Sherrie A. Inness, Palgrave Macmillan, 2004, pp. 153–78.
Crow, Liz. "Including All of Our Lives: Renewing the Social Model of Disability." *Exploring the Divide: Illness and Disability*, edited by Barnes and Mercer, The Disability Press, 1996, pp. 55–73.
Cushing, Pamela, and Tanya Lewis. "Negotiating Mutuality and Agency in Care-giving Relationships with Women with Intellectual Disabilities." *Hypatia*, vol. 17, no. 3, 2002, pp. 173–93.
Dahl, Marilyn. "The Role of the Media in Promoting Images of Disability—Disability as Metaphor: The Evil Crip." *Canadian Journal of Communications*, vol. 18, no. 1, 1993.
Daly, Kathleen. *Norse Mythology A-Z*. Chelsea House, 2010.
Damon, John Edward. "Desecto Capite Perfido: Bodily Fragmentation and Reciprocal Violence in Anglo-Saxon England." *Exemplaria*, vol. 13, no. 2, 2001, pp. 399–432.
Dark Angel. Created by James Cameron and Charles H. Eglee, Fox, 2000–2002.
Davidson, Joy. "Whores and Goddesses." *Finding Serenity: Anti-heroes, Lost Shepherds and Space Hookers in Joss Whedon's* Firefly, edited by Jane Espenson, BenBella, 2004, pp. 113–29.

Davies, Stanley P. *Social Control of the Feebleminded: A Study of Social Programs and Attitudes in Relation to the Problems of Mental Deficiency.* National Committee for Mental Hygiene, 1923.

Davis, Lennard. "Bodies of Difference: Politics, Disability, and Representation." *Disability Studies: Enabling the Humanities,* edited by Sharon L. Snyder, Brenda Jo Brueggeman, and Rosemarie Garland-Thomson, Modern Language Association, 2002, pp. 100–106.

Davis, Robert A. "*Buffy the Vampire Slayer* and the Pedagogy of Fear." *Slayage: The Journal of the Whedon Studies Association,* vol. 1, no. 3, 2001.

"Definition of Intellectual Disability." *American Association on Intellectual and Developmental Disabilities,* 2011, https://www.aaidd.org/intellectual-disability/definition.

Deleuze, Gilles. "Transcript of Deleuze's Lecture on Spinoza's Concept of Affect." *Webdeleuze,* Accessed 25 Sept. 2011.

Dennett, Daniel. *Consciousness Explained.* Little, Brown, 1991.

DeRogatis, Amy. "'Born Again Is a Sexual Term': Demons, STDs, and God's Healing Sperm." *Journal of the American Academy of Religion,* vol. 77, no. 2, June 2009, pp. 275–302.

DerSarkissian, Carol. "What is Obesity?" *WebMD,* 30 April 2017, https://www.webmd.com/diet/obesity/qa/what-is-obesity.

Deutsch, Helen, and Felicity Nussbaum. Introduction. *Defects: Engendering the Modern Body,* edited by Helen Deutsch and Felicity Nussbaum, University of Michigan Press, 2003, pp. 1–30.

Dicker, Rory, and Alison Piepmeier. *Catching a Wave: Reclaiming Feminism for the 21st Century.* Northeastern University Press, 2003.

Diefenbach, Donald L. "The Portrayal of Mental Illness on Prime-Time Television." *Journal of Community Psychology,* vol. 25, no. 3, May 1997, pp. 189–302.

"'Dirty Girls' Episode Commentary." *Buffy the Vampire Slayer: The Complete Seventh Season DVD Collection.* Featuring Nicholas Brendan and Drew Goddard, 20th Century Fox, 2006.

Dix, Dorothea. "Memorial to the Legislature of Massachusetts Protesting against the Confinement of Insane Persons and Idiots in Almshouses and Prisons." Address, 1843, printed by Munroe & Francis, 1843, retrieved from the Library of Congress, lccn.loc.gov/11006306.

Dr. Horrible's Sing-Along Blog. Director Joss Whedon, Writers Joss Whedon, Maurissa Tancharoen, Jed Whedon, and Zack Whedon, Mutant Enemy, 2008.

Dr. Kildare. Executive Producer Norman Felton, MGM Television, 1961–1966.

Dr. Quinn, Medicine Woman. Creator Beth Sullivan, CBS, 1993–1998.

Dohnt, Hayley, and Marika Tiggemann. "The Contribution of Peer and Media Influences to the Development of Body Satisfaction and Self-esteem in Young Girls: A Prospective Study." *Developmental Psychology,* vol. 42, no. 5, 2006, pp. 929–936.

Dollhouse. Created by Joss Whedon. Fox, 2009–2010.

du Pré, Athena. *Communicating About Health: Current Issues and Perspectives.* 3rd ed., Oxford University Press, 2010.

Dunlop, Richard. *Doctors of the American Frontier.* Doubleday, 1965.

Dunway, Dustin. "Genius, Billionaire, Playboy, Prometheus: Transhumanism and Proxemics in the Works of Joss Whedon" in *At Home in the Whedonverse: Essays on Domestic Place, Space and Life,*" editor Juliette C. Kitchens, McFarland, 2017, pp. 11–26.

Early, Frances. "The Female Just Warrior Reimagined: From Boudicca to Buffy." *Athena's Daughters: Television's New Women Warriors,* editors Frances Early and Kathleen Kennedy, Syracuse University Press, 2003, pp. 55–65.

Eberly, Susan Schoon. "Fairies and the Folklore of Disability: Changelings, Hybrids and the Solitary Fairy." *Folklore,* vol. 99, no. 1, 1998, pp. 58–77.

Edelstein, David. "Now Playing at Your Local Multiplex: Torture Porn." *New York Magazine,* 28 January 2006, nymag.com/print/?/movies/features/15622, Accessed 18 Aug. 2011.

Elwick, James. "The Philosophy of Decapitation: Analysis, Biomedical Reform, and Devolution in London's Body Politic, 1830–1850." *Victorian Studies,* vol. 47, no. 2, Winter 2005, pp. 174–87.

Emerson, Eric, Chris Hatton, and William E. MacLean, Jr. "Self-Reported Well-Being of Women and Men With Intellectual Disabilities in England." *American Journal on Mental Retardation,* vol. 113, no. 2, March 2008, pp. 143–55.

Emerson, Ralph Waldo. *May Day and Other Pieces*. Ticknor and Fields, 1867.
Eramo, Steve. "Sci-Fi Blast From the Past—Christian Kane (Angel)." *SciFiAndTvTalk*, 25 Mar. 2011, https://scifiandtvtalk.typepad.com/scifiandtvtalk/2011/03/sci-fi-blast-from-the-past-christian-kane-angel.html.
Erickson, Gregory, and Jennifer Lemberg. "Bodies and Narrative in Crisis: Figures of Rupture and Chaos in Seasons Six and Seven." *Buffy Goes Dark: Essays on the Final Two Seasons of* Buffy the Vampire Slayer *on Television*, edited by Lynne Y. Edwards, Elizabeth L. Rambo, and James B. South, McFarland, 2009, pp. 114–29.
"Experts Call on Media to End Glamorization of Underweight Models." *Mental Health Practice*, vol. 13, no. 7, 01 April 2010, https://journals.rcni.com/doi/abs/10.7748/mhp.13.7.6.s7.
Family Matters. Creators William Bickley, Robert L. Boyett, Thomas L. Miller, and Michael Warren, Warner Bros., 1989–1998.
Feinstein, Sandy. "Losing Your Head in Chrétien's *Knight of the Court*." *Arthuriana*, vol. 9, no. 4, 199, pp. 45–62.
Fernald, Walter E. "Description of American Institutions." 1893, *The History of Mental Retardation: Collected Papers*, edited by Marvin Rosen, Gerald R. Clark, and Marvin Kivitz, vol. 1, University Park, 1976, pp. 323–325.
_____. "Farm Colony in Massachusetts." 1903. *The History of Mental Retardation: Collected Papers*, edited by Marvin Rosen, Gerald R. Clark, and Marvin Kivitz, vol. 2, University Park, 1976, pp. 119–26.
Finkelstein, Vic. "The Commonality of Disability." *Disabling Barriers—Enabling Environments*, edited by John Swain, Vic Finkelstein, Sally French, and Mike Oliver, SAGE Publications, 1993, pp. 9–16.
Finkelstein, Vic, and Sally French. "Towards a Psychology of Disability." *Disabling Barriers—Enabling Environments*, edited by John Swain, Vic Finkelstein, Sally French, and Mike Oliver, SAGE Publications, 1993, pp. 26–33.
Firefly. Created by Joss Whedon, Fox, 2002–2003.
Firefly: The Official Companion: Volume One. Titan Books, 2006.
Firefly: The Official Companion: Volume Two. Titan Books, 2007.
Fixler, Alex. "'The Hardest Thing in This World Is to Live in It': Identity and Mental Health in *Buffy the Vampire Slayer*." *Slayage: The Journal of the Whedon Studies Association*, vol. 16, no. 2, 2018.
Fletcher, Lawson. "'Is She Cold?': Telasthetic Horror and Embodied Textuality in 'The Body.'" *Slayage: The Journal of the Whedon Studies Association*, vol. 9, no. 1, 2011.
Folk, Moe. "Slights and Slants: Visual Representation in *Carnivàle*." *Mediascape: UCLA's Journal of Cinema and Media Studies*, Spring 2007.
Forster, E.M. *Howard's End*. Edward Arnold, 1810.
Foucault, Michel. *Discipline and Punish: The Birth of the Prison*. Translated by Alan Sheridan, Vintage, 1979.
_____. *Madness and Civilization: A History of Insanity in the Age of Reason*. Pantheon Books, 1965.
_____. *Mental Illness and Psychology*. Translated by Alan Sheridan, University of California Press, 1954.
Freeman, Melvyn, et al. *WHO Resource Book on Mental Health, Human Rights and Legislation*. World Health Organization, 2005, https://ec.europa.eu/health/sites/health/files/mental_health/docs/who_resource_book_en.pdf, Accessed 4 Feb. 2011.
French, Sally. "Can You See the Rainbow?: The Roots of Denial." *Disabling Barriers—Enabling Environments*, edited by John Swain, Vic Finkelstein, Sally French, and Mike Oliver, SAGE Publications, 1993, pp. 69–77.
_____. "Disability, Impairment, or Something In Between?" *Disabling Barriers—Enabling Environments*, edited by John Swain, Vic Finkelstein, Sally French, and Mike Oliver, SAGE Publications, 1993, pp. 17–25.
_____. "What's So Great about Independence?" *Disabling Barriers—Enabling Environments*, edited by John Swain, Vic Finkelstein, Sally French, and Mike Oliver, SAGE Publications, 1993, pp. 44–48.
Frey, Hillary. "Slain, at Last: The Late, Great *Buffy the Vampire Slayer*." *Slate*, 21 May 2003,

https://slate.com/news-and-politics/2003/05/remembering-buffy.html, Accessed 25 Jan. 2011.
Friends. Creators David Crane and Marta Kauffman, Warner Bros., 1994–2004.
Funk, Michelle, et al. "Mental Health and Development: Targeting People with Mental Health Conditions as a Vulnerable Group." World Health Organization, 2010, https://www.who.int/mental_health/policy/mhtargeting/development_targeting_mh_summary.pdf, Accessed 4 Feb. 2011.
Garbett, Christine. "Often Invisible: Disability in *Pushing Daisies*." *The Television World of Pushing Daisies*, edited by Alissa Burger, McFarland, 2011, pp. 43–53.
Garland-Thomson, Rosemarie. *Extraordinary Bodies: Figuring Physical Disability in American Culture and Literature*. Columbia University Press, 1997.
Geller, Len. "'Normal Again' and 'The Harvest': The Subversion and Triumph of Realism in *Buffy*." *Slayage: The Journal of the Whedon Studies Association*, vol. 8, no. 4, 2011.
Gilbert, Sandra M., and Susan Gubar. *The Madwoman in the Attic: The Woman Writer and the Nineteenth-Century Literary Imagination*. Yale University Press, 1979.
Gilman, Charlotte. "The Yellow Wall-Paper." *The New England Magazine*, 1982.
Ginn, Sherry. "Memory, Mind, and Mayhem: Neurological Tampering and Manipulation in *Dollhouse*." *Slayage: The Journal of the Whedon Studies Association*, vol. 8, nos. 2–3, 2010.
Gleeson, Brendan. "Community Care and Disability: The Limits to Justice." *Progress in Human Geography*, vol 21, no. 2, April 1997, pp. 199–224. *SAGE Journals*, Accessed 31 Jan. 2011.
Godfrey, Mary F. "*Beowulf* and *Judith*: Thematizing Decapitation in Old English Poetry." *Texas Studies in Literature and Language*, vol. 35, no. 1, 1993, pp. 1–43.
______. "*Sir Gawain and the Green Knight*: The Severed Head and the Body Politic." *Assays: Critical Approaches to Medieval and Renaissance Texts*, vol. 8, 1995, pp. 69–100.
Goffman, Erving. *Stigma: Notes on the Management of Spoiled Identity*. Simon & Schuster, 1986.
Golden, Christopher, and Holder, Nancy. *The Watcher's Guide*. Pocket Books, 1998.
Gorton, David Allyn. *Neurasthenia: or Nervous Exhaustion*. London, G.P. Putnam's Sons, 1894.
Gosling, Francis George. *Before Freud: Neurasthenia and the American Medical Community, 1870–1910*. University of Illinois Press, 1987.
Goulart, Ron. *Comic Book Encyclopedia: The Ultimate Guide to Characters, Graphic Novels, Writers & Artists in the Comic Book Universe!* HarperCollins, 2004.
Grabe, Shelly, L. Monique Ward, and Janet Shibley Hyde. "The Role of the Media in Body Image Concerns among Women: A Meta-analysis of Experimental and Correlational Studies." *Psychological Bulletin*, vol. 134, no. 3, 2008, pp. 460–476.
Green, Sharin P., and Mary E. Pritchford. "Predictors of Body Image Dissatisfaction in Adult Men and Women." *Social Behavior and Personality*, vol. 31, no. 3, 2003, pp. 215–222.
Grey's Anatomy. Created by Shonda Rhimes, Touchstone Television and ABC Studios, 2005present.
Groce, Nora Ellen. *Everyone Here Spoke Sign Language: Hereditary Deafness on Martha's Vineyard*. Harvard University Press, 1985.
Grogan, Sarah. *Body Image: Understanding Body Dissatisfaction in Men, Women and Children*. Taylor & Francis, 2016.
Guinea Piggy. "Health Dangers of Being Overweight." *Weight-Loss-Center*, 15 June 2009, http://www.weight-loss-center.net/weight-loss-blog/2009/06/health-dangers-of-being-underweight/.
Hacking, Ian. *Rewriting the Soul: Multiple Personality and the Sciences of Memory*. Princeton University Press, 1995.
Hahn, Kelsie. "Lady Killer: Death of the Feminized Body in the Whedonverse." *Slayage: The Journal of the Whedon Studies Association*, vol. 10, no. 1, 2013.
Halfyard, Janet K. "Singing Their Hearts Out: The Problem of Performance in *Buffy the Vampire Slayer* and *Angel*." *Slayage: The Journal of the Whedon Studies Association*, vol 5, no. 1, 2005.
Hamilton, Jennifer. "Pylean Idol: L.A.'s De(con)struction of a Postmodern Bard." *The Literary*

Angel: Essays on Influences and Traditions Reflected in the Joss Whedon Series, edited by AmiJo Comeford and Tamy Burnett, McFarland, 2010, pp. 41–53.
Haraway, Donna. "A Manifesto for Cyborgs: Science, Technology, and Social Feminism in the 1980s." *The Haraway Reader*, Routledge, 2004, pp. 5–45.
Hargreaves, Duane, and Marika Tiggemann. "Longer-term Implications of Responsiveness to "Thin-ideal" Television: Support for a Cumulative Hypothesis of Body Image Disturbance?" *European Eating Disorders Review*, vol. 11, no. 6, 2003, pp. 465–477.
Haslam, David, and Fiona Haslam. *Fat, Gluttony and Sloth: Obesity in Literature, Art and Medicine*. Liverpool University Press, 2009.
Hawk, Julie. "Hacking the Read-Only File: Collaborative Narrative as Ontological Construction in *Dollhouse*." *Fantasy Is Not Their Purpose: Joss Whedon's* Dollhouse, edited by Cynthea Masson and Rhonda V. Wilcox, special issue of *Slayage: The Journal of the Whedon Studies Association*, vol. 8, nos. 2–3, 2010.
Helford, Elyce Rae. "'My Emotions Give Me Power': The Containment of Girls' Anger in *Buffy*." *Fighting the Forces: What's at Stake in* Buffy the Vampire Slayer, edited by Rhonda V. Wilcox and David Lavery, Rowman and Littlefield, 2002, pp. 18–34.
"'Helpless' Episode Commentary." *Buffy the Vampire Slayer: The Complete Third Season DVD Collection*. Featuring David Fury, 20th Century Fox, 2003.
Henry, O. *Let Me Feel Your Pulse, Or Adventures in Neurasthenia*. Doubleday, 1910.
Heroes. Created by Tim Kring, NBC, 2006–2010.
Hills, Matt, and Rebecca Williams. "*Angel*'s Monstrous Mothers and Vampires with Souls: Investigating the Abject in "Television Horror." *Reading Angel: The TV Spin-off with a Soul*, edited by Stacey Abbott, I.B. Tauris, 2005, pp. 203–217.
Holliday, Ruth, and John Hassard. "Introduction." *Contested Bodies*, edited by Ruth Holliday and John Hassard, Routledge, 2001, pp. 1–17.
The Hospital Baby. Essanay Film Manufacturing, 1912.
Hostel. Director Eli Roth, Next Entertainment, 2005.
House. Created by David Shore, Universal, 2004–2012.
Howe, Samuel G. "On the Causes of Idiocy." 1848. *The History of Mental Retardation: Collected Papers*, edited by Marvin Rosen, Gerald R. Clark, and Marvin Kivitz, vol. 1, University Park, 1976, pp. 33–60.
Howson, Alexandra. *The Body in Society: An Introduction*. Polity, 2004.
Hunt, Paul. *Stigma: The Experience of Disability*. Catholic Book Club, 1966.
"'Hush' Episode Commentary." *Buffy the Vampire Slayer: The Complete Fourth Season DVD Collection*. Featuring Joss Whedon, 20th Century Fox, 2003.
"'Hush' Episode Script." *Buffy the Vampire Slayer: The Complete Fourth Season DVD Collection*. 20th Century Fox, 2003.
Hyler, Steven H, et al. "Homicidal Maniacs and Narcissistic Parasites: Stigmatization of Mentally Ill Persons in the Movies." *Hospital and Community Psychiatry*, vol. 42, no. 10, 1991, pp. 1044–48.
_____. "Stigma Continues in Hollywood." *Psychiatric Times*, vol. 20, no. 6, 2003, https://www.psychiatrictimes.com/stigma-continues-hollywood, Accessed 4 Feb. 2011.
I, Robot. Director Alex Proyas, 20th Century Fox, 2004.
Idiocracy. Director Mike Judge, 20th Century Fox, 2006.
"Interviews—Christian Kane—Evil Lawyer Lindsey McDonald—Right Turn." BBC, archived 18 June 2014, www.bbc.co.uk/cult/buffy/angel/interviews/kane/page11.shtml.
Invasion of the Body Snatchers. Director Don Siegel, Walter Wanger Productions, 1956.
James, Henry. *The Spoils of Poynton*. Houghton, Mifflin, and Co., 1897.
Janes, Regina. *Losing Our Heads: Beheadings in Literature and Culture*. New York University Press, 2005.
Jefferson, Deana L., and Jayne E. Stake. "Appearance Self-attitudes of African American and European American Women: Media Comparisons and Internalization of Beauty Ideals." *Psychology of Women Quarterly*, vol. 33, no. 4, 2009, pp. 396–409.
Jenkins, Alice, and Susan Stuart. "Extending Your Mind: Non-Standard Perlocutionary Acts in 'Hush.'" *Slayage: The Journal of the Whedon Studies Association*, vol. 3, no. 1, 2003.
Johnson, Máire. "Preserving the Body Christian: The Motif of 'Recapitation' in Ireland's

Medieval Hagiography." *The Heroic Age: A Journal of Early Medieval Northwestern Europe*, vol. 10, May 2007.
"'Joss Tours The Set' Featurette." *Firefly: The Complete Series DVD Collection*. 20th Century Fox, 2003.
Jowett, Lorna. "Biting Humor: Harmony, Parody, and the Female Vampire." *The Literary Angel: Essays on Influences and Traditions Reflected in the Joss Whedon Series*, edited by AmiJo Comerford and Tamy Burnett, McFarland, 2010, pp. 17–29.
_____. "Lab Coats and Lipstick: Smart Women Reshape Science on Television." *Geek Chic: Smart Women in Popular Culture*, edited by Sherrie A. Inness, Palgrave, 2007, pp. 51–88.
_____. *Sex and the Slayer: A Gender Studies Guide for the Buffy Fan*. Wesleyan University Press, 2005.
Kaveney, Roz. "A Sense of Ending: Schrodinger's *Angel*." *Reading Angel: The TV Spin-off with a Soul*, edited by Stacey Abbott, I.B. Tauris, 2005, pp. 57–72.
Kerlin, Isaac N. "Manual of Elwyn." 1891. *The History of Mental Retardation: Collected Papers*, edited by Marvin Rosen, Gerald R. Clark, and Marvin Kivitz, vol. 1, University Park, 1976, pp. 313–319.
Kessler, Ronald C., et al. "Lifetime Prevalence and Age-of-Onset Distributions of *DSM-IV* Disorders in the National Comorbidity Survey Replication." *Archives of General Psychiatry*, vol. 62, no. 6, June 2005, pp. 593–602.
King, Derrick. "The (Bio)political Economy of Bodies, Culture as Commodification, and the Badiouian Event: Reading Political Allegories in *The Cabin in the Woods*." *Slayage: The Journal of the Whedon Studies Association*, vol. 11, no. 2/vol. 12, no. 1, 2014.
Kinsella, Frank. *The Degeneration of Dorothy: A Novel*. 1912. Forgotten Books, 2017.
Kirkup, John. *A History of Limb Amputation*. Springer, 2007.
Klein, Ian G. "'I Like My Scars': Claire Saunders and the Narrative of Flesh." *Inside Joss Whedon's Dollhouse: From Alpha to Rossum*, edited by Jane Espenson, Benbella, 2010, pp. 117–131.
Koontz, K. Dale. *Faith and Choice in the Works of Joss Whedon*, McFarland, 2008.
Kowalski, Dean A., and S. Evan Kreider, editors. *The Philosophy of Joss Whedon*, University Press of Kentucky, 2011.
Kregloe, Karman. Interview with Amber Benson. *AfterEllen*, 19 August 2007, https://www.afterellen.com/tv/22075-interview-with-amber-benson, Accessed 7 Jan. 2011.
Kriegel, Laurence. "The Cripple in Literature." *Images of the Disabled, Disabling Images*, edited by A. Garner and T. Joe, Praegar, pp. 65–78.
Kristeva, Julia. *Powers of Horror: An Essay on Abjection*. Translated by Leon S. Roudiez, Columbia University Press, 1982.
Kromer, Kelly. "Silence as Symptom: A Psychoanalytic Reading of 'Hush.'" *Slayage: The Journal of the Whedon Studies Association*, vol. 5, no. 3, 2006.
Lacey, L. B. "What Size is the "Average" Woman?" *Full & Fabulous*, https://www.fullandfabulous.org/single-post/2015/07/14/What-Size-is-the-Average-Woman, Accessed 29 Jan. 2011.
LaFrance, Marc. "Skin and the Self: Cultural Theory and Anglo-American Psychoanalysis." *Body and Society*, vol. 15, no. 3, 2009, pp. 3–24.
Laughlin, Harry. "The Eugenical Sterilization of the Feeble-Minded." *Mental Retardation in America*, edited by Stephen Noll and James W. Trent, Jr., New York University Press, 2004, pp. 225–231.
Lavery, David. "'A Religion in Narrative': Joss Whedon and Television Creativity." *Slayage: The Journal of the Whedon Studies Association*, vol. 2, no. 4, 2002.
Lawrence, John Shelton, and Robert Jewett. *The Myth of the American Superhero*. Grand Erdmans, 2002.
Le Fanu, Joseph Sheridan. *Carmilla*. Serialized in *The Dark Blue*, 1871-1872.
Lederer, Susan E. *Flesh and Blood: Organ Transplantation and Blood Transfusion in Twentieth-Century America*. Oxford University Press, 2008.
Lee, Michael J. Interview with Jewel Staite. *RadioFree.com*, 15 September 2005, http://www.radiofree.com/profiles/jewel_staite/interview02.shtml, Accessed 7 Jan. 2011.
Levers, Lisa Lopez. "Representations of Psychiatric Disability in Fifty Years of Hollywood Film: An Ethnographic Content Analysis." *Theory & Science*, vol. 2, no. 2, 2001.

Levine, Elana. "*Buffy* and the 'New Girl Order': Defining Feminism and Femininity." *Undead TV: Essays on Buffy the Vampire Slayer*, edited by Elana Lerine and Lisa Parks, Duke University Press, 2007, pp. 168–189.

Levine, Michael P., and Sarah K. Murnen. "'Everybody Knows that Mass Media Are/Are Not [Pick One] a Cause of Eating Disorders': A Critical Review of Evidence for a Causal Link between Media, Negative Body Image, and Disordered Eating in Females." *Journal of Social and Clinical Psychology*, vol. 28, no. 1, 2009, pp. 9–42.

"Life is the Big Bad—Season Six Overview." *Buffy the Vampire Slayer: The Complete Sixth Season DVD Collection*. 20th Century Fox, 2004.

Lifton, Robert Jay. "Advocacy and Corruption in the Healing Professions." Edited by William R. Rogers and David Barnard. *Nourishing the Humanistic in Medicine: Interactions with the Social Sciences*, University of Pittsburgh Press, 1979, pp. 53–72.

Lindquist, Lisa K., Holly C. Love, and Eric B. Elbogen. "Traumatic Brain Injury in Iraq and Afghanistan Veterans: New Results from a National Random Sample Study." HHS Public Access Author Manuscripts, 25 January 2017, https://www.ncbi.nlm.nih.gov/pmc/articles/PMC5501743/, Accessed 21 Apr. 2020.

Livingston, Kathy. "Viewing Popular Films about Mental Illness through a Sociological Lens." *Teaching Sociology*, vol. 32, Jan. 2004, pp. 119–28.

Lloyd, Christine. "Spike and Willow: Unleashing the Monster to Hide the Geek." *The Collected Musings of Shadowkat: Character Studies and General Themes in Buffy the Vampire Slayer*, 13 Mar. 2004, http://www.oocities.org/shadowkatbtvs/part_one_two.html.

Lombardo, Paul A. *Three Generations, No Imbeciles: Eugenics, the Supreme Court, and Buck v. Bell*. Johns Hopkins University Press, 2008.

Longino, Charles F. "Beyond the Body: An Emerging Medical Paradigm." *American Demographics*, vol. 19, December 1997, pp. 14–18.

Love, I. N. "Neurasthenia." *The Journal of the American Medical Association*, 14 Apr. 1894, pp. 539–544, doi:10.1001/jama.1894.02420940015002b.

Lutz, Tom. *American Nervousness 1903: An Anecdotal History*. Cornell University Press, 1991.

Lynch, Brian, and Joss Whedon. *Angel: After the Fall*, IDW Publishing, 2007–2011.

Mac Suibhne, Seamus, and Brendan D. Kelly. "Vampirism as Mental Illness: Myth, Madness and the Loss of Meaning in Psychiatry." *Social History of Medicine*, 2010.

Mann, Caroline E., and Melissa J. Himelein. "Factors Associated with Stigmatization of Persons with Mental Illness." *Psychiatric Services*, vol. 55, no. 2, Feb. 2004, pp. 185–87.

The Many Loves of Dobie Gillis. Creator Max Shulman, 20th Century Fox, 1959–1963.

Marano, Michael. "River Tam and the Weaponized Women of the Whedonverse." *Serenity Found: More Unauthorized Essays on Joss Whedon's* Firefly *Universe*, BenBella, 2007, pp. 37–48.

Marrs, William Taylor. *Confessions of a Neurasthenic*, F. A. Davis Company, 1908.

Masson, Cynthea, and Marni Stanley. "'Evil's Spreading Sir … And It's Not Just Over There': Nazism in *Buffy* and *Angel*." *Monsters in the Mirror: Representations of Nazism in Post-War Popular Culture*, edited by Sara Buttsworth and Maartje Abbenhuis, Praeger, 2010, pp. 179–99.

_____. "Queer Eye of that Vampire Guy: Spike and the Aesthetics of Camp." *Slayage: The Journal of the Whedon Studies Association*, vol. 6, no. 2, 2006.

_____. "What the Hell?: *Angel*'s 'The Girl in Question.'" *Reading Joss Whedon*, edited by Rhonda V. Wilcox, Tanya R. Cochran, Cynthea Masson, and David Lavery, Syracuse University Press, 2014, pp. 34–146

McColl, MaryAnn, and Brickenbach, Jerome. *Introduction to Disability*. WB Saunders Company, 1998.

McGee, Masani. "Big Men in Spangly Outfits: Spectacle and Masculinity in Joss Whedon's *The Avengers*." *Slayage: The Journal of the Whedon Studies Association*, vol. 11, no. 2/vol. 12, no. 1, 2014.

McKeon, J. Michael. "Love the One You're with: Developing Xander." *The Truth of Buffy: Essays on Fiction Illuminating Reality*, edited by Emily Dial-Driver, Sally Emmons-Feathestone, Jim Ford, and Carolyn Anne Taylor, McFarland, 2008, pp. 131–41.

McMahan, Jeff. "Cognitive Disability and Cognitive Enhancement." *Cognitive Disability and*

its Challenge to Moral Philosophy, edited by Eva Kittay and Licia Carlson, Wiley-Blackwell, 2010, pp. 345–367.
McRuer, Robert. *Crip Theory: Cultural Signs of Queerness and Disability.* New York University Press, 2006.
"Mental Health: Strengthening Our Response." *World Health Organization,* 30 Mar. 2018, https://www.who.int/news-room/fact-sheets/detail/mental-health-strengthening-our-response.
Merikangas, Kathleen Ries, et al. "Lifetime Prevalence of Mental Disorders in U.S. Adolescents: Results from the National Comorbidity Survey Replication—Adolescent Supplement (NCS-A)." *Journal of the American Academy of Child and Adolescent Psychiatry,* vol. 49, no. 10, 2010, pp. 980–89.
Metropolis. Director Fritz Lang, Universum Film, 1927.
Miller, Laura. "Bye-Bye, Buffy!" *Salon,* 21 May 2003, https://www.salon.com/2003/05/20/buffy_6/, Accessed 25 Jan. 2011.
_____. "The Man Behind the Slayer." Interview with Joss Whedon, *Salon,* 21 May 2003, https://www.salon.com/2003/05/20/whedon/.
Mitchell, David T. "Narrative Prosthesis and the Materiality of Metaphor." *Disability Studies: Enabling the Humanities,* edited by Sharon L. Synder, Brenda Jo Brueggeman, and Rosemarie Garland-Thomson, Modern Language Association, 2002, pp. 15–20.
Mitchell, Silas Weir. *Fat and Blood: An Essay on the Treatment of Certain Forms of Neurasthenia and Hysteria.* 1884, J. B. Lippincott, 1893.
_____. *Wear and Tear, Or Hints for the Overworked.* J.B. Lippincott, 1871.
Mo Pie. "Dollhouse, *Fat Willow, and Joss Whedon.*" *Big Fat Deal,* 17 August 2009, http://www.bfdblog.com/2009/08/17/dollhouse-fat-willow-and-joss-whedon/, Accessed 31 Jan. 2011.
Modern Times. Director Charlie Chaplin, Charles Chaplin Productions, 1936.
Morris, Barry. "Round up the Usable Suspects: Archetypal Characters in the Study of Popular Culture." *Buffy in the Classroom: Essays on Teaching With the Vampire Slayer,* edited by Jody Krieger and Meghan Winchell, McFarland, 2010.
My So-Called Life. Creator Winnie Holzman, ABC Productions, 1993–1994.
The Nevers. Creator Joss Whedon, HBO, starting 2021.
"'Normal Again' Episode Commentary." *Buffy the Vampire Slayer: The Complete Sixth Season DVD Collection.* Featuring Rick Rosenthal and Diego Gutierrez, 20th Century Fox, 2004.
Norris, Fran H., and Martie P. Thompson. "Applying Community Psychology to the Prevention of Trauma and Traumatic Life Events." *Traumatic Stress: From Theory to Practice,* edited by John R. Freedy and Stevan E. Hobfoll, Plenum, 1995, pp. 49–71.
"The Numbers Count: Mental Disorders in America." National Institute of Mental Health. http://www.lb7.uscourts.gov/documents/12-cv-1072url2.pdf, Accessed 4 Feb. 2011.
Nussbaum, Emily. "Must-See Metaphysics." *New York Magazine,* 22 Sept. 2002.
Oliver, Mike. "Defining Impairment and Disability: Issues at Stake." *Exploring the Divide: Illness and Disability,* edited by Barnes and Mercer, The Disability Press, 1996, pp. 39–54.
_____. *The Politics of Disablement.* Macmillan, 1990.
_____. "Re-Defining Disability: A Challenge to Research." *Disabling Barriers: Enabling Environments,* edited by Swain, Finkelstein, French, and Oliver, SAGE Publications, 1993, pp. 61–67.
Olney, Marjorie F., and Karin F. Brockelman. "Out of the Disability Closet: Strategic Use of Perception Management by Select University Students with Disabilities." *Disability & Society,* vol. 18, no. 1, Jan. 2003, pp. 35–50.
Owen, A. Susan. "Vampires, Postmodernity and Postfeminism: *Buffy the Vampire Slayer.*" *Journal of Popular Film and Television,* vol. 27, no. 2, 1999, pp. 24–31.
Owens, Margaret E. *Stages of Dismemberment: The Fragmented Body in Late Medieval and Early Modern Drama.* University of Delaware Press, 2005.
Pateman, Matthew. "'That Was Nifty': Willow Rosenberg Saves the World in *Buffy the Vampire Slayer.*" *Shofar: An Interdisciplinary Journal of Jewish Studies,* vol. 25, no. 4, 2007, pp. 64–77.
Peeling, Caitlin, and Meaghan Scanlon. "'What's More Real? A Sick Girl in an Institution… Or Some Kind of Supergirl…': The Question of Madness in 'Normal Again,' A Feminist

Reading. Presentation. The Slayage Conference on *Buffy the Vampire Slayer* (Slayage Conference on the Whedonverses 1). Nashville, TN, 2004, https://www.whedonstudies.tv/uploads/2/6/2/8/26288593/peeling_and_scanlon.pdf.

Pender, Patricia. *"I'm Buffy and You're...History": Buffy the Vampire Slayer and Contemporary Feminism.* I.B. Taurus, 2016.

_____. "'I'm Buffy and You're...History': The Postmodern Politics of *Buffy.*" *Fighting the Forces: What's at Stake in Buffy the Vampire Slayer,* edited by Rhonda V. Wilcox and David Lavery, Rowman and Littlefield, 2002, pp. 35–44.

Perdiago, Lisa K. "This is the Next Me: The Evolution of AI in the Whedonverses" in *Transmediating the Whedonverse(s): Essays on Texts, Paratexts, and Metatexts,* editors Juliette C. Kitchens and Julie L. Hawk, Palgrave McMillian, 2009, pp. 87–116.

Philo, Greg. "Changing Media Representations of Mental Health." *The Psychiatrist,* vol. 21, 1997, pp. 171–72.

Pickering, Neil. *The Metaphor of Mental Illness.* Oxford University Press, 2006.

Pirkis, Jane, et al. "On-Screen Portrayals of Mental Illness: Extent, Nature, and Impacts." *Journal of Health Communication,* vol. 11, 2006, pp. 523–41.

"Playing Worst Clips." *Parents Television Council.* 31 Jan. 2011, http://parentstv.com/PTC/clips/WorstClips.asp.

Potvin, Jacqueline. "Pernicious Pregnancy and Redemptive Motherhood: Narratives of Reproductive Choice in Joss Whedon's *Angel.*" *Slayage: The Journal of the Whedon Studies Association,* vol. 14, no. 1, 2016.

Priester, Paul E. "The Metaphorical Use of Vampire Films in Counseling." *Journal of Creativity in Mental Health,* vol. 3, no. 1, 2008, pp. 68–77.

Proust, Marcel. *In Search of Lost Time.* Grasset and Gallimard, 1913–1927.

"'R. Tam, Session 416' Viral Marketing Shorts." *Serenity: Collector's Edition DVD.* Universal, 2007.

Rabb, J. Douglas, and J. Michael Richardson. "Memory and Identity in Whedon's Narrative Ethics: Reading the Whedonverses through *Dollhouse* and *Dr. Horrible.*" SC4: Slayage Conference on the Whedonverses, Flagler College, St. Augustine, FL, 6 June 2010.

Rambo, Elizabeth L. "'Queen C' Goes to Boys' Town: Killing the Angel in Angel's House." *Slayage: The Journal of the Whedon Studies Association,* vol. 6, no. 3, 2007.

Recht, Marcus. *Der sympathische Vampir: Visualisierungen von Männlichkeiten in der TV-Serie* Buffy, Campus-Verlag, 2011.

Richardson, J. Michael, and J. Douglas Rabb. *The Existential Joss Whedon: Evil and Human Freedom in* Buffy the Vampire Slayer, Angel, Firefly *and* Serenity. McFarland, 2007.

Riess, Jana. *What Would Buffy Do? The Vampire Slayer as Spiritual Guide.* Jossey-Bass, 2004.

Robinson, Tasha. Interview with Joss Whedon. *The Onion A.V. Club,* vol. 37, no. 31, September 2001.

Rogers, William R., and David Barnard. "The Interaction Between Humanistic Social Sciences and Medical Education." *Nourishing the Humanistic in Medicine: Interactions with the Social Sciences,* edited by William R. Rogers and David Barnard, University of Pittsburgh Press, 1979, pp. 3–24.

Romesburg, Rod. "Buffy Goes to College: Identity and the Series Based Seminar Course." *Buffy in the Classroom: Essays on Teaching With the Vampire Slayer,* edited by Jody Krieger and Meghan Winchell, McFarland, 2010.

Rosa's Law. Pub. L. 111–256, 5 Oct. 2010.

Ross, Gina. *Beyond the Trauma Vortex: The Media's Role in Healing Fear, Terror, and Violence.* North Atlantic Books, 2003.

Ross, Sharon. "'Tough Enough': Female Friendship in *Xena* and *Buffy.*" *Action Chicks,* edited by Sherrie A. Inness, Palgrave Macmillian, 2004, pp. 231–256.

Rotundo, E. Anthony. *American Manhood: Transformations in Masculinity from the Revolution to the Modern Era.* Basic Books, 1994.

Ruditis, Paul, and Diana G. Gallagher. *Angel: The Casefiles, Volume 2.* Pocket Books, 2004.

Rybarczyk, Bruce, and Jay Behel. "Limb Loss and Body Image." *Psychoprosthetics,* edited by Pamela Gallagher, Deirdre Desmond, and Malcolm MacLachlan, Springer, 2008, pp. 23–31.

Sanchez-Hucles, Janis, and Kimberly Gamble. "Trauma in the Lives of Girls and Women." *Handbook of Girls' and Women's Psychological Health,* edited by Judith Worell and Carol D. Goodheart, Oxford University Press, 2006, pp. 103–12.
Saw. Director James Wan, Evolution Entertainment, 2004.
Scaer, Robert. *The Trauma Spectrum: Hidden Wounds and Human Resiliency.* 1st ed., W. W. Norton & Co., 2005.
Scarry, Elaine. *The Body in Pain: The Making and Unmaking of the World.* Oxford University Press, 1985.
Schlozman, Steven C. "Vampires and Those Who Slay Them: Using the Television Program *Buffy the Vampire Slayer* in Adolescent Therapy and Psychodynamic Education." *Academic Psychiatry,* vol. 24, no. 1, 2000, pp. 49–54.
Schooler, Deborah, L. Monique Ward, Ann Merriwether, and Allison Caruthers. "Who's That Girl: Television's Role in the Body Image Development of Young White and Black Women." *Psychology of Women Quarterly,* vol. 28, no. 1, 2004, pp. 38–47.
Schumitz, Kali. "Fairfax Woman Fights to Eradicate 'R Word': Mental Retardation." *Fairfax County Times,* 14 Oct. 2010, p. 3.
Serenity. Director and Writer Joss Whedon, Universal, 2005.
Sgt. Fury and His Howling Commandos, #13, Written by Stan Lee, Art by Jack Kirby, Marvel, 1964.
Shade, Patrick. "Screaming to be Heard: Reminders and Insights on Community and Communication in '"Hush."' *Slayage: The Journal of the Whedon Studies Association,* vol. 6, no. 1, 2006.
Shakespeare, Tom. "The Social Model of Disability." *The Disability Studies Reader,* edited by Lennard J. Davis, 2nd ed., Routledge, 2006, pp. 197–203.
Shane, Margaret A. "River Tam as Schizoanalysand in Joss Whedon's *Firefly* Narratives." *Slayage: The Journal of the Whedon Studies Association,* combined vol. 12, no. 2/vol. 13, no. 1, 2014/2015.
Shelley, Mary. *Frankenstein, or the Modern Prometheus.* Lackington, Hughes, Harding, Mavor & Jones, 1818.
Sherman, Yael. "Tracing the Carnival Spirit in *Buffy the Vampire Slayer*: Feminist Reworkings of the Grotesque." *Thirdspace,* vol. 3, no. 2, March 2004, pp. 89–107, Accessed 28 Jan. 2011.
Showalter, Elaine. "Hysteria, Feminism, and Gender." *Hysteria Beyond Freud,* edited by Sander L. Gilman, Helen King, Roy Porter, and Elaine Showalter, University of California Press, 1993, pp. 286–344.
Siebers, Tobin. "Disability as Masquerade." *Literature and Medicine,* vol. 23, no.1, 2004, pp. 1–22.
_____. "Tender Organs, Narcissism, and Identity Politics." *Disability Studies: Enabling the Humanities,* edited by Sharon L. Synder, Brenda Jo Brueggeman, and Rosemarie Garland-Thomson, Modern Language Association, 2002, pp. 40–55.
Sigman, Aric. "A Source of Thinspiration? The Biological Landscape of Media, Body Image and Dieting." *The Biologist,* vol. 57, no. 3, 2010, pp. 117–21.
Simmel, Georg. "The Metropolis and Mental Life." 1903. *The Nineteenth Century Visual Culture Reader,* edited by Vanessa R. Schwartz and Jeannene M. Przyblyski, Routledge, 2004, pp. 51–55.
Simmons, Rachel. *Odd Girl Out.* Harvest, 2002.
Singer, Peter. *Animal Liberation.* 1975. HarperCollins, 2009.
"Size 14 Is the Average American Woman's Size, but Not the Average Shopper's: Kim Crow." *Cleveland,* 25 August 2010, http://www.cleveland.com/style/index.ssf/2010/08/size_14_is_average_american_wo.html.
"'Smashed' Episode Commentary." *Buffy the Vampire Slayer: The Complete Sixth Season DVD Collection.* Featuring Drew Z. Greenberg, 20th Century Fox, 2004.
Smeesters, Dirk, Thomas Mussweiler, and Naomi Mandel. "The Effects of Thin and Heavy Media Images on Overweight and Underweight Consumers: Social Comparison Processes and Behavioral Implications." *Journal of Consumer Research,* vol. 36, no. 6, 2010, pp. 930–949.
smith, s.e. "Hipster Ableism." *Disabled Feminists,* 5 November 2009, http://disabledfeminists.com/2009/11/05/hipster-ableism/, Accessed 20 Feb. 2011.

______. "Language Matters: Language Matters, But It's Not the Most Important Thing." *Meloukhia.net,* 25 Feb 2011, http://meloukhia.net/2011/02/language_matters_language_matters_but_its_not_the_most_important_thing/.
Snyder, Sharon, Brenda Jo Brueggemann, and Rosemarie Garland-Thomson. Introduction. *Disability Studies: Enabling the Humanities,* edited by Sharon Snyder, Brenda Jo Brueggemann, and Rosemarie Garland-Thomson, Modern Language Association, 2002, pp. 1–12.
Snyder, Sharon L., and David T. Mitchell. *Cultural Locations of Disability.* University of Chicago Press, 2006.
______. "Re-engaging the Body: Disability Studies and the Resistance to Embodiment" in *Public Culture* vol. 3, no. 13, 2001, pp. 367–89.
Sontag, Susan. *Illness as Metaphor and Aids and Its Metaphors.* Penguin, 1991.
______. "The Imagination of Disaster." *Against Interpretation and Other Essays.* Dell, 1969, pp. 212–28.
______. *Regarding the Pain of Others.* Picador, 2003.
Spicer, Arwen. "'It's Bloody Brilliant!' The Undermining of Metanarrative Feminism in the Season Seven Arc Narrative of *Buffy.*" *Slayage: The Journal of the Whedon Studies Association,* vol. 4, no. 3, 2004.
______. "'Love's Bitch But Man Enough to Admit It': Spike's Hybridized Gender." *Slayage: The Journal of the Whedon Studies Association,* vol. 2, no. 3, 2002.
Spinoza, Baruch. "Ethics." 1883. www.sacred-texts.com/phi/spinoza/ethics/index.htm, Accessed 25 Sept. 2011.
Stafford, Anika. "Feminist Abuse Survivor Narratives in *Angel* and Sarah Daniel's *Beside Herself.*" *The Literary Angel,* edited by AmiJo Comerford and Tamy Burnett, McFarland, 2010, pp. 85–97.
Stafford, Nikki. *Bite Me! The Unofficial Guide to* Buffy the Vampire Slayer. *The Chosen Edition.* ECW Press, 2007.
______. *Once Bitten: An Unofficial Guide to the World of Angel.* ECW, 2004.
Stagecoach. Director John Ford, Walter Wagner Productions, 1939.
Star Trek: The Original Series. Created by Gene Roddenberry, Paramount Television, 1966–1969.
Starr, Moses Allen. *Organic and Functional Nervous Diseases: A Text-Book of Neurology,* 4th ed., Lea & Febiger, 1913.
Stevens, Katy. "Battling the Buzz: Contesting Sonic Codes in *Buffy the Vampire Slayer.*" *Music, Sound, and Silence in* Buffy the Vampire Slayer, edited by Paul Attinello, Janet K. Halfyard, and Vanessa Knights, Ashgate, 2010, pp. 79–89.
Stice, Eric, and Heather E. Shaw. "The adverse effects of the media portrayed thin-ideal on women and linkages to bulimic symptomatology." *Journal of Social and Clinical Psychology,* vol. 13, no. 3, 1994, pp. 288–308.
Stoker, Bram. *Dracula.* Archibald Constable and Co., 1897.
Stone, Alby. "Bran, Odin, and the Fisher King: Norse Tradition and the Grail Legends" *Folklore,* vol. 100, no. 1, 1989, pp. 25–38.
Stout, Martha. *The Myth of Sanity: Divided Consciousness and the Promise of Awareness.* Penguin, 2001.
______. *The Sociopath Next Door: The Ruthless vs. the Rest of Us.* Broadway, 2005.
Streeting, Jessica, Mike Lehane, Mandy Allison, and Linda Drake. "Readers Panel—Curb the size zero." *Nursing Standard* 24.30 (2010): 28–29.
Stuart, Heather. "Media Portrayal of Mental Illness and Its Treatments: What Effect Does It Have on People with Mental Illness?" *CNS Drugs,* vol. 20, no. 2, 2006, pp. 99–106.
Sullivan, Shannon. *Living Across and Through Skins: Transactional Bodies, Pragmatism, and Feminism.* Indiana University Press, 2001.
Sutherland, Sharon, and Sarah Swan. "Lilah Morgan: Whedon's Legal Femme Fatale." *The Literary Angel: Essays on Influences and Traditions Reflected in the Joss Whedon Series,* edited by AmiJo Comeford and Tamy Burnett, McFarland, 2010, pp. 54–65.
Tarnoff, Brooke. "Amber Benson on Books, Body Image, and Why *Buffy* Kicks *Twilight*'s Butt." *TV Squad,* 21 Apr 2009, Accessed 12 Feb. 2011.
Tasker, Yvonne. *Spectacular Bodies.* Routledge, 1993.

_____. *Working Girls: Gender and Sexuality in Popular Cinema*. Routledge, 1998.
TBI: Get the Facts." *Centers for Disease Control and Prevention*, https://www.cdc.gov/traumaticbraininjury/get_the_facts.html, Accessed 21 Apr. 2020.
The Thing From Another World. Directors Christian Nyby and Howard Hawks (uncredited), RKO Radio Pictures and Winchester Pictures, 1951.
THX 1138. Director George Lucas, Warner Bros., 1971.
Tiggemann, Marika, and Amanda S. Pickering. "Role of television in adolescent women's body dissatisfaction and drive for thinness." *International Journal of Eating Disorders*, vol. 20, no. 2, Sep. 1996, pp. 199–203.
Titchkosky, Tatiana. "Coming Out Disabled: The Politics of Understanding." *Disability Studies Quarterly*, vol. 21, no. 4, Fall 2001. *The Ohio State University Libraries Knowledge Bank*.
TNH Videos. "Joss Whedon: Cultural Humanist." *The New Humanism*. The Humanist Chaplaincy at Harvard, 2010, http://thenewhumanism.herokuapp.com/authors/video/articles/joss-whedon-cultural-humanist, Accessed 28 Nov. 2010.
Tong, Rosemarie. *Feminist Thought: A More Comprehensive Introduction*. 3rd ed., Westview Press, 2008.
"Transhumanist Declaration," Humanity+, https://humanityplus.org/philosophy/transhumanist-declaration/, Accessed 18 May 2020.
Trapper John, M.D. Created by Don Brinkley and Frank Glicksman, 20th Century Fox Television, 1979–1986.
Tregaskis, Claire. *Constructions of Disability: Researching the Interface of Disabled and Non-Disabled People*. Routledge, 2004.
Trent, James W., Jr. *Inventing the Feeble Mind: A History of Mental Retardation in the United States*. University of California Press, 1994.
24. Creators Robert Cochran and Joel Surnow, 20th Century Fox, 2001–2010.
U.S. Census Bureau. "Facts for Features: 20th Anniversary of Americans with Disabilities Act: July 26." *U.S. Census Bureau Newsroom*, https://www.census.gov/newsroom/facts-for-features/2019/disabilities-act.html, Accessed 19 Aug. 2011.
Vaughan, Brian K. "No Future for You." *Buffy the Vampire Slayer*, Season Eight, no. 6–9, Dark Horse, 2007.
Vickroy, Laurie. *Trauma and Survival in Contemporary Fiction*. University of Virginia Press, 2002.
Vint, Sherryl. "'Killing Us Softly?': A Feminist Search for the 'Real' Buffy." *Slayage: The Online International Journal of Buffy Studies*, vol. 2, nos. 1, May 2002.
Wälivaara, Josefine. "Welcome to Buffydale: Mutual Construction of Bodies and Space in *Buffy the Vampire Slayer*." *Slayage: The Journal of the Whedon Studies Association*, vol. 14, no. 2, 2016.
Wall, Brian, and Michael Zryd. "Vampire Dialectics: Knowledge, Institutions and Labour." *Reading the Vampire Slayer*, edited by Roz Kaveney, I. B. Tauris, 2001, pp. 53–77.
Wardell, K. Brenna. "Actors Assemble!: The Intertextual Pleasures of the Joss Whedon Ensemble." *Slayage: The Journal of the Whedon Studies Association*, vol. 14, no. 2, 2016.
Weaver, Roslyn. "Metaphors of Monstrosity: The Werewolf as Disability and Illness in *Harry Potter* and *Jatta*." *Papers: Explorations Into Children's Literature*, vol. 40, no. 2, 2010, pp. 69–82.
"'Welcome to the Hellmouth' Episode Commentary." *Buffy the Vampire Slayer: The Complete First Season DVD Collection*. Featuring Joss Whedon, 20th Century Fox, 2002.
Wells, H.G. *The Island of Doctor Moreau*. Heinemann, Stone & Kimball, 1896.
Wendell, Susan. *The Rejected Body: Feminist Philosophical Reflections on Disability*. Routledge, 1996.
_____. "Unhealthy Disabled: Treating Chronic Illnesses as Disabilities." *Hypatia*, vol. 16, no. 4, 2001, pp. 17–33. *Project Muse*, Accessed 4 Mar. 2005.
Whaley, Katherine E. "'There's Nothing Wrong with My Body': Xander as a Study in Defining Capability of the Disabled Body in *Buffy the Vampire Slayer*." *Slayage: The Journal of the Whedon Studies Association*, combined vol 12, no. 2/vol. 13, no. 1, 2014/2015.
"What Is Mental Illness?" Department of Health, Australian Government. https://www1.health.gov.au/internet/ ublications/publishing.nsf/Content/mental-pubs-w-whatmen-toc~mental-pubs-w-whatmen-what, Accessed 4 Feb. 2011.

"What is the Definition of Disability under the ADA?" *ADA National Network*. https://adata.org/faq/what-definition-disability-under-ada, Accessed 4 May 2005.
Whedon, Joss. *Buffy the Vampire Slayer,* Season Eight, Dark Horse Comics, 2007–2011.
_____. The Chain." *Buffy the Vampire Slayer,* Season Eight, no. 5, Dark Horse Comics, 2007.
_____. *Fray,* Dark Horse Comics, 2003.
_____. "Let's Watch a Girl Get Beaten To Death." *Whedonesque,* 20 May 2007, http://whedonesque.com/comments/13271, Accessed 15 Jan. 2011.
_____. "The Long Way Home." *Buffy the Vampire Slayer,* Season Eight, no. 1–4, Dark Horse, 2007.
_____. *Willow: Goddesses and Monsters*. Dark Horse, 2009.
"Whedonesque Commentary on PTC Report." *Whedonesque.com*. 28 March 2005, http://whedonesque.com/comments/6390, Accessed 31 Jan. 2011.
When World Collide. Director Rudolph Maté, Paramount Pictures, 1951.
Wider, Todd. "The Positive Image of the Physician in American Cinema During the 1930s." *Journal of Popular Film and Television,* vol. 17, no. 4, 1990, pp. 139–52.
Wilcox, Rhonda V. "'Every Night I Save You': Buffy, Spike, Sex and Redemption." *Slayage: The Journal of the Whedon Studies Association* vol. 2, no. 1, 2002.
_____. "'I Do Not Hold To That': Joss Whedon and Original Sin. *Investigating Firefly and Serenity: Science Fiction on the Frontier,* editors Rhonda V. Wilcox and Tanya Cochran, I. B. Tauris, 2008, pp. 155–166.
_____. "'Set on This Earth Like a Bubble': Word as Flesh in the Dark Seasons." *Buffy Goes Dark: Essays on the Final Two Seasons of* Buffy the Vampire Slayer *on Television,* edited by Lynne Y. Edwards, Elizabeth L. Rambo, and James B. South, McFarland, 2009, pp. 95–113.
_____. "There Will Never Be a 'Very Special' *Buffy: Buffy* and the Monsters of Teen Life." *Journal of Popular Film and Television,* vol. 27, no 2, 1999, pp. 16–23.
_____. *Why Buffy Matters: The Art of* Buffy the Vampire Slayer. I. B. Tauris, 2005.
_____, and David Lavery. "Introduction." *Fighting the Forces: What's at Stake in* Buffy the Vampire Slayer. Edited by Rhonda V. Wilcox and David Lavery, Rowman and Littlefield, 2002, pp. xvii–xxix.
Wilentz, Gay. "Instruments of Change: Healing Cultural Dis-Ease in Keri Hulme's 'The Bone People.'" *Literature and Medicine,* vol. 14, no. 1, 1995, pp. 127–45.
Wilfond, Benjamin S. and the Seattle Growth Attenuation and Ethics Working Group. "Navigating Growth Attenuation in Children with Profound Disabilities." *The Hastings Center Report,* vol 40, no. 6, Nov./Dec. 2010, pp. 27–40.
Williamson, Graham. "Mean Length of Utterance." *Speech Therapy Information and Resources,* 2009, https://www.sltinfo.com/wp-content/uploads/2014/01/mean-length-of-utterance.pdf, Accessed 15 Mar. 2011.
Wilson, Claire. "How Mental Illness Is Portrayed in Children's Television: A Prospective Study." *The British Journal of Psychiatry,* vol. 176, May 2000, pp. 440–43.
_____. "Mental Illness Depictions in Prime-Time Drama: Identifying the Discursive Resources." *Australian and New Zealand Journal of Psychiatry,* vol. 33, no. 2, Apr. 1999, pp. 232–39.
_____, Raymond Narin, John Coverdale, and Aroha Panapa. "Constructing Mental Illness as Dangerous: A Pilot Study." *Australian and New Zealand Journal of Psychiatry,* vol. 33, no. 2, Apr. 1999, pp. 240–47.
Wilson, Derek. *The Tower: The Tumultuous History of the Tower of London from 1078*. Charles Scribner's Sons, 1979.
Wolfensberger, Wolf. *The Principle of Normalization in Human Services*. National Institute on Mental Retardation, 1972.
The Wonder Years. Creators Carol Black and Neal Marlens, New World Television, 1988–1993.
World Health Organization. *International Classification of Diseases: 11th Revision*. 2018.
Youngner, Stuart J. "Some Must Die." *Organ Transplantation: Meanings and Realities,* edited by Stuart J. Youngner, Renée C. Fox, and Laurence J. O'Connell, University of Wisconsin Press, 1996, pp. 32–55.
Zenderland, Leila. "The Parable of the Kallikak Family." *Mental Retardation in America,* edited by Stephen Noll and James W. Trent, Jr., New York University Press, 2004, pp. 165–85.

About the Contributors

J. **Bowers** is an assistant professor of English at Maryville University in St. Louis, where she teaches courses in creative writing, literature, and film/television studies. She holds a Ph.D. in English from the University of Missouri, and has previously published scholarship in *Poe Studies.* Her short fiction has appeared in numerous national journals, including *StoryQuarterly*, *The Indiana Review*, and *Big Muddy* as well as in several anthologies.

Tamy **Burnett** is an associate director of the University Honors Program at the University of Nebraska–Lincoln, where she teaches courses on television, popular culture, gender, and social movements. She has published on *Angel*, *Buffy the Vampire Slayer*, *Veronica Mars*, and *The X-Files*. She is coeditor, with AmiJo Comeford, of *The Literary Angel* (McFarland, 2010). She is also a member of the leadership team of the Southwest Popular/American Culture Association.

Brian **Cogan** is an associate professor of communications at Molloy College. He is the author of ten books and dozens of other articles and chapters. He has written about Punk Rock, *South Park*, and especially *Buffy*. He wanted to be Angel or Spike, but has settled on being Giles.

AmiJo **Comeford** is a professor of English at Utah Tech University in southern Utah, where she teaches courses in early British literature, Shakespeare, and Milton. She also serves as university ombuds. Her previous publications have focused on *Angel* and *Buffy the Vampire Slayer*. She is coeditor, with Tamy Burnett, of *The Literary Angel* (McFarland, 2010).

Sherry **Ginn** received her Ph.D. from the University of South Carolina and retired in 2018 after 35 years of teaching. She is the author/editor of several books on women in science fiction, sex in science fiction, time-travel, and various popular culture topics. She is the Co-Chair of the Science Fiction and Fantasy Area of the Popular Culture Association.

Emily James **Hansen** earned her MA in English from Middle Tennessee State University where she wrote her thesis, "Love, Loss, Death, and Hope: The Egyptian Voice of Edgar Allan Poe" (2011), under the direction of Philip Edward Phillips. She contributed an essay on Poe and Egypt to *Poe and Place* (2018).

Cynthia **Headley**, a surfer turned scholar, started as a high school teacher in Oceanside, California, became a surf instructor in Costa Rica, and then earned a

Ph.D. at the University of Arizona. She is a full-time lecturer at California State University San Marcos and specializes in body studies, early modern drama, and composition pedagogy.

Erin **Hollis** is an associate professor in the Department of English, Comparative Literature, and Linguistics at California State University, Fullerton, where she teaches modernism, Irish literature, disability studies, and pop culture. She has taught courses on single authors such as James Joyce and Virginia Woolf, as well as broader courses on Irish literature, disability studies, and 20th-century literature.

Mary Ellen **Iatropoulos** is an author and educator who has thrice won the Mr. Pointy Award for Best Work in Whedon Studies. She is the coeditor of *Joss Whedon and Race* (2017). Her scholarship on media and popular culture informs her work as Director of Programs at The Art Effect, a New York–based arts education nonprofit.

Lorna **Jowett** is a reader in television studies at the University of Northampton, UK. She is the author of *Dancing with the Doctor* (2017) and *Sex and the Slayer* (2005), co-author with Stacey Abbott of *TV Horror* (2013), and coeditor of *Global TV Horror* (2021), *Joss Whedon vs. The Horror Tradition* (2018), and *Time on TV* (2016). Her research engages with issues of representation and inequality in the television industry.

Cynthea **Masson** is a professor in the English Department at Vancouver Island University, where she teaches writing and literature courses. Her academic work includes the coedited volume *Reading Joss Whedon*, along with various articles and conference papers in both television and medieval studies. Her novels (*The Elijah Tree*, *The Alchemists' Council*, *The Flaw in the Stone*, and *The Amber Garden*) are anchored in concepts of medieval mysticism and alchemy.

Madeline **Muntersbjorn** is an associate professor in the Department of Philosophy and Religious Studies at the University of Toledo, where she teaches logic, philosophy of science, and philosophy of science fiction. She has studied *Buffy the Vampire Slayer* for over two decades and is especially drawn to the series' depictions of the constitutive relations between persons.

Kelly L. **Richardson** is a professor of English at Winthrop University. She is the Director of Composition and teaches courses in American literature, language, and writing. Her primary scholarship focuses on 19th-century American literature and constructions of gender. Her study of *Buffy* arises from an ongoing interest in portrayals of women and power, notably spiritual power, in popular culture.

Frances **Sprout** enjoys an active retirement in Vancouver, BC, but before that taught in the English Department at Vancouver Island University. Her research and teaching interests include Canadian literature, First Nations literature, British Columbian literature, elegiac fiction and the photograph, coastal boating and intersectional identity in British Columbian literature and Whedon studies (specifically, *Buffy the Vampire Slayer* and *Angel*).

Brett S. **Stifflemire** teaches courses in cinema studies at the University of Montevallo. He received a Ph.D. in communication and information sciences from the University of Alabama. His publications examine the postapocalyptic genre and its relationship with history and culture. He has also written on the topics of science fiction and the depiction of medicine and physicians in popular culture.

Barbara **Stock** completed a Ph.D. in philosophy at Syracuse University and is an associate professor in the School of Arts and Humanities at Gallaudet University. Her areas of interest include animal ethics, moral psychology, philosophy of disability, and history of early modern philosophy. She specializes in using popular culture—particularly science fiction and fantasy literature and visual media—to wrestle with philosophical issues.

Elizabeth K. **Switaj** is the Vice President for Academic and Student Affairs at the College of the Marshall Islands. She is the author of *James Joyce's Teaching Life and Methods* (2016) and two collections of poetry: *Magdalene & the Mermaids* (2009) and *The Bringers of Fruit: An Oratorio* (forthcoming 2022).

Roslyn **Weaver** has a Ph.D. in English literature from the University of Wollongong, Australia, and she completed a postdoctoral fellowship in medical humanities at Western Sydney University. She is the author of *Apocalypse in Australian Fiction and Film* and co-author of *Werewolves and Other Shapeshifters in Popular Culture* and *Mental Health Disorders on Television*, both with Kimberley McMahon-Coleman.

Katheryn **Wright** is an associate professor of interdisciplinary studies at Champlain College. Her book *The New Heroines* (2016) examines teen and YA heroines in popular culture as models of posthuman subjectivity. She also writes about media convergence, screen culture, and critical pedagogies.

Index